Jan. '73

To Gordon Willis with best wishes

William R Peterson

THE VIEW FROM COURTHOUSE HILL

by

William R. Peterson

DORRANCE & COMPANY

Philadelphia

ISBN 0-8059-1650-4
Library of Congress Catalog Card Number: 76-181751
Printed in the United States of America

TABLE OF CONTENTS

Page

PART III: THE FINISHING YEARS: 1882-1900

PREFACE

Explaining an interest in local history is a little like trying to explain how you caught cold. Who knows where, when or by whom you were exposed to the germ; perhaps there has to be a susceptibility to the disease. At any rate, suddenly it's there. Curiosity about one's ancestors plays a part, of course. A grandfather who came from Canada as a boy to work the log drives on Michigan's rivers and went on to primitive railroading left interesting stories and a desire to explore them. Great-grandparents, Swedish immigrants who homesteaded in a wilderness and survived its hardships to surpass ninety years compel one's attention. An aunt's elderly father, vaguely remembered for fervent lectures on the law and public service, suddenly comes alive years later as an aggressive young editor in a few random surviving issues of the *Democrat*. All these create some personal exposure to the history virus.

Curiosity about one's profession, too, plays a part, particularly when that profession so often deals with old things newly litigated. New questions can and do arise about old titles to land, a George Mitchell gift for a school, the legal status of a cemetery, or governmental enactments—today's problems blooming from ancient roots. Lawyers, too, no less than others, are disposed to thumb through old records and see who was doing what to whom and why. Curious, skeptical and nosey, they are born historians, stubbornly unwilling to accept "I don't know" as an answer.

And so you start—and promptly run into the challenge of sources, the problem of where to search and what to believe, essentially the problem that every lawyer faces in the preparation of a case for trial. Almost at once, a familiarity with Courthouse Hill *now* led to misassumptions of related fact and then the discovery that the Courthouse Hill of the past was not that of today.

Unlike the seven hills of Rome, Cadillac's denomination of its hills has been fickle and unenduring. Today's Courthouse Hill was sometimes Observatory Hill, sometimes Orchard Hill, and in the distant past, when it was a garbage dump, was called Pig Farm Hill.

The original Courthouse Hill around which the story of early Clam Lake and Cadillac is centered, block F of George A. Mitchell's plat of the village of Clam Lake, has been deforested, raped, shaped, whittled down, renamed, improved, and built upon, and now is just another one of the hills in a hilly city, undistinguished by any particular name.

Piety Hill, at the intersection of Simons and East Mason streets, was not so named because of the religion of its hard drinking occupants but because those occupants commanded most of the public offices of the village. The name didn't last long—only until another election. Schoolhouse Hill became Standpipe Hill and now is Diggins Hill. Cemetery Hill, alone, has been enduringly named, a subject of appropriate philosophical reflection.

And so it is with the identification and location of villages and townships. Ghost towns abound, some of consequence in their time. The village and the township of Thorp, both named for Col. Thomas Thorp, cannot be found on a modern map. The village has long since disappeared; the township was renamed. Haskins became Boon. Clam Lake Village became the city of Cadillac. Bond's Mill, Greenwood and Viola, among others, became nothing, and even the location of the latter two cannot be determined.

Differences in spelling are sometimes historically explained, sometimes merely typographical errors. Harring township and village, after an early logger, soon lost an "r." The village of Harriette, after confusion with other names, ends as Harrietta. Manton Station in Cedar Creek township, was occasionally Cedar Creek village but finally ended as Manton.

It is even more difficult to verify early individuals by name. One man in a lifetime can call himself, or be called, by an infinite variety of names. Clam Lake township's third settler, Lester Cornelius Sha, not only signed his name "L. Shay," but as "L. C.," "L. Cornelius," "Lester C." and "Lester Cornelius," and varied his last name as "Shay," "Sha" and "Shea." Little wonder that he, John Shay (also appearing as "John Sha" and "J. Shay") and Ephraim Shay, who usually signed his name "E. Shay," got each other's mail. The author's greatgrandfather, who bought land from L. C. Sha, had an even worse time. Olaf Lindberg saw his first name as "Ola," "Ol," "Ole," "Oley" and "Olaff," and his last name as "Linberg," "Linburg," "Linnburg," "Lindeberg" and "Lineberg." One good Scandinavian appeared in print as "Y' Anson!" The Dayhuff family appeared as "Dahuff" and with other variants, and one homestead patent went to Amos DerHuff. Job Hoxie was also "Hoxsie" and "Hoxey." From immigration and language change, phonetics, illiteracy and bad handwriting, many variants can follow.

I have tried to avoid misunderstandings that might arise by changes in name through the passage of time. For instance, an 1880 reference to the state university speaks of the University of Michigan and not to Michigan State University, which was then the Michigan Agricultural College. Locally, Big Clam Lake and Little Clam Lake have been referred to for a century as "big lake" and "little lake," but they have been changed to Lake Mitchell and Lake Cadillac.

With these changes in mind I have tried to avoid confusion by adhering to consistent usage, but at times simplicity has conflicted with consistency. When I say that Lester C. Sha settled in Clam Lake Township in 1869, I know that there was no Clam Lake Township legally existing then. I hope the explanation of the organization of the townships in chapter eleven will suffice.

For convenience, newspaper references are shortened. The *Wexford County Pioneer* later became the *Sherman Pioneer*. It is generally referred to simply as the *Pioneer*. Through all the name changes and mergers, the original *Clam Lake Weekly News*, coming down to us as the *Cadillac Evening News* of today, is referred to simply as the *News*.

Some of the interests of the author, involving events essential to a history of the area and a feeling for its times, must await future publication. This is a beginning, intended to recount the settling of the county, its townships, cities, villages, and crossroads settlements; the physical building of Cadillac; the county seat struggle that preoccupied a generation, and the main personalities involved. But the story is essentially the story of the coming of the railroads and the evolution of the lumber industries. They are touched on here only briefly as they are necessary to the limits of this book. Hopefully, a second volume will deal with them in detail, along with a look at the fascinating newspaper history of Cadillac in the nineteenth century. Time permitting, a third volume will deal with the life and times of the nineteenth century residents of the area.

ACKNOWLEDGMENTS

An immense debt is owed to Earl and Tom Huckle of the *Cadillac Evening News* for access to the old files of the *News*. The kind people at the *News* and the public officers who have tolerated me underfoot, digging in their files and asking questions, have made this possible. The Michigan Historical Collection at the University of Michigan, the Burton Historical Collection in Detroit, and the Cadillac, Kendallville, and Michigan State libraries, have been invaluable sources of information. To the helpful librarians there, and the many people who have furnished photographs, old letters, books, and accounts of the early day, I am most appreciative.

PART I:
THE SETTLEMENT OF THE COUNTY

Chapter One

WOLVES AND SHIN-TANGLE

When Gov. Henry P. Baldwin put his name to Act 386 on March 30, there were no photographers present, nor were any of the sponsors of the legislation on hand. It would be over a week before they would learn that Wexford County had been legally organized. News, and the people who carried it, traveled slowly in 1869. Getting from Lansing to Grand Rapids and then on to Morley was relatively simple on the new railroads, but it was a rough ride on the stage from there to Sherman. The trip over the Newaygo and Northport State Road would take at least three days, and perhaps five at this time of the year, when snow, ice, and mud left the ungraded trail virtually impassable at many points.

The people who lived near Sherman—and there was scarcely anyone else in the county—had been assured, however, that passage of the act would be just a formality, and that they could schedule the first spring election of the new county even though they might not have definite word that the county bill had become law. So, schedule it they did, and 129 people cast their first ballots as citizens of the new county on April 5 without knowing for certain that the election was legal. It was, and the glory of politics and local self-government had come to the North Woods.

Except for occasional trappers along the rivers, the forest wilderness that was to become Wexford County had seen few white men before the government surveyors came to northern Michigan in 1836 and 1837. Except for a few settlements along the Great Lakes, this was Indian country. It was acknowledged as such by the legislature when, in 1840, it used the government survey to lay out the northern part of the state into counties and gave Indian names to the vast areas of vacant space shown on the map. The name attached to the block of survey townships 21 through 24 north and ranges 9 through 12 west was Kautawabet, meaning "broken tooth," after a chief of the Potawatami Tribe who had been a signatory to the Great Peace Treaty of 1825. In 1843, repenting of its generosity, the Indian-giving legislature took it all back and renamed sixteen of the counties.[1] Most of the changes honored Michigan's early explorers and political leaders, but, in an un-American moment, five counties, including Wexford, were given the names of Irish counties.

The early designation of the area as Kautawabet and then as Wexford County, however, was purely a matter of geography. The administration of governmental matters, justice, and taxation was first assigned to the newly organized county of Grand Traverse in 1853, and then to Manistee County upon its organization in 1855. As a practical matter, however, such questions did not soon arise. With no permanent residents in the area, there was little government to administer and no privately owned property to be taxed.

The Indian population had no permanent settlements. Small bands moved about from campsite to campsite, living off the land. Several well-established trails crossed the county. One running across the southeast corner of the county branched around Little Clam Lake, while a north-south trail ran between the Big and Little Clam lakes, up the center of the county, across the Manistee River in section 32 of Hanover Township and on north to Traverse Bay.[2]

1. It was of little consequence in any event, since it was discovered that most of the Indian names used had no meaning in either the Chippewa or Potawatami tongues. Kautawabet was one of the few names properly used.

2. Both trails seem to have followed those of earlier mound-building tribes that roamed the area centuries before. On Little Clam Lake, mounds were found in the Sunnyside area on the southeast, and in Taylor's Grove, now called Kenwood, on the north. The largest concentrations were in the area between the lakes and along the south shore of the Big Lake.

The mounds were great curiosities to the early settlers and were looted without any attempt at preservation or systematic exploration. Bones, particularly skulls, were home and office decorations. An 1895 *News* description of the mounds between the lakes said that twenty years of exploration had left the area littered with bleached and crumbling bones. The shape of the mounds led to the assumption that they were old fortifications, and the abundance of stone arrowheads suggested fierce battles. Charles Manktelow thought them fortifications at the perimeter of a large city inhabited by a lost people that had been destroyed in a cataclysmic battle, like Rome sacked by the Goths. He published the thesis in

In January of 1854, Perry Hannah of Traverse City, firm in the white man's belief that the shortest distance between two points is a straight line, scorned the Indian trail and ignored the advice of his Indian guides in making the first known overland trip by a white man from Traverse City to Grand Rapids. His time of six and a half days, made on snowshoes, was considered a prodigal feat, unequaled for many years, but was probably a good day longer than the time required by the Indians over their meandering path of less resistance. At that, his trip may have been hastened by an escort of a large pack of wolves which followed him almost the entire distance. They surrounded his camp the first night, and "a tremendous howl was set up and continued during the whole night." He said the wolves did not prove troublesome, but it was a sleepless journey. It was also a lonely one, for he saw no sign of human habitation or civilization from the limits of Traverse City until he stopped at the tiny settlement of Big Rapids for supplies.

2.

The opening of the area was made possible by an 1857 act of the legislature appropriating funds for the laying out of a state road, first called the Muskegon and Northern Pike, but later known as

several brochures and made it the setting of a romantic novel.In 1881 a hunter known as "Hungry Lou" discovered mounds at the confluence of the Mosquito Creek and Clam River, digging out skeletons and pieces of iron. Dr. D. J. Irwin pronounced the site typical of seventeenth century European earthworks and thought it proved the presence of white men in the area before the explorations of LaSalle. Some years later, Irwin said he had been told by John Ching Wash, an old Ottawa, that "many grandfathers before" the Ottawas had captured six white men in the north and held them captive. The leader of the whites was called Stargazer because he traveled by watching the stars. Attacked by Hurons, the story went, Stargazer had directed the building of the fort, but they had been overwhelmed and the defenders all perished. The iron scraps, said Irwin, were remnants of an English cutlass and helmet. Stargazer, he concluded, was none other than explorer Henry Hudson, who had been cast adrift on Hudson Bay with a few loyal supporters by a mutinous crew in 1611.

the Newaygo and Northport State Road. To the early settlers, it was always "the trail." Surveyors began marking out the route the same year, working south from Traverse City and north from Newaygo. It took three summers to finish the survey, but clearing work was commenced in the south in 1858 and in Grand Traverse County in 1859. It was slow going. Most sections were at least passable by 1863, and the road was considered officially open when the Manistee River was bridged in 1864.

The opening of the road, however, did not in itself insure a rush of new settlers to the area. Few veterans of the British or Mexican wars were still looking for free homestead land at this late date. There were large tracts of public land in more choice locations still available for those with cash in hand. Under the Preemption Law, public lands could be purchased by settlers at $1.25 per acre. That was a reasonable price for grasslands but hardly attractive where the work of clearing a forest was involved.

As the state road was opened, some speculative purchases were made along the right-of-way at what were hoped would be strategic locations. It was not until 1862, however, that the first settler, Benjamin W. Hall, followed the "trail" north from Newaygo to see what could be found. He almost turned back when he discovered that the road had not been cleared north of the Pine River and was only a path marked by "blazed" trees. He went on, however, found the going easier a few miles north, and located an appealing site in section 30 of Hanover Township on the high ground a half mile north of the Manistee. He cut a dozen trees along the trail to mark the north and south limits of his claim, went on to Traverse City to record the claim in the land office there, and then returned to Newaygo for the winter. The following May, with wife, pigs, chickens, and a few household possessions, he set forth by ox team and wagon for his new home. The trip took three weeks.

On arriving at their "farm," the Halls immediately began clearing the land to get in their first crop, turnips on which to feed themselves and the stock during the coming winter. They lived out of the wagon until August, when Hall put up the framing for his house. It was merely a pole-framed one-room shanty made of elm bark, at one end of which was a loose fieldstone hearth, with a crude tin smoke funnel to serve as a chimney. There was no floor.

Perhaps it was not surprising that Mrs. Hall "ran away with Mr. Anise, the stage driver," two years later.[3]

When Hall reached the river in early June of 1863 en route to his farm, he met another traveler going in the opposite direction in search of land to settle. He was Dr. John Perry, already seventy years old, looking for new scenery. He had passed Hall's site and not cared for the area. South of the river he found a spot in section 6 of Antioch Township that Hall had bypassed but which suited him, and he and his wife soon had a log cabin up. The county has perhaps never since been so healthy as when half of its male population engaged in the medical practice. Actually, "Doctor" John had neither medical schooling nor degree.[4] He was typical, however, of the all-sufficient man of the pioneer period in which necessity drove people to the literate man who was resourceful, who had both books and tools and the nerve to use them. So it was with Perry.

He was born in New York in 1793, had farmed, fought in the War of 1812, learned carpentry, and traveled widely. Supposedly he had been thrice married and twice widowed, twice wealthy and twice ruined. Whatever and wherever else he had been in his varied career, at some point he had acquired more than a passing acquaintance with drugs and medicine. By the time he came to southern Michigan in the fifties, he was a physician along with his other trades. He wandered on west and in 1862 came back to Michigan, turning up in Traverse City with a twenty-nine-year-old

3. Thirty-six years later, a narrow majority of those present at a meeting of the Pioneer Society concluded that it was neither Hall's habits nor the charms of Mr. Anise, but the bark house, that caused the desertion. In 1867, on the assumption that wife One had died or divorced him, Hall remarried. Wife Two endured the bark house two years before leaving. Wife Three was made of sterner stuff. Sarah refused either to leave him or to live in the place, leaving him no choice but to build a frame house in which the presumably happy family lived until Hall's death in 1882. Their only child, Ben, Jr., had died in infancy. Sarah sold the farm and moved to Cadillac, where she died in 1887.

4. There was no state regulation of medicine in Michigan until 1883, and anyone choosing to practice medicine and to call himself a "doctor" was free to do so. At the center of the county, "Grandma" Dayhuff was the primary source of medical care in and around Meauwataka for thirty years. The county still had "unlettered" physicians practicing after the turn of the century.

bride from Iowa. The next year, at seventy, he made his new start in Wexford County.

He farmed a little. He helped his neighbors build as they settled. He brought a daughter by a prior marriage and her husband to the county, helped them locate and build, and then looked after her when her husband was killed. He persuaded Moses Cole, who had homesteaded in Wexford Township in 1867, to come to the settlement growing up around the Perry residence, then built a sawmill for him a mile to the east on what came to be known as Cole's Creek, and ran the business end of a fatherly partnership. He became postmaster. But above all, he doctored. For seven years, he was the only physician in the county, and he continued to practice actively until his death in 1875 at age eighty-two. His daughter, his wife, and their son, born in his eightieth year, all survived him only briefly.

3.

It was not long after Dr. Perry's arrival that he had patients. The new Homestead Act allowed a man to acquire up to 160 acres of public land free. All he had to do was improve it and live on it for five years. By the end of 1863, Lewis Cornell, Edward Morgan, William Masters, and Robert Myhill, Perry's son-in-law, had homesteaded in Wexford Township.[5] During 1864 another fifteen families joined them, all in the northwest part of the county, and all within two miles of the state road. The Mesicks—Howard, Jesse and Walter—were there too, along with another trapper

5. Morgan was just twenty-one and only discharged from the army. He cleared part of his land in 1864 and then re-enlisted, the only man to enlist from Wexford County during the Civil War. Dr. Perry had taken a fancy to the lad and tried to discourage the enlistment, urging him instead to learn to read and write and seek a good trade. In 1870 Perry received a letter from the newly literate Morgan, thanking him for his advice which had been sensibly followed, and further promising that when next they met he, too, would be a doctor. In 1877 Dr. Morgan returned to the county to find Perry dead. Morgan had no degree, but he had attended medical school. He practiced in Cadillac and Kalkaska, and ultimately settled in Manton, where he practiced until his death in 1912.

known only as "Eli Red," but they hardly counted as settlers. They had worked on the state road and stayed to live off the land Indian-style.

All of the first settlers were New Yorkers, and over the next few years their relatives, in-laws, and friends joined them—the Bakers, Dunhams, Kelloggs, Carpenters, Skinners, Copleys, Deans, Wheelers, and Davises; and in 1867 and 1868, the Coles, Clarks, Dodges, Jewetts, Devoes, Fletchers, Foxes, Worths, Usewicks, and Northrups. With them came the flood of discharged Civil War veterans, a few of whom had heard about the area from friends, but most of whom just drifted in looking for a likely place to settle, like Captain Finch and Captain Champenois at Sherman, and the colony of comrades who came in 1867 and called their Colfax settlement Unionville in commemoration of their service in the Great Rebellion. They were the first settlers to get away from the state road, which was no mean task in itself.

Travel away from the road was laborious and, at places, impossible. The height and density of the forest blocked out the sunlight so as to create a perpetual twilight, at best, and the brush and trees were so thick that it was impossible to see more than eight or ten feet. On his trip in 1854, Perry Hannah found the woods so dark, even with the leaves off the trees, that he had to make constant use of his compass to maintain his direction.

Another account involves a homesteader, Columbus Durbin, who found the path leading from the state road to his cabin blocked by a windfall. Leaving the path to circle the fallen tree, he found himself lost and after some wandering found himself back on the state road. A second attempt brought the same result. He finally passed the windfall by crawling through the tangle of fallen limbs and brush, inch by inch, like a dog sniffing out a scent to be sure that he would not lose touch with the cleared path.

The areas first settled were largely covered by hardwoods in which deadfalls and windfalls, interwoven with ground brush, had created an impenetrable tangle. In places, all ground growth seemed choked out by an evergreen vine growing multiple, tentacle-like vines three to six feet in length.[6] A species of ground

6. In one view, the vine's nature was such as to choke out other ground growth. Another theory is that it was the only ground growth to survive in areas

hemlock, it was appropriately referred to by the settlers as "shin-tangle," and some reports describe masses of it piled head-high and completely impassable. Another settler described it as "where to go if looking for bears, but where not to go if you ain't."[7]

Dr. Perry acquired two close neighbors in 1865. South of him on the same section, Harmony J. Carpenter homesteaded early in the summer while his younger brother, Isaac, located a short distance away in section 24 of Wexford Township. Perry aided them in putting up their cabins, which were typical of all those going up.[8] Logs were cut into twelve- or fifteen-foot lengths, notched at the ends and stacked to the height of seven or eight feet. The spaces between the logs were chinked with carefully whittled pieces of wood, covered over on the exterior by moss or by clay where available. The roof was sometimes of bark, but more often split pole ribs were laid across the rafters and covered with hand-hewn shingles, or "shakes." Except for the base tier of logs, there were no foundations. If there was a floor, it was "puncheon," or thin

in which the migratory passenger pigeons roosted. The flights were so immense that the acrid droppings sometimes covered the ground to a depth of two to three inches and killed most plant life.

7. The settlers soon learned that hungry stock would browse on shin-tangle. It was sometimes jokingly called "Michigan clover" and used for winter feed if nothing better was available. The milk of cows feeding on the stuff had a distinctly tangy taint but could be endured. Stock would also browse on the smaller branches of maple trees, so that winter felling of maples provided food at the same time that it helped clear the land. Turnips and rutabagas could be planted fairly late and provide a crop serving equally well for stock and family purposes. The author's intense dislike of "beggies" perhaps stems from childhood, when he overheard oldsters describing them as pigs' winter feed.

8. At least one dugout home is known to have existed in Antioch Township in the late sixties. It was nothing more than a hole dug into the sheltered slope of a hill with woven brush fitted around poles to reinforce the earth wall, and covered over with poles and bark for a roof, but it served for over a dozen years. More than twenty years later, during hard times, squatters built a number of such dugout houses in the woods around Cadillac. Bricks were easily filched from the Mosser brickyard to provide a fireplace and crude chimney, and lumber from the mill yards was easily liberated to provide door framing and a roof. In one instance, a house was found in this low-rent district with a roof made of pieces of sheet iron.

slabs of wood, usually elm or bass, laid on the earth, and leveled and fitted as snugly as possible. Since openings in the log walls complicated construction, they were few. It was rare that a cabin had more than one window, and in many the doorway was the only opening. Glass was unique at first, and the usual window covering was either oiled paper or a deer hide. The former admitted some light. The latter was rolled back during the summer, admitting light and everything else, but was never removed during the winter. Even the best of cabins were dark places.

Perry's second neighbor arrived in late fall with a wife and five small children and located on the east side of the trail a short distance north of Perry. The land was a "railroad" section and not open to homesteading, but he chose it nonetheless, perhaps in the hope of acquiring the title by continued possession. We don't know his name, surviving accounts referring to him only as "the squatter." We know little else of him, save that he didn't like advice. Suggestions that there were good homestead sections nearby were disregarded. He rejected the idea of a small cabin, which could be put up quickly and added to later. Instead, he insisted on putting up a huge twenty-by-thirty-foot cabin that wasn't fully roofed until mid-January. During the winter, three of the children died, and all would have starved had it not been for generous gifts of venison from the Mesicks, and as much salt pork, turnips, and potatoes as other settlers could spare. That spring, his wife ailing, the squatter loaded his wagon, abandoned his prized cabin, and disappeared. The trail which opened the area to the settlers was a means of retreat for some.

4.

It is doubtful that the thought of retreat occurred to many of the settlers. The trail that brought them in wasn't a way "out" but was their connection with "home," wherever that might be, and with the commerce of Traverse City. Traverse was the port of entry to which most of the settlers had come by boat. By 1864 the population of Grand Traverse County was over 2,000, and the city had become a fairly civilized commercial center. There was, as yet, no significant amount of produce coming off the homestead farms to move to market, but what there was had to go north over the trail to Traverse. For building supplies, goods and staples of all kinds, there was no place to go except to the supplier at Traverse. And the city, of course, continued to be the funnel through which an increasing flow of new neighbors were coming down the trail to settle the area.

During 1865 considerable improvement was made on the road. North of the Manistee it was almost completely stumped, and some grading and filling was done. Early that year, Jacob York started a weekly dray service to Traverse City, the round trip taking from two and a half to three and a half days, depending on the weather. The settler who made the trip usually did so with ox team rather than horses and found it even slower.[9] Even on the improved trail, travel by wagon was no pleasure, complicated in the best of weather, by soft sand and mud holes. South of the Manistee there were fewer settlers, no convenient trade centers, and little use of the road. Its improvement in that direction was accordingly neglected, and the early stage runs on that part of the trail must have been bone-jarring. It was not until 1874, seven years after the first regular mail route south, that stumping was completed on the trail in the southern part of the county.

The York dray service originated at the home of William Masters in section 12 of Wexford Township, a little over a mile south of the county line. By 1864 his home had grown into something of a gathering point for the settlers. He was one of those seemingly ever-cheerful souls who never fail to appear genuinely delighted at seeing a visitor at their door. He was noted for his hospitality and was one of the best loved men of the area.

9. Few settlers had horses, oxen being useful all-purpose beasts more adaptable to pioneer needs. There were, of course, many settlers who had neither. As small centers grew up with general stores, no one thought it uncommon to walk eight or ten miles to the nearest store to carry seventy-five to a hundred pounds to his home on a back pack. One early settler, R. U. Updike, regularly did the twenty-eight mile trip to Traverse monthly with a hundred-pound pack. As late as 1887, the *Pioneer* commented on a Mr. Whipple of Henderson Township, who walked fourteen miles from his home to Sherman to take out a back-load of groceries, quoting him as saying that "the walking was easier to Sherman than it was to Cadillac," and noting that he was doing right smart for a man eighty-seven years old!

As the early settlers went to and from Traverse City, his home became a way-station. A settler going to Traverse would stop at Masters' house to see if anyone had left any mail or messages to be taken to Traverse. At Traverse, the traveler would inquire for mail for his neighbors and would leave it with Masters on his return. Settlers traveling by wagon would frequently bring back extra supplies and leave them with Masters for some particular person or for anyone who might stop by and have need of them.

Before long, formality caught up with practice, and Masters was in the grocery business, paying York to bring him regular supplies from Hannah, Lay and Co. in Traverse. York found he could make a profit by making a regular trip, and the government acknowledged the settlement by designating "Wexford" as a post office, naming Masters the postmaster. He was, of course, essentially a farmer, with over 100 acres of cleared land on his homestead, but he remained postmaster for seven years, served as the county's second treasurer in 1871-72, held almost every township office that there was to be held, and was a sort of community host at his little general store until his death at age eighty-three in 1887.

At first, the mail service was locally paid, the government furnishing free delivery only to and from Traverse. People sending mail out paid postage and also paid to have it taken to Traverse by York. At Traverse, York would pick up the mail for the Wexford post office and be paid for its carriage by Masters, who charged the addressee in turn. Before the year was over, York was running two trips a week and had hired a driver.[10] In 1886 the government established a free mail route, provided York with the official mail bag, and paid him for three weekly trips between Wexford and Traverse. In 1867 York's service became part of a Traverse City-Cedar Springs mail route, and daily service began in 1868.

The significance of the opening of the southbound mail route in 1867 can be understood only in view of the isolation of the area,

10. York's first driver did not remain in the area long enough to leave a lasting memory of his first name, although long enough to entice Mrs. Hall to leave with him. Mr. Anise was replaced by Israel Sutton, a tiny man only slightly over five feet in height, but reputed to have been capable of carrying 150 pounds on each shoulder and to be an equally prodigous drinker.

particularly in the winter. Mail moving to Traverse City by the York wagon in 1865 would find its way by boat to Chicago or Detroit, where a railroad would speed it to or near its destination. An answer might be forthcoming in as little as two and a half to three weeks. During the winter, however, when the Great Lakes were frozen and closed to navigation, communications to the outside world were virtually cut off. Until 1867 no attempt was made to maintain dray service on a regular basis during the winter, and it generally ceased altogether from around Christmas until the end of March or mid-April. During that time, any mail or supplies that were brought in came by back-packing on snowshoes.

Even Traverse City, cosmopolitan as it was in the mid-sixties, suffered from the isolation. In the winter of 1866-67, for instance, an exceptionally late spring delayed the opening of lake traffic so long that merchants resorted to rationing of flour, sugar, and pork to customers until late in May.

The opening of the year-round mail route to the south changed all that. The establishment of the formal government mail route meant the expenditure of funds to improve the road. In the fall of 1867, one could leave Traverse City and two and a half days later be in Cedar Springs, then the northern terminus of the Grand Rapid's and Indiana Railroad. Winter travel was slower and unreliable but was maintained. In 1868 the stage service was described as running "Each way daily except Sunday and as weather permits." The road from the Manistee River north to Traverse had by now been so improved that York's stage could make the round trip in a day, weather and the driver's drinking habits permitting.

5.

To the settlers, then, the state road was their lifeline, the umbilical cord nourishing the new settlements during the gestation period of their development. The need for such nourishment, for a simple feeling of assurance that civilization was reasonably near at hand, can be understood. Self-reliance was necessary for survival, but the most independent of the settlers grasped desperately at other human contacts. Meeting at the Masters "store," letters from family and friends, Sunday services, and "neighboring" kept the primitive world around them from encroaching too heavily into their humanity.

A look at the pattern of settlement is necessary to an understanding of the isolation and loneliness of the backwoods homesteads. At this time, the only people coming into the area were homesteaders looking for free government land. By the time they came, a few large tracts had been acquired by timber speculators, who had no intention of settling there. More important, over half of the county had already been set aside for specific government grants and was not available for homesteading. Half of the land in the county was reserved for the land grant to the Grand Rapids and Indiana Railroad to subsidize the construction of a railroad from Grand Rapids to some point on Little Traverse Bay.[11] The grant was for alternate square-mile sections of land for a distance of six miles on each side of the railroad, but the route had not been surveyed and construction was over a decade away. Until then, the whole county was subject to the grant, which turned the map into a giant checkerboard, with every odd-numbered section of land reserved for the railroad. Only those even-numbered sections not already sold or otherwise set aside were available for homesteading. As a result, most sections were to remain in their natural state for ten or twenty years after the first settlers entered the county.[12]

Then, too, these settlers were farmers. The limit on a free homestead or preemption purchase was 160 acres of land, or a

11. The G. R. & I. grant of 1856 was but a small part of the land subsidy program by which the federal government gave away over 214 million acres of land to railroads as an incentive to new railroad construction between 1850 and 1871. Actually, Uncle Sam had over a billion acres of public land going begging at $1.25 an acre. Thirty years later, after the railroad grants, general education grants to the states, Morrill Act grants to support state colleges (another 200 million acres), and the Homestead Act of 1862, the government had succeeded in disposing of only half of the available land. Homesteaders claimed less than 50 million acres in the first twenty-five years after passage of the act.

12. In 1884 there were almost 30,000 acres of government owned land in Wexford County in its natural state, and the G. R. & I. still owned over nine thousand acres, of which over two-thirds had not been logged.

quarter of a square-mile section. Most claimed the full amount. This meant that in a section available for homesteading, there would be generally only four families at most, and that section, in turn, would be squared by four "railroad" sections, in which there would be no settlers. The areas cleared for farming were small, and the work of clearing was laboriously slow. Life in the confining and dark cabin must have been emotionally trying, particularly in the winter, when there was little escape outdoors. The huge forest provided berries and game to supplement the diet, but it also was an enemy, cutting off the sunlight from all but the largest clearings for most of the day and harboring unpleasant surprises, from poison ivy and oak to predators who killed the farm animals and kept the settler awake at night with howls and screams.

Each homestead, then, was a remote island, the dark isolation of which is hard to imagine in this modern day of instant communication and constant illumination. There were no lights to be seen at night, no sounds to be heard except those of the forest. It is little wonder that the homesteaders so hated the night-howling of the wolves and an occasional panther, so earnestly attacked the forest, and so prized their neighbors, remote though they were.

There were a few, like Hall, who scorned help. When he died, half of his 160 acres were under cultivation, and it was his boast that he had cleared it all himself. But it took him most of his life to do it, and his neighbors didn't think they had that long. The raising of a house or barn was a neighborhood affair, and work bees for building or land clearing were turned into social affairs whenever possible.[13] One is worth mention, not because of the social festivities, but because of the ingenuity of the host, Lewis Cornell.

In the winter of 1866-67, Cornell cut twenty acres of hardwood on his homestead in section 12 of Wexford Township. It was heavily covered by shin-tangle through which passage was impossible, so the preparatory work was done on snowshoes when

13. The first work bee planned in the county for a public project turned to tragedy as it resulted in the county's first accidental death. Dr. Perry's son-in-law Robert Myhill donated an acre of land on section 24 of Wexford Township for the county's first school. During the clearing, he was struck by a falling tree and killed.

the growth was weighted down by snow. The trees were cut and trimmed. Larger limbs were cut into poles, and three or four were laid across the logs at ten-foot intervals and surrounded by smaller branches and the chopped brush. The following July, when all was thoroughly dry, he fired the area. The dry brush and shin-tangle kept the poles burning down into the logs, sometimes completely severing them. When the fire burned out, the shin-tangle and brush were gone, and nothing remained but twenty acres of scorched but undamaged hardwood logs, neatly marked out into ten-foot lengths by the burned-out poles. At the logging bee, a dozen neighbors came in with several ox teams, finished sawing through the logs that hadn't been completely severed by the burning poles, and hauled the lot to Wheeler's sawmill. In one day, Cornell had sold a handsome lot of hardwood timber and had twenty acres "completely done up" except for stumping.[14] The wives had spent the day berrying and cooking, and a "sumptious [sic] repast in late afternoon allowed much singing and fun and a return home before nightfall."

14. Several attempts to clear pine land in the same fashion were something less than successful, as the pine logs were burned beyond value and the fire spread to "clear" more land than was intended.

Chapter Two

"AT OR NEAR MANISTEE BRIDGE"

When the early settler came to Wexford County, it was as if he were stepping a half century backwards in time. It was an inventive society, already beginning to be a mass-production industrial society. The sewing machine, reaper, automatic corn planter, telegraph, and railroad made life easier—elsewhere. In his log cabin in the backwoods, the homesteader lived, hunted, and farmed little differently from his grandfather. He was Daniel Boone, with a modern rifle and a better axe, but still Daniel Boone.

But it was only temporary. The first big step into civilized living came with the skill John Harrison Wheeler brought with him in 1865. Like his neighbors, Wheeler was from New York. Like many of them, he was a veteran of the Union Army. Born and reared on a New York farm, he was trained as a carpenter and learned something of the machinist's trade.

When the Civil War broke out, Wheeler enlisted and saw most of the early fighting of the war in Maryland and Virginia. After a convalescent leave, during which he met and was smitten by a charming young teacher, Georgianna Fox, he was transferred to an engineering detail and had charge of the construction of some hospitals of the Army of the Potomac. Several men in his construction brigade were from Michigan and described their state in such glowing terms that he resolved to see the place after the War. As chance would have it, within days after his return home from service, Wheeler met the brother of Benjamin Hall. Hall had visited relatives in his home state after being deserted by his wife, and he so praised the paradise of northern Michigan that several families were planning to homestead there. The second-hand, and probably exaggerated, account convinced Wheeler.

He organized his affairs, conducted a whirlwind courtship of Georgianna, and left for Michigan on their wedding day. They shipped by boat from Buffalo to Traverse City, where he bought a horse and wagon, loaded his furniture, consisting of a bed, rocker, chair, and tool chest, and headed south along the trail, which was not then fully stumped. On October 30, 1865, he picked out a homestead site just north of the Manistee on section 30 of Hanover Township on what was logically known thereafter as Wheeler Creek. At that late date, it was a race to get up shelter, but a twelve-by-sixteen-foot cabin with a window and the luxury of a floor was completed before the first snowfall.

Wheeler never forgot the cheerfulness with which his wife helped him through that first winter. He had a little more money than the average homesteader and could afford a trip to Traverse to bring back some chickens and a cow, real glass for the window, and a good supply of flour, sugar, salt, pork, oats, and other dried foods that would get them through the winter along with the game and fish that he would catch. For Georgianna, he brought yard goods and books. That winter she sewed, he made furniture, and they took turns reading to each other. Even so, it was a lonely time, with the nearest neighbor over a half mile back through the woods, reached by a path marked with blazed trees. From Christmas to Easter, they saw only a half dozen other people.

Chickens and a cow he might have, but a farmer he had no intention of being. Before starting his westward journey, he had hit upon the idea of building a sawmill which would give him a source of income as well as provide him with lumber for the building business he planned to follow. The homestead site had been chosen because of the creek which would provide water power for the sawmill.

It was the right idea at the right place. Until his arrival, frame construction was impossible. The nearest mill was on the Boardman River at Traverse, and the cost of finished lumber was not only high but the expense of hauling it from Traverse was prohibitive. At the same time, no one lived in log cabins by choice. They were crude. They were uncomfortable. The effort in putting them up was all out of proportion to the product obtained, and there was virtually no construction of outbuildings. If any shelter for livestock was put up at all, it usually consided only of a crude lean-to.

As might be expected, Wheeler's announced intention of

building the sawmill was greeted with enthusiasm by his neighbors. He shrewdly offered future milling for help now and managed to enlist the neighbors in a volunteer effort to build his dam and help him put up his works. When the mill started operation in 1867, he was kept almost continuously at work getting out lumber for the surrounding settlers, and those who had helped put up the mill got more than they expected from John. Busy as he was, he put up a five-room frame house for Georgianna that summer. It was the first frame building completed in the county.

That same summer Oren Fletcher settled on the north side of the Manistee farther downstream. He was a miller, and he soon had a host of volunteers busy clearing land for his home and helping in the construction of a grist mill. The dam, on what was thereafter "Fletcher's" Creek, was quickly completed, and, with the help of Wheeler's lumber, the mill was rapidly put up and ready for operation before the end of the year. Civilization was coming to the woods.

2.

The coming of John Wheeler to Wexford County brought a far larger gift than just his skills as a builder and mill operator. In 1888 the new editor of the Clam Lake *News & Express*, Perry F. Powers, made his first acquaintance with Wheeler and was sufficiently impressed to make it a matter of record in the *News*:

> We had the pleasure of meeting Wheeler, the editor of the Sherman *Pioneer* yesterday. Wheeler lays no claim to beauty, but he is an unusually useful man. He is a druggist, a dry goods merchant, a grocer, an editor, a supervisor, a husband and father, and the time not occupied in fulfilling the duties of these vocations are given to doing good on general principles.

This was hardly the first mention of Wheeler in the county's papers. His "press" had ranged from adulation to derision, from approval to excoriation. An earlier editor of the *News* had called him an "ape," and Cooper at Manton had called him worse. But the Powers account was accurate; Wheeler was all he said, and more.

A photograph of Wheeler taken while he was in his early fifties shows a handsome, sandy haired man with a contrasting white goatee and enormous mustaches extending seven to eight inches in each direction. His eyes hint at humor, and the portrait accurately reflects an intelligent, benign, and tolerant disposition. It is, perhaps, not a complete portrait, nor wholly accurate, for he was certainly not guileless, and nothing in the picture gives any clue to his ambition or his shrewd skill in business and politics. He could be clever, but he was always honest. He could drive a bargain, but he never overreached.

For thirty-five years, there was little that happened in the county affairs in which he was not involved. He was the first county treasurer and later served two more terms in the same office from 1899 through 1902.[1] During his career of public service, he was justice of the peace, county superintendent of the poor, deputy county clerk, and deputy sheriff. He was postmaster of Sherman from 1880 to 1886.

He served as a Republican district delegate, as chairman and for many years secretary of the county Republican committee. He was twice chairman of the county board of supervisors during the ten years he spent as a supervisor from the townships of Antioch, Sherman and Concord.

During the many years of the county seat struggle, he was spokesman for and dominated the Sherman faction. His knowledge of parliamentary law and some innovations of his fertile mind were instrumental in prolonging Sherman's losing fight to keep the county seat. The townships of Sherman and Concord were such innovations, created from parts of other townships for the sole purpose of increasing the representation of the northwest part of the county on the board of supervisors. The supervisor

1. He was defeated for the same office in 1884 by Democrat James Haynes, partly as a result of the "greenback" split within the Republican party, and partly because of the residual bitterness from the county seat battle in which he played a dominant role—and partly because Haynes was rather more personable than Democrats were usually allowed to be.

from each of these short-lived townships was none other than John Harrison Wheeler, battling tooth and nail on the board, in the courts, and in the press, by every means, to keep political power in Sherman. Judge Fallass called him a great lawyer.

To strengthen his hand in the county political war, Wheeler bought an interest in the Wexford County *Pioneer* in 1878 and was its sole editor and publisher from 1880 until 1891. Even before becoming personally involved in the newspaper business, he was a frequent editorialist. A fierce competitor, he was also an intelligent loser. When the county seat battle was lost to Cadillac, his good judgment was not clouded by his emotions, and he did much to heal the wounds remaining from the long fight.

Besides running the sawmill and newspaper, he was a successful contractor and builder. He operated a general store and a drugstore. He made his share of timber deals, and, in partnership with Judge C. C. Chittenden, he became involved in real estate investment, which included a subdivision in the city of Cadillac and gave us Wheeler Street.

Throughout such a career, he remained a man of great good humor. He took politics seriously, and he had a deep feeling for the historic events of the period, large and small. Some thought him overly sober, even pompous, but those who thought he took himself too seriously may well have been missing the subtle humor which, often as not, was directed at them. He was a prolific and entertaining letter writer, both private and public. The mind that could produce a keen memorandum on township law and author a scathing editorial could equally produce sentimental and tender poetry for the wife he so dearly loved.

In the 1880s he commenced the recording and preservation of the history of the people of the area and organized what came to be the Sherman Pioneer Society. The publication of the *Pioneer* under his editorship and the notes of the Pioneer Society were candid and earthy. He could easily have been a gossip, for he had a keen eye and ear for the people around him. After he sold the newspaper, its new editor, R. D. Frederick, described one paper given by Wheeler at the Pioneer Society as recounting "many spicy doings among the early settlers." And it is John whom we must thank for preserving the accounts of the Gasser adultery trial, the Preston scandal, and the conclusion that the marital problems of Ben Hall were more likely caused by the bark of his house than the bite of his personality.

Over the years, even those who opposed him most violently, in the political fashion of the times, found it impossible to maintain a feud with him, excepting only Thomas A. Ferguson (briefly) and Charles Cooper, who never forgave him for buying the *Pioneer* out from under him in 1878. We shall meet both elsewhere. In 1903 Wheeler published a history of Wexford County in which both Ferguson and Cooper are, typically, generously portrayed, and in which the role of John Wheeler is but modestly mentioned.

3.

By 1866 there were enough people in the new settlement to merit political notice. For several years the county had been attached to Brown Township of Manistee County for administrative purposes. In the fall of 1866, however, the Manistee County board of supervisors organized the entire area as a single township called Wexford and provided that the first elections would be held in April of 1867. Over the next few years the political activity of the county was largely that involved in nominations within the Republican party, no significant Democratic vote existing. In 1867 Lewis C. Dunham was elected supervisor, defeating Hiram Copley. In the following year, Dunham was re-elected, defeating Enos C. Dayhuff from the Unionville settlement. At the time of the election, it was estimated that there were about 450 people living in the area, and everyone expected an increasing influx of settlers. It was not surprising, then, that talk should commence about the possibility of setting off the area from Manistee and organizing it as an independent county.

One man who had seen this eventuality was George W. Bryant of Traverse City, who was speculating in real estate throughout the northwestern part of the state. During the period when the state road was being surveyed, Bryant made a point of cultivating the acquaintance of Perry Hannah, a Traverse City merchant. Hannah had been appointed by the governor as one of the commissioners to lay out the route. Bryant managed to get sufficient survey information to find where the right-of-way would be located and made land purchases at various strategic points along the way. One such purchase in Wexford County was at the point where the Manistee River would be bridged. Something of his nature is disclosed in a story told by Hannah. When the comissioners contracted for the building of the bridge, Bryant sought out the builder, Godfrey Greilick, to threaten suit should Greilick trespass or cut any trees on Bryant's property. Greilick's response was to build the entire bridge out of timber cut from Bryant's land.

As the road was improved and the area settled, Bryant commenced an ambitious campaign. Late in 1867 he started construction of a two-story hotel and grocery store at the bridge. At the same time he had started a campaign to convince postal authorities that the "Manistee Bridge Settlement" was of such a size as to warrant its own designation as a post office. Apparently in the belief that this was true, the authorities approved the new post office in January of 1868. "Manistee Bridge," however, did not seem an appropriate name to the postal superintendent. Since there was no organized village at the spot, it was his recommendation to name it in honor of Gen. William T. Sherman. To Mr. Bryant's further disappointment, it was not he but Dr. John Perry who was designated as the first postmaster of Sherman.

Recognizing the post office as a community center in itself, Bryant put down his disappointment and made a deal with Perry. Instead of using the Perry home as the point at which the mail stage would make pickups and deliveries, Bryant House could be used without charge, and if Perry wished to name an assistant postmaster to be there, Bryant would give that person employment. He probably hoped for the appointment for himself. It developed that the man appointed by Perry was Lewis J. Clark, named simultaneously for both great American explorers. Clark was the carpenter who had built Bryant House, and, with Bryant's facility for antagonizing people, their relationship had not been altogether smooth. Swallowing hard, Bryant made his apologies to Clark and persuaded him to come to work for him as manager of his hotel-grocery store.

Clark went, liked the work, disliked Bryant, and quit within a few months. He put up a store of his own about a mile south of the Manistee at the point where Antioch, Springville, Wexford, and

Hanover townships corner. It was the first frame building in what was to become the village of Sherman. Perry kept Clark as his deputy postmaster, and the mail stage began using the Clark store as the mail distribution center. It became a real post office. Within a year Perry resigned as postmaster, and Clark was named his successor. In the immediate vicinity were the homes of Clark, Perry, and H. J. Carpenter, while Moses Cole was putting up a home just to the east on the way to the sawmill which he and Perry had just completed.

Bryant House, without the post office, had few guests and fewer customers for groceries. The potential of the area still appeared good even though the post office had been moved away. Most of the 450 people in the county were within a six-mile radius of the bridge, so Bryant persisted in his efforts on behalf of "Manistee Bridge."

So far as river travel was concerned, the picture of a water highway that we sometimes gather from historical novels is pure fiction. The river in 1868 bore little resemblance to its appearance today. It is true that trappers and Indians moved into the interior of the state by canoe. The trappers were on the river by the nature of their business, however, and not because river travel was convenient. Early descriptions of the Manistee disclose that it was rare to find so much as a mile of open river in any one stretch. Overhangs, rocks, and tipped trees collected floating brush and trees, which the current wedged into tightly matted "jams," around which the river traveler had to portage. Some such "jams" had become so thick as to form natural bridges. One "jam" several miles upstream from the state road bridge was the river crossing for the old Indian trial and was so solid that, with reasonable care, it could be crossed by horses and livestock.

But the Manistee did hold promise in 1868. In the 1840s the first sawmills had been built where the river emptied into Lake Michigan at Manistee City. Logging had begun along the river in the 50s, and now the loggers were flourishing. The investment of capital in new mills and in the purchase of timber lands was accompanied by a cooperative effort of the loggers to clear the river "jams" so that logs could be floated down to the mills. The realization that the upper reaches of the river would soon be open to logging led to optimistic ideas of steamer traffic on the river, ideas that continued to beguile promoters and investors for another twenty years.

Bryant House, then, seemed to be strategically located where the river was bridged by the only inland road on the west side of the state. As Bryant said in a letter to State Rep. William H. Mitchell of Traverse City regarding the proposed incorporation of Wexford County, the population of the territory "now approaches 500 souls, all within ten miles of Manistee Bridge."

4.

The distribution of population around the north end of the state road was reflected in the township organization proposed by Representative Mitchell's bill. Not only did Act 386 organize the county and authorize the first county election, but it also divided the county into four political townships: Hanover, Wexford, Springville, and Colfax.

Hanover Township included the present-day township of the same name, together with the area comprising the present townships of Greenwood and Liberty.[2] Springville Township included the present township of the same name, together with the area comprising the present townships of Antioch, Boon, Slagle, Henderson, and South Branch. Colfax Township included the area of the present township of the same name, together with Clam Lake, Cherry Grove, Haring, Selma, and Cedar Creek. Of the four townships, only Wexford exists in the same form today, reflecting the fact that it was then the most heavily settled area of the new county. The act directed that the first caucus of Wexford Township be held at the home of William Masters, with Isaac U. Davis, Isaac Cornell, and Lewis Carpenter designated as election inspec-

2. The act ordered the holding of the first township caucuses. That for Hanover was to be held at the home of Lewis C. Dunham, with Dunham, Robert Henderson, and John Wheeler as election inspectors. The first caucus for Springville was ordered held at the Clark store, with Aaron Baker, Daniel Jewett, and H. C. Dunning named as election inspectors. The Colfax caucus was ordered held at the home of Lucas Gates, with Gates, William Goff, and Nathan Dayhuff named as election inspectors.

tors. It must have been a spirited caucus, because a fight ensued between Jay J. Copley and Myron Baldwin, resulting in the prosecution of Copley for assault and battery.[3] The trial itself, in addition to being the first judicial proceeding in the new county, must have had some interesting overtones, for election inspector Davis helped break up the fight, was elected justice of the peace at the caucus, and was a witness at the trial of Copley over which he was the presiding justice. He undoubtedly sentenced Copley with complete impartiality.[4]

Act 386 also attached Missaukee County to Wexford County for purposes of administration, taxation, and justice until such time as it might be given its own independent county organization. The top tier of surveyed townships were attached to Hanover Township for that purpose and the remaining three-quarters of the county to Colfax Township. At the annual meeting of the county supervisors in 1869, Reeder Township in Missaukee County was organized, and Daniel Reeder attended the Wexford board meetings for the next year and a half, until the legislature organized Missaukee County as an independent political unit in 1871.

3. There was considerable bad blood in the area over the Copleys' political activities, going back to the first election of 1867 when the area was part of Manistee County. Prior to the election, said Wheeler, the Copleys and Skinners, "considering themselves the best qualified Republicans, thought to dominate the nominating caucus" and had nominating slips prepared with which Hiram Copley was to be nominated for supervisor and justice of the peace, Jay Copley for clerk, H. H. Skinner for road commissioner and school inspector, and Mrs. Skinner for treasurer. The Copleys did dominate the caucus but so antagonized everyone that a rump session was held outside, led by John Wheeler, in which a separate slate was put up headed by Lewis Dunham which won the election. The Copleys never ceased to consider it a personal affront, and to be perpetually feuding thereafter. When Jay Copley's wife ran away with Dr. Preston, Copley "lit into" any number of people who he thought were laughing at him. Perhaps they were.

4. The trial was held in the log school on the Myhill property. The deputy sheriff in charge of the jury was John Wheeler, and when the jury was ready to deliberate, there being but the one room, everyone left the building except the jury. Just after the building was cleared, a thunderstorm drenched spectators, witnessses, and court officers alike to the great delight of the jury, one of whom said they withheld their verdict only long enough to get everyone well soaked.

5.

Act 386 was unique in one particular. Acts for the incorporation of counties generally left location of the county seats to the first county board of supervisors. Section 9 of Act 386, however, reflected the influence which George Bryant was able to bring to bear upon Representative Mitchell:

> The county seat of said county shall be and is hereby located in township 24 north, range 12 west, at or near what is called Manistee Bridge; and Henry I. Devoe, Isaac U. Davis, and E. C. Dayhuff are hereby appointed commissioners to locate the same. If said commissioners, or any two of them, shall fail to locate said county seat within one year from June next, then the board of supervisors and county clerk of said county shall locate the same.

Dayhuff apparently did not participate in the survey. He lived in the southern part of the Unionville settlement, and it was not an easy trip to Manistee Bridge. Later events suggest that he did not favor the site anyway and considered his homestead at the center of the county to be an ideal site for location of the county seat. It does not appear that the survey took long. Davis was paid four dollars and Devoe five dollars for mileage and one day of services in making the selection. It also appears that they probably had already made up their minds as to the site. As Wheeler put it, the commissioners shared "the feeling of all settlers that in view of Bryant's parsimony, no village could thrive on a site at which Bryant owned all the land."

We can imagine Bryant's concern when the commissioners neglected to respond to his written invitation to meet to discuss the sale of land for the courthouse site, and we can understand his anguish and despair when a trip to Manistee Bridge disclosed that the two commissioners living closest to the site had selected land owned by Henry Clark behind the Lewis Clark store. They had taken advantage of the language of Act 386 to select a site "*near* what is called Manistee Bridge" rather than *at* Manistee Bridge. Instead of having to buy a site, the county was receiving it as a gift from Clark,[5] who was also adding a contribution of $400 towards the cost of constructing a courthouse. Exit Mr. Bryant from Wexford County history. His Bryant House proved unprofitable and was soon sold.

The site selected was about a mile down the state road from the Bryant store and was just west of the Lewis Clark home and store. In the previous year, Sylvester Clark and his nephew, Henry, had come to the area. Henry was a "land-looker," scouting out pine lands for lumbermen with an eye to northern operations, and doing some speculative buying on his own. Young and single, he had no intention of settling in one place for long. But some of John Wheeler's in-laws had come to homestead. Henry met Alice Fox, looked at things a little differently, and bought some land.

Sylvester Clark had a wife and was looking for an opportunity to settle. Just up the trail from the post office was the big log cabin that "the squatter" had put up and abandoned a few years before. He moved in, found he could buy the land, and set about improving it by replacing the roof, putting in a floor and some partitions, cutting some windows, and building a good fireplace. On the back he built a frame addition containing a dining room and kitchen, and the Sherman House hotel was in business. In future years the original log structure was sided over and another addition made, creating a very presentable place that bore no resemblance to a pioneer cabin. It was still serving the public at the end of the century.[6]

5. Clark's deed contained language that it was only "so long as it shall be used for county purposes." The language was later to be seized upon by Clam Lake partisans as evidence that the county's title was defective and used as a reason for moving the county seat from Sherman.

6. For judicial purposes, Act 386 placed Wexford County in the thirteenth judicial district, then presided over by Judge J. G. Ramsdell of Traverse City. The first court session was held in the Sherman House in August of 1869. The only case on the calendar was an appeal from Justice Davis in a civil suit, *Milliman v. Cornell*, which was settled by the parties several days before the term opened. As became customary, however, until the new courthouse was constructed, the little log Sherman House became the courtroom and the lodging for the judge, court officers, and attorneys who followed the judge from county to county around the circuit. John Wheeler said: "The first session was not very interesting, as there

At that first county election in 1869, the following officers were elected at salaries set by the board of supervisors: sheriff, Harrison H. Skinner, $100 per year; treasurer, John H. Wheeler, $50 per year; clerk and register of deeds, Leroy P. Champenois, $150 per year; and probate judge, Isaac N. Carpenter, $100 per year. All were Republicans except Carpenter, who defeated Solomon C. Worth by a quirk of the election laws. The ballots were poorly prepared, and some named the Republican candidate only as S. C. Worth, while others carried his full name. Election law required the differently worded ballots to be treated as if they named two different candidates. Since neither S. C. Worth nor Solomon C. Worth alone drew more votes than Carpenter, he won, although receiving a minority of the votes.[7]

Supervisors elected were Henry I. Devoe of Wexford Township; William E. Dean of Springville Township; L. Clarence Northrup of Hanover Township, who was also elected county superintendent of schools, and Rascelas S. McClain of Colfax, who was also elected county surveyor.

As there was no county building, the supervisors met immediately and authorized the county officers to conduct county business from their homes. They also authorized the sale of bonds to meet the first year's county expenses, levied taxes of $4,703.75 on an equalized valuation of $941,279.03, contracted for a second bridge across the Manistee at a cost of $400, and added a county supplement of $5 to the state bounty on wolves.[8] Sheriff Skinner, piqued at the failure of the board to provide a jail and sheriff's

was no calendar, no cases to try, and no lawyers in the county." O. H. Mills of Traverse City had been named acting prosecuting attorney for the county, and he and Judge Ramsdell were joined by three other Traverse City attorneys, who made the trip to see the new county and meet the new county officers.

7. Worth had come in by ox team to homestead with his brother-in-law Henry Devoe in 1867. Like Devoe, he went on to long service on the county board of supervisors and held office as township clerk and as superintendent of the poor.

8. The wolf packs were soon decimated, Lucas Gates and the Mesick brothers collecting large bounties. In 1877 the Lansing Republican reported that during debate on a bill to repeal the wolf bounty, the charge was made that wolves were being bred in Wexford County for the profit to be made on the bounty. Coincidentally, the last large pack was reported in the county that year, although bounties were still being paid in the nineties.

residence immediately, named John Wheeler as deputy and Sanford Gasser as under-sheriff, and largely sat out his term on his farm near the county line. Wheeler and Champenois, however, could see the coming growth of a village at the county seat. They immediately bought land near the courthouse site and put up homes.[9] The village of Sherman was being born.

9. It is unfortunate that space does not permit a better acquaintance with Capt. Leroy P. Champenois, a peculiar mixture of backslid Methodist and backslid Republican, who moved through life with a casual grace and self confidence that were sometimes criticized but undoubtedly envied by all who knew him. Born in Adrian in a devoutly orthodox Methodist family, he soon rebelled at the disciplines and beliefs then current in the Methodist Episcopal church. Although always a Methodist and one of the founding members of the first Methodist congregation in the county, he seldom attended and seldom bothered to explain his absence. He seems to have represented a challenge to each new pastor at the church; each in turn sought him out, tried to convince him of the error of his ways, and withdrew in confusion at his excellent understanding of, and indifference to, theology.

His childhood exposure to abolition, however, made a permanent impact. The Champenois family home had been part of the underground railroad in the 1840s, helping to hide and transport escaped slaves to safety. As a boy, he had helped in some midnight "shipments" to Canada. When the Civil War broke out, Champenois was among the first volunteers, saw action in many battles, and was raised from enlisted man to captain because of his leadership and bravery. At the battle of Tupelo in 1864, most of his right hand was shot away. It was said of him "that he slept that night in a bloody shirt, and he has been waving it ever since," because he remained among the most radical of Republicans in his view as to the treatment that should have been accorded to the conquered rebels of the south. His other political views, however, involved a touch of "greenback" heresy. He supported the Women's Suffrage constitutional amendment of 1874, and he disagreed with the Republican position on tariffs and labor organization.

After serving his term as the county's first clerk and register of deeds, he was not renominated and never sought office again. In spite of it, he was from time to time elected to different township offices by his friends and neighbors. He was appointed postmaster at Sherman in 1897, serving until shortly before his death in 1902. He seems to have been comfortably fixed financially, worked when, as, and if he felt like it, and preferred to devote his time to hunting, fishing, and reading. His wife was an early activist in the W.C.T.U. movement at Sherman, but he was as tolerant of this foible as he was of the differing political and religious views of his friends and neighbors, and she lovingly reciprocated.

Chapter Three

MAKING A VILLAGE: SHERMAN

As might be expected, the news that a new county had been organized attracted a different type of newcomer, the businessman anticipating the growth of a community around the county seat and hoping to make a profit from it. It was a reasonable anticipation. Every county seat attracted business and professional people, drew commerce, and prospered. Those looking over Wexford's new county seat could see the prospect of growth ahead. Most of the county's 500 population lived within a radius of ten miles, and this would be their trading center. It was natural to expect future settlement to grow outward around this beginning.

The first farming experiences in the area had been successful, and the nature of the sterile sand underlying the thin topsoil and forest humus had yet to be revealed. Early accounts of county farming described the area as a garden spot and predicted that the county would rival any state in the Union in the growth of grain and fruit. The movement of the logging business upriver indicated that the area would be the site of a new industry and the Manistee a possible inland waterway. Somewhere through the area a railroad would be located, and it was inconceivable that it could bypass the county seat. To this apparent hub of new growth, center of government, and future center of trade and commerce, came those who wished to be in on the ground floor of its prosperity.

Two who came somewhat reluctantly were the Maqueston brothers, Edward and Isaac. They were New Yorkers and previously acquainted with some of the settlers in the area. In New York, Isaac had only recently sold a business and was at loose ends, trying to make a decision about a new venture, more or less of a mind to reject the suggestions of his brother Edward that he come to Michigan and join him in a land venture. Working as a land-looker, Edward had gradually moved northward through lower Michigan, selecting pine lands for his employers and doing some buying and selling on his own account. By 1867 he was operating out of Big Rapids with Henry Clark. We do not know if he had been through the Sherman area, but he had acquired a familiarity with the pine lands in the eastern part of the county before 1869 and had bought some good pine lands for himself in various locations.[1]

Henry Clark's uncle, Sylvester Clark, was the owner of the Sherman House and intended to make Sherman his permanent residence. Henry, a bachelor, was doing well as a land-looker, but he hadn't had the capital to do much buying on his own account. He was uncertain as to what he might do at this point, and his donation of the land for the county seat had been an impulsive thing. He could ill afford the $400 pledged towards the cost of the courthouse. But he was taken with the idea of building a community, and his enthusiasm for that was contagious. At his urging, Edward Maqueston wrote to his brother in New York. Isaac agreed to come, at least for a visit. They went to Sherman, agreed it had a good business future, and Isaac agreed to "stay for awhile." As matters developed, they both stayed, while Henry Clark soon drifted back to Big Rapids, then briefly back to Sherman, and finally to Minnesota.

The Maquestons bought a few parcels of land as an investment in what they thought would be the village. They put up a two-story frame building along the state road, beside the courthouse site, and started a general store, selling groceries, feed, and manufactured products of all kinds, from dry goods to hardware. They designed the second floor as a community hall, and it became the social center of the village—the lodge rooms, church, dancehall, and all-round meeting place. They prospered as merchants and, with Edward's land buying experience, did well in buying and selling pine lands. When Isaac decided in 1878 that his visit had lasted long enough and was about to go home to New York, the two-year-old gristmill of Shackleton & Bennett burned with little insurance. He stayed to buy the site, hired John Wheeler to rebuild

1. One parcel around the east end of Little Clam Lake was subsequently part of the site of the city of Cadillac.

the mill, then decided that he had to stay long enough to help someone learn the business, and ended by letting his manager gradually buy it from the earnings. He was a particularly kindly man who went out of his way to help people who were down on their luck, and to lend money that he could never reasonably expect to be repaid. He was still helping his gristmill manager buy the mill when, one day in 1886, after helping neighbors fight a fire, he returned to his store, collapsed, and died. The entire village followed the hearse which carried his body to Manton, whence he finally went home to New York.

2.

Sanford Gasser, another acquaintance of Clark in the Big Rapids area, also came to the new county seat in 1869. He was born in Ohio, and his family moved to an Indiana farm, where he spent his boyhood. His search for a living had then brought him to the Big Rapids area when he was twenty-two. He began as a hunter of passenger pigeons, shipping thousands of barrels out of Big Rapids each year during the migration. In other seasons, he hunted and trapped for fur and meat, supplying local restaurants and markets, and ultimately opening his own restaurant. This enterprise he expanded into a billiard hall and saloon.[2] In order to supply domestic meats, he leased a small farm and expanded his farming operation into the harvesting of marsh hay, which was sold to lumber camps for their horses and oxen.

Hearing of Clark's interest in Sherman, he made the trip on the state road, liked what he saw, and bought eighty acres of land adjoining the proposed courthouse site on the west. Anticipating the growth of a village in that direction, he set to work surveying and clearing his land, and the following year subdivided a portion of it as the plat of the village of Sherman. Unfortunately, the village grew along the state road and to the east, and the sale of his lots was slow. He borrowed heavily for timber land speculation which didn't produce prompt returns. He farmed, but the effort was handicapped by his lack of interest in agriculture and his

2. And developed an obsessive hatred of whiskey and those who used it.

preference for spending his time looking for land deals.

Judging from the number of lawsuits brought against him by his creditors, one would be tempted to conclude that during his early years in the county, Gasser was always just a step ahead of the sheriff. Actually he served as under-sheriff and jailer while the county seat was at Sherman, boarding prisoners in his home while a jail was built. The fees for this service may have been all that permitted him to stave off his creditors. On the other hand, the frequency with which the county supervisors refused payment for claims which he submitted may have caused his chronic insolvency. Their repeated disallowance of all or a portion of his charges and fees suggests either that he regularly attempted to perpetrate petty frauds upon the county or that he was grossly abused by the supervisors. His tolerance of their action without suit suggests the former, but his tenure as under-sheriff during the term of several sheriffs and the fact that he remained a deputy sheriff most of his life indicate confidence in his probity by those best able to make such judgments. Among the neighbors there were sharp differences of opinion attributable in part, perhaps, to an incident in 1871 that had people choosing up sides.

To assist him in the operation of his farm while he was away looking over prospective land and timber deals, Gasser hired Myron Baldwin.[3] Baldwin soon joined the ranks of those aggrieved by Gasser's failure to pay promptly, and he ultimately took his complaint against his employer to the prosecuting attorney. A warrant was issued charging Gasser with fraud, and he was convicted in justice court. He appealed to circuit court, where the matter was allowed to die without trial, since the complaint was essentially a civil action for debt and not actually a violation of criminal law.

Gasser did more than appeal, however. Whether from justifiable indignation or, as some people felt, merely because he thought the best defense to be a strong offense, Gasser also went to the prosecutor's office to make a complaint against Baldwin. While he was off looking at pine land, said Gasser, Baldwin had

3. Baldwin will be remembered as the subject of the assault by Jay Copley at the first Wexford Town caucus, and the complaining witness in the county's first criminal trial which resulted.

neglected his duties on the Gasser farm but had not neglected Mrs. Gasser. The prosecutor agreed that the latter, at least, was criminally wrong. On Gasser's sworn complaint, Baldwin was charged with adultery. After some reflection it occurred to the prosecutor that such an offense is not committed alone, and he advised Gasser that the complaint would have to be against both Baldwin and Mrs. Gasser or against neither. So a second complaint was signed, Mrs. Gasser was arrested, and the stage was set for the county's first circuit court jury trials.

The first case, that of Baldwin, was heard at Clark's Sherman House on February 14, 1872. The jury found Baldwin not guilty. The trial of Mrs. Gasser was never heard. She had left her husband's home after the arrest and became dependent upon her friends. An attorney was appointed by the court to defend her, but, while staying with her family in southern Michigan, she died suddenly—of a broken heart, said her friends.[4]

At the next term of court, Gasser returned to defend himself against a civil suit brought by Baldwin for the wage claim which had started the series of court appearances. The second jury took the same view of things as had the first, and gave Baldwin a judgment against Gasser, which was eventually paid, ending their litigious relationship. The last official record in connection therewith is the claim submitted by Gasser to the board of supervisors for a twenty-five dollar attorney fee, represented to have been paid in connection with the prosecution of his wife and Baldwin. The board found it had been for his defense of Baldwin's wage suit and refused payment.

Eventually things took a better turn for Gasser. His land deals began to return a profit. His new wife was well accepted and became a leader in the W.C.T.U. and various social organizations of the village. He opened an office as a real estate and insurance agent and extended his personal land and timber investments. From inauspicious beginnings as Sherman's chief debtor, he acquired a reputation as one of the shrewdest and busiest private lenders in northwestern Michigan. He built the largest home in Sherman and ended his career, according to John Wheeler, "in

4. Mr. Gasser remarried promptly, to the surprise of some.

the respectability of Republican politics and the temperance movement."

3.

During the summer of 1869, two men, brothers-in-law, made the trip to Sherman to look it over and judge its prospects. They were Thomas A. Ferguson, just graduated from the law school at the state university at Ann Arbor, and Heman B. Sturtevant. Sturtevant had been born in Vermont into a poor but well-educated farm family. His grandfather had been a close friend of Ethan Allen and had served for a time as Allen's second in command during the Revolution.[5] As a grown man of nineteen, Sturtevant came to Livingston County, where he was employed briefly on a farm, and then enrolled at the normal school at Ypsilanti. After graduation he taught until the outbreak of the Civil War, then enlisted in the army. After the war he returned to the state university at Ann Arbor briefly, and then resumed farming near Owosso. A chance encounter with a merchant led him to part-time employment, and he soon opened his own store and was an immediate success.

Ferguson was born in Livingston County, received a good education, and resumed that education after army service during the Civil War. He entered the law school at the University of Michigan, graduating in 1869. One of Ferguson's teachers at the university was Judge H. J. Beaks of Ann Arbor, who had received a letter from Judge J. G. Ramsdell of Traverse City noting the opportunities for attorneys in the new settlements of northern Michigan. Ramsdell mentioned the organization of several new counties, naming Wexford County as one in which there were no attorneys. Judge Beaks suggested to Ferguson that he might do well to look at some of the counties in the Grand Traverse vicinity. As it developed, he never looked farther than Sherman.

Ferguson invited his brother-in-law to accompany him on the trip. From Grand Rapids they traveled on the G. R. & I. to its

5. And each successive generation had at least one Ethan Allen Sturtevant.

then northern terminus, Morley, making the rest of the trip by stage. Arriving, they found a tiny settlement with a gristmill and two sawmills nearby, a hotel, two stores, a doctor, a post office with a daily mail stage, but no lawyer. Dr. Perry told them that logging crews were busy clearing the river and undoubtedly many camps would be established throughout the county before the year was out. It was apparent to Sturtevant that there was a good opportunity for a merchant as supplier for the camps and that there were also many opportunities for the purchase of inexpensive land. Inquiries about several parcels disclosed the railroad land grant, and the two concluded that Sherman would undoubtedly be a "stop" on the G. R. & I. The decision was made, and Sturtevant returned home to liquidate his affairs, while Ferguson went on to Traverse City, met Judge Ramsdell, and was assured that an appointment as prosecuting attorney was his for the asking. He returned to Sherman, contracted to purchase land for himself and his brother-in-law, posted a letter to Judge Ramsdell announcing his location in the county, and went after his wife. The letter, though legible enough to state his intent, resulted in an order by Judge Ramsdell appointing *J.* A. F*u*rguson. Within six weeks, both men were back in Sherman and had houses under construction.

Sturtevant had a long and distinguished career as a merchant, business man, and political figure. He was elected county clerk and register of deeds in 1870, '72, and '74 on the Republican ticket.[6] As a former teacher, he was soon pressing for the construction of a good school building. When it was built, he was its first teacher, and he was a school officer for years. He held office as justice of the peace continuously from 1870 until 1901. For eight years he was the supervisor of Hanover Township and played an important role in the county seat struggles between Sherman and Cadillac. In 1877 he was the Sherman postmaster.

Sturtevant started a general store in Sherman which he operated alone or in partnership with others for over thirty years. In addition, he dealt extensively in real estate, operated another store at Manton, and bought into partnership in the Cole sawmill

6. During the "greenback" split in the Republican party, he ran for probate judge as a Democrat and was defeated.

after the death of John Perry. While county clerk, he "read law" in the office of his brother-in-law and was admitted to the bar. He appeared in court occasionally, but he does not seem to have carried on an active law practice. In 1892 he started a lumber business in Owosso and in 1901 he moved there from where he managed his diverse investments.

4.

Ferguson's ambitions were political. He dominated the area's Republican politics briefly and won two terms in the House of Representatives. Had it not been for tuberculosis which cost him his wife, his tact and good judgment, and ultimately his own life, he would undoubtedly have gone much further.

He had only nicely settled in his new home when he was busy canvassing the county, making friends and building an alliance of political friendships which would have done credit to a big city organization, but was quite unexpected in a pioneer community. In company with his brother-in-law, Sturtevant, he planned nothing less than a clean sweep of the county officers for the coming year. Even township supervisors who weren't compatible were to be purged. One supervisor who went was McClain, from Colfax, who was later to come back onto the board at a crucial time and cast his vote against Sherman in the county seat battle.

One supervisor who stayed was Clarence Northrup of Hanover. He was particularly drawn to Ferguson, and Ferguson seemed to have put great trust in him. Early in 1870 another attorney, E. W. Stewart, moved into Sherman and opened an office for the practice of law. He came without contacting Ferguson, made no move to get acquainted, and appeared to pose a political threat as a potential candidate for prosecuting attorney and a legal bastion around which political opposition to Ferguson might form.[7]

7. The lawyer was assumed to have some special qualities or opportunities for political leadership. Many people sought admission to the bar for this reason and not because they intended to be active practitioners. At that time, an applicant could prepare by "reading law" with another lawyer, or by serving as a probate judge or justice of the peace. He had to pass an examination in open court con-

Northrup entered the Ferguson office and "read law" for the purpose of diluting Stewart's position as the only other attorney in Sherman.

Ferguson had gauged Stewart's intentions correctly. An opposing faction did begin to form around him, and it was apparent that he would seek the Republican nomination for prosecuting attorney. Shortly before the nominating caucus, however, it was rumored that Lewis Clark would be resigning as postmaster and that Stewart might be his successor. Stewart's name was not submitted for prosecutor, Ferguson had no opposition, Clark did resign after the fall election, and Stewart was named postmaster shortly thereafter. One explanation might be that Stewart's backers pushed him for postmaster in an effort to give him a position of prestige from which to operate and to keep the job out of the hands of the Ferguson faction. Another explanation is that Ferguson had hit upon a neat means of derailing Stewart without a direct confrontation.

Another Ferguson alliance was with Isaac Carpenter, the Democratic probate judge, running again in 1870 for the balance of the unexpired term. When the nominating caucus was over, the new politicians, Ferguson, Sturtevant, & Co., had made their clean sweep to the surprise of those who considered themselves the "Old Settlers." John Wheeler was out as county Republican chairman. In a particularly adroit move, Ferguson had prevailed upon the much loved William Masters to accept the nomination for county treasurer, and Wheeler, who had found himself attacked by Ferguson for his courthouse contract, was dumped. It hadn't been hard to displace Skinner, who had made few friends as sheriff, and his deputy, Joseph Sturr, had the nomination. For county clerk and register of deeds, Captain Champenois had lost the nomination to Sturtevant. Even more surprising, at the fall

sisting of questioning by the circuit judge or by a committee of attorneys. Undoubtedly many courtesy admissions were made with a minimum of questioning for applicants who obviously had no intention of practicing. Newspaper editors, legislators, and teachers were among those admitted who never seriously practiced, but one, Prof. H. B. Groesbeck, the Cadillac school superintendent, surprised everyone, moved to Wyoming, won several spectacular cases, and ten years later was chief justice of the Wyoming Supreme Court.

election, a large part of Ferguson's Republican alliance deserted the Republican candidate for probate judge to support Judge Carpenter, who was the only Democratic candidate elected.

Wheeler was mightily offended. The insult was more keenly felt when the new officers were installed and it appeared that Masters had no intention of doing the work of the treasurer's office. He named Ferguson his deputy, leaving all of the records in Ferguson's office and leaving Ferguson to do the work.[8] Probably more important to Wheeler was the support given by Ferguson to the Democratic candidate, Carpenter. Wheeler and Carpenter got along well and were to work together well on the board of supervisors in future years, but political loyalty was one of the highest virtues honored by Wheeler, and he never completely trusted Ferguson again. But the bitterness of these years wore off quickly, and Wheeler was not one to hold a grudge. He and Ferguson worked together closely in future political activities and in the county seat campaign, and Wheeler cheerfully gave Ferguson credit for his many accomplishments.[9]

The Stewart-Ferguson political rivalry came to an early end, but not because of Stewart's appointment as postmaster. One of his supporters was William Mears, who had homesteaded in Wexford Township and who had entered into a partnership with Israel

8. Ferguson's experience as deputy treasurer while he was prosecutor may well have influenced his view towards railroads. The G. R. & I. railroad refused to pay taxes on the property which it had acquired under land grant as a subsidy for construction. Hundreds of thousands of acres of land were involved, and Ferguson introduced legislation during his first term in the House of Representatives to compel such payment. Litigation resulted and the legislation was upheld.

9. Someone was not so gracious, however. When Ferguson died, the G.A.R. Post, which he helped organize at Sherman, was named after him. Within a few years, however, the post was renamed the Abram Finch Post, after a veteran who had homesteaded section 12 of Springville Township, a little over a mile south of Sherman, and who died in 1873. We do not know the contemporary gossip after the name change, but Ezra Harger took pains to dispute reports that it was either Wheeler or Champenois who had expunged Ferguson's name, and such spite would not seem to be consistent with the disposition of either. The G.A.R. was but one of many groups in the founding of which Ferguson was instrumental. The varied list includes the Methodist Episcopal Church of Sherman, the County Agricultural Society (sponsoring the first "fair"), and the baseball club.

Foust at Wexford Corners, where they ran a small grocery store. Stewart invited Mears to come to Sherman and start a similar business and to "read law" with him in preparation for admission to the bar. The idea of being a lawyer and the prospects of a political career appealed to Mears. He made the move and commenced his studies with Stewart after opening a grocery store. Inexplicably, in January of 1872, Stewart decided tht there were greener pastures elsewhere, resigned as postmaster, and moved away from Sherman and out of our history, leaving his pupil to "read" alone. Mears opened another store in Manton later that year, and, having broadened his business and political base, ran for probate judge and was elected. He was never admitted to the bar in Wexford County,[10] but later moved to Boyne Falls, where he held several public officcs and was finally admitted to practice. With this treasured asset, he was elected to the Senate in 1892.

5.

During 1870 work in clearing the Manistee reached and passed Sherman. The river was badly jammed with centuries of accumulations of overhangs, logs, and debris, and over forty men with several ox teams were at work with saws, axes, and block and tackle to remove the obstacles and clear the river beds for future

10. It was not for want of trying, however. The Clam Lake News carried the following story on June 16, 1876: "The people of this county probably don't know what a narrow escape they had to having another lawyer in the county. If the applicant had only been able to answer a few more questions, we should have been compelled to suffer the affliction. The gentleman alluded to is the Hon. William Mears of Sherman, the present judge of probate, who probably in anticipation of retirement from that office thought to fit himself for the profession. He thought his golden opportunity had come when he learned that at the recent special term of circuit court of Missaukee County, there was not a single case on the calendar and no lawyers from abroad would be in attendance and there is only one attorney in the county, A. C. Lewis, Esq. The last named gentleman was named a committee by the circuit judge to examine the applicant, who near succeeded in getting away with one question but the balance got away with him. The circuit judge, in the kindness of his heart, allowed the disappointed applicant to withdraw his petition."

log drives. The first logging camp was located in Springville Township that year, and when they put in their supplies for the winter, Sturtevant and Maqueston Brothers both had a handsome profit.

More homesteaders were coming into the area, and the village had a minor building boom as it acquired the population which would make it a real county seat. Besides its three lawyers, it had acquired a second physician. Dr. H. D. Griswold, university trained, arrived, built a home, took over the operation of Clark's drugstore, and settled down to almost thirty years of practice as the picture of the county doctor—quiet, kindly, no case too minor, no hour too late, and no distance too great to keep him from answering a call, catching up on his sleep in the buggy while his horse, "Partner," brought him safely home. The new stores, the new homes, kept Clark busy as a carpenter, and the Wheeler and Cole-Perry sawmills couldn't keep up with the demand. And it must have been a pleasant looking place, although perhaps so only by comparison with the forty miles of wilderness along the state road to the south. Seven stage drivers quit at Sherman to make it their home. Two drifted on and one died suddenly, but William Derr, Ben Woods, Frank Hopkins, and Esedore Gilbert all went into business and played a prominent part in Sherman's building.

Elsewhere in the county, people were gradually finding their way to homesteads farther away from the state road. At least thirty families came into the southern and central portions of the county in 1869, and by 1870 every survey township had at least one homesteader, Taylor Gray reaching what is now Liberty Township late in the summer of 1870.[11] The census was taken and it showed

11. The Unionville settlement had gradually spread out, and settlers were scattered across most of Colfax Township. Joining the earlier settlers were Lucas Gates, E. D. Abbott, the McClains, John Goldsmith, and Ezra Harger. The Reverend A. L. Thurston and Eli Woodward were in what is now Selma Township, and the Denikes were in what is now Boon. The years 1869 and 1870 brought even more families. In Cedar Creek, were George Manton and Warren Seaman. Along the southern end of the state road, the first settler had been Thomas Henderson, followed by Job Hoxie, the Caswells, Bankers, and Conants. In 1870 a post office designated as Clay Hill became the third post office in the county. The first settlement in the southeast corner of the county was by John Gane on section 36 of Clam Lake early in 1869, followed a little later by Thomas

the county population to be 650 people. They were still largely settled around Sherman, less than 10 percent living more than ten miles from the county seat.

Whaley, Lester C. Sha, and Chauncey Hollister. These homesteaders came in overland from Hersey rather than from the Newaygo-Northport Pike.

Chapter Four

THE COURTHOUSE IS BUILT

At a special meeting of the county board of supervisors early in 1870, the board took up the question of construction of a courthouse. Devoe, Dean, and Northrup were all in favor of immediate construction on the site which Devoe and his fellow commissioner Davis had selected.

Rascelas McClain tried to postpone a decision. Consider the possibility, he argued, that a site near the center of the county (not too far from his homestead in Colfax Township) might do more to encourage the future growth of the county by the very fact of its equal accessibility to all sections of the county. The village of Sherman had not sufficiently developed that the construction of a courthouse elsewhere would hurt it, nor would delay. At the very least, a final decision should not be reached until it was learned definitely where the G. R. & I. railroad was going to be located. The others would not hear arguments; a site had been selected. The only thing that remained to be done was to build. They thought it foolish to talk about accommodating future settlers. It was the people who were there now who voted and who were interested in the county's government.

Those people viewed the courthouse construction as a double guarantee of their prosperity. A railroad was the doorway to the world and would insure the prosperity of any community through which it might pass. New cities could spring up along its right of way, but a bypassed city would wither away. As far as the railroad was concerned, it would be most apt to locate where there was a thriving community, and the construction of the courthouse would go far towards insuring the future growth of the village. But even without a railroad, a completed courthouse could be insurance against a possible move to relocate the county seat closer to the center of the county. There were no settlements in the eastern part of the county, but the thought that there would be was realistic.

The apprehension of future rivalry was prophetic. They were anxious to get the courthouse built as a means of nailing down the county seat at Sherman permanently.

McClain was outvoted. The board named chairman Devoe, Northrup, and Prosecutor Ferguson as a special building committee. Plans were secured from W. C. Holdsworth of Traverse City at a cost of $25, and on February 21, 1870, the board voted to advertise for bids in the nearest newspaper, the Traverse City *Eagle*. In March, bids were opened and the successful bidder at $4,500 was found to be county treasurer John Wheeler.

The distinguished Wheeler career nearly died aborning before the contract was completed. It was a financial disaster to both Wheeler and the county and left room for hard feelings and suspicions. Part of the problem was prosecuting attorney Ferguson. The contract which he prepared for the courthouse construction contained no provision regarding site preparation and cleanup. Nor did it set a time for completion of the building. There was an immediate argument about the site preparation and, on Wheeler's refusal to do anything but build a courthouse according to the plans bid on, the county hired the work done.[1] By the time the site was ready, the 1870 building season was over.

The next spring saw good progress made in preparation of the foundation and framing in the building, but then a disastrous series of fires ravaged the area during the summer and fall. The summer of 1871 was exceptionally dry and was perhaps the worst for fires in American history. Large forest and prairie fires, swept by high winds, destroyed hundreds of thousands of acres of timber and grass-land. It was said that sparks from the fires in Wisconsin that summer, or the great Chicago fire in October, or the conflagration that destroyed Manistee at the same time, started a large number of fires in the Sherman area. There were some suspicious souls who thought it possible that arson might be involved. A grudge against public officers could explain the fire that destroyed prosecutor Ferguson's home and that which destroyed Wheeler's mill. Perhaps it was only a deranged

1. The records of laborers hired reads like a Who's Who of the oldest families of the area: Baker, Morell, Jewett, Finch, Kellogg, and Carpenter.

Democrat, said Wheeler years later, but that didn't explain the loss of so many other buildings. Whatever the cause, the mill was destroyed. Before the fires started, Dr. Perry had contracted to furnish lumber for a new hotel that Ferguson was putting up and for a new school to be built in the village. Besides those needs, the entire capacity of the Cole-Perry mill was used to supply lumber to rebuild burned-out homes and barns, and the men of the area were too busy rebuilding those homes and barns to hire out to work on the courthouse.

It might have been thought that Ferguson, having lost a home to fire, would have been sympathetic to Wheeler. Such was not the case, however. As prosecutor and deputy treasurer, Ferguson claimed that Wheeler's failure to complete the courthouse promptly was grounds for forfeiture. Another dispute arose over the hiring of a stone mason, who was eventually hired directly by the supervisors—at Ferguson's direction, according to Wheeler.[2] The minutes of the 1870 sessions of the supervisors contain repeated resolutions for Wheeler to complete the building and threatening to hold him liable for damages for delay.[3]

The courthouse was finally occupied in November of 1872, although finishing work was not completed until the next spring. The building and site work had cost over $7,500, and Wheeler had yet to be paid for extra work authorized by the board. When the supervisors refused to allow the claim, he ultimately sued and prevailed, notwithstanding the county's plea that the contract price had been intended to include construction of a jail as well. By the time the courthouse was furnished, the grounds landscaped, a jail and woodhouse built, and a well dug, the county investment exceeded $12,000.[4]

2. It was an unfortunate choice, for the minutes of the supervisors over the next few years reveal repeated attempts to correct the chimneys so that they would draw properly and not smoke out the county employees.

3. What the actual damages would have been, of course, is speculative since they were renting no other space. Sylvester Clark was making no charge for the use of the Sherman House for Circuit Court sessions. The county officers were using their own homes as offices, prisoners were bordered as guests in the home of under-sheriff Gasser, and the munificent salaries set by the county were presumed to include compensation for this arrangement.

4. A curious oversight appears in the records of the supervisors, perplexing in

Wheeler, of course, was paid only for the construction of the courthouse proper, plus some agreed extras, amounting in all to slightly over $5,000. He always maintained that he lost money on the contract, although perhaps the loss of his mill by fire was the main source of any loss. He did, however, sustain a very real loss in that he did not actually realize the full amount of the contract price. Wexford County had no money. Payment of county bills was made by giving orders, a form of promissory note, payable after the annual meeting of the board of supervisors each October. Thus, the installment payments made to Wheeler as work progressed actually were in the form of such orders.

Public credit generally, and that of new counties in particular, was so poor during those years that public orders were usually unacceptable except at interest rates of 10 percent or more. Even then, banks and merchants refused to accept them in trade without discounting them from 25 percent to 35 percent. Wheeler specifically mentioned one order in the amount of $1,000. There was no bank at Sherman, and neither of the merchants was in a position to negotiate the order. It was refused by the bank at Traverse. It was finally discounted to Perry Hannah for $800, and then only upon condition that Wheeler take $400 in cash and $400 in future trade with Hannah, Lay & Co. It is very possible, therefore, that Wheeler may have realized as little as $3,500 from the $5,000 in orders issued by the county for the courthouse contract.

2.

At any rate, by the time the courthouse was occupied, Sherman was a thriving village. H. B. Sturtevant had been reading law with his brother-in-law Ferguson and was admitted to the bar that winter so that the village again had three attorneys. It had two doctors. It had a school, the Maqueston and Sturtevant general

the sense that such a pressing need would go unnoticed for several months. The courthouse had been occupied for that length of time before anyone brought the problem to the attention of the supervisors, and they voted to add to the county building complex by construction of a path and two outhouses.

stores, Clark's grocery and drugstore, and a blacksmith. It had two hotels, The Sherman House, and Ferguson's Grant House. Surprisingly, it had no saloons.[5] Perhaps the reason was the predominantly Methodist complexion of the early settlement. From time to time, the homesteaders had gathered in their homes or at the log school to conduct their own devotions. Now, if they were going to have a regular village at Sherman, they would have regular church services. They were commenced in 1869 in the new Maqueston Hall, led by the Reverend Almond K. Herrington, who had homesteaded in Wexford Township in 1866.[6] In 1870 the Methodists organized a formal charge with a supply pastor, the Reverend Mr. Cayton, traveling from Traverse City to Sherman for the weekly services. Later that year, the Reverend A. L. Thurston, from the central part of the county, took over the church.[7] In 1871 church meetings were moved to the new school in Sherman, where they remained until a church was built on land donated by Isaac Maqueston. Among the original members of the congregation were Moses Cole, John Perry, Captain Champenois, Thomas Ferguson, H. B. Sturtevant, and Esedore Gilbert. The Congregational church was organized in 1871 under the Reverend Jonas Denton and built its church in 1873.

3.

Perhaps the most significant event of 1872 in Sherman was the establishment of a newspaper by A. W. Tucker and Charles E.

5. "Sherman has always been noted for the purity of its morals, and in matters of temperance particularly, the people have taken a lively interest." H. R. Page & Co., *The Traverse Region,* 1884.

6. Herrington was not an ordained minister but was typical of many who filled the need of the people for religious leadership. Particularly well read and intelligent, he was elected county surveyor in 1872 and county superintendent of schools in 1874.

7. Thurston was one of the first homesteaders in what is now Selma Township. A Civil War veteran, he had become a licensed minister several years before. When a Methodist congregation was later formed in the village of Clam Lake, he served that church and still later supplied the Methodist Church at Kingsley and other small communities in Grand Traverse County. In 1876 he was an unsuccessful candidate for probate judge, but did serve as a school commissioner for several terms.

Cooper. The Wexford County *Pioneer*, later named the Sherman *Pioneer*, made its first appearance in May, narrowly beating the Clam Lake *News* (now the Cadillac *Evening News*) to press. By then, of course, there was another community in the county. An early edition of the *Pioneer* described the new building going on in Sherman in glowing terms, particularly noting the near completion of the courthouse and the existence of a "most proper school." With some superiority and seniority, the *Pioneer* referred to the new settlement at Clam Lake as "a few log huts put up for the gangs laying iron on the G. R. & I. R. R. and hardly fit for anyone else." How sophisticated Sherman had become!

Editor Cooper was to spend another twenty-five years in the county, during most of which he was in print at Sherman or Manton, yet surprisingly little about his personal life is known, other than what is reflected in his editorial policies. He soon bought out Tucker at Sherman and ran the paper alone until 1877, when he sold it to a new attorney in town, Charles S. Marr.[8]

It was customary for newspapers to adhere to one party or the other, and many communities had both Republican and Democratic newspapers. Cooper made the *Pioneer* both a Republican journal and a temperance paper. He never wavered in the latter but strayed into political heresy when he actively supported the greenback movement before leaving Sherman. He was reincarnated as a Republican again at Manton but eventually claimed the Democratic party as his own for reasons of monetary policy, and he actively sought office as a Democratic candidate.

8. At this time, it was the practice to award postmasterships in small communities to local political leaders, preferably newspaper editors; so in Sherman and in Manton over the next twenty-five years, a change in the control of the newspaper meant a change of postmaster. Cooper was succeeded as postmaster by Marr, who bought the paper. In turn, Marr was succeeded by H. Frank Campbell, who followed Marr as editor of the paper, and Campbell was subsequently followed by John Wheeler when Wheeler assumed sole control of the *Pioneer*. In the meantime, Cooper had bought the Manton *Tribune* and became postmaster at Manton. In 1883 Cooper sold the *Tribune* to Campbell, who became Manton's postmaster, and when Cooper later re-purchased it from Campbell, he again became the Manton postmaster. Thus, both Campbell and Cooper were postmasters at both Sherman and Manton, with Cooper serving twice at Manton.

His views on money were, perhaps, derived from his chronic insufficiency thereof.

Cooper's papers were always in financial difficulty. Getting out the *Pioneer* was a constant struggle, and its sale in 1877 was solely the result of Cooper's lack of cash. His hopes of recovering it from the purchaser, Charles S. Marr, were thwarted by John Wheeler, who ended the paper's greenback line and restored the *Pioneer* to its orthodox Republican identification. Wheeler thereby earned the bitter enmity of Cooper, who thought he had been cheated out of the paper.[9] Cooper's financial success was not much better with the *Tribune* in Manton, and he sold to H. F. Campbell in 1883. Some fortunate dealings in timber lands and, ironically for a "Greenbacker," some dealings as a money lender enabled him to repurchase it a few years later.

4.

Over the next few years, the fortunes of Representative Ferguson took a turn for the worse. His election to the House of Representatives in 1872 had been by an overwhelming majority, and he seemed to have as much, if not more, strength in Manistee than in his own county. Shortly after his election, however, his wife began to show signs of serious illness, and he himself was already showing some of the symptoms of the same disease, tuberculosis. Under constant stress, and sometimes overmedicated with morphine, he displayed an unpredictable temperament and made rash statements easily. He made inconsistent promises to the Republicans in Manistee and in the new settlement of Clam Lake. He lost all support in Clam Lake by introducing legislation which took Cleon Township from Manistee County and added it to Wexford County, a move obviously designed to increase the

9. Cooper's antagonism towards Wheeler continued until Cooper left the county in the nineties. It perhaps reveals something about both Wheeler and Cooper to note that with all of Wheeler's political battles over the next twenty years, Cooper seems to be the only person who could stay mad at him. The fact that Wheeler was only one of many on Cooper's hate list suggests that he may have been wrong about Wheeler and tells us something about Cooper.

population and political strength of the Sherman area at the expense of Clam Lake. In 1874 the Clam Lake Republican organization supported Democrat George Holbrook against Ferguson, and Feguson narrowly won reelection. A month after the election, his wife died, leaving him with a young daughter to rear. He lost his zest for political life.

In 1876 he sold the Grant House Hotel and actively entered the business of buying and selling pine lands. In 1877 he moved to Manton and impulsively bought into the partnership of Brandenburg, Backus & Co., which was engaged in the lumber business. The business failed within a year. He accused his partners of fraud, while the Clam Lake *News* openly accused him of crooked land grabbing and being a log thief. He attempted to block thc incorporation of thc village of Clam Lake as the city of Cadillac and participated ineffectually in the maneuvering to keep the county seat at Sherman or move it to Manton. His efforts seemed less a matter of conviction, however, than of animosity towards Cadillac, and he was frequently bed-ridden by his illness. In 1878 he moved to Grand Rapids, practicing law there and continuing his dealings in timber lands in Wexford, Missaukee, and Kalkaska counties. His health continued to deteriorate and he died in 1883. His daughter Teenie was adopted by his sister and brother-in-law, the H. B. Sturtevants.

5.

Sherman grew somewhat more in the seventies. In 1872 another physician, the dapper Dr. W. H. Preston, arrived, charmed the ladies, and left, having added much scandal and subtracted Mrs. Copley from the village. With the incursion of logging camps, the merchants prospered, and there was soon a main street of grocery and general stores, two drugstores, a bank, a livery stable, and a wagon shop. George Shackleton and William Bennett erected a large gristmill, which was constructed by John Wheeler in 1876. Two years later the partners were wiped out when the mill burned. Isaac Maqueston purchased the site and constructed an even larger mill.[10]

10. The mill stood until 1932, when fire again leveled the site, this time permanently.

It has proved impossible to find accurate figures of the population of Sherman over the years. One estimate put its peak population at over 600 residents, but the largest figure shown by a census was fewer than 450. In 1897, R. D. Frederick, then and for many years thereafter, editor of the *Pioneer*, described the village as having a population of about 500 and enjoying steadily increasing prosperity. It then had three hotels, three general stores, three drugstores, two hardware stores, two blacksmith shops, two grocery stores, a bank, a millinery store, a flour mill, and a planing mill. There was even a suburb, West Sherman, better known as Claggettville, where a railroad spur served a sawmill, kiln, and lumber yard, about a mile west of Sherman proper. Along the river were busy sawmills and gristmills. Frederick noted the two active church congregations, Methodist and Congregational, and pointed out that Sherman had only one saloon, enjoying what was then a unique position for northern Michigan, with twice as many churches as saloons. His comment reflected his continuation of a long editorial policy of the *Pioneer*, which was temperance first and Republicanism always. In the first it never wavered, and over the years the *Pioneer* on many occasions commented piously on the lack of temperance on the other side of the county.

The census figures, however, were showing something else about Wexford County as early as 1874. The county had grown from 650 to 3,011 in just four years. Sherman had grown but slightly. Most of the new residents were locating where the transportation was, along the new railroad in Clam Lake, Haring, and Cedar Creek townships. It was true that there was a new state road started to the east between Sherman and Cedar Creek, and west into Manistee County. But road travel at best was slow going, and the trails that passed for the back roads in the county were covered almost as fast on foot as by horse. In 1874 John Denike sent a neighbor on an emergency trip to the city in an attempt to get a doctor for his ailing wife. By the best possible route it was almost twenty miles and took four hours.[11]

11. Ten years later, the Ben Woods stage over the state road took three hours to make the trip between Sherman and Manton in good weather. Twenty years later, even the back roads were much improved, as witness this account in the

The first baseball team was organized in Sherman in 1874, but it was hardly worth the trip to get to another community for a game. The first county agricultural fair was held in Sherman the same year, but, again because of transportation problems, the fair was never representative of the south and east part of the county while it was held at Sherman. Transportation was time and money, power and prestige, and Sherman was to starve for its lack. During the battle for removal of the county seat, the Clam Lake *News* mentioned the departure of area supervisors for their annual meeting "at Sherman, which is twenty-six miles from somewhere."

For years Sherman entertained hope of steamship travel on the Manistee River. In 1876 the Manistee River Navigation Company was organized, and an attempt was made to raise $50,000 capital. There wasn't that much money in Sherman, only $12,825 being pledged, and those in Clam Lake and Manton who had money weren't interested. Similar proposals thereafter never got off the ground. In 1877 a better effort was made in raising money in Sherman for the expenses of a survey for a railroad route between Sherman and Clam Lake. The Sherman businessmen had apparently been led to believe that capital for the project would be forthcoming in Clam Lake. The survey was made and was in fact the basis for part of the Ann Arbor railroad route plans ten years later. After some delay, a corporation called the Cadillac-Sherman Railroad Company was formed, only to find that there were no subscriptions for its stock in Cadillac or elsewhere.

In 1887 Sherman was incorporated as a charter village so as to have the legal power to issue bonds. The Ann Arbor Railroad was planning its northwest extension and had a definite route established as far as Harrietta. A bond issue was proposed to subsidize

News in 1892: "Elijah Smith, the farmer, merchant, and postmaster at Meauwataka, has a fine driving horse of his own raising which brings him to Cadillac, a distance of fourteen miles over the newly improved roads, in an hour's drive, but he does not attempt to make quite as rapid speed as that when he brings in his fresh eggs during the season of unsettled weather." Even so, travel was unpredictable until after the turn of the century, and an axe and saw were standard equipment for the traveler to cut through windfalls which frequently blocked the roads.

the extension of the road to Sherman. A decision of the Michigan Supreme Court, however, denied villages the power to use public credit for private corporations. The Sherman bond issue could not be marketed. A later borrowing by Wexford Township to subsidize the location of the Ann Arbor to Sherman resulted in something of a deception on the part of the railroad. Track was laid in its present location, and the place now known as Mesick was called Sherman Station. Considerable bitterness arose in the Sherman area when the Ann Arbor demanded additional funds to run a spur to the village but came no closer than the industrial spur that later ran to Claggettville. A similar attempt to help finance a route for the Manistee and Northeastern Railroad through Sherman also failed.

By 1880 the county population was 6,815, compared to 650 in 1870 and 3,011 in 1874. That population was largely located along the railroad on the east side of the county. The lowly village of Clam Lake had been transformed into the rowdy but dynamic city of Cadillac, and even Manton had outgrown Sherman.

Chapter Five

FOR PINE AND THE G. R. & I.

While the state road was opening up the western side of the county to settlement in the mid-sixties, a handful of men were prowling the hills on the eastern side of the county for different reasons. They had no interest in farming or in settling for any reason. Some of them were railroad surveyors; the others, land-lookers like Henry Clark, were scouting out choice pine lands for speculative purchase.

The Civil War had not restored the old Union of 1860; rather, a whole new nation had been born. Sections of the South were devastated and its agricultural lands laid waste, but the West was ripe for opening. The North was on the verge of the great machine tool revolution that would create an industrial society and a mass production economy that would transform small villages into cities and cities into burgeoning urban centers.

Northern Michigan was a vast reservoir of raw material for the building industry. Even before the war, communities were springing up around the sawmills where the rivers emptied into the Great Lakes, and Bay City, Alpena, Manistee, Ludington, and Muskegon were shipping large quantities of pine. Everyone knew that after the war the interior would be opened up by railroads. If the land grant pattern continued, construction would be subsidized by blocks of free land which would make the railroads the largest land owners in the state. One such grant had already been approved before the war for a line to be constructed by the Grand Rapids and Indiana Railroad from Grand Rapids to the Straits of Mackinaw. The knowledge that large tracts had been set off for the G. R. & I. touched off a scramble to claim the best of the remaining pine lands.

There seems to have been no concept of "conflict in interest" between the land buyers and their scouts, or land-lookers, who were crossing and re-crossing the upper part of the lower peninsula.[1] His own resources permitting, the land-looker bought also. Finding a good area of pine, he would, depending upon the extent of his capital, stake out only a portion of the tract in the name of his employer and take the remainder in his own name. Far from being frowned upon, it seems to have been acceptable practice, a means, perhaps, of encouraging the land-looker to range far and wide as rapidly as possible. Other pine buyers entered into incentive arrangements by which the land-looker would have a share in everything he claimed for his employer. The choicer the stand of pine, the more he stood to gain from his share.

One of the major land buyers was Martin Ryerson, a partner in Ryerson, Hills & Co., for which Henry Clark was employed.[2] We do not know if Edward Maqueston was also working for Ryerson, but we do know that Clark and Maqueston were operating out of Big Rapids together. We also know that both picked up random forty-acre parcels of pine land for themselves in Missaukee,

1. The land-looker, also called a "timber-cruiser," had to be able to judge a stand of pine in terms of its age, quantity or board footage of lumber it would produce, and its quality. He had to be able to locate government survey markers and get a legal description of the land, and he also had to weigh other factors, such as accessibility to water, transport problems, and the like, in making a judgment as to what tracts to claim and which ones to pass by. Most land-lookers covered the ground on foot, as it was too difficult to move by horse into the areas they had to get into to get a good "look."

2. Another land-looker employed by Ryerson was Thomas B. Stimson, who fared somewhat better than Clark. He spent the better part of two and a half years walking northern Michigan with a pack on his back, sleeping in the woods and living off the land. His agreement with Ryerson gave him half of everything he found. At the end of the two and a half years, Stimson was a wealthy man. He sold or traded the northernmost portions of his share to Ryerson and others and acquired more pine land in Newaygo, Mecosta, and surrounding counties. Having centralized his holdings he logged, sawed, and dealt in lumber in and around Big Rapids for another twenty years. He retired to California, where he died, having reduced his estate by gifts to less than one and a half million dollars. His brother, W. B. Stimson, was a civil engineer with the G. R. & I. R. R. and was its roadmaster for many years. He supervised construction in the Cadillac area and lived at the Mason House for almost a year. Tips from him assisted Thomas in making some of his earlier purchases along the middle stretch of the railroad, and he shared in the profits. George Mitchell gave the Stimson name to a street in his new village of Clam Lake.

Osceola, and Wexford counties.

In the search for pine lands, the man who got there first and moved the fastest was Delos A. Blodgett. Like Stimson, Maqueston, and Clark, he lived off the land, sustained by what he could shoot and carry on his back. However, the main difference between Blodgett and the others was not merely that he got here first, but that he was working solely for himself and not for someone else. He did have backers to assist him with the financing, but the risks were all his. The gain would be all his, and, if he was wrong, the loss would be all his.

The risk didn't deter him. To judge from his comments in later years, they scarcely occurred to him. He had no doubt that the demand for pine lumber would increase. He had no doubt that the economy would boom after the war. As a judge of pine, he didn't doubt for a moment his ability to pick the right land in the right place. And he didn't doubt that he would make a fortune. He was right on all counts. It was the right time.

More than thirty years later, Blodgett stopped at Cadillac on his way to his summer home on Mackinaw Island. He was accompanied by a representative of *The Timberman*, a lumber journal published in Chicago,[3] who recorded his reflections as they stood at the top of the hill above the new Masonic and Cummer buildings. Known as "Courthouse Hill" because of the expectation that someday it would be the site of the county courthouse, it provided an imposing view across the city, the mills bordering the shore, and the expanse of lake beyond. The view from Courthouse Hill was the more impressive as Blodgett pointed out the portions of the town which had belonged to him before Cadillac had appeared on the map. When he had first seen it, he had already bought huge tracts farther south and east and had made some purchases in southern Missaukee County as early as 1863. He was already the largest landowner in Osceola County, having purchased heavily there.

But when he saw the stand of pine in the Clam Lake area in 1866, he knew he must have it. As he went on for miles and discovered its quality and the extent of it running northeasterly into

3. The *Timberman* offices, coincidentally, were located in one of Chicago's first and largest skyscrapers, put up in the Loop by Delos A. Blodgett.

Missaukee County, the only question in his mind, he said, was how he could get it all. It sounded very easy in the 1898 interview. He simply undertook to get as much of the land as he had cash, or could borrow money, to pay for, then bought more on the credit of associates willing to advance money for a minor share of future profits. As it was, of course, every other section of land along the possible railroad route was set aside for the land grant,[4] and other sections were already set aside for other government grants, but he got the best of the rest. The purchase included the major portion of eight sections, and parts of others, in Richland and Lake townships of Missaukee County, over 5,000 acres in all. In Wexford County, he acquired government lots 4 and 7 on Clam Lake, and, with the exception of a few scattered forty-acre parcels, acquired all of sections 2, 10, and 12 in Clam Lake Township, and sections 14, 20, 22, 24, 26, 32, 34, and 36 of Haring Township, the line of purchases generally following the direction of the forest. All told, his acquisition came to almost 15,000 acres.

2.

The earliest settlers of northern Michigan came by boat, and the first communities of consequence grew up where there were

4. After the G. R. & I. route had been established, Blodgett tried to buy all of the railroad sections in this pine tract. Some of the railroad's stockholders and officers were in the competition for pine lands, and his offers were declined. One, George A. Mitchell, had plans of his own for the area and bought some key sections from the railroad. He undoubtedly intended to pick up the rest over a period of time but was prevented from doing so by his death. Those sections were then sold to his nephews and associates, Cobbs & Mitchell, and Mitchell Brothers, and to the Cummer interests. Blodgett held off logging many of his sections, and the Cummers who had bought the alternate railroad sections which matched, did likewise, leaving one last block of virgin pine in the area on both sides of the Wexford-Missaukee county line east of Cadillac. Both sought to buy out the other; neither would budge. The Cummers were the more stubborn. Blodgett finally gave up and sold to them in 1892. By then, choice pine was becoming scarce, and the value of the stand had increased immensely. The huge Blodgett-Cummer reserve kept the pine operation of the Cummer and Diggins mills in continuous operation for almost nine years.

natural harbors. Ludington, Frankfort, Manistee, Traverse City, Petoskey, and Alpena were footholds of civilization on the edge of the wilderness. The lakes were their highways. Shipping was inexpensive and provided the quickest mode of travel except, of course, during the winter. As settlers moved inland, these communities became the port of entry for the newcomers and the merchandising centers to supply them. Even after the opening of the main north-south state roads, most travelers and freight moved on the lakes.

By 1850, however, it was apparent that a great era of railroad building was commencing which would revolutionize transportation and open up great expanses of land to new settlers. In that year Congress passed the first railroad land grant act. More followed quickly. The extent of the grants varied in different cases, but as the grant policy became standardized, the usual grant gave the railroad the alternate sections amounting to half of all the acreage for a distance of six miles on each side of the railroad route. It accomplished its purpose as an incentive for railroad construction. Many railroads were built for the money to be made from the sale of the land subsidy and not because of anticipated operating profits. Many were hastily improvised and poorly planned, inefficiently operated, and laid out over economically unsound routes. On the other hand, in opening up a new area, who could say with certainty what routes would prove economically sound? The government got payment of its bargain just by the opening of the territory. The railroads served to bring in new settlers then, increasing the demand for purchase of both railroad and government land. So great was this demand along the land grant railroads in Illinois and through the plains states that the government land office was able to double the price for public land from $1.25 per acre to $2.50.

The Civil War slowed railroad construction, but after a brief economic pause, the country suddenly erupted in a surge of business activity. There was no question that the railroads would come to northern Michigan and bring with them new settlers, industry, and commerce. The only questions were where and when. The assumed golden truth of the moment was that prosperity beyond wildest dreams followed the railroads. Existing communities desperately hoped that the coming railroads would not pass them by. Many communities worked desperately to influence the location of a new railroad's route by subsidies, offers of land, and bribes to survey and road engineers.[5]

In 1853 a young civil engineer from New York, William P. Innes, came to Michigan to lay out a route and superintend the construction of the Oakland and Ottawa Railroad. The job was efficiently done, and he acquired something of a reputation for tight management of the rough and tough construction crews working under his supervision. As a result, he was in demand for construction of other lines and made his home in Grand Rapids while supervising construction on various lines in southern Michigan. He rapidly became known as one of the outstanding construction experts in the Midwest and was frequently hired as a consultant for existing or proposed railroad projects. Two such instances, quite unrelated, were to have important consequences.

In the first, he met at Grand Rapids with a group of investors who had organized the Grand Rapids and Southern Railroad to construct a line to the Indiana border, where it would connect with the line of an Indiana corporation in which most of the same men were officers. Among the investors was William Mitchell, who had come to northern Indiana from New York State and built the town of Kendallville. Everything he touched had turned to profit. His wealth, ambition, and personality made him a force to reckon with in Indiana business and political affairs.

He was engaged in a variety of business affairs. He was the founder and president of the Kendallville Bank. He built plank roads and then, as technology revolutionized transportation, turned his interests to railroad construction. He was a member of the Indiana legislature, a leader of the Whig party, and later one of the founders of the Republican party. A close friend of Congressman Abraham Lincoln, he actively worked for Lincoln's

5. When the land grant system ended, new railroads went directly to the communities, playing one against another, promising to go through the ones which raised the most money. A large part of the Toledo and Ann Arbor Railroad was built by the communities along the route that had outbid other communities to get the railroad. The subsidies were usually financed by bonds. Some communities defaulted in payment. Others contested the bonds when they thought better of it at a later date, or concluded that they had been "had." Fifteen years of interesting litigation up and down the T. & A. line resulted.

nomination as president and capped his own career as a member of the Congress and one of the influential policy makers in Washington.

We cannot be certain that Mitchell attended the Grand Rapids meeting at which Innes first was consulted regarding the Grand Rapids and Southern, but we do know that he was an early backer of the Indiana venture and that he had two things in mind beyond investment for investment's sake. He wanted to insure location of the Indiana line through Kendallville, and he was interested in acquiring land along the proposed route for speculative purposes. We also know that within a matter of months after the initial meeting, the Grand Rapids and Southern was merged with the Indiana corporation under the name of the Grand Rapids and Indiana Railroad. Mitchell was one of the directors, and Innes was retained as the consulting engineer for the new corporation.

The other matter in which Innes was consulted involved some preliminary route surveys for a Kalamazoo group which was interested in the construction of a railroad from Grand Rapids to the Straits of Mackinaw. A group of Grand Rapids investors, under the leadership of John Ball, was also interested in a route to the straits, and a race developed to incorporate. Congress was busily handing out land grants to subsidize construction, but where there were competing corporations between the same points, only one corporation would have a grant. Each group therefore was anxious not only to incorporate but to arrange financing and beat the opposition to Capitol Hill for the probable grant. By the time the two groups had incorporated as the Grand Rapids and Mackinaw, and the Grands Rapids and Northern, respectively, they discovered that Mitchell and associates had already made the first move and that a bill was pending in Congress to award the grant to the Grand Rapids and Indiana Railroad. The Indiana group, in hiring Innes, had also bought his knowledge of the northern route for which the Kalamazoo group had paid.

Both Michigan factions appealed to the Michigan congressional delegation. House members, led by Rep. George W. Peck, were persuaded to intervene upon the ground that new construction in Michigan ought to be in the hands of Michigan investors. The bill was passed providing for the land grant for a route north from Grand Rapids, but with the added provision that the Michigan legislature was to select the recipient and set the conditions of the grant. Ball seemed to have things well in hand when a bill was immediately introduced in the Michigan legislature to award the grant to the Grand Rapids and Northern. But somehow, when the bill was signed by the Governor, it read "Grand Rapids and *Indiana* Railroad." The deception was masked by an amendment which provided that it was the purpose of the act to provide for the construction of a railroad between Grand Rapids and a point on Little Traverse Bay, the grant for continuance to the Straits of Mackinaw being taken care of later. Ball was furious. Grand Rapids newspapers alleged fraud, but the matter was closed.

The act made the grant on condition that at least twenty miles of road was to be built each year, with an overall completion deadline of seven years. It also prohibited the issuance of any stock except for full cash value in an attempt to limit the financial abuses that were prevalent in the corporate world at the time. The G. R. & I. was nearly broke from the expenses of construction in Indiana and from lobbying (Ball called it bribery) in Washington and Lansing. The maneuvering that followed could illustrate a book on the corruption of railroad financing, but it was typical of the era. Briefly, a new Grand Rapids and Mackinaw Railroad was incorporated, rewarding some of the Kalamazoo investors who had swung over to support the Indiana faction. Another dummy corporation, the Grand Rapids and Fort Wayne Railroad, was organized, and assets were switched around between the existing G. R. & I. and these corporations. Finally, in 1857, they were all merged into a new corporation also called the Grand Rapids and Indiana, and the law had been circumvented. The new corporation was so badly underfinanced, charged Ball, that it could barely afford the bribery necessary to obtain a stay of the construction conditions of the grant. But this it did, and the first track north was not laid until 1867, eleven years later. It didn't reach the Straits of Mackinaw until 1882, twenty-six years after the original congressional grant.

It is likely that Innes had a role in the shift of position of some of the Kalamazoo group which had consulted with him. He had become closely allied with Mitchell, and this friendship and his work for the Indiana group make this conclusion believable. At any rate, he continued as consultant for the G. R. & I., and, immediately upon completion of the corporate reorganization, made the preliminary survey for the route north. There matters rested while the railroad sought to raise more capital. It received the time it needed when the Civil War broke out. When it was over, Innes, the Mitchells, and the G. R. & I. turned towards northern Michigan.

3.

Congressman Mitchell of Indiana was one of twelve children born to Charles T. Mitchell, a merchant-farmer of Montgomery County, New York. Intelligence, energy, and a resourceful imagination had characterized the Mitchells throughout a family history dating back to the early days of colonial settlement. A grandfather had served with distinction in the Revolutionary War, and Mrs. Mitchell was descended from one of the early colonial governors of New Jersey.

The Mitchell children continued to distinguish the family name. Besides William, there was John who served for some years as prosecuting attorney of Montgomery County, New York, spent some time assisting his brothers in Kendallville, and then moved to Adrian, Michigan, where he practiced law successfully and played an active role in public affairs in Lenawee County. Another son, Charles T. Mitchell, Jr., joined his brother William in Indiana, got some experience in the construction of the Indiana railroad, and then moved to southern Michigan where he was involved in the constructon of a portion of the Michigan-Southern Railroad. He settled in the new village of Hillsdale and played a large role in its development. He was a merchant, grain dealer, banker, and land developer. Like all the Mitchells, he was an active community builder, and like them all he was a passionate abolitionist. With his brother William, he was instrumental in the founding of the Republican party in the famous "meeting under the oaks" at Jackson in 1854, was a Lincoln presidential elector, and with his younger brother, George, served on the Michigan Republican Committee. Two of his six children, William W.

Mitchell and Austin W. Mitchell, were later to figure prominently in Cadillac history.

The youngest Mitchell brother, George, tried his hand at various enterprises in his home state and had acquired a fair nest-egg by 1861. In that year, when he was thirty-seven years old, he sold all of his New York properties and moved to Kendallville to join his brother, William. He had barely settled there when the Civil War broke out and he was commissioned as a paymaster. He soon was deputy paymaster of the Armies of the West. His financial and administrative responsibilities grew as the army grew, and he was headquartered at various times in Missouri, Arkansas, Tennessee, and with General U. S. Grant at Vicksburg, Mississippi. At the end of the war, he had twenty regional deputy paymasters serving under his command, his accounts were in meticulous order, and he had acquired a broad grasp of finance.

He was mustered out of the army in 1867 and returned to Kendallville to pick up the pieces of his business interests.[6] Those interests were varied. A mercantile business had proved particularly profitable. More important, his life was changed by a logging partnership into which he had entered shortly before going into the army and which had returned a steady profit all during his absence through the war. One of the reasons for that success had been the sale of large quantities of railroad ties to the government for the construction of army railroads. A large part of these had been shipped to the railroad division of the Army of the Cumberland, whose engineering superintendent was William P. Innes. There is nothing to indicate what contacts there may have been between Innes and George Mitchell before the war, but it is possible that his acquaintance with William Mitchell had something to do with the volume of business placed by the army.

Congressman Mitchell and some associates had acquired land in various places along the right-of-way between the state line and Grand Rapids and also in northern Kent County and Montcalm County. He died unexpectedly while on a business trip to the South

6. Those interests had been well managed by him despite the war. Except while stationed in Arkansas, he had been free to get back to Kendallville regularly. While in St. Louis and Memphis, he had been able to spend at least a week at home every month.

at the end of the war, and the task of cutting and milling the timber on his Michigan lands was undertaken by George Mitchell and his partners.

We don't know exactly how George Mitchell came into contact with General Innes, although his brother's friendship with Innes and the partnership's dealings with the Army of the Cumberland while General Innes was superintending military construction suggest that it is not impossible that they met during the war. We do know that before the railroad's first year of construction was over, George Mitchell was not only logging his brother's lands along the right-of-way but had contracted to cut some of the timber from railroad lands as well.

4.

At the end of the Civil War, the northern terminus of the Grand Rapids and Indiana Railroad was still Grand Rapids. Not an inch of right-of-way had been cleared for its authorized line to the Straits of Mackinaw. The deadline for completion, which was a condition of the land grant subsidy, had been extended before the war, and the war added a cogent reason for further extensions. In 1865 the deadline had been extended to 1874. Besides the additional time, the war, with its profitable freight on the southern branch of the line, had enabled the corporation to recover some measure of financial health.

General Innes was separated from the service during the winter of 1865-66 and immediately rejoined the G. R. & I. as its construction engineer. Surveyors were hired and the task of making the final survey was undertaken. Different men worked on different sections, but it was General Innes' boast that he personally covered every inch of the line on foot at least twice before the final survey work was completed on the north end in 1873. One of the surveyors who worked in the middle section of the route in 1867 was S. H. "Lee" Beardslee of Kendallville, Indiana.[7]

7. The other two working with Beardslee were William Ash, after whom the village of Ashton in Osceola County was named, and Delos Kerstetter of Lagrange, Indiana, after whom Delos Kerstetter, Jr., was named.

In making the preliminary survey of this part of the road, Innes had relied heavily upon the government survey. Through Wexford County, the survey called for a route northward on an almost straight line from the south county line near Hobart, passing between Big and Little Clam lakes and then swinging north-northeast towards what is now Manton. This was the route followed by Beardslee's crew in making a final survey. Months later, Beardslee chanced to be a passenger with Mitchell on the train from Grand Rapids to Kendallville, and Mitchell eagerly picked his brain about the pine lands of the north and what lay along the right-of-way.

When Mitchell began commuting between Kendallville and Kent County to supervise the partnership's logging operations in the summer of 1867, the G. R. & I. track had not yet reached Cedar Springs. Progress was slow, and while Cedar Springs was reached by the end of that year, it took almost two more years to get to Morley and another fifteen months to get to Reed City.[8] Mitchell worked his way north with the construction crew. Several biographers and some contemporary accounts refer to him as having participated in the railroad construction. While it is not impossible that he was employed by the railroad in some capacity, it would appear more likely that the references were to the logging operations in which he engaged and which may well have included some right-of-way clearing under contract with the railroad. He was not content, however, to follow the road. He was looking ahead of it.

8. Patrick J. Walsh, for many years an engineer on the G. R. & I., started to work for the railroad on a construction train shortly before it reached the area that became Morley. He described the casual nature in which Morley was born: Two men got off the train with fourteen kegs of beer and two bottles of whiskey to establish a saloon for members of the construction train. Many of the men got drunk, among them the camp cook, that night and went to sleep on the ground around the outdoor saloon. Seeing further opportunity, the two entrepreneurs wangled enough provisions from the supply car to feed their customers the following morning, which they managed to do with the use of "borrowed" pans from the railroad cook house. They never left the site, and the town grew up around their saloon and grocery store. The account is not dissimilar from that of the first business activity at Clam Lake, and Alba supposedly had its beginnings in like manner.

During the summer of 1868, he got in touch with Beardslee and invited him to meet at the Mitchell home in Kendallville, asking Beardslee to bring his survey notes for Osceola, Wexford, Kalkaska, and Antrim counties. When Beardslee arrived, Mitchell had copies of the maps and field notes of the original government survey. He told Beardslee that he had eliminated Antrim and Osceola counties from his plans. The two spent the better part of a weekend examining the lands through which the road would pass in Wexford and Kalkaska counties.[9]

In Wexford County in 1870, the county's new officers and the people buying land and putting up buildings at the new county seat were quite aware that the G. R. & I. was northward bound. The Land Grant Act had indicated only that a railroad was to be constructed to a point on Little Traverse Bay. They were convinced that it could not afford to bypass so important a place as a county seat, and the Maquestons, the Clarks, Sturtevant, Ferguson, and others raised as much money as they could to purchase land in the vicinity. The railroad had reached Big Rapids in 1869, and E. G. Maqueston, Henry Clark, and Sanford Gasser, who had all done business in Big Rapids, kept in close touch with their friends there about the railroad's progress.

9. After the founding of Clam Lake, Beardslee lived at the Mason House with Mitchell for several years and did surveying and some land-looking for Mitchell. During at least one winter, he supervised a Mitchell logging camp. He was the county surveyor for four years, but after Mitchell's death didn't stay put in any one place very long. Although maintaining a residence in Cadillac for another nine or ten years, he was employed in surveying the Toledo and Muskegon Railroad and part of the Grand Trunk system in central Michigan. In 1887 and 1888, he was surveying in southern Michigan and then for several years was engaged in laying out logging railroads in Antrim, Emmett, Otsego and Cheboygan counties. He came back to central Michigan in connection with construction of the Toledo and Ann Arbor, had real estate holdings around Harrietta and Marion, serving briefly as station agent at Marion for the T. & A. and then headed for the Upper Peninsula, where he was a construction superintendent for various logging railroads and for part of the Soo Line Railroad. He seems to have been a jovial, happy-go-lucky individual, and at one time Cadillac boasted that it had in his person the Michigan champion roller skater. He was thoughtful enough to record, and fate was sufficiently kind to preserve, his accounts of several incidents in connection with the building of the G. R. & I. and the founding of the village of Clam Lake.

There may have been some second thoughts in Sherman when it was learned that crews clearing the railroad right-of-way had bypassed the Osceola County seat at Hersey and swung to the west to pass through what later became Reed City. If this was bad news in terms of the importance of county seats, it could also be explained as evidence that the road was maintaining a northwesterly direction towards Traverse City. Further assurance came that summer when it was learned that the G. R. & I. was buying property for a depot site in Traverse City. That seemed to resolve any doubt as to the railroad route, and Sherman was almost on a straight line between Reed City and Traverse City.

It was with more than a little surprise that Sherman came out of hibernation in the spring of 1871 to learn that during the winter, camp sites had been established for construction crews in the areas that are now Ashton, Leroy, Tustin, Hobart, Cadillac, and on to Fife Lake. Traverse was not to be on the main line but would be served only by a branch from Walton, and Sherman was bypassed. But if the route had been a secret to the people around Sherman, it had not been to George Mitchell.

Chapter Six

A SITE FOR A CITY

One of the pleasant legends of county history is that the site of Cadillac was "stolen" in 1871. It appears in John Wheeler's *History of Wexford County,*[1] as follows:

> The first effort to clear away any portion of the forests which covered the ground where the City of Cadillac now stands was for the building of camps used in the construction of the extension of the Grand Rapids & Indiana Railroad. Col. J. C. Hudnutt was the railroad company's civil engineer at that time and when he was ordered to swing around the eastern end of Little Clam lake, instead of passing between the two lakes, as was first intended, he concluded that it meant the building of a town at that point. With this idea in view, he decided to buy any or all land bordering on the eastern shore of the lake and for this purpose he started for the government land office, then located at Traverse City, in the fall of 1871, to ascertain what there was in that locality that could be purchased. The only road to Traverse City then was the State road, running through Sherman, and as the stage was the only conveyance it took two days to make the trip from the northern end of the railroad, which was then just this side of Big Rapids, to the land office.
>
> The colonel stopped over night in Sherman and in conversation with some of the business men of that village casually remarked that he was on his way to the United States land office "to buy a city." I. H. Maqueston, one of Sherman's first merchants, boarded at the hotel and, overhearing this

1. The Wheeler story was accepted without question by Perry F. Powers and George Fuller.

> remark of the Colonel's, adroitly drew out the facts that the "city" was yet in embryo, but that it was to be built on the eastern shore of the Little Clam Lake, so while the Colonel was enjoying a much needed night's rest, Mr. Maqueston started for Traverse City, where he arrived in the middle of the night. How he found the residence of the register of the land office or how much he gave him to leave his warm bed and go to the land office at that unseemly hour of the night will probably always remain a mystery, as both have been dead for many years, but certain it is that when Col. Hudnutt reached the land office the next day he discovered the fact that government lots, 1, 3 and 5 of section 4, in Clam Lake township, or rather what is now Clam Lake township, had been sold to L. J. Clark and I. H. Maqueston of Sherman. This was the land upon which the original village of Clam Lake was platted. The village has now become the city of Cadillac, so that Mr. Hudnutt's facetious remark about buying a city proved the truth of the old adage that "many a truth is spoken in jest." Messrs. Clark and Maqueston sold their "city" purchase to George A. Mitchell, who soon after platted it into the village of Clam Lake.

It makes a nice story, which reflects the devil-take-the-hindmost competition of those days. But the story has many flaws. By the fall of 1871, the G. R. & I. right-of-way had been logged all the way to Fife Lake, a large part of it in Wexford County had been stumped, and the track had passed Tustin. There was already a settlement on the east end of Little Clam Lake half as big as that at Sherman. Even if one were to assume a year's error in memory and set the story in the fall of 1870, it isn't consistent with other facts.

There was a J. C. Hudnutt who had served under General Innes in the Army of the Cumberland and had gone to work for him as a construction supervisor of the G. R. & I. It would not have been unusual had he decided to patent some land for himself along the right-of-way; that was not an uncommon practice among those with inside knowledge of the right-of-way location. But had he attempted to do so in the fall of 1871, he would have found the property already owned by Maqueston and Clark. He could have found that out by simply asking some questions in the settlement of Clam Lake. The information was available at the government land office and in the county records at Sherman, and this would have been evident even in 1870. He would also have found that Maqueston and Clark were not the only owners involved. They held government lots 1-3 and 5, while the rest of the land at the end of the lake was owned by others. None of the land in question remained public land by 1870.

An examination of land title records shows that it was not Isaac H. Maqueston who acquired land around Clam Lake but his brother Edward, who, covering the area as a land-looker, had purchased timber lands for himself in Wexford and surrounding counties. He had claimed the land along Little Clam Lake long before the patent was finally issued on July 1, 1870.

The story is peculiarly mixed up as to the Clarks also, if one assumes that Sylvester H. Clark, the owner of the hotel at Sherman, was involved in the plot. Edward Maqueston and Sylvester's nephew Henry Clark had been land-lookers operating out of Big Rapids together for several years before locating in the Sherman area. Henry wasn't involved either. The title inconsistency, however, is that the Clark who became a co-owner of the property on Little Clam Lake was neither Henry nor Sylvester, but Lewis J. Clark, the storekeeper and postmaster at Sherman. When the Maquestons decided to move to Sherman in 1869, they looked for land for a store and made a trade with Lewis Clark by which they acquired land at Sherman in return for a half interest in the pine land along the Clam Lake on which Edward Maqueston had applied for a patent. The deeds to accomplish the trade were executed even before Maqueston's patent was approved.

Mitchell did get a deed on October 4, 1871, from Edward Maqueston and Lewis J. Clark for the property which they owned, but it is apparent that they had contracted to sell much earlier than the date of the deed. By then the village of Clam Lake had already been born. The property which they sold was but a small part of the tract that Mitchell had put together to make a city. The care with which the city was conceived is more fascinating than the legend of its theft.

2.

The legend of the theft of the city really does an injustice to Mitchell. The most significant part of Wheeler's account of the legend is the casual reference to a change in the location of the G. R. & I. right-of-way from the route originally planned between the Big and Little Clam lakes to a position at the east end of Little Clam Lake. When the rest of the story is disproved, this fact remains: there was a change in the planned route. Wheeler's account dismisses it without detail and leaves the reader to speculate why and by whom the change was made.

When Mitchell had finished his talk with Lee Beardslee, he had three possibilities in mind for investment purposes. One was a river site which would bridge the Manistee, permit the construction of a mill operated by water power, and allow the floating of logs to the mill on the river. The possibility of acquisitions around, and the establishment of a mill at, Fife Lake also was considered. The third possibility was the one at Clam Lake. The railroad location at Fife Lake did not appear favorable but could have been changed. Any advantage at Fife Lake, however, existed two-fold at Cadillac. The possible connection of the two lakes and the larger area of water would permit the floating of logs a greater distance to a mill, and the Fife Lake possibility was soon discarded.

Sometime during the summer of 1869, Mitchell set out on horseback from Big Rapids to survey the area himself. The first settlers in Clam Lake Township, the Ganes, were surprised in their solitude one evening to hear the sounds of an approaching horse and were happy to share their new log home with the rider. They always remembered his courtesy and he particularly appreciated theirs. There was only one other homestead from there to the Manistee River, that of Warren Seaman, near what was to become Manton.

We do not know the duration of this trip or why Mitchell arrived at his conclusions. We do know that he apparently reached the river and gave up the possibility of locating a mill site there. Later in 1869 or early in the spring of 1870, Mitchell and General Innes traveled from Big Rapids to Fife Lake over the proposed right-of-way.[2] In retrospect, it would appear that Mitchell could have had no other purpose in persuading Innes to retrace the survey of the railroad route than to persuade him to make a change.

Man-made changes make it difficult to picture the area around the lakes as it must have appeared to the travelers in 1870. The shoreline and contours of the lake as they exist today are largely the result of erosion and the shaping action of waves and ice, since variations in the water level of the lakes have been minimized by a dam controlling the Clam Lake River outlet. Most of the marsh areas around the lakes have dried up or been filled. The small lakes southeast of the city have largely disappeared or been filled, and only some muck and occasional standing water show where a natural drain ran in that direction from Little Clam Lake during the spring runoff. Buildings now stand in the city where fish were caught eighty years ago.

Perhaps the area which today most nearly resembles its 1870 appearance is the swamp north of the canal through which the Black River runs between the lakes, and extending northward across the township line. And some portions of this are even now being filled. It was apparently either a dry year, or during the dry season, when Innes first surveyed the route between the lakes. In contrast, when he and Mitchell surveyed the scene, it must have been during an unusually wet year or during the spring runoff, for the marsh running from the west end of Little Clam Lake south of Big Clam Lake was so full of water that passage was almost impossible. The Black River, which connected the two lakes, was at flood, and there seemed to be standing water for several miles to the northeast. These were not serious obstacles to the filling of a railroad grade, according to the survey. The condition did provide an argument which Mitchell could and did advance, and which Innes cited as justification for moving the right-of-way to the east end of the smaller lake.[3]

2. Innes later gave conflicting dates for the trip, but the latter date appears more likely, since the G. R. & I. track reached Big Rapids and Innes made his headquarters there that year. The description of the area between Little and Big Clam lakes also seems to indicate that it was during the spring season.

3. Having re-routed the right-of-way, Innes disappears from our story, though not from the Cadillac scene. He soon left the G. R. & I. and was a pioneer in western Michigan in the relatively new insurance business. He left the

In fact, the change of the right-of-way was made because Mitchell wanted it made. The cost of a few extra miles of construction was probably insignificant in the face of his persuasion. He was in a good position to persuade. Apart from his friendship with Innes, his brother William was an organizer of the G. R. & I. and had known and worked with Innes as early as 1854. Mitchell and his partners were stockholders in the railroad; one was a director, and Mitchell was about to become one.

What was Mitchell's interest in the route? When he had looked at the maps and discussed the survey with Beardslee, he had pictured the lakes as a vast floating pond for pine sawmills. Even the smallest mill operation was ideally located on water. Water was an ideal storage area in which the logs could be floated, easily moved, and sorted as to size and quality. Beyond that, water was a means of transporting logs. Little Clam Lake, with prevailing westerly winds and a current towards its outlet, could be used to float logs dumped around its perimeter to sawmills at the east end, and was even large enough to permit rafting and towing of logs. Beyond that, there was a connecting river between the two lakes which could be opened, making the larger lake a tributary of the smaller.

Beardslee's observations confirmed that the lakes were surrounded by a fine stand of pine. When Mitchell came through and saw the area, everything Beardslee had told him appeared true, and more. In studying the maps and the surveys, he had pictured an industry around which a city would grow of necessity. A personal inspection changed nothing of that plan. In fact, as he later told Beardslee, when he came to the lake through the trees, he could picture a city growing around its banks. A survey of the area proved that the hills at the east end of the lake were the approximate center of the prime stand of pine forest covering almost 150 square miles of land. He was too late, he discovered, to acquire the lands which were not railroad sections. Others, notably Maqueston and Blodgett, had beaten him to it. But his associations with the G. R. & I., he was confident, would give him

Republican Party and became Chairman of the Michigan Greenback Party. He held high office in the G. A. R. and various fraternal groups, particularly the Masonic organizations. Over the years, he was a regular caller in Cadillac on business, and on political, fraternal, veteran's, and social calls.

first call on the railroad sections. It would be ideal, then, to route the railroad right-of way to the east end of the lake, convenient to where mills ought to be located, and convenient to where it could service a city located along its right-of-way.

Time proved the accuracy of the vision. The railroad went where he wanted it, where it would serve the mills. The mills followed and with them the city. In only one respect was he wrong. The Black River could not be improved enough to provide passage between the lakes, but if nature wouldn't oblige, Mitchell would improve on nature.

3.

The railroad route relocated, Mitchell proceeded to do what he could to acquire the land that he wanted for his purposes. Sections 3 and 9 in Clam Lake Township, and section 33 in Haring Township, were railroad sections. Mitchell could have them for the asking. Indeed, Delos Blodgett attempted to purchase them from the G. R. & I. but was refused. Blodgett had all of section 34 in Haring Township, except forty acres of pine land on high ground where Diggins Park and the new McKinley School are presently located. Mitchell immediately applied for a government patent on the forty.

Around the east end of the lakeshore, section 4 was divided into government lots running clockwise around the lake. Government lot 1 included Harris Point. Government lot 2 was that part of the northeast shore of the lake through which the Clam River outlet ran. Government lots 3 and 4 covered the extreme end of the lake in what is now downtown Cadillac, while 5, 6, and 7 ran around the southeast corner of the lake and out the Sunnyside area. Government lot 2, through which the Clam River outlet ran, had been strategically identified and purchased several years earlier by Levi O. Harris, who, with his brother, had built Harrisville on the Lake Huron shore. The Harrises planned the erection of a sawmill and sought control of the river outlet with a view to possible damming and utilization of the flowage for water power. Government lot 4 had been picked up by Delos Blodgett. Lots 1, 3, and 5 had been acquired by Edward Maqueston, who had subsequently traded a half interest to Lewis Clark at Sherman.

Mitchell approached Maqueston and Clark, made an offer, and a contract of sale at a price of $5,000 was agreed upon for their lots. He next contracted Blodgett and contracted to purchase government lot 4 from him. Blodgett also owned other government lots farther down the lakeshore but wasn't interested in selling them, and they weren't necessary for Mitchell's plans. He had the land he needed to insure development around the lake and so proceeded to close his deal with the G. R. & I. for the purchase of sections 3 and 9 in Clam Lake and 33 in Haring—almost 2,000 acres of pine land.

The dates of the deeds on these purchases may have made possible the idea that Mitchell didn't come to the area until late in 1871 and did not discourage the legend that Maqueston "stole" the site of the city that fall. But as any buyer of land knows, the date on a deed indicates only when the seller parted with his title and perhaps the date when he got paid. It shows nothing about when he agreed to sell it or when the buyer may have taken posession of the land. In fact, what was happening on the land early in 1871 indicated that Mitchell already had his real estate package put together, for as the railroad came through, a survey of a new village plat was in process, and people were contracting to buy property from Mitchell.[4]

In the winter of 1870-71 camp sites were prepared at various points along the G. R. & I. right-of-way between Reed City and Fife Lake for the use of construction crews who would commence clearing operations as soon as the weather broke. At Little Clam Lake, the camp consisted of log huts along the lakeshore between Cass and Mason streets. During the winter the greater portion of the right-of-way was logged and the timber skidded out.

4. Mitchell made no attempt to acquire government lot 2 from Harris. He had no desire to do so. A mill operated by Harris, or anybody else on the lake, was exactly what he wanted for the purpose of sawing his logs. Mitchell had decided not to engage in the mill business himself but only to engage in the logging business and the sale of pine lumber. In fact, Mitchell had committed himself to give additional land to the Harris brothers at a nominal price if they would locate in Clam Lake. He was so sure they would come that he gave their name to one of the streets in his new village. They came, built a mill, and also gave their name to Harris Point and Harristown, the settlement west of the mill.

Mitchell's men stacked the logs on the lake, and when the ice went out in the spring of 1871, his great log pond, Little Clam Lake, received the first of the millions of pine logs which were to float in it over the next thirty years.

It is said that the first business establishment of Clam Lake was a pine stump on which sat a barrel of whiskey, reminiscent of the origins of Morley.[5] The first business properly called such was the Clam Lake House, a rude log hotel, put up in early March of 1871, which appears to have been located just east of where Lake and Cass streets now intersect, near the construction crew huts. Two other log buildings went up nearby late in March, the Mason House at what is now the southeast corner of Mason and Lake streets, and Holbrook and May's general store, between Lake Street and the water's edge at the foot of Mason Street. During the summer, a fourth building went up, a log home put up by John S. McClain and located along the west side of the railroad right-of-way about half way between Mason Street and Pine Street. The only other structure built that summer, except for the crude crew camps, was a sawmill put up by J. R. Hale at the foot of South Street. In September it began sawing logs for Mitchell from the railroad right-of-way and from sections 3 and 9.

Mitchell made the Mason House his headquarters and spent a good deal of time in Clam Lake during 1871. County surveyor R. S. McClain and his cousin John McClain, assisted by Beardslee,

5. About 1900, Samuel J. Wall said that from what he had been told, the probable site of this enterprise was at about the then location of the Haynes brothers' office on the south side of Chapin Street between the railroads. In 1886, however, Lee Beardslee, who had been here at the time, placed it on the bank of the lake just south of the foot of Chapin Street. He declined to identify the entrepreneur, saying that he had become a respectable Cadillac businessman. Of those few who were here during the first months of 1871, only Morris Bunyea and John Mosser were in business here in 1886. Bunyea came with the railroad crews, then late in the summer started a grocery store on the lake front at about the location Beardslee assigns for the whiskey stump, and later owned several businesses on Mitchell Street. Mosser, a bridge builder for the railroad, was a skilled builder, contractor, owner of a brickyard and building supply house, and the subject of a great mystery when he disappeared in 1893. During the first few years of the village, he owned a saloon-boardinghouse on Mason Street. Take your pick.

went to work for Mitchell early in the summer surveying his plat of the village of Clam Lake. It was completed by fall. Thus the year 1871 saw the commencement of the city he foresaw. Before Mitchell's death in 1878, a booming and boisterous mill town had proved the accuracy of his vision. One detail of Mitchell's plat of the village of Clam Lake discloses the thoroughness of his planning and foreshadows a fascinating story ending after his death, but in which he played a strenuous part of his lifetime. The plat was centered around a high hill giving a commanding view of the area. The hill was designated as Block F on the plat and set aside as a site for the county courthouse.

4.

At the beginning of 1871, the site presently occupied by the city of Cadillac was covered by a dense pine forest. There was nothing to indicate the presence of man except an occasional marker from the government survey and the blazed trees left as survey markers by the railroad and private surveyors. These were but small indication of the onslaught that was to change the face of the land, minute guides for the army of laborers, loggers, and settlers which would sweep through the forest in the coming year.

During the winter, the camp sites had been prepared and the timber cut from the right-of-way. In March the work began in earnest, and two log buildings were added to the campsites to provide shelter and storage for the railroad contruction crews. These buildings, log bunk houses, went up on the right-of-way between Harris and Mason streets and were quickly surrounded by four or five smaller huts. By the end of the year, they had served their purpose and had been demolished and replaced by two frame buildings, the larger of which served as a railroad depot until 1878.

Before the summer was over, the central part of Michell's plat of the village of Clam Lake was completed in the sense that a large part of it had been cleared and a decision made as to the major lines along which the streets would be run, fitting the design of the proposed village to the contours of the land. Perhaps it is misleading to refer to the area as having been cleared. To picture it, one must begin by noting that Michell's loggers were at work that spring, along with the railroad crews. From the swamp below Cemetery Hill to the Clam River, the pine was quickly cut along the lake and for a distance of from 300 to 500 yards east of the railroad right-of-way. There was left a desolate looking expanse of brush, slashings, and pine stumps. Photographs taken several years later show stumps and brush piles still cheek-by-jowl with buildings on Mitchell Street.

Through the center of this forlorn scene only the railroad right-of-way was truly "cleared" to the ground. As the streets were laid out by the surveyor R. S. McClain, they were "brushed" to their full width, but only enough stumps were removed to permit passage of a wagon and team. In this sense, by late fall Mitchell Street and Lake Street were "cleared" thoroughfares from Harris Street to Pine Street, and Harris, Mason, and Pine streets were cleared for the one block between Lake and Mitchell. It was another eight years before even those sections were completely cleared of stumps.[6]

The Mitchell plat covered roughly eighty acres of land, about twenty acres lying between the railroad right-of-way and the lake and the remainder running up the slopes east of the right-of-way. The street marking the north limit was appropriately named North Street. The east boundary was Park Street and the south boundary was Howard Street.[7] Other streets had names appropriate to time and place, such as Mitchell, Lake, Pine, Beech, and Spruce. Neither of Michigan's illustrious governors, Lewis Cass or Stevens T. Mason, gave his name to a street. Cass Street took its name from Edgar Cass, a G. R. & I. official, while Mason Street was named for Mitchell's friend S. C. Mason, a Big Rapids innkeeper, who came to Mitchell's new village and whose Mason House fronted on that street. Mitchell's Indiana partners,

6. The delay was costly, for Mitchell's death in 1878 resulted from a skull fracture suffered when he was thrown from his buggy on Pine Street near the railroad crossing and struck his head on one of the stumps still standing in the street.

7. William Howard was the land comissioner for the G. R. & I. and the man with whom Mitchell arranged the purchase of the railroad land necessary for his village.

Oscar A. Simons and Augustus A. Chapin, were likewise remembered to posterity, as were logging and railroad associates Bremer, Nelson, Shelby, and Stimson.

Not the least of the exceptional features of the plat was the unusual width of Mitchell Street, far exceeding any reasonable needs of that day. It permitted the development of a business district which could grow and expand into the modern era of automobile without traffic congestion, with fewer parking problems than most communities, and without the necessity of costly widening projects and relocation of buildings.

Several other features distinguished the plat. One was the designation of a block centrally located between the railroad and the lake as a public park, which it still remains. Another, the centrally located block F, bounded by Mitchell, Shelby, Spruce, and Beech streets, was not subdivided into lots but was set aside as a site for the location of the county courthouse, although the county seat had already been located at Sherman, and the presumptuous village of Clam Lake was not yet legally organized. Block F was never used as intended, but it was not for want of Mitchell's efforts, and those efforts made possible the move of the county seat to Cadillac after his death.[8] Neither the park block nor block F, of course, were prime building sites. The park was almost entirely swamp, and large amounts of fill were brought in to raise it to its present grade. Block F, on the other hand, was the opposite, an exceptionally high prominence with slopes so steep as to make impractical the opening of Beech and Spruce streets, which were platted on its western slope. At its highest point, it

8. Block F was also called Courthouse Square, or Courthouse Hill, the name by which it is referred to earlier in the account of the visit of Delos Blodgett to Cadillac. Had the county seat been moved to Cadillac during Mitchell's lifetime, block F would have been the site of the county buildings. In the expectation of such use, it remained undeveloped for years and served as a commons on which farmers grazed their horses while in town. It was ultimately acquired by the Cummers from the Mitchell heirs and subdivided. The Cummers would let someone else donate a courthouse site. Dr. John Leeson said he would do so, but *sold* the present site at the head of Harris Street to the county. Ironically, before construction of the present courthouse, block F became the seat of county government for twenty years when the county leased office space in the Masonic building erected on the square.

once stood twenty feet higher than it does today. Over the years it was gradually whittled down and provided fill dirt for the park, along the lakeshore, and for the channeling of the Clam River. But the crown of the hill remained free of buildings until almost the very end of the century, providing a parklike commons, to which visitors were directed for "the view from Courthouse hill."

Sherman Courthouse—Built by John Wheeler and occupied as the Wexford County Courthouse from 1872 until 1881. In 1938 an N.Y.A. relief project, looking for work to do, razed the old courthouse while the county board of supervisors was planning its renovation as a historical museum.

George A. Mitchell, founder of the village of Clam Lake and first mayor of the city of Cadillac.

The Clam Lake House—September 1871.

The County Seat Combatants.

John H. Wheeler, editor of the *Pioneer*.

Rep. Thomas A. Ferguson.

County Clerk Heman B. Sturtevant.

Judge Silas S. Fallas.

DR. JNO.

Dr. John Leeson.

Mayor Daniel McCoy.

Mayor Jacob Cummer.

Mayor Byron Ballou.

Harristown, Aug. 12, 1882—Forerunner of Industralization. The *James Thomas*, a Shay locomotive built at Cadillac's Michigan Iron Works, stops near the company store of the Cummer Lumber Co. for a historic photograph. It drew a record load of 45 heavily loaded cars with 393 white pine logs from Haring Township scaling 60,937 feet.

C.T. Stoner collection.

Chapter Seven

MAKING A VILLAGE: CLAM LAKE

By the end of September of 1871, the surveying had been completed for Mitchell's plat of the village of Clam Lake, and a handful of buildings were scattered between the lake and the railroad right-of-way. Besides the bunk houses for the construction crews, there was the home of John McClain, as well as the two hotels—the Clam Lake House and Mason House—and two stores, that of Holbrook and May near the Mason House, and that of Morris Bunyea farther south along the lakeshore. South of the Bunyea store, the Hale Mill was in operation, and the buildings that were to go up thereafter would be of frame rather than log construction.

Several articles refer to George Mitchell as having commenced his operation at Clam Lake in October of 1871. The statement is true only in the sense that this marks the date at which the plat of the village was completed and filed. Although the track had gone no farther than Tustin by October, the right-of-way from there to Clam Lake had become a well-traveled road for settlers, suppliers, and homesteaders. Construction engineer W. B. Stimson had already moved his headquarters to the Mason House and was making his preparations for the winter camps. The hotels were jammed with teamsters and provisions using Clam Lake as a base for the next step north.[1] Mingled with them were laborers, homesteaders, loggers, and lumbermen looking over the area, and railroad officers and investors. At the hub of the activity was

1. An April visitor to Clam Lake in 1871 described the Mason House as being fully occupied before the cracks between the logs had been chinked, with spring snow blowing in on the guests who slept side by side on the floor. The Clam Lake House was fancier, with real beds, but an account by owner Charles Teller says that guests were often four to a bed, rousted out in the middle of the night to allow a second set of guests to recline in similar luxury.

George Mitchell's office in the Mason House, from which railroad business, logging activities, and the selling of a city were directed.

During October and November, construction was commenced on more than twenty commercial buildings in the new settlement. Among those persuaded to locate in the village were three carpenters, John Tracy, Adam Gallinger, and Ira White. They, with John G. Mosser, the bridge-builder for the G. R. & I., were to start the physical construction of the city. Tracy, Gallinger, and White looked on the place as a permanent residence, although all three were to leave within a few years. Mosser, on the other hand, was eventually to become a permanent resident and the area's leading contractor but at the moment was simply looking for winter work to keep himself occupied until he resumed railroad work the following spring. In partnership with White, he acquired two lots from Mitchell on the east side of Mitchell Street between Cass and Chapin streets, and put up a two-story store building, the first frame building in the city. The second floor, called the Empire Hall, was soon being used on weekdays for the first school classes of the village and on Sundays by Methodist and Presbyterian congregations. White and Mosser lived in the first floor and used it as a carpenter shop until spring, when it was leased to Cornwell and LaBar as a grocery store.[2] For Morris Bunyea, the lakeshore grocer, they started two other buildings on Mitchell Street between Cass and Harris streets. South of Bunyea's log grocery, they put up a boardinghouse along the lakeshore for William Parks, one of the owners of the Clam Lake House, and a saloon and boardinghouse on the corner of Cass and Mitchell streets for R. P. Thurber, who operated it as the Ohio House.

The main business district, however, was at the intersection of Lake and Mason streets. Across Lake Street from the Mason House, by Holbrook and May's log store, Gallinger put up a building which served as a carpenter and wagon shop and as his residence.[3] To the east, Gallinger erected several buildings for

2. It remained a grocery store for various tenants, Crawford Brothers, Wilcox Brothers, Cowin and Baker, and others, for almost ninety years, and was finally demolished to make way for the Oleson parking lot.

3. And in which he eventually ran a saloon. Mosser, too, tried his hand at the saloon business from 1874 to 1876.

Andrew Larcom: a store building, a blacksmith shop occupied by Reed and Ferris, and a small building occupied by John Duval, a bootmaker.[4] Immediately across the street on the east side of Lake Street, Mosser and White built a large boardinghouse for Lewis G. Lawson, known as the Lakeview House, but frequently referred to in early years as the "Sweed House." Confusingly, Lawson's wife ran the Scandinavian House, which was built next door the next year. East of the Mason House, a horse barn was erected for the hotel's guests, and across the street next to McClain's building a livery stable and harness shop was put up by Alonzo McCardy. South of the Mason House, Mosser built a small saloon for John Davis[5] at the corner of Harris and Lake streets, and just to the south of him another was put up by Robert Goldman.[6]

In an effort to reach the new village before the end of the year, workmen continued laying track into winter, and temporary trestles were laid to permit the running of a supply train into Clam Lake in mid-December. On January 8, 1872, he first passenger train arrived. Engineer William Smith said, "The road was so rough that I broke the tender loose from my engine while passing over one of the pitfalls into which a portion of the track had sunk

4. By 1873, Duval had also found that whiskey was gold, and he too was running a saloon.

5. The Davis saloon had an interesting history. The lots on which the building was put up had been sold by George Mitchell to Levi Harris, so another lot was purchased by Davis on Mason Street early in 1872, and his building was moved to that location. Davis subsequently entered into two partnerships, one with E. Arthur Bowen, buying the Mason House, and the other for the operation of the saloon with Alonzo McCardy, the harness maker. A bigger saloon was built in 1875, and the original building was moved onto Mitchell Street. It is believed to be the building presently occupied by Johnson's photography shop.

6. Goldman had considerable difficulty with the law. His building was on the park grounds and was torn down by Mitchell's men in 1873. Goldman set up shop on the west side of Lake Street near Pine with a saloon and boardinghouse which soon became known as The Robbers Roost. About 1876, Goldman moved to the Ohio House, where his troubles with the law continued, and he disappeared after it burned down under circumstances suggesting arson. The Robbers Roost became an even worse den, a recognized house of prostitution, and the scene of frequent disorders. When it burned down in 1894, part of the city was surprised to learn that the owner of the building was Dr. John Leeson, staunch Methodist and temperance leader.

before I had gone far, and I had to couple them together with a chain which held during the trip."[7]

2.

In March, 1872, three different visitors described the new community. The editor of the Midland *Independent* was brief:

> Having been to the new village of Clam Lake as a guest of its proprietor, Mr. George A. Mitchell, Esq., we found it a very loosely constructed city with sandy bottom, stumpy streets, and not very streety. We visited the Clam House and saw several old clams around there. Had imbibed too much mountain dew the night previous and looked now as if waiting for high water. The last named hotel was built of logs and does not look just like a hotel after all. The lake itself is a beautiful sheet of water some three miles long by perhaps a mile in width. It is surrounded by a forest of pines and appears like a crystal set in emerald.

Another newspaper account of 1872 is as follows:

> Clam Lake is the present terminus of the Grand Rapids and Indiana Railroad. It is a place of about five month's growth, but remarkably active and go-head-a-tive.
>
> Mr. George A. Mitchell, proprietor of the village plat, commenced operations there in October last. Now the village contains about 60 families and a population of some 300.
>
> The plat of the village covers over 50 acres. It is divided into some 200 lots, 150 of which have already been sold.
>
> The village contains two hotels, the Mason House and the Clam Lake House, four or five general stores, one hardware,

7. Beardslee says that the train of January 8, however, was a freight train to which one passenger car had been attached, and indicates that for another two months passengers were brought in only irregularly, as often as not in freight cars. Railroad records indicate that scheduled passenger service was established on a daily basis February 20, 1872.

blacksmith shops, shoe shops, wagon shops. One steam saw-mill, that of J. R. Hale with the capacity of about 20,000 feet per day is already in operation. Mssrs. Harris brothers are building a mill that is expected to cut 1 million feet per month. Shackleton and Green are also soon to erect a mill that will cut 750,000 in a month. Mssrs. M. H. and J. P. Hawley are building a planing and shingle mill which they expect to have in running order on or before the 1st of May. A Mr. Anderson is constructing a dock and has made arrangements for putting a small steamer on the lake.

Among the mercantile establishments, we would make special note of the general store of Mssrs. Holbrook and May and the hardware store of Mr. H. W. Hicks. The firm first named consists of two young men from Plymouth, Mich., who have come to Clam Lake to stay and build up their business as the country developes. Mr. Hicks, formerly of Big Rapids, has a nice new store and doubtless understands his business. A school district has been formed and a school is in successful operation. The Methodists have weekly religious services and a Presbyterian Church is likely to be organized soon.

It is said that the railroad company has 300,000,000 feet of pine timber that may be worked up at the Clam Lake and that other parties have nearly as much more. This being the case, there will necessarily be a large amount of lumber manufactured each year for a long time to come. This insures business to the village and business, too, of a paying character.

There is said to be a large amount of excellent farming land in the vicinity that will be tributary to the place, help to build it up and sustain it when the pine is gone.

The location of the village is a pleasant one. Little Clam Lake, on the borders of which the village stands, is a beautiful sheet of water of crystal purity and abounding in fish. The village site ascends very gently from the water, spreading out into a plain covered with a heavy growth of pines. There is a border of young pines along the shore of the lake which we trust "the powers that be" and that may be hereafter, will carefully preserve. Woodmen, spare those trees!

There is talk of opening the channel between the Little and Big Clam so as to admit the passage of steamers between them. Sooner or later this will doubtless be done.

Mrs. George Mitchell described her visit to the new village in this fashion:

It was in March, 1872, I accepted Mr. Mitchell's invitation to visit Clam Lake (now Cadillac), it being then about six months old. We took the G. R. & I. road at Kendallville, Ind., came to Grand Rapids and remained over night, as Mr. Mitchell had business to attend to. Next morning resumed our journey, and as there was but one coach for the passengers it was soon crowded full of men, but few women, and the further we came the less in number. We passed through a new rough-looking country, and after leaving Reed City there were no clearings, just the track through a wilderness of tall pines. After much jolting about we reached Clam Lake, tired and hungry. There were two places where food and lodging could be had, one a log house near where the sash and blind factory now stands, and the other also a log structure, but larger, stood just north of McAdie & Co.'s Foundry, fronting on Lake Street, and was called the "Mason House." There were very few divisions, on the first floor, one sleeping room and the kitchen, the remainder was used for general purposes. Across one end was a long table with benches for seats, where food was served, always the best the town afforded. On the upper floor a small room was partitioned off for Mr. Mitchell, the remainder of the floor being occupied by beds.

There were the usual buildings that start a town, the general store, blacksmith shop and postoffice, with plenty of energy. My first visit was limited to a few days on account of the accommodations, but as the town grew rapidly, better accommodations could be found, and I enjoyed spending several weeks with Mr. Mitchell, particularly in the summer. Finally, in December, 1876, we decided to make Cadillac our home.

3.

The hotels, rooming houses and boarding houses of the new village, and the Mason House in particular, deserve some special mention. The log house of John McClain was the only home to be built in the new settlement in 1871! Most of the first businessmen came ahead of their families. Even if the buildings they put up didn't provide permanent living quarters, they lived temporarily in their stores as a matter of convenience and boarded out. In these early months, the boarding table was the social and communal center, affectionately remembered in later years for comradeship and tall tales.[8]

More significant, however, the new village was shaped from the beginning, as it was for many years thereafter, by the transient nature of its population, largely railroad men and woodsmen. In consequence, the business district was peculiarly adapted to that kind of population, and largely consisted in the beginning of provisioners, hotels, rooming houses and boardinghouses, saloons and red-light houses. In 1871 the two hotels, the Mason House and Clam Lake House, had been built, along with three boardinghouses, the Ohio House, the Lakeview House, and William Parks' boardinghouse. They were joined in 1872 by another hotel, the American House, located on the southeast corner of Mitchell and Harris streets and operated by William Currie and William Bennett. Its advertisements proclaimed it a "temperance hotel." In that particular it was unique. In those days it was a hard drinking country. Except for taxation, the state had neither entered into the liquor business itself nor into the regulation or licensing of the liquor trade. Sales were unrestricted, and liquor was available at all hotels and public eating places—except, of course, at the American House, a "temperance hotel." In a town that soon had the reputation of being the toughest town in Michigan, the American House was a real exception.[9]

8. To say nothing of the fare—beans, potatoes, turnips, salt pork, salt horse, and all the bread you could eat, at twenty-five cents a day or $1.40 a week. Eggs were a delicacy at five cents each. Whiskey was a dime, beer five cents.

9. It was also soon insolvent, perhaps for want of the revenue which might have been obtained from liquid gold. Bennett gave up and sold his interest to

Boardinghouses and saloons soon multiplied on Mason Street and for several blocks in each direction on Lake Street. Parks built a better boardinghouse on the north side of Mason Street and sold his old place of business to a man by the name of Merchant, who operated it as the Merchant House. Merchant in turn also built a better boardinghouse on South Mitchell Street, and his successor soon gave the old place a bad reputation, doing business as the Swamp House. Morris Bunyea started the construction of some store buildings on Mitchell Street between Harris and Cass. He leased part of his old building on the lake to Gil Cook for a saloon and the remainder to LaBar and Cornwell briefly as a grocery store.

The Scandinavian House was built on Lake Street. It burned down a few years later and was rebuilt on Harris Street. On the north side of Mason Street, Bergstrom's Sweed Saloon and Boardinghouse was built. Mention is soon made of other "Sweed" boardinghouses along the west side of Lake Street, north of Mason, notably the Lake House,[10] and a few years later the *News* referred to "the French boardinghouse on Mason Street," which suggests that it was not only the Swedes who were clannish in seeking accommodations. In 1873 Duncan McKinnon and Daniel Beaton built a hotel on the northeast corner of Harris and

Captain L. J. Newson and joined lumberman George Shackleton in the gristmill venture at Sherman. Newson "hedged" his temperance investment carefully, pairing it with two other ventures, a saloon, and a partnership in selling liquor wholesale. In 1879, the hotel was sold to C. K. Russell, and was as well known by the name "Russell House."

10. The Lake House, not to be confused with the neighboring Lakeview House, went up in the spring of 1872 and soon became the hangout of gamblers and prostitutes. It was also the place of business of the city's first barber, H. M. Wall. Wall put up a little barber shop nearby the following year and built a dock at the foot of Harris Street in 1878 from which he rented boats. Beardslee vows that Wall was never seen in a wholly sober state, nor other than cheerful. When he died in 1890 at age fifty-six, the *News* said: "He had yielded to his seemingly ungovernable appetite for intoxicating drink until his vitality could no longer sustain the strain and the inebriated stupor in which the officers found him at the G. R. & I. Railroad station at 7 o'clock a.m. was followed a few hours later by an entire cessation of all of his physical forces and death ensued without any apparent return to consciousness."

Mitchell streets. The McKinnon House, predecessor of our present Northwood Hotel, was to be the most enduring and best remembered of the village hostelries.

But the place that was best known in the early days, through good reputation and bad, was the Mason House. Many of the hotels and boardinghouses acquired unsavory reputations as the mill hands, loggers, and rivermen made Clam Lake a boom town, and ladies of doubtful virtue came to help them spend their time and money. The ups and downs of the Mason House tell the story, as it and Mason Street were the center of activity in the new village.

Spencer C. Mason had been the proprietor of a hotel at Big Rapids (also the Mason House) and had become friendly with Mitchell, who stayed there with him for many months. He was persuaded by Mitchell that there would be a town at Clam Lake, that it would thrive, and that a hotel was both a necessity and a good investment. To encourage Mason to make the move and the investment, Mitchell employed a practice which he also used to encourage other key professional and business people to locate in his new village. He gave Mason the land on which to build his inn. Mason accepted, selected the land at the southeast corner of the intersection of Lake and Mason streets, and put up the log hotel in late March of 1871.[11]

Although the building was of log construction, it was large and well built, and designed with a view to further enlargement. In June of 1872, shortly after Mrs. Mitchell's visit, an addition was made, and the interior was partitioned. The *News* described the improvements:

> The rooms are all being newly ceiled, papered and finished in the most comfortable manner. The walls, which are now known to be made of logs, are sided on the outside so it will appear to be a log building no more. Mr. Mason is a pleasant and obliging landlord and is ready to do anything for the comfort and entertainment of all who are so fortunate as to stop with him. He has placed on the lake for the entertain-

11. Mitchell did not yet have a deed to the land, but it was subsequently platted as lots 7, 8, and 9 of block 1 of the plat of the village of Clam Lake.

ment of his guests, a fine pleasure boat that is truly delightful to ride in. The tables are spread with the very best the market affords and everything presents a tidy and tasty appearance.

The Mason House was headquarters for George Mitchell, who had the privilege of a room of his own, from which he and Lee Beardslee planned the development of the village and managed Mitchell's lumber business. It was the headquarters for the G. R. & I. officials, notably construction engineer W. B. Stimson and assistant superintendent H. D. Wallin, Jr.[12] It was the stage house for the line to Traverse City and the dispatch center for the government mail route to Sherman until the railroad reached Manton. In short, it was the hub of activity in the new village, peopled by the village leaders and visited by all those doing business with them.

The Mason House had its good days, but they were brief, and its reputation derives as much from the bad times as from the good. During 1872 and 1873, the *News* referred to Mason on several occasions as suffering ill health, with recurring chills and fevers (perhaps malaria?) If the place was frequented by the better people during the good years, it was also, of necessity, shelter for those of ruder ways, and they weren't always easy to handle. Mason was badly bruised on one occasion for refusing to sell whiskey to a drunken logger. On another occasion he was in trouble for making such a sale. The *News* carried this note: "S. C. Mason, proprietor of the Mason House, was arrested on charges of selling whiskey to an old whiskey sucker. The people of Clam Lake consider the charges untrue. He is well liked and has never been known to sell to a drunken man." Notwithstanding the local confidence, he was apparently convicted.[13]

12. Wallin's familiarity with the area eventually led to his purchase of the Levi Harris lots adjoining the Mason House property. In partnership with James Henderson, Wallin put up the Michigan Iron Works factory there and manufactured logging locomotives.

13. Mason was apparently charged with the misdemeanor of selling liquor to an already intoxicated person, one of the few laws then dealing with liquor sales. Justice court records are gone, the newspaper made no further reference to the

Mason sold the hotel early in 1873. The contract indicates that he had borrowed from Mitchell to make the 1872 improvements, the loan being secured by a mortgage which his purchasers, Davis & Bowen, agreed to pay. The character of the place immediately changed for the worse. Newspaper accounts of brawls and worse crimes over the next ten months frequently describe the Mason House as the place of the disorders, and it became the favorite haunt of those of poor repute. Mitchell found himself unable to tolerate the place and found other living and office accomodations.

On occasion, newspaper references to events at the Mason House during this period display an editorial sense of humor. Thus the *News* of November 15, 1873, carried a story with the alarming headline: "CHOLERA IN CLAM LAKE." The story described in ghastly detail the excruciating symptoms suffered by a number of men who were apparently seized with "Asiatic cholera" at the Mason House. The cries, retching, and dysentery of the "dying victims" were described in starkly realistic language. The unavailing efforts of Drs. Leeson and Dillenbeck, who made the diagnosis of cholera, and the summoning of ministers to ease the transit of the poor suffering souls into the Great Beyond, were recounted in terms evoking horror and pity. And then, after building such suspense and emotion in the reader, the paper casually stated that "all the poor victims will recover," and disclosed that it had been found that the boys had helped "the girls of the house cook up a batch of beans in Old Rye and got some croton oil by mistake." For the younger readers, croton oil was a cathartic of considerably greater potency than castor oil.

The change of the Mason House from a well-run hotel to a well-

matter, and the county records do not disclose any payment of justice fees. The latter may be circumstantial evidence—or rather the circumstance of a lack of evidence—supporting conviction. Justices of the peace were paid by fee and were supposed to account in every case. In practice they seldom did so in case of conviction, merely keeping the fine as their fee, and filing a report only in those cases where there was an acquittal, and they looked to the county for payment. John Wheeler tells of coming to Clam Lake as deputy sheriff in this period to make two arrests for liquor violations, and says that both men were convicted, although the evidence was scanty.

run bordello was accompanied by a total absence of payments by its new proprietors, either to Mason or on the Mitchell mortgage. Mason was compelled to evict his purchasers—and their tenants—and resume the management of the business himself. Neither the evicted proprietors nor their tenants and guests had been gentle with the building, and Mason was forced to borrow further from Mitchell to finance the repairs and renovations necessary to make the place fit for decent people again.

On December 13, 1873, the *News* noted: "C. S. Mason has resumed the management of the Mason House. The star boarders who made their headquarters there have been discharged. It will be put in first class running order and fit to serve the public." On December 20, the paper added this note: "Work is coming well on the Mason House. It will be just as genteel and accommodating as in former times."

Unfortunately, the "genteel" trade was not quick to return to the place which had acquired such a notorious reputation, while drunken loggers and rivermen still continued to call there at all hours of the night, frightening respectable patrons. Business declined for Mason and he fell further behind in his mortgage payments to Mitchell. His wife divorced him for good grounds. Eventually, even friendship had to end in the face of such adversity, and Mitchell foreclosed the mortgage in 1876. The Mason House passed into the hands of others who restored both its prosperity and its excellent reputation for vice.

The log Clam Lake House had been built in part on the right-of-way that would be Cass Street, and in part on the block set aside for a city park. Its proprietors, Charles Teller and William Parks, soon parted company as Parks devoted his efforts to his own boardinghouse.[14] Teller entered into a partnership with Abner Steward, who had contracted for the purchase of three lots on the southeast corner of Chapin and Mitchell streets, and during the summer of 1872, they commenced the construction of a

14. And, a few years later, to the practice of law. Parks had been prosecuting attorney in Ottawa County, but did not practice law here until 1880, after taking a turn at logging in the Upper Peninsula. He practiced rather creditably until 1885, when he contracted a fatal case of pneumonia after being caught in a storm while returning to Cadillac from a court session at Lake City.

new Clam Lake House on that location.[15] Finding the Mason House intolerable, George Mitchell took quarters in their new building as soon as it opened, and it was immediately renamed the Mitchell House. Originally constructed with an eighty-foot frontage on Mitchell Street, it was further enlarged in 1873 and boasted cab service to the depot, a fine dining room, a billiard parlor, and a barber shop.[16]

In 1875, with the nation involved in a financial panic, and with its owner in financial distress, the Mitchell House was destroyed by fire. General W. P. Innes, newly in the insurance business, investigated, and found proof of arson. The claim was never paid, and Steward disappeared. Teller promptly started a new business on Mason Street, as—what else?—a saloon keeper.

15. Some early histories indicate that the old log hotel was moved to the new site and improved, but this is in error. After the new building was completed, the log building was burned.

16. The Mitchell House barbershop provided the first employment for another new settler, who was first noticed by the press in the following account from the *News* early in 1873: "On Thursday evening last, Charles Studley and John Sheridan—not Phil—being of different opinions in regard to some question concluded to settle it by the code of 'ye fiste.' Some innocent (?) blood was spilt but further no harm done." Restaurant and saloon keeper Studley was but the first of many to encounter the thirty-six-year-old barber, newly arrived from Ireland, and this was to be but the first of many such accounts in the *News*. Like his fellow barber, Wall, he had no quarrel with whiskey, but differed from Wall in two respects: where Wall was in a perpetual haze, Sheridan's bouts with the bottle were periodic; and while both men were well liked, Sheridan's good nature disappeared with the second drink. He appeared in court frequently for assaults and disorderly conduct. Neither family nor friend nor foe were safe when John had overindulged in "tanglefoot" or "scorpion juice," as the *News* was fond of commenting. He seemed to take particular delight in breaking up church meetings or street gatherings of the Volunteers or Salvation Army. Surprisingly, he survived seventy-six years, dying of a heart attack in 1913.

Chapter Eight
THE MILLS

In the development of his city, Mitchell was businessman, salesman, promoter, and talent scout. His business, of course, was timber, and first things come first. To insure that the city would develop according to his plans and to provide mills to cut his timber, he sought out experienced mill operators, persuaded them to locate at Clam Lake, and helped them select their sites. His persuasiveness was increased by the sale of the sites at nominal prices.

The first mill operators to agree to locate at Clam Lake were the Harris brothers, Levi and Henry, although their mill was not completed until several others were already in operation. Although relatively young men, they had already made a name in Michigan as pine mill operators. With their father, Benjamin, they had built a mill on Lake Huron in Alcona County in 1854, gradually enlarged their operation, and around it had built the community of Harrisville.

Levi was particularly gifted mechanically. An expert machinist, he patented many devices which were adapted to the lumber industry, many of them devised in a small machine shop in Cadillac after he had retired from the lumber business. At Harrisville, he had constructed an intricate system of mill races and reservoirs to harness water power for their mill. A man of many talents, he had served as postmaster there, and was a combination doctor, dentist, lawyer, engineer, and banker. Above all, both he and his brother were quiet, studious, and gentle men, neither of whom is ever known to have made an enemy.

On the death of their father in the early sixties, both brothers were still bachelors with business interests of many kinds scattered across the country. They had a farm and rental properties in their home state of New York, a half interest in a linseed oil processing company in Omaha, Nebraska, a lumber yard in Chicago, a large farm engaged in agricultural research and processing corn oil in Iowa, a machine shop in Jacksonville, Illinois, and interests in banks in three states. In 1866 Levi married, and the brothers sold their Harrisville interests, lock, stock, and millrace. Perhaps to satisfy a new bride's desire for more genteel surroundings, Levi went to Buffalo and entered upon the sedate life of a banker, while looking after their New York properties. Henry moved to Chicago and continued the partnership's lumber business there while overseeing their other midwestern businesses.

Both were soon itching to get back into the mill business. On a trip to Chicago in 1868, Levi left the boat at Petoskey and traveled overland through the still largely unexplored pine country, selecting tracts in key positions on the Sturgeon, Boardman, Manistee, and Pine rivers, and government lot 2 on Little Clam Lake, through which the Clam River outlet flowed. Two years later, Henry heard stories in Chicago that George Mitchell was acquiring immense tracts of pine in northwest Michigan along the route to be taken by the G. R. & I. railroad. He wrote to Levi suggesting that they might look into the matter, and Levi set about contacting Mitchell, finally arranging a meeting in Grand Rapids.

The rumors about Mitchell's holdings, of course, proved to be exaggerated. Mitchell didn't own whole counties. As a matter of fact, at the time of the meeting he owned only a little pineland, but he planned to get more. Levi knew first hand that there was good pine there, a lot of it, and what Mitchell didn't get, somebody else would. No matter who owned it, it would be milled. The men arrived at a tentative agreement. For a token payment, the Harris brothers could purchase government lot 1 to the east of the land already acquired by Levi, and they would also have the right to three lots centrally located in the village plat, on which it was contemplated that Levi would erect a machine shop. In return, except for a reasonable amount of work on their own account, the Harris Brothers mill was to be devoted exclusively to milling pine for Mitchell for a three-year period. When Levi and Henry came to Clam Lake in the fall of 1871 to arrange for construction of the mill, the village plat was being completed, and they were flattered to note that there was already a Harris Street in the village.[1] The mill they erected was the biggest on the lake and started operation July 1, 1872.

2.

The first mill to commence operation on Little Clam Lake was owned by an Indiana resident named John R. Hale, with whom Mitchell had been previously engaged in some lumber transactions. The mill, known as the Pioneer Mill, went up at what is now the west end of South Street, but was constructed on pilings driven in the shallows of the lake, the better to permit the handling of floating logs. Over the years the surrounding area was gradually filled in with sawdust, slabs, cinders, and sand.[2]

Hale was an Indiana lumberman who apparently never saw Clam Lake. He had the mill built as an investment on the recommendation of Mitchell, and it was operated for him by Andrew Liddell, who also set up and operated a portable mill at the foot of Pine Street briefly in 1872 for another Indiana partnership, J. Slinger and Company. Having no real interest in northern Michigan, Hale decided to sell the mill and discussed it with a former employer of his, Jonathan W. Cobbs. Knowing that Cobbs was casually acquainted with Mitchell, he suggested that Cobbs might like to take the mill off his hands and do Mitchell's sawing. He did.

1. The lots for the machine shop were at the intersection of Lake and Harris streets. Levi bought a lot on "his" street, built a house which still stands, and made the town his home. When the contract to grade Harris Street was let, he bid it to "make sure it was done right." Levi held many public offices, puttered in his machine shop, patented more inventions, and became one of the city's most familiar and best loved figures. Henry died of tuberculosis in 1875, coincident with the financial panic sweeping the country in which two of the Harris banks failed. Levi gradually liquidated the Harris enterprises. In 1882 the Harris mill was sold to Jacob Cummer.

2. A large portion of the shoreline in that vicinity, as well as in the northeastern corner of the lake, represents filled-in lake bottom. Construction of the Cadillac Manor Apartments in the early 1960s on the former mill site disclosed the forgotten original state of the site as former lake bed, and extensive excavations were necessary to remove the muck and accumulated debris to provide a solid footing for the construction.

Cobbs was hardly the type to be an industrialist in the days of the great capitalists. He was a fun-loving Quaker, believing in hard work as necessary but not as an end in itself. He had no platitudes about the dignity of labor, no speeches about God entrusting the destiny of the workingman to free capitalism. He genuinely thought of his employees as his friends and partners and not as raw material from a labor market. He was in some ways almost naïve, with an open and trusting disposition. His association with George Mitchell and Mitchell's nephew William was a happy one of kindred spirits, and he came to dread the solemn, single-minded, and relentless drive for profits that later developed in the Cadillac lumber community.

His father was a cabinet-maker and he said that he cut his teeth on hardwood and his meat with a saw. The family lived on a farm near Salem, Ohio, and the boy farmed, learned something of woodworking, and got a better than average education for the times. At seventeen he was apprenticed to a wagon-maker in Valley, Ohio, at six and a half cents a day plus board. He soon started his own business and invented a dump cart, which he sold in quantity to the Pennsylvania Railroad then being constructed through Ohio. He moved to southern Indiana, where he started a sawmill, and soon had several mills in various parts of the state. Almost inadvertently he found himself growing wealthy and gradually turned over the operation of his mills to his employees, allowing them to share the profits and use them to buy shares in the mills. By 1871 he was a minority owner and sold the remainder of his interest, intending to retire on his farm.

It was at this point that Hale approached him about buying his mill at Clam Lake. Cobbs turned him down, having made a decision to go into business at Grand Rapids, but after several visits with Mitchell decided to buy Hale's mill as an investment. A year and a half in Grand Rapids was disappointing, and in April of 1874 Cobbs moved to Clam Lake to make his home.

He was a happy influence in the new community. He took a great interest in the problems of the immigrant Swedes and secretly endowed their churches and their Benefit Association. The partnership bought tracts of land near the mill sites and platted it for homesites to be sold to employees at nominal cost. And the lots were of unusually large size to permit each employee to have land enough to be self-sufficient, with a garden and grazing room for a cow or two. "Cobbtown" was born.

In community affairs, he took a particular interest in education, served repeatedly on the board of education, and made large donations toward general expenses or for particular school purposes. Although not a temperance fanatic, he viewed the saloons as the enemy of his employees and thought it was his duty to sponsor any form of cultural and recreational activity that would provide a wholesome alternative to whiskey sellers. He financed a roller skating rink for the Oddfellows Lodge. An ardent baseball fan, he backed the city's first amateur and semi-pro baseball teams, made frequent trips from Petoskey to Detroit and Chicago to watch games, and provided winter employment for several of the states's better players to insure their summer participation for the Cadillac nine.[3]

At one time it was believed that Mitchell owned all the sawmills operating on Clam Lake in 1872. John Wheeler's *History* refers to Mitchell as owning three sawmills, and contemporary accounts refer to Mitchell as owning the Hale or Pioneer Mill. An 1874 account refers to William W. Mitchell as "running the Cobbs mill on Clam Lake for his uncle George A. Mitchell, who also operates two other sawmills there." Some confusion may have arisen about the Pioneer Mill during its first few years, since neither of its owners lived in the village until Cobbs arrived in 1874.

The presence of William Mitchell as mill foreman in 1874 may also have led to the conclusion that he was doing his uncle's work. George Mitchell had brought his nineteen-year-old nephew to Clam Lake from Hillsdale the preceding year to work for him as a talleyman and to learn the lumber business. He was learning more as Cobbs' employee in 1874, learning so well that he soon became Cobbs' partner in what was to become one of the largest logging and milling operations in Michigan.

There is no evidence to indicate that George Mitchell had any

3. And was sadly disappointed in the lack of loyalty in the professional athlete when the Gordon brothers, hired away from the Chicago "Ansons" by Cobbs, jumped the Cadillac team in mid-season of 1886 to return to the National League. Nevertheless, he seldom missed a chance to see them play against Detroit or Chicago during the next few years.

interest in the Pioneer Mill, or any other mill, with the exception of a shingle mill on the lakeshore at the foot of Pine Street, which he financed and had to take over later when it's owner failed. Certainly, had Mitchell wanted to set up one or more mills for his own operation, he could easily have done so. The evidence, however, is that he did not consider a sawmill to be particularly profitable, or that he at least thought it less profitable for him and more profitably done for him by others. He was concerned with buying and cutting standing timber and with selling finished lumber. Milling was a technical middle step that he would leave to others. The belief that he owned all the mills may understandably have arisen from the fact that all of the Clam Lake mills were almost exclusively devoted to milling his lumber.[4]

3.

Wherever he went, George Mitchell was selling his future city, and from Indiana all the way north along the railroad, people were being sold on Clam Lake. It was more than just salesmanship, however. Particular business and professsonal people were actively recruited and offered inducements to make Mitchell's city their home. Almost before the first railroad crews had started working around the end of Little Clam Lake, Mitchell had made his first trip to Manistee trying to interest people there. As many as thirty-five or forty men made trips to Clam Lake at his invitation, and some were convinced.

One mill operator, George Shackleton, wasn't particularly interested in coming, but he suggested that Mitchell talk to his partner, Holden A. Green, hoping perhaps to terminate the partnership, which was successful but not particularly compatible. Green was in Chicago, visiting relatives of his wife, so Mitchell

4. The extent of Mitchell's activities are reflected in the shipping records of the G. R. & I. From the beginning of its freight records in early 1872, through the month of October following Mitchell's death in 1878, over 70 million feet of pine lumber were shipped on his account. It has been estimated that 60 million feet of this total represents his own timber, milled for him by the three mills mentioned above, and by Ephraim Shay at Haring.

wrote to him a few weeks later. Green wasn't particularly interested in leaving Manistee, and he had no great interest in starting a business venture elsewhere. He wrote Mitchell a courteous response to that effect. Events were to change both views.

Green is another example of the all-sufficient, multi-talented men who moved through the period and moulded it in their image. He was born in New York in 1827 but started a series of moves as his father continually sought greener pastures "a little farther west." In 1847 young Green came to Chicago, then with less than 20,000 population but booming, and took a job as a machinist's helper in the shops of a new railroad being constructed to Galena. He soon found himself involved in a variety of engineering tasks for the railroad. Two years later he bought a stage line in partnership with a livery stable operator and acquired a mail contract on the route from Chicago to Joliet. In another year, he was dealing in lumber with a yard on the waterfront, supplying the thriving building trade in the rapidly growing city.

His taste for the lumber business suggested that there was more money to be made in its manufacture, and he visited the cities along the shores of Lake Michigan, finally selecting Manistee as the new home for himself and his bride, Adeline. Manistee at the time was only a collection of houses clustered around a few sawmills and was on the verge of insurrection against the government because of Uncle Sam's annoying complaints that the mills were operating with pine clandestinely cut from federal land.[5] The area was rough wilderness, without any semblance of government. Green helped civilize it. He was one of the founders of the first Methodist congregation. He helped found the first temperance groups in the city. He was admitted to the bar after reading law briefly. In 1855 he was elected the first prosecuting attorney of

5. The loggers ignored the complaints of government land agents, resulting in the first act of the famed "Timber War" when an invasion by a single U. S. marshal and two agents was repulsed by the local defenders of liberty. They drove the marshal from the hotel and burned down half of the small hotel by throwing pitch fireballs through his window. Then they sank the marshal's boat. Uncle Sam returned with reinforcements and finally prevailed, convincing the loggers that they were not entitled to cut all the pine from public lands merely because they were members of the public.

Manistee County when it was organized, and he prosecuted liquor violations severely.

By 1871 Green was relatively well fixed financially. He practiced law in a leisurely fashion, deriving his main livelihood from his mill partnership with Shackleton. He had a healthy family of seven children and had just settled comfortably in a new home.[6]

On October 9, 1871, fire started ın the slashings at the edge of Manistee. Before the day was over, the entire city hd been leveled with the exception of a handful of homes. Green's home was one of the few spared, but his office and the sawmill were destroyed. Within a week Mitchell had written to both of the partners expressing sympathy, selling Clam Lake, and pointing out that it would be an opportune time to consider a move.

Green and Mitchell met, were impressed with one another, and began a warm friendship. Green liked his home and still had no intention of leaving it, but he and Shackleton thought Clam Lake looked promising and decided to build a sawmill there rather than to rebuild at Manistee. Shackleton and his brother William[7] immediately set out for Clam Lake and selected a site on the

6. After the Greens moved to Clam Lake, the children's marriages related the family to most of the other prominent pioneer families, and provided some family aspects to local government. Daughter Ella May married Donald McIntyre, an excellent attorney. She died in childbirth, and he later took a second wife, George Mitchell's divorced daughter, Sophie Moyer. Daughter Ruby married a son of Attorney James R. Bishop. The youngest child, Fred, married Helen Kelley, her father William Kelley having been one of the earliest settlers, a supervisor, sheriff, and owner of considerable Mitchell Street property. Daughter Grace married banker-lumberman Jared Hixson, mayor in 1886. McIntyre, Kelley, Bishop, and Holden Green were all to serve on the board of supervisors during its most tempestuous sessions from 1877 to 1882.

7. The two Shackletons and a third brother, Jeremiah, all moved to Clam Lake. William stayed only briefly, then returned to Manistee. When the Manistee & Northeastern Railroad was built, he took a job as brakeman, fell between the cars and was decapitated. Jeremiah was elected the county's fourth sheriff in 1874, built a home at the northeast corner of Cass and Shelby streets, then decided to return to Manistee. In 1877 he sold his home to W. W. Mitchell for $1,200. After it was heavily damaged by fire in 1881, it was rebuilt and served as the Mitchell home until 1890, when Mitchell sold the building to Capt.

northeast shore of Little Clam Lake in government lot 3, adjoining the Harris property. Construction of the mill by John Born commenced in late winter, and it was in operation late in June of 1872.

As fate would have it, within a month after the new mill went into operation at Clam Lake, another fire swept Manistee, this time devastating the residential area previously spared. Twenty-three homes, including Green's, and his newly rebuilt office, were destroyed. He decided that perhaps Clam Lake might make a nice home, after all, and moved his family to the village. For several years they lived in an apartment over the A. M. Lamb grocery store on Mitchell Street, separated by a vacant lot from the building in which two old Manistee neighbors had their places of business: Dr. John Leeson's drugstore and Clark Frazier's newspaper.

Green never actively practiced law in Clam Lake, although he kept offices for many years with attorneys McIntyre and Rice in the Mitchell building. He held a variety of village and city offices, was tax collector, school inspector, served several terms as justice of the peace and several more as coroner. He represented his ward on the board of supervisors during some of the years of the county seat struggle. In 1880 he defeated former judge Isaac Carpenter in the election for probate judge. With his fellow ex-Manistee-ites, he organized the Clam Lake Methodist Church and the following year organized a Union Sunday School in which he taught for years. He was one of the organizers of the Bay View Assembly, a Methodist chautauqua-type camp association near Petoskey, and he helped organize the Good Templars, Clam Lake's first temperance group.

Although strongly aware of the need for the moderating

Lawrence Newson, the saloon keeper. Newson moved it across the street to the southeast corner of Cass and Shelby, where it stood until 1971, changed only by a third story addition put on by Newson about 1896. George Shackleton was thrice village president, then ran for sheriff in 1876, when his brother Jeremiah did not seek re-election. He was badly beaten, took it personally, and decided to leave Clam Lake. He and Green were temperamentally incapable of working at close quarters anyway, and he sold his interest in the mill to Milton J. Bond who also bought his home on Harris Street. He went to Sherman but was ruined when the gristmill he owned with William Bennett burned in 1878.

influences of religion and temperance in the rough-and-ready society of a milltown, Green was an unusually sophisticated and urbane man.[8] His views on religion were remarkably progressive for the time. His self-education extended into a variety of fields, and his library was undoubtedly one of the best in northern Michigan. He organized a debating society. His support of temperance didn't extend to abstinence, church dogma notwithstanding. He was particularly fond of racing horses, bred them, trained them, and frequently raced them himself. He saw nothing wrong with attending the Bay View camp meetings and taking along one of his prize horses to race for prize money at Petoskey or Charlevoix. He was a knowledgeable bettor. Over the years he traveled widely to race his horses or to attend the theater or opera in Chicago, Detroit, or Grand Rapids. In 1878 he designed and built Cadillac's first waterworks and operated it for many years.[9] He was, all in all, a most fascinating man, and there are those who contend that his son Fred, who went on to become governor of Michigan, was only a fair copy of his father.

By midsummer of 1872, the Harris Brothers, and Shackleton and Green mills were in operation. With the Cobbs mill and the portable Slinger mill, their combined capacity was estimated at four million feet a year, a figure which proved modest in the light of subsequent performance.

4.

Reference was made earlier to a newspaper account indicating that an M. H. and J. P. Hawley were building planing and shingle mills at Clam Lake in the spring of 1872. No other reference to the

8. In 1888 the *News* described him as being equally at home "at the bottom of a seven-foot ditch exploring the intricacies of a water pipe or mixing with the social and first circles with kid gloves and imported ice cream." Noting his expertise in mechanics, horses, Bible scholarship, and baseball, the *News* still probably didn't do justice to his catholic tastes.

9. In 1879 Bond and Green sold their sawmill to Jacob Cummer of the Cummer lumber interests, introducing a new personality to the city's lumber manufacturing industry, and changing it completely.

name can be found, and it is believed that the account is a garbled reference to James Haynes and his sons, who were in the process of putting up a planing mill.

Haynes was born in Gorham, New York, in 1825, the son of Joseph Haynes, a farmer-businessman of Dutch ancestory.[10] The family, like so many others of the period, was unsettled, moving on the average of every three years, and ultimately finding its way to Michigan, where Haynes farmed in Van Buren County. James' first business venture was at Lawrence, where he dealt in feed and produce. In 1862 or 1863, he moved to Decatur, continuing in the same business and later getting into the lumber business as well. It is not certain how he and George Mitchell got together, but sometime in the spring of 1872 he visited Clam Lake and selected a site for a planing mill and home just west of the Clam River in Haring Township at about the spot where the National Guard Armory now stands. By mid-September, the mill was up and in operation. Five years later, it burned, threatening his residence, so when he rebuilt he moved the mill to the other side of the river and to the north side of the road which now bears his name.

Haynes apparently had a wait-and-see attitude about the new village. His doubts were soon resolved by the success of his first mill, however, and he moved his family to Clam Lake the following year to occupy a large residence built adjoining the mill. In 1881 he built another mill between the railroad and the lake south of Chapin Street. The first mill was sold to the Cummer interests after his death, but the "new" mill was kept in operation as part of a family enterprise that continued at the same site until the property was sold in 1968 as the location of Cadillac's new library.

However he was persuaded, when Haynes came to Clam Lake it was a great addition to Mitchell's city, both industrially and in human leadership. Haynes was a Democrat, without any of the sympathy for slavery which had destroyed the effectiveness of the

10. Coincidentally, the Haynes and Harris families both lived in Gorham at the same time and, it being but a small village, must have been acquainted. Benjamin Harris moved to Henrietta, N.Y., in 1826. Joseph Haynes left Gorham about the same time, going to Rochester, then to Parma, and ultimately moving on the way west to Michigan.

party for a generation. The minority party could not have been better represented in the new community. He was a jovial giant of 260 pounds, without reserve or self-importance, to whom everyone was a friend and neighbor. He stood with Jonathan Cobbs in notions about wages and treatment of his employees, and the two were a constant irritant to Jacob Cummer, whose idea of industrial management was to give his employees hard work, more hard work, and wages, in that order. Lacking the subtle Haynes wit, Cobbs was no match for Cummer after Haynes' death, and Cadillac became "Cummer Town."

But while he lived, Haynes was the leaven of the community. He was an early and loyal member of the local fraternal orders. He was always promoting something for the village. He served five terms as township treasurer, a term as justice of the peace, and at his death was both county treasurer and mayor of Cadillac, positions which constituted a unique expression of confidence for a Democrat in an overwhelmingly Republican community. He was perhaps the most popular man ever to live in Cadillac. When he died, over 300 out-of-town members of the Masonic and Oddfellow orders attended the services, and a mile-long procession which included two bands followed the hearse to the cemetery. His sons, Norman, Charles, and Elbert, distinguished themselves in their own right in public service, logging, industry, and the social life of the town.

5.

We have previously noted that when Mitchell first saw the lakes, he pictured them as a storage reservoir and floatway for sawmills to be located at the east end of the Little Clam Lake. He thought that the Black River connecting the two lakes could be cleared to float logs so that both lakes could service such mills. During the summer of 1872, as the Harris Brothers mill went into operation, its superintendent, Silas Pelton, a versatile mechanic, constructed a small steam tugboat and put it in operation rafting logs on Little Clam Lake. The tug had a shallow draft, and it was thought that it could be used on both lakes once the Black River channel was cleared.

Work on clearing the channel rapidly bogged down, however. It proved to be shallower than originally thought, and the prevailing westerly winds filled the mouth of the outlet with sand almost as rapidly as it could be dredged. The meandering course of the stream made it difficult to navigate. Mitchell concluded that a canal cut on a straight line would be less susceptible to silting and easier to dredge than the natural channel. The logical place for such a canal, across the narrowest part of the strip of land between the lakes, also had the advantage of being farther south than the natural channel and, accordingly, somewhat less susceptible to silting from wind and wave action.

Adam Gallinger had put up a boathouse and dock behind his carpenter shop on Lake Street and set to work constructing a dredge which could be used in digging the canal. Having determined the project feasible, Mitchell bought the forty-nine-acre strip of land between the lakes for $2,000. The Clam Lake Canal Improvement and Construction Company was incorporated with Mitchell and Adam Gallinger as its first officers.

On August 21, 1873, a survey party headed by Gallinger and Lee Beardslee set out to lay out the line of the canal. The Harris Brothers tug, operated by "Captain" Silas Pelton, carried the crew across the lake but promptly returned under different command. One of the first acts of the party had been to fell a tree inartfully on the head of the unfortunate Pelton. Said the *News*, "His body was brought back a corpse but a few hours after he left in perfect health and strength."

Another jack-of-all-trades, Eugene Saunders, who had just opened a grocery store on Mason Street, undertook supervision of the construction work and had the job underway by mid-September. State law then, as now, required permission from the county board of supervisors before commencement of any canal, dam, or water diversion project. On November 8, 1873, the Wexford County board of supervisors received a petition from Mitchell on behalf of the canal corporation. A committee was appointed, boated out to the site, found the canal already half completed, and cheerfully recommended that the petition be granted. It was, and the work was completed December 20, 1872. Thereafter the Clam Lake Canal Improvement and Construction Company was paid a toll, figured by estimated board feet of all logs that passed through the canal except those owned by Mitchell.[11]

The opening of the canal so increased the flow of water from Big Clam Lake that the Little Clam Lake outlet flooded. The railroad bridge across Clam Lake River withstood the flood, but the log "road bridge" into Haring Township was submerged and had to be rebuilt. The level of Big Clam Lake was lowered over a foot and not restored until the outlet was dammed a few years later. An attempt was made to control the level of the two lakes separately by the construction of a dam and locks in the middle of the canal, but the engineering was imperfect, and, after being washed out and rebuilt in three successive springs, it was abandoned.

11. We have no records indicating how the canal corporation fared financially. We do know that by Mitchell's death six years later it had ceased to be an operating company, and no revenues were being collected for logs floated through the canal. In the inventory of Mitchell's estate, no value is assigned to his shares in the corporation; the appraiser's warrant briefly stated the condition of the business with one word—"busted." The lack of revenue may well have been due to the fact that the great majority of the logs floated through were Mitchell's own and exempt from the toll.

Chapter Nine

MITCHELL'S RECRUITS

It would take more than sawmills, of course, to make a city, and Mitchell was giving some thought to the other essential ingredients of a good community. As the presence of the mills, with good operators, was assured, an increasing amount of time and thought went into the recruiting of key business and professional people who would provide the services necessary to a city. Given such a nucleus, he knew, the settlement could not help grow and acquire substance. He was virtually a talent scout; and he was a powerful persuader.

To some it was merely a matter of salesmanship. To others there were inducements: the gift of a business site to Spencer Mason and a promise of help in financing the Mason House; for the Harris Brothers, it was good land cheap and a mutually advantageous milling contract; for merchants Holbrook and May, and Cornwell and LaBar, it was land at a nominal price and the assurance of business from logging camps; for lawyers Fallass and Rice, it was free office space for two years; for the first doctors, Leeson and Dillenbeck, it was a free lot; for Clark L. Frazier, printer and teacher, it was a free homesite, lumber for a house, and a promise of subscriptions for twenty-five copies of a weekly newspaper.

Both Drs. Leeson and Frazier had visited with Mitchell at Manistee in 1871. Later in the year they had visited Clam Lake with two other Manistee men, coming 'cross country through the forest until they hit the railroad right-of-way near LeRoy. At the time, they had come to no decision, perhaps because Mitchell, up to that point, had spoken only in generalities about helping them locate. They came again early in 1872, made their arrangements, and moved.

Frazier was a particularly desirable settler to Mitchell. A teacher, with some experience as a printer he could fill a two-fold need in the new community. He would supply a newspaper, which every community worthy of its name required and which would publicize the village. As a teacher, he would be invaluable in organizing a school district, and the influence which he could command through the newspaper in support of education and other community projects could make his role doubly influential.

The two came. Frazier selected a residential lot at the corner of Simons and East Mason streets, while Leeson picked a business lot at the southeast corner of Beech and Mason streets. The two were friends, and it was agreed that Leeson would construct a drugstore and office building on his property, the second floor of which Frazier would lease for the operation of his newspaper. The residential lot was large enough to be divided and provide a home for each, or it could be sold and the proceeds divided. Until the Leeson building was constructed, they took space in Lorenzo Ballou's grocery and feed store on the north side of Mason Street, adjoining the railroad on the west. By late June, Leeson's building was up, and the friends moved their operations during the first few days of July.[1]

Dr. Leeson may or may not have been a graduate of a medical school, but he attended both the medical school at the university at Ann Arbor, and the Detroit Medical College. Born in England and reared in Canada, he had a fascination for drugs and herbs. In 1869 he came to Manistee and practiced with another physician who owned a drugstore.[2] The line of distinction between the medical profession and the pharmacist was not clearly defined as yet, and the two frequently went together. It was not surprising,

1. At the time, Courthouse Hill and Beech Street had not been graded, and the hill extended into Mitchell Street so that its level at the foot of Beech was roughly ten feet higher than it is today. The grading process on the hill began in 1881, and Beech Street was cut down substantially. At the same time, the grade of Mitchell Street was leveled, leaving Dr. Leeson's drugstore up in the air. It was simply jacked up, the half-basement beneath it enlarged and another story built on the new ground level. This lead to the local riddle: "Where is the first floor the second floor, and the third floor the first?"

2. The burning of the drugstore in the Manistee fire left Leeson without a base from which to operate and undoubtedly made him receptive to Mitchell's sales talk.

then, that the first few doctors in Clam Lake also established drugstores.

During his early years in Clam Lake, Dr. Leeson began to bottle his own special medicines, the most famous of which was Tiger Oil, guaranteed to cure everything from cholera to weak ankles. He soon had so much demand for his medicines that he constructed a separate building on the back of his lot, paralleling the alley, in which he located his medical office and manufactory. By the early eighties, his patent medicine business had grown to such an extent that he left the management of his Central Drug Store to O. L. Davis and finally sold it to Davis in 1893. Although he continued to be an active practitioner until his death in 1922 at age eighty-six, the last thirty-five years of his life were largely devoted to the manufacture and sale of Tiger Oil. He was a staunch Methodist, prohibitionist, and successful real estate investor, and he gloried in the self-bestowed title of "the workingman's doctor." He was also controversial, argumentive, and a pain in the neck to his more orthodox brothers of the medical profession who expressed doubt as to the efficacy of Tiger Oil, applied internally and/or externally.

Dr. Leeson's medicines unfortunately were ineffective against the consumption of his friend Frazier. The teacher-editor did all that Mitchell expected of him and more. He helped Mitchell organize the Clam Lake-Haring fractional school district, was its superintendent, and ultimately became the county school superintendent. In emergencies, he taught. And he was a constant nag, prodding and needling the village to build a school, hire more teachers, and put its money on the line for education. His newspaper, the *Clam Lake Weekly News*, made its first appearance June 1, 1872, and was a lively, earthy mirror in which the community could see itself, for better or for worse. Reflecting the views of its main sponsor, Mitchell, the paper was actively Republican, consistent with the journalism of the day in which most newspapers adopted firm political affiliations. Recurrent bouts of illness, however, left Frazier dependent on friends to edit the paper for protracted periods of time,[3] and only the help of other

3. Friends who were called on most frequently to fill in as editor and who impartially kept the paper in its Republican image were attorneys Silas S. Fallass

printers from neighboring towns kept the paper going. He soon was forced to sell out, and he left the state.[4]

Dr. Leeson was soon joined by other physicians during the summer of 1872. A Dr. DeNoyes stayed but briefly and left for more civilized surroundings before the end of the summer. Dr. George Dillenbeck was given a lot on the east side of Mitchell Street next to the new stores being put up by Morris Bunyea between Harris and Cass streets. He built his drugstore and made it not only his office but also the site of an almost continuous poker game for the next twenty years.[5] Dr. Royal McTaggart and Dr. Hiram Wilcox were next. We know little of Dr. McTaggart except that he apparently had little respect from his colleagues. His office was first at the Mason House, then in Turner's store on Mitchell Street, then at the McCardy saloon, and finally he bought Duval's saloon on the west side of Lake Street, dispensing whiskey and medicines with an impartial and, we hope, steady hand.

Dr. Wilcox took space for his office and a drugstore in the Holbrook & May building. Late in 1873 he took a partner, Dr. Joshua M. Wardell, newly graduated at eighteen from the medical school at Ann Arbor, the only physician in the village other than Dr. Leeson to have had formal medical school training and the first who we can say with assurance had the medical degree. The partnership lasted only a few years. Dr. Wilcox had a greater interest in hunting and trapping than in attending his patients. Dr. Wardell had little interest in running a drugstore and was infuriated to find his office filled with hides and animal carcasses. The partnership was dissolved, and Dr. Wardell took quarters elsewhere, becoming one of Cadillac's most prominent citizens. He

and Eugene F. Sawyer, and Dr. Hiram Wilcox, all Democrats.

4. Having apparently recovered his health after some years in the South, Frazier returned to Michigan and located in Muskegon. His tuberculosis was only quiescent, however, and he suffered a relapse and died in 1898, at age fifty-five.

5. Somewhat the worse for whiskey, Dr. Dillenbeck was committed to the Traverse City State Hospital in 1895. His successor, Louis Finn, continued the poker game in the public interest until the drugstore burned down under circumstances suggesting that there might have been some relationship between Finn's gambling losses and the fire insurance proceeds.

was a shrewd investor in real estate, a patron of music and the theater, but above all, for fifty-nine years he was to be a leader in the medical profession during its transition from the age of the patent medicine man to the disciplined, scientific calling that it has become. Dr. Wilcox continued the drugstore until 1876,[6] then moved to Manton, where he opened another drugstore, practiced medicine indifferently, and continued his fur trade.

2.

All things considered, it may well be that Mitchell's greatest contribution to his city was his ability to attract some outstanding men who stayed, prospered, and built a substantial community. In an age of strongly held and loudly contested religious and political views, Mitchell was interested only in ability and integrity. He shared the Republican views of his brothers, became a member of the state Republican committee, and insisted that Clam Lake's newspaper was to be a Republican organ. Yet many of the people he sought out to bring to Clam Lake were ardent Democrats. Among them were James Haynes and the Fallass brothers, Silas and William, Jr.

The beginning of the acquaintance between Mitchell and W. A. Fallass, Sr., isn't known. Fallass was from a family of early Kent County settlers, founders of Fallassburg. In correspondence with Mitchell in 1871, he was discussing the opportunities for his sons at Clam Lake. The brothers were then students at the state university at Ann Arbor and, on the graduation of Silas from law school in the summer of 1872, they came to Clam Lake and looked

6. While there were other doctors who came and went, Drs. Leeson, Dillenbeck, and Wilcox were the only proprietors of drugstores for some years. It was thus more than embarrassing when editor Frazier exercised the newspaperman's prerogative as keeper of the community's morals with the following item: "If our local druggist who spent Wednesday night last at the hotel in Big Rapids with a lady not his wife should repeat such a performance, his name will be published in this column." Probably no one at the time thought he was speaking of his friend, landlord, and fellow Methodist, Dr. Leeson, so life must have been interesting for Drs. Wilcox and Dillenbeck when that edition came out.

over the village. They apparently liked what they saw, for Silas opened the first law office in the village and William stayed for four years, replacing Clark Frazier as superintendent of the school district.

Over the next few years, though violent political opponents, Silas S. Fallas and George A. Mitchell were closely associated—in friendship, as attorney and client, and as co-conspirators in the maneuvering to move the county seat. Where Mitchell made his office, there Fallass made his, at first in the Mason House, then at the Mitchell House, and when Mitchell built a large four-story office building on the northwest corner of Cass and Mitchell streets, the Fallass office adjoined that of Mitchell there. Fallass was elected circuit court commissioner and prosecuting attorney in the fall election of 1872. Two years later he was named U. S. district court commissioner. He handled the legislation organizing the village of Clam Lake. In 1877 he drafted the bill to incorporate the city of Cadillac and spent over a month in Lansing managing its passage through the legislature. He was the Third Ward supervisor on the county board for four of the next five years and was Cadillac's strategist and spokesman on the board in the county seat battle.

In 1882, the county seat battle won, Cadillac's newly elected circuit judge, John Rice, suddenly announced his resignation, in order, he said, that a better man, Fallass, might be appointed to the judgeship. The appointment of Fallass was promptly made by the governor, and Fallass was recognized as one of the state's most able jurists. Early in 1887, however, M. L. Dunham of Cadillac began a quiet campaign to get the Republican nomination to run against Fallass. Fallass had resigned from the state Democratic committee upon being appointed to the bench, but he had run for Congress in 1884 and had narrowly been defeated by the incumbent, Civil War hero Gen. Byron Cutcheon. Partisan politics being what they were, some Republicans felt it a duty to put up a candidate against Fallass, even though they admired him as a man and as a judge. No one else at the bar being disposed, apparently, to run against Fallass, Dunham appeared to have the Republican nomination in the bag.

Suddenly, the Reed City *Clarion* published a letter brought to it by an outraged Osceola County lawyer. Written by Dunham in the belief that the lawyer was an enemy of Fallass, it asked his help in circulating reports of the most scurrilous kind against Fallass. The Clarion had been asked, it said, to print material of like kind and had turned down Dunham. Over the next few weeks, reports of similar incidents came in from around the circuit, and it became apparent that Dunham had been conducting a vicious whispering campaign of gossip and slander against the judge. Fallass told his friends that if Dunham was nominated he would decline to run. The leaders of the bar called on Dunham and asked him to disavow the reports and issue a statement that he was not a candidate. Dunham refused and announced his candidacy as the judicial nominating caucus was about to convene. Fallass wrote a brief note stating his belief that a partisan and personal campaign would demean the bench and announcing that he would not be a candidate for reelection.

The community was stunned. The bar almost unanimously petitioned him to reconsider. He refused.[7] After leaving office at the end of the year, he remained in Cadillac only briefly, probably because he had been chosen grand master of the Oddfellow order and felt obliged to fulfill his responsibilities there. In 1889 he moved to Chicago, where he became one of the most successful corporate lawyers in the Midwest. At the turn of the century, he was an officer and director of a half dozen railroads and many other industrial corporations and banks, and his law firm represented the largest corporations of American industry, banking and insurance.

Fallass soon had company in the legal profession as David and Rolin Rice, William Cavanagh, Eugene F. Sawyer, and Donald E. McIntyre came to the village in the next year and a half. In

7. In his anticipation that he would have no opposition with Fallass out of the race, Dunham was rudely disappointed. He was nominated at a supposed Republican nominating caucus at Kalkaska but was immediately accused of fraud and corruption. Another caucus was held which nominated a young attorney named Fred Aldrich, setting the stage for a bitter campaign. Dunham found himself an outcast in his profession because of his conduct, and the community as a whole turned against him. The result was the same throughout the circuit, and Aldrich was elected by an overwhelming margin. He proved to be a scholarly and capable judge. Dunham moved to Grand Rapids.

another two years they were joined by George Worth, John Rosevelt, John Rice, and James R. Bishop. All except Cavanagh, who moved to Missaukee County in 1873, were to hold a variety of public offices and play an active part in the building of the city.

3.

Every civic need was anticipated by Mitchell. Every church organized during his lifetime was given a free lot of its selection. The cemetery site was a gift. A block was set aside for a park. He organized the fractional school district for Haring and Clam Lake townships, served on the school board continuously until his death, hired its first teacher and donated block 24 of the village plat as a school site. Block F was set aside for a courthouse, and he worked tirelessly to procure the county seat for his city. In 1874 he led the move to legally incorporate the village, and he was largely responsibile for its incorporation as the city of Cadillac in 1877. It was appropriate that he was elected to be its first mayor.

Indeed, there was little of interest or concern in the community that did not engage his attention. For a time, letters signed G. M. appeared in the *News* to prod the city or the county, or their officers and citizens, to awareness of a need. In 1876 a weekly series of comments signed "Street Correspondent" began in the *News*, covering everything from personal conduct to public expenditure. They are very likely the work of Mitchell, urging, scolding, pleading, and praising, and, as events unfolded, getting results. Although never a church member, Mitchell actively supported the Presbyterian church. Though not averse to a social drink, he fully recognized the potential for danger in the unbridled saloon trade and advocated strict limitations on the saloons. He helped prod the community into its first successful temperance movement by encouraging local participation in the Red Ribbon Reform Crusade that was sweeping the country in 1878.

Surprisingly, Mitchell's early plans did not include making Clam Lake his own home. His family was happily situated at Kendallville, and he maintained his residence there for some years. He spent an increasing amount of time attending to his business interests in Clam Lake, however, and gradually disposed of his Indiana properties. On his shorter trips to Clam Lake, Mrs. Mitchell would occasionally accompany him, and beginning in 1873 the entire family spent from two to six weeks in the village each summer. In 1874 Mitchell commenced the construction of a large four-story office building on the northwest corner of Cass and Mitchell streets and, while it was only partly completed, had its builder commence the construction of a home for his daughter and her husband, Mr. & Mrs. Andrew Keller Moyer, on North Shelby Street at the head of Beech Street. Mrs. Mitchell saw it, thought it a better residence for the Mitchell family, and Clam Lake became their permanent home.[8]

8. After Mitchell's death, the home was purchased by Wellington Cummer, eldest son of Jacob Cummer. Now remodeled, the residence is the location of the Yearnd Funeral Home. In what was an unusually long story by the newspaper practices of those days, the *News* said: "October 31, 1874: A palatial residence. Probably no building which has been erected since the foundation of the village has attracted so much notice as the beautiful dwelling which Mr. Geo. A. Mitchell has been building for his son-in-law and daughter, Mr. & Mrs. A. K. Moyer. Located on an eminence nearly in the center of the town, it is almost the first object that meets the view. The building is attractive in itself, being a large square structure facing the west with a bay window on the south extending through [sic] stories. The exterior of the building is finished in the best possible manner and in an index of excellence within. The style of architecture belongs to no regular class but is a graceful and pleasing combination of the French with the Italian, the former predominating. The interior is arranged almost faultlessly. On the lower floor is the parlor 14 x 22, a sitting room 14 x 15, a family room 14 x 15 and a dining room 12 x 18 and kitchen, bathroom, et cetera. The hall is 8 x 26, the foot of the stairs being at the rear end. The upper floor has four large bedrooms 14 x 15 with a servant's room over the wing. Above all this covering the whole extent of the main building is a large room lighted by the dormer windows in the mansard. The rooms are all high. Those on the lower floor being 11 feet and those on the second floor 10 feet and are all well ventilated. The whole building is supplied with all the modern improvements which characterize a palatial residence. In looking over the house one is struck with the almost absolute completeness of everything that pertains to comfort and convenience. The basement is devoted to the laundry and furnace. The latter is capable of heating the entire building."

4.

The *News* of July 25, 1878, reported that Mitchell was ill and had been suffering chills and fever for some days. The reported prevalence of similar illnesses suggests that malaria may have been common in the early days of the community, and this might well be the nature of his illness. It persisted, and it was against the advice of his wife and physician that he resumed his business affairs. On the morning of August 5, 1878, he fell or was thrown from his buggy near the railroad crossing on Pine Street, striking his head on a pine stump. A brain specialist, Dr. DeKamp, was immediately summoned from Grand Rapids, but Mitchell died three days later, having recovered consciousness but briefly.

One can only speculate as to what more Mitchell might have accomplished had he had additional years, but there was no doubt in the minds of his fellow townsmen about their loss or the value of what he had built in seven short years. Every mill and place of business in the village was closed on the day of his funeral, and it was said that there was total silence for over an hour in the village as virtually every inhabitant, with countless state and county dignitaries, followed his body to the cemetery.

After Mitchell's death, a document was recorded in the office of the county register of deeds which escaped many historians. It was an 1872 agreement whereby Mitchell acknowledged that the lands platted as the village of Clam Lake, with other lands, and the business he was conducting, were actually held by him under a secret trust for an Indiana partnership with Charles E. Gorham, Oscar A. Simons, and Augustus A. Chapin,[9] in which he held only a two-ninths interest. He had bought out Chapin's one-ninth share in 1876, but at his death, instead of being the sole owner of the unsold city lands and other properties, he was only a one-third owner, drawing a salary of $1,500 a year for management of the business.[10] The profits, of course, had been substantial, as they

9. Chapin, who gave his name to Chapin Street, was Mitchell's attorney in Kendallville, where he was also the city clerk. He became politically prominent in Indiana and ended his career as a judge in Fort Wayne.

10. The partnership interest constituted the largest single asset in the Mitchell estate, conservatively valued by the appraisers at $156,161.76.

continued to be for some years after his death, as Simons assumed management until his suicide or murder in 1887.

The fact that Mitchell was not, and had not been, the sole owner of the properties in his name, while surprising to many, does not detract from the magnitude of his efforts and the brilliance of his management. His imagination and effort started the venture and made it successful. The disclosure of the identity of the other interested parties, however, helped explain the ease with which the G. R. & I. right-of-way had been relocated and the vital tracts of land deeded to Mitchell—as well as a reason for the secrecy. All three partners were substantial stockholders in, and one a director of, the G. R. & I. Railroad.[11]

11. Mitchell's descendants have scattered over the years, but two great grandchildren, George Atchison and Virginia Atchison Dontje, still reside in the community he founded.

Chapter Ten

SHERMAN OUTGROWN

Before the new settlement at the end of Little Clam Lake was a year old, it had already outstripped the county seat at Sherman, both in population and in commerce. By June of 1872, there were about 125 families in the village, with a permanent population of over 600 persons. The railroad and logging camps added a large number of transients, accommodated by its many hotels and boardinghouses, a condition that continued as the logging industry grew and brought more and more men to its camps and mills. This volatile labor force supported a business district substantially larger than a population of 600 people would normally warrant, and the growth continued during the year.

By the end of the year, Mason Street was solidly built up. John McClain had been appointed postmaster in January, and he built a frame addition onto his log house, at which he conducted a small business. For some reason he decided to return to his homestead farm in Colfax Township. Lorenzo Ballou bought his building and added onto it still further for the operation of a grocery and feed business. As one proceeded west towards the lake, Ballou's building was adjoined by McCardy's livery stable and harness shop. Then came Eugene Saunder's grocery store, Cloud's hardware store, the residence of house painter J. E. Kelly, William Park's boardinghouse, and Bergstrom's Sweed Saloon.

On the south side of Mason, from the railroad towards the lake, could be found a small saloon and boardinghouse owned by John Mosser, Liddell's blacksmith shop, Jonas' boardinghouse and saloon, Charles Studley's restaurant, McCardy and Davis' saloon, the Mason House barn, and the Mason House.

On West Harris Street, the Scandinavian House, a livery stable and veterinarian, a residence, and the John Davis saloon were located across from the park, with the Goldman saloon in the park.

Along the lake, the Bunyea grocery store and Merchant House stood between the Pioneer Mill and Chapin Street. Then came the Clam Lake House, and north of Harris Street there were the Reed & Ferris blacksmith shop, Holbrook & May's store (which was now the post office, Henry May having been named postmaster when John McClain resigned), Gallinger's carpenter shop, Larcom & Mott's general store,[1] W. H. Hicks hardware store, Duval's boot shop, Fred Hector's blacksmith shop, and the two boardinghouses to be so well known over the coming years, F. H. Vosburg's Lake House and the Robbers Roost. Across from them on the east side of the street, near Pine, was Lawson's Lakeview House.

On the east side of Mitchell Street, there was a residence near Pine Street, then Dr. Leeson's drugstore at the corner of Beech. To its south was Lamb's grocery, the shoe shop of Tobias Born, and the Reynolds & Adams meat market.[2] In the next block, the American House was at the southeast corner of Harris and Mitchell. Behind it on Harris were the residence and furniture factory of G. W. Kirkbride. To its south on Mitchell Street, Morris Bunyea had two buildings, occupied by Hill & Olney, clothiers, and John Bissell's meat market. Then came Dillenbeck's drugstore. South of Cass Street was the Ohio House, adjoined by the Mosser and White building in which was LaBar and Cornwell's grocery, and at the corner of Chapin was J. M. Ridlon's clothing and dry goods store. In the following block was the Mitchell House. South of that there was nothing except John Born, builder and house mover, at the corner of Stimson and Shelby.[3]

The west side of Mitchell built up more slowly. At the south was LaBar & Cornwell's gristmill on Chapin. In the next block there was nothing. Between Cass and Harris, the only structures were

1. They also had a dock and boat service, and Motts had begun a dray service called the City Express Wagon.

2. The market was torn down the next year to make way for the McKinnon House.

3. Born built Shackleton and Green's mill, the Leeson drugstore, and many other buildings, but is best remembered as the man who moved houses around like chess pieces. He also patented and manufactured a refrigerator.

the residence and building in which attorney William H. Cavanagh and his brother James had a law office and real estate business. Between Harris and Mason streets, store buildings were going up for Goodenough & Foster, clothiers, and Abbott & Turner, grocers, the residence of William Kelley, and Willard S. Kendall's insurance and real estate office.

Supposedly there were nineteen saloons in business by the fall of 1872. Even crediting the boardinghouses as saloons, the list of business places we have noted falls short of that number. It is hard to find an accurate listing of the saloons in the early years of Clam Lake. With the adoption of the licensing laws, it would seem that they could be easily identified. On the contrary, there are frequent references in the newspaper to saloons for which there are no records of licenses. Saloons changed hands often, and sometimes there were apparently several partners in a business, so that references to the Culver saloon and the McCardy saloon in 1874 refer to the same place of business, it being the same as that of McCardy and Davis of 1872, but distinct from the Davis saloon of the same year.

The saloons and other places of entertainment are subjects in themselves. Suffice it to say at this point that there were such places in abundance from the beginning of the village and that at one time there may have been as many as thirty-six saloons in operation, if hotels and boardinghouses serving liquor are taken into account.

2.

The coming of the railroad not only serviced the mills and brought the people to run them but increased the business of the village in other ways. The railroad opened up the eastern side of northern Osceola County and western Missaukee County to settlement, creating a trading district of considerable size around Clam Lake. In addition to homestead lands, railroad and state lands were available cheap. The railroad advertised and marketed its land vigorously. The fourth issue of the Clam Lake *Weekly News*, June 22, 1872, carried an advertisement of the G. R. & I. R. R. offering land to be chosen by the buyer from 900,000 acres of pine land or farm land available in northern Michigan, at four dollars an acre, one-fourth down, the balance at 7 percent interest over ten years or more, and claiming that "northern Michigan is famous for its garden lands and the salubrity of its climate."

The land was sold and the settlers came. The population of the northern Osceola townships of Highland, Sherman, and Burdell increased from an estimated 50 persons to over 500 from 1870 to 1874. In southern and western Missaukee County, over 450 new settlers came in the same four-year period. But in Wexford County the population jumped from 650 to 3,011, the new settlers locating almost entirely in the eastern half of the county.

To the southeast the Sherman settlement in Osceola County and the Whaley-Hollister settlement in southeast Clam Lake Township built up rapidly. The *News* mentioned a Hollister picnic at the Thomas Whaley farm in August of 1873, attended by 75 people of the neighborhood.

Mention was made earlier that the unorganized county of Missaukee was at first attached to Wexford County, being divided between what was then called Hanover and Colfax townships for purposes of administration. By early 1870, there were enough people there to warrant the organization of a township called Reeder, which sent Daniel Reeder to the Wexford County board of supervisors as its representative. Later that year, Clam Union and Riverside townships were organized under the direction of John Vogel, John Koop, Otto Schaap, Gillis McBain, William Cavanagh,[4] and Ira and Henry Van Meter.

In the spring of 1871, Missaukee County was given independent status by the legislature and disappeared from Wexford County history save for a lingering dispute over the honesty of Wexford's tax accounting to the new county, a matter which was ultimately resolved by a lawsuit.

The first county seat of Missaukee County was originally at Pinhook, later known as Falmouth. A state road to Falmouth was

4. Cavanagh, an attorney, moved to Clam Lake in 1872, but moved back to Missaukee County after the county seat was moved from Falmouth to Lake City, setting up a law office in Lake City and serving briefly as prosecuting attorney. By 1882 he was back in Cadillac, the first of many prosecuting attorneys to complain of the niggardly salary policy of Missaukee County.

begun in 1872 and the area along the road was rapidly opened to farming as the railroad brought a rush of settlers. The *News* was soon reporting the regular passage of Netherlands immigrants to southern Missaukee County, where John Vogel was helping them to settle.[5] By 1873 a good sized settlement existed at Lake City, and an election on June 7, 1873, resulted in the Missaukee County seat being moved there.

To the west, settlers were clearing land in what was to become Cherry Grove and Boon townships and the existing township of Selma. In July of 1873, a post office was opened at Meauwataka and Enos C. Dayhuff was named postmaster. That settlement attained sufficient size that, with its advantage of location at the approximate center of the county, it was seriously considered over the next few years as a possible location for the county seat, and fully expected to have its own railroad running through it cross-county.

For all these new settlers, Clam Lake was the railhead and trading center, a fact as fully appreciated by the Clam Lake merchants as by the settlers. In 1873, advertisements in downstate newspapers promoting Missaukee County, for instance, pointed out the existence of an improved state road between Falmouth and Clam Lake (almost before it was "improved") and mentioned the good access that Missaukee County residents had to stores and shipping of Clam Lake. In turn, the Clam Lake *News* preached constantly of the necessity of improving roads and bridges "as a courtesy to those who come to trade with us."

3.

The coming of the railroad ended the dominant position of Traverse City as a wholesale distribution center. Merchandise

5. The new settlers were described by the newspaper as matter of factly as if they were freight. One *News* account, for instance, said: "There were quite a number of Hollanders arriving in town Monday being shipped en route to Falmouth by John Vogel." The death of George Mitchell disclosed that he financed Vogel and was a silent partner in Vogel's business affairs in Missaukee County, including the sale of land to the immigrants.

could be brought to Clam Lake as economically by rail as to Traverse City by ship, and more quickly, and Clam Lake's merchants took business from Traverse City's wholesalers and distributors. The proliferation of grocers noted in the list of early merchants tell but half the story. They were all of the "general store" type business, carrying not only packaged foods but produce, grain, hay, and feed, and almost everything that could be used on a farm, in a lumber camp, or in the household. Several, like Holbrook & May and LaBar & Cornwell, dealt both wholesale and retail from the beginning, but almost all of them were soon engaged in the wholesale trade to some extent. Morris Bunyea, Lorenzo Ballou, and A. M. Lamb were soon joined by High Brothers, Corneil & McDonal, Martin & Clary, Crawford Brothers, and McAdam & Brown.[6]

We have mentioned that George Holbrook and Henry May built the first permanent building at the east end of Little Clam Lake early in 1871. Boyhood neighbors in Plymouth, Michigan, they had tried several ventures together before working as provisioners for G. R. & I. construction crews around Big Rapids. In the process, they met George Mitchell frequently and were privy to his plans for a village at Clam Lake. Accordingly, they built their log store on the lake front, intending it as a permanent home and place of business.

6. In the uncertain economic conditions of the day, with recurrent "panics" and bank failures, the failure of a commercial business was often not so much the result of incompetence as it was the result of having extended credit to others who failed. This was particularly true of wholesalers and logging camp provisioners, who having committed themselves to large credit extensions to one major customer, found themselves unable to meet their notes to suppliers or banks when that customer failed. In 1877, E. J. Copley, logging extensively in Haring Township, built a shingle mill at the foot of Pine Street, financed by George Mitchell, and with it constructed tenant houses and a boardinghouse for his employees. When he failed, Mitchell took over the mill in foreclosing the mortgage, but Copley's failure caused the collapse of High Brothers, operating out of the old Holbrook & May log store, who had supplied all of his camps and the village boardinghouse. When he failed again, a few years later, he again took his supplier, Crawford Brothers grocery. Mayor James McAdam failed for the same reason. McDonal and Corneil weathered their financial storms by the assured income of their other businesses. Each partner had a saloon.

They prospered from the beginning, supplying the train crews and the early logging camps and operating both a retail store and a wholesale business. Their prosperity is attributable not merely to opportunity, but undoubtedly rested on reputations as gentlemen and honest merchants. For a decade, they were an influence for good in the community. They held a variety of elective offices. They volunteered for every civic program. They were organizers of the Presbyterian church and conducted a "rescue" operation for drunken loggers before the organization of the Good Templars, which they supported generously. When postmaster John McClain resigned in June of 1872, May was appointed to replace him. When the area was looking for someone to run against Rep. Tom Ferguson of Sherman later that year, it turned to Holbrook and supported him enthusiastically, even though he was a Democrat.

In 1873 the partners built a new store at the northwest corner of Mitchell and Mason streets. It was a large, frame, two-story building, thirty by eighty feet in size, with its length parallel to Mitchell Street.[7] The south end was occupied by the post office and Dr. Wilcox's drugstore, with an entrance from Mason Street. The rest of the first floor was occupied by the retail and wholesale store, with a Mitchell Street entrance. There was a full basement and a huge storage attic. For a short time the two families lived on the second floor, but it was soon converted into an "opera hall," which was the scene of public gatherings, dances, and opera and other theatrical and musical performances. The Holbrook & May Hall also became the meeting chambers for the village and city council and was to be the scene of many stormy meetings of the county board of supervisors.

May had a farm "east of town" and later joined with George Mitchell's son Alvin in platting the surrounding area.[8] He held

7. The building lay across the east end of lots 1 and 2 of block D of the village plat. They sold land along Mason Street on the west end of lot 1 to three lumber companies who built their offices between the Holbrook & May store and the railroad track: Levi Harris, J. Cummer & Son, and McCoy & Ayer.

8. May's and Mitchell's subdivision embraced the hill area east of the original George Mitchell plat of the village. Presidents Washington and Lincoln each had a street named for them. The recently assassinated Garfield had four: North, East, South, and West Garfield streets. Non-presidents May, his partner,

office in the village as treasurer and trustee, was a member of the school board, and was appointed a superintendent of the poor. In 1878 he was elected to the House of Representatives. He had a variety of investment interests in lumbering and furniture manufacturing. The growth of these interests led him elsewhere, however, and in 1881 he sold his interest in the partnership and moved to Grand Rapids.

Holbrook held a number of village offices and served as city alderman from the second ward for several years.He built a home on the southeast corner of East Mason and Simons streets. About six months after his partner had sold his interest to Fred Kieldsen, Holbrook did the same, selling Kieldsen his home as well and leaving the area.

Kieldsen came to this country from Denmark as a young man of twenty and found employment hauling supplies for construction crews on the G. R. & I. It was in that manner that he first saw Clam Lake early in 1871. He soon decided to make it his home and took employment with Holbrook & May as a clerk in their store. Within a few years, he branched off on his own and had a grocery store on the west side of Mitchell Street a half block south of Holbrook & May. A heart attack in 1877 led him to sell the stock and rent out the building, and he bought a Haring Township farm

Holbrook, and lumberman Delos Blodgett, were remembered in like fashion.

As an alternative to Courthouse Hill (block F) of the original plat, two blocks were left undivided as possible sites for a future courthouse. Perhaps with his 1883 promise to donate a courthouse site in mind, Dr. Leeson bought a portion of block 2. On it he built a home with a commanding view of the city, and set out the rest to an orchard and called it Orchard Hill Farm. In 1886 Austin Mitchell bought a portion at the northwest corner of Holbrook and Division streets and erected a huge home now owned by Judge Frank Miltner. For many years, until the planting of shade trees began to reduce visibility, the Leeson and Mitchell homes caught the eye from every direction. Notwithstanding Dr. Leeson's Orchard Hill designation, the *News* persisted in calling it Observatory Hill. After Dr. Leeson *sold* the property to the county for $7,000 in 1911, it became Courthouse Hill. The Leeson house was moved onto a lot behind the new courthouse, stood empty for many years during the depression, and was finally torn down in 1935 or 1936. The rest of the hill was known to children of several generations as Bunker Hill, serving as ballfield, battleground, and play area until graded down in 1948 for construction of the Christian Reformed Curch, now the intermediate school offices.

where he could live in more leisurely fashion. He raised Holsteins and got into the milk business. Soon he was raising thoroughbred race horses. Next he was dabbling in pine and found himself operating a lumber business. In 1881 he bought out first May's interest in the big store and then Holbrook's six months later.

Kieldsen's operation of the store proved every bit as successful as that of Holbrook & May, and he continued his logging and lumber operations profitably. In 1892 he shared the general optimism of the area's larger lumber firms but without their resources. In anticipation of a rising economy and higher pine prices, he put everything he could raise into purchase of some of the few remaining pine stands in Missaukee and Kalkaska counties. The panic of 1893 nearly destroyed him financially and did destroy him physically. He was left with little except his home and the store. He had had continuing heart problems, for which liberal doses of morphine had been prescribed. As the panic continued into 1894 and Cadillac's mills remained largely idle, his condition worsened. On September 29 he was found dead. Deliberately or accidentally, he had taken an overdose of morphine.

In 1892 the store building was turned and moved so that it lay lengthwise on lot 2, the narrow end fronting on Mitchell Street.[9] The store became Nordstrom and Lofgren's Hardware. The second floor Kieldsen's Hall became Nordstrom's Hall, the meeting place of the Swedish Society which later organized as the Gotha Lodge, and a gathering place for meetings of all kinds. In later years, the building had a succession of diverse tenants, ending as Johnson's Auto Body Repair Shop before it was torn down in 1949.

4.

Clam Lake's second large merchant house founded in 1871, LaBar and Cornwell, was to prove its most enduring.[10] After

9. Plans to build a modern brick office building on the vacated corner lot were abandoned because of the panic, and the lot was later sold to Delos Blodgett of Grand Rapids. It was purchased from him in 1900 for the site of city hall.

10. Accounts differ as to the date of their first operation. LaBar said he

operating through the first winter from the log Bunyea building near the lake, they moved in May to the Mosser & White building on Mitchell Street. The move was only temporary, however, as the partners already had a store building going up on the west side of South Mitchell Street and a large gristmill under construction on West Chapin Street, which were ready for use by late fall.

Charles H. LaBar was an experienced miller. He supervised construction of the mill and ran that part of the operation. It was the then customary grinding-stone operation and was one of the largest in northern Michigan, with three stones in constant operation. The original mill was destroyed by fire in 1877 but promptly rebuilt. In 1880 the Lenawee roller mills at Adrian began the first successful experiment with grinding rollers instead of millstones, and the following year a mill at Sand Beach adopted the principle. LaBar visited both and experimented with rollers of his own design. In 1884 the entire operation was converted to the roller method, and the name of this division of the business was changed from Cadillac City Mill to Cadillac City Roller Mills, and finally to Cadillac City Flouring Mills. Under LaBar's management, the firm added a mill in Shephard and operated as grain brokers and dealers throughout Michigan.

Jacob Cornwell was an excellent business manager, and he and LaBar had the good sense to make one of their employees, Martin Heath, a partner in 1873.[11] Cornwell and Heath both knew groceries, merchandising, and money, and they soon had expanded their wholesale business into several divisions dealing with retailers and loggers. Their own retail operation was expanded to include stores in Lake City and Manton and a second retail store in Cadillac.

By 1884 the firm had outgrown its Mitchell Street building and

walked into the village on December 10, 1871, and that the first supplies came with the first freight train several weeks later. Cornwell put his arrival in summer, when the trees hadn't yet been cut off Mitchell Street. LaBar's reference to snow might be explained as late spring of '71, but why the positive date? Perhaps he came after his partner. They do seem to have been selling that fall and can be placed in Bunyea's building by December 1 at the latest.

11. No articles of partnership were filed to show the proper name. A variety of versions appear in the newspapers: LaBar & Cornwell, Cornwell & LaBar, LaBar & Heath & Co., etc.

plans were made to put up a larger building which would house the South Cadillac retail store and the business offices of the firm. The lot at the southeast corner of Cass and Mitchell streets, where the Ohio House had formerly stood, was acquired, and contractor John Mosser was hired to put up a large three-story brick building which boasted the city's first elevator. By January of 1885 it was ready for occupancy. The Masonic order, which had previously leased space in the bank building, took the third floor, while the entire second floor was leased to the county for a five-year term at $1,000 a year for use of the circuit court and county officers. Both floors were vacated in 1890, when the county took a long lease on space in the new Masonic Temple, but the LaBar & Cornwell building was still considered to be the city's choicest office site, and its second floor was promptly occupied by business, insurance, and law offices, while the Maccabees leased the third floor. In later years, as newer buildings provided even more modern office suites, the second floor became a sort of publishers' annex. Several newspapers, the *Michigan Advance,* the *Democrat,* the *Daily Citizen* and the *Arbitaren,* a Swedish language paper, had their headquarters there, as did a number of monthly journals, including the *Pythian*, the *State Oddfellow,* the *Journal of Foresters,* and several other publications devoted to the lumber and milling industries.

Both Heath and LaBar suffered from periodic bouts of ill health. Heath left the firm in 1880 and LaBar retired in 1893. In the interim, Cornwell's sons, Monroe, Willis, and Frank, entered the business, and the firm name was changed to J. C. Cornwell & Sons on LaBar's retirement. Eventually, after the death of the father and the dissolution of the business, the LaBar-Cornwell building was acquired by furniture dealer Chris Kryger. The third floor was removed, and the exterior was later substantially refinished by his son and successor, Henry Kryger, giving it its present appearance as the home of Gately's furniture store.

5.

The Lorenzo Ballou store on Mason Street was part of a family partnership that had its main branch at Otsego in Allegan County.

Lorenzo's father, Byron, was born in Cleveland in 1827 and came with his father by ox team to Ypsilanti when that area was still wilderness. They were desperate years and when the father died Byron was sent to live with an aunt in Kalamazoo, where he was apprenticed to a carpenter. They put up a gristmill on the river and he stayed to learn the miller's trade. Several moves finally brought him to Otsego, where he started a general store in which his sons Henry and Lorenzo became partners.

Somehow, Clam Lake came to their attention, and Lorenzo moved north in the spring of 1872 and bought John McClain's property adjoining the railroad on the north side of Mason Street. It was further improved, and the grocery, flour, and feed store was conducted as part of the family partnership. Within a few months his brother Henry joined him.

In 1873 the father closed out the Otsego business and moved to Clam Lake, buying a half interest in the retail hardware business of John Cloud, which was also located on Mason Street. The hard times of the mid-seventies left the grocery business on the edge of failure for several years. Lorenzo was not the manager to put it back on its feet, and Henry had no real interest in the business.[12] In an effort to save the business, the father sold his interest in Cloud & Ballou to George Mitchell's son Andrew[13] and went back to the store fulltime. He built another addition to the building and expanded the wholesale operation of the building. The old McClain home at the back of the lot was destroyed, and a flour mill, the Banner mill, was erected, which was later sold to John Wade. Unfortunately, Lorenzo's personal financial affairs were in

12. Henry left the store in 1877 and went to work for the G. R. & I., then joined Cobbs and Mitchell as their bookkeeper. Lumbering stimulated him as groceries hadn't, and he was soon superintendent of the Cobbs & Mitchell plant operations. He married Jacob Cornwell's daughter, Sarah, and held a variety of public offices, including that of city clerk, alderman, and member of the school board.

13. Cloud bought out Mitchell two years later after moving the business to the west side of Mitchell Street, midway between Cass and Harris streets. He later took another partner, Edward Morgan, and finally retired in 1897, selling his interest to J. H. Murray. Morgan & Murray continued at the same location for another decade. The building is presently occupied by Carlson's Jewelry Store and Steve Fowler's Beauty Salon.

worse condition than those of the store, and he gave up and left the area. Byron's health was not the best, and the business was only maintained at great effort. But like many others, he dabbled in logging and profited. He started a shingle mill on the Sunnyside shore of the lake, and this also proved profitable. When it burned in 1887, Ballou called it quits. His grocery inventory and wholesale business were sold to LaBar and Cornwell, and the store building was rented out for a few years. In 1889 he sold it to John Mosser, who used it as a warehouse for building materials and ultimately converted it to a building supply business. It has since been used for the same purpose by C. J. Manktelow and others and eventually was acquired by Leo Brehm, who returned it to its original use as a wholesale grocer business. Now, largely rebuilt and remodeled by Brehm, it is the headquarters of Brehm Tree and Land Corporation.

Byron Ballou left quite an imprint on the early village. He was one of the first Republicans when that party was born and participated vigorously and bluntly in the political activities of the day. In Allegan County, he had been chairman of the county board of supervisors and of the county Republican committee. In his new home, he was chairman of the county Republican party for several terms. Notwithstanding the fact that he had a speech impediment which became aggravated when he was excited, as he usually was in political debate, he was accounted a powerful and convincing speaker. John Wheeler said he was a man of plain, blunt truths, bluntly spoken.

The views he held would probably be considered "progressive" or "bull moose" type Republicanism by later generations. Wheeler described him as a "Radical Republican" in a period when that label designated strong views on civil rights, reconstruction of the south, and regulation of railroad and monopolies. On the other hand, he advocated a state monopoly of the liquor business as the only means of controlling saloons and striking a happy medium between prohibition and a population reduced to delerium tremens. He shocked the churchly population (small) of the early village with one of his "bluntly spoken" truths by advocating legalized prostitution in an 1877 letter to the *News*. It was a carefully thought out analysis of sin in Clam Lake which was flourishing on the business of the single or separated men working in the mills and logging camps. It suggested debate of the issue as to health, public morals, and offenses, and the protection of the resident community. It was widely noted, helping to bring Clam Lake its reputation as a modern Sodom and Gomorrah.

The letter may have brought scorn from afar—Detroit, Sherman, or Manton—and from the clergy and ladies' societies of the village, but it didn't lessen the esteem and affection in which he was held by most of his contemporaries. He was appointed postmaster for a four-year term during the presidency of General Grant and received another such appointment during Harrison's administration from 1889 to 1893. He served as the Clam Lake Township supervisor before the city was incorporated. In 1882 he was elected Cadillac's mayor. In retirement he held several appointive city positions before moving to a farm on the south shore of Big Clam Lake. In 1892 a small settlement in Selma Township was given a post office and named Ballou in his honor. When he died in 1901, the county mourned the loss of an honest, fiercely independent, and forthright man.

6.

Early in 1872, a twenty-six-year-old Irishman named William Kelley came to the village to supervise a logging crew for George Mitchell and try his own hand at the lumber business. Born in Ireland, he had come to New York with his father at the age of seven, and then virtually raised himself when the father died two years later. At age sixteen, he enlisted in the Union Army, spent most of the first four months in the stockade for insubordination, and then went into battle. At Bull Run, he and four comrades volunteered to hold an outflanked position in a delaying action. The only one to survive, he was captured after being knocked senseless by a spent musket ball. After almost a year's captivity, he was returned to the north in a prisoner exchange and discharged. He joined a fellow prisoner for a visit in Greenville, married the friend's sister, and re-enlisted, serving until the end of the war and winning several citations for bravery.

At the end of the war he had joined his Nancy at Greenville, tried several jobs, and soon convinced himself and his employers that he wasn't meant to take orders. Several business ventures were successful, and he read law with a Greenville attorney for the sake of the learning and not with any intention of practicing law. From Greenville he went to Lakeview and made a quick profit in buying and selling land there. At some point he met Mitchell and accepted an offer to work for him. His main purpose was to learn about logging, in which he supposed that there was money to be made.

As an advance against his wages, Kelley took a lot on the west side of Mitchell Street midway between Harris and West Mason streets, and built a two-story home during the summer of 1872. He quickly learned all he thought he needed to know about logging, disagreed with Mitchell in various matters, and quit the job. He had been a better crew boss than he had been employee, and many of the crew went to work for him in future seasons. He bought another lot adjoining the first one and put up a store building for investment. He contracted with Mitchell and Delos Blodgett to cut their pine in sections 32, 33, and 34 of Haring Township on a footage basis. He did it cheaper than Mitchell had been doing it with his own labor, and he made a profit.

In the course of the contract, he made a wager with Mitchell on the delivery of logs to the lake, then built the area's first logging railroad, a pole road running up Pine Street from the lake, with horse-drawn carts. The bet was paid with two more lots. On one, at the southwest corner of Pine and Shelby, he built another home, still standing, into which he moved his family, converting the Mitchell Street home into a store.[14]

He entered into several other logging deals, bought and sold pine lands, built logging railroads for Ephraim Shay and Thomas Graham, invested in real estate in the village, operated a livery stable, did building and was the contractor for various street improvements, including the construction of the first board sidewalks and crosswalks. He was elected to several offices as a

14. Kelley's Mitchell Street properties were badly damaged by fire in 1875. In October, 1877, the entire block burned, taking his stores and the livery stable behind them. The Kelley block, which he rebuilt in brick still stands, presently housing Ted J. Brown's Men's Wear, Reed & Wheaton's Jewelry, and Henne's Shoe Store.

Republican, including that of supervisor from Clam Lake Township, where he managed to aggravate and be aggravated during some of the county seat battle sessions. When the village was organized, he held several village offices, was a member of the school board, and was elected alderman and school inspector when the city was incorporated. In the election of 1878, he was elected county sheriff, but he died of a heart attack before he could take office. He left three children, Mrs. Edith Morgan, Edwin V. Kelley, and a daughter, Helen, who married Holden Green's son Fred, later to be governor of Michigan.

7.

The man who replaced William Kelley as sheriff was Charles C. Dunham. He was an exceptional man, intelligent, full of zest for life, and gregarious. Yet it would be hard to find a more modest, down to earth, and unpretentious man among our early settlers.

Born in Ohio in 1845, his family had moved to Michigan in the fifties. Both he and his father had enlisted in the Union Army. After the war, the father had moved to Manistee, had been elected county clerk and register of deeds, had prospered as a banker, and had moved to Grand Rapids, where he had an interest in a wholesale house and was president of a bank. Active in political and fraternal affairs, the senior Dunham had been a presidential elector for Rutherford B. Hayes.

After the war, the younger Dunham also went to Manistee, where he ran a sawmill and dealt in lumber. In 1874 he came to the village of Clam Lake and lumbered, held office as justice of the peace for four years, and was in and out of the grocery business several times. As a boy, he had read law at Wayland, Michigan, with Judge Charles Godwin, and he was admitted to the bar here in 1885, although he never actively engaged in the practice of law. In later years, he engaged in the undertaking and furniture business.

Dunham's election as sheriff was the first of six such elections, and he was later to be elected probate judge and three times mayor of Cadillac. He was absolutely fair in treatment of his prisoners and completely honest. It is doubtful that a county could ever want more in a sheriff than it had in Dunham. Although not a large man, he was absolutely fearless. He was more than competent with a gun, but he scorned the use of a pistol as endangering others needlessly. On at least three occasions, he subdued and disarmed wanted men, two of whom shot at him and missed. On another occasion, he was attacked by one of the worst brawlers among the rivermen, a 280 pounder who declined to be arrested peaceably at Jacobson's saloon. When the fight was over, Dunham apologized for his inability to carry his senseless prisoner to the jail without help.

The energetic and fun-loving side of Dunham is revealed in this comment from the *News* in 1888:

> Charles Dunham came in 1875 from Manistee. He has been in the lumber business and a grocer, but has spent the greater part of his time being sheriff and the chairman of four committees for fireman's balls. He is chief of the fire department, first baseman in the Masonic Lodge, zealous toiler in the Knights of Labor, and ornamental drum major on horse back in street parades for 4th of July processions. He is so adept at running to fires and directing the manipulation of the nozzles that his more timid friends fear that he will try to organize a hose company in Paradise the first night of his arrival, there to do service on the historic flames of the lower wards.

All in all, he was an unusual man. His only child, Eva, married jeweler Errol Wheaton, and a granddaughter, Mrs. Dorothy Sorenson, lives in Cadillac today.

8.

Over the next few years, the village of Clam Lake continued to grow rapidly. In 1874 it was legally incorporated as a village[15] and in 1877 incorporated as the City of Cadillac. New industries multi-

15. And re-incorporated the following year when the village incorporation act was held unconstitutional and had to be re-enacted by the legislature.

plied. In 1873 George Mitchell's son-in-law, A. K. Moyer, started the Clam Lake Brickyard at the edge of the swamp south of the village. That same year, two lumber dealers, Daniel McCoy and Charles Ayers, opened an office in the village.[16] They built a sawmill between the railroad and Haring Road, a quarter of a mile north of the Clam River. A handful of homes and a boarding-house were soon located east of the mill, and the settlement became known as McCoy's Siding, although its location is marked today by Ayers Street.[17]

In 1877 E. J. Copley built his shingle mill on the lake at the foot of Pine Street, and William Saunders put up a planing mill several hundred yards to the northwest. On the east side of the Clam River, near the Haynes planing mill, W. W. Cummer and his father-in-law, the wealthy lumberman Nathaniel Gerrish, put up another planing mill.[18] Several lumber dealers built offices in the village, among them Jacob Cummer, who soon got into the mill business.

16. Ayers is the originator of the name "Cadillac" for the new city in 1877. McCoy was thrice mayor, later one of Grand Rapids' leading bankers and businessmen, and twice treasurer of Michigan.

17. There was one place of business "in the woods between Crippen's Foundry and McCoy's Siding," the North Star House. This seemingly remote description refers to a location near North Street between the road north and the railroad! The North Star House soon became one of the more notorious places in a community becoming famous for notorious places.

18. Another Gerrish daughter married Delos Diggins, whose brother Fred had married Wellington Cummer's sister Carrie. It proved a solid consolidation of lumbering power. Gerrish and his son Winfield Scott Gerrish are credited with being the first men to use a locomotive to move their timber on a logging railroad between the Doc and Tom Creek and the Muskegon River. They soon found that the railroad could move logs not only to water but straight to the mill. Gerrish logged extensively in Montcalm, Osceola, and Clare counties, establishing a rather substantial fortune. His death certificate listed his occupation simply as "capitalist!" Gerrish moved to Cadillac on retirement, living next to his daughter and son-in-law, the W. W. Cummers, in a large home on the southwest corner of East Mason and Simons streets. Cummer had acquired the George Mitchell home which, it will be recalled, had been originally built by Mitchell for his daughter and son-in-law, Sophie and Andrew Keller Moyer. When the Mitchells decided to move to Cadillac and pre-empted the home, Mitchell had built an almost equally large home just to the east for the Moyers. When Gerrish came to Cadillac, the Moyers were approaching divorce, and the home was available.

In 1876 William Crippen started a small foundry and machine shop at what was then the northernmost part of the village, Bremer Street, and four years later another metal-working shop, the Cadillac Division of the Michigan Iron Works, was built at the northeast corner of Harris and Lake streets by H. D. Wallen, Jr., assistant superintendent of the G. R. & I. and owner of the parent Michigan Iron Works of Grand Rapids. In 1878 Judge Holden Green put in the first waterworks for the city, and the following year the Banner Gristmill was built by Byron Ballou along the west side of the railroad track between Mason and Pine streets on the site of the old McClain log cabin. On the south shore of the lake, in the area already known as Sunnyside, a brewery was built in 1876 by Westover & Co., a partnership which later included Delos Blodgett.[19] The ice business was already an important part of the economy of the village by 1873, when the first storage shed was built by George Mitchell at the end of Harris Street where the city dock is now located. A few years later, he put up a huge storage shed along the shore between Cass and Chapin streets, and hundreds of tousands of tons of ice were shipped on the G. R. & I. over the next fifteen years.

Other new hotels went up: The Bay City House on Pine Street in 1877; in 1875 the twin hotels facing each other across Harris Street on the east side of the railroad tracks: on the north side of the street, Larson and Nelson's Arnold House,[20] and on the south side, the Balfour House.[21] Another dozen boardinghouses and as many more saloons, a bowling alley, more livery stables, harness

19. The brewery was apparently no great financial success, notwithstanding the huge amounts of alcohol being consumed locally, and it ceased operation after a fire in 1884. The building was acquired by Cobbs & Mitchell and used for a small machine shop until it was destroyed by fire in 1888.

20. The Larson and Nelson Hotel was destroyed by fire in October, 1877. It was rebuilt as a three-story building and called the Arnold House. From 1879 until 1883 it was called the Cadillac House. Later owners chose to give it their own names, the Jackson House and the Burke House. As the latter, it was destroyed by fire in 1899. The Anheuser-Busch Brewery rebuilt it as a combination beer-storage house and saloon, with rooms to let on the upper stories. It eventually became a hotel again, last known as the Royal Hotel, and is now incorporated as part of the Cadillac State Bank Building.

21. The Balfour House later became the Cadillac Hotel.

shops and blacksmiths, and two dozen new retail establishments filled out the central business district of the city.[22] Around the edges, residences edged outward toward the forest, and four churches gave some solace to the hardships and uncertainties of nineteenth century milltown life.

At the end of the seventies it was a strange community, pulsing with energy, strident, aggressive, and boisterous. It had a well-developed cultural community, with theatrical, literary, and musical groups and a debating society. Among its citizens were persons who were to go on to a variety of positions of political and industrial leadership in the state. But it was better known throughout the Midwest as the home of such brawlers as Kicking O'Neill, Wild John, Barney the Lather, Sweet William May, Comer Haley, Mike Corbitt, Tom Crow, and the notorious prostitutes, Swede Min, and Mame Ten.

9.

Other settlements were springing up along the railroad. Hobart had a post office, blacksmith shop, and several stores. On October 25, 1873, the *News* reported that "Harring Station, 3 ½ miles north, is putting on a real town-like appearance. The McKinnon Brothers mill will run all winter. The E. Shay mill is busy." The E. Shay mentioned was Ephraim Shay, inventor of the Shay logging locomotive, of whom we shall hear more later. The McKinnon brothers logged widely, were engaged in various commercial ventures, and built the McKinnon hotels in Cadillac and McBain. In addition to its mills, Haring Station had a depot, post office, general store, boardinghouse, and the Shay machine shop.

In the northwest corner of Haring Township, the Bond

22. The most intriguing of the new businessmen was blacksmith Robert Christensen, newly arrived from Denmark. Fred Kieldsen took him under his wing, saw that he got business, and tutored him in English, finally taking him into his store to clerk, the better to learn the language. In 1880 Christensen was admitted to citizenship, admitted to the bar, and elected supervisor from the First Ward! He prospered as a lawyer, then moved away in 1882 and disappeared from our view.

brothers, Milton,[23] Myron, and Eber, dammed the outlets of some springs near the railroad to create a logging pond which they called Umbrella Lake. The community springing up around their sawmill soon had its own post office, and Bond's Mill had two stores, the usual blacksmith shop, a hotel, and a Swedish Lutheran church. To the east, there were settlements around the mills at Long Lake and Round Lake, while further to the north, the community of Gilbert grew up around another sawmill and had its own post office, general store, and church.

By the end of 1872, the railroad had reached Manton Station. The stop was named after George Manton, supervisor of Colfax Township, which then included the area which was to be set off as Cedar Creek Township. In 1872 Manton saw the possibilities of the area for a city, primarily because of his knowledge of road law. State law provided for eventual construction of roads along all section lines, but as a practical matter, the first roads would be built along the township lines. It was felt a community at the intersection of a town line and a railroad would have a good chance of prospering. Furthermore, the north town line of Colfax Township was almost due east of Sherman, the county seat.

In the summer of 1872, Manton and Ezra Harger walked the area and resolved to start the settlement first called Manton Station, sometimes called Cedar Creek, but eventually known officially as the village of Manton. They bought and platted twenty acres of land along the railroad. Harger put up the first store building, followed shortly by Manton, who put up a shoe store, and by William Mears of Sherman, who built a grocery store.

Early in 1873, the railroad depot was opened, a hotel went up, and the G. R. & I. stationmaster, Harry Brandenburg, started a sawmill. As George Manton had foreseen, the legislature appropriated money to build a state road along the town line west-

23. The same Milton Bond who was partner to Judge Green in operating the former Shackleton & Green sawmill on Clam Lake, and who operated a mill of his own on the Sunnyside shore of Little Clam Lake. He went on to log in Mississippi in the late eighties, but soon came back to logging in northern Michigan. He also had an interest in the Cadillac Machine Company with Daniel and Walter Kysor.

ward towards Sherman, and the mail route to Traverse City, via Sherman, was changed to depart from Manton Station. By 1877, the village had another sawmill, a planing mill, the drugstores of Dr. Wilcox and Dr. Taplin, five more retail stores, two churches, three hotels, and five saloons. To these refinements of civilizaton, the community added governmental independence in 1877, when the legislature incorporated it officially as the village of Manton. By then, Manton had dreams of becoming the county seat.

The new settlements were reflected in the political structure of the county. The legislature organized the new townships of Clam Lake and Cherry Grove in 1872, Haring and Cedar Creek in 1873, and Liberty in 1874. The drift of the wind was obvious from the first at Clam Lake. At its first township election, held at the Mason House, an even 100 votes were cast, with the suspicion that some extra and unlawful effort was made to reach that magic number. Several credible accounts relate that transients at the Mason House and "its colored employees" were made to vote to reach that figure. The township's first supervisor, Chauncey Hollister, promptly rocked the county boat at the next meeting of the board of supervisors by introducing a resolution to move the county seat to Clam Lake, and editor Frazier of the *News* reported the event in one cocky sentence: "Owing to deep snow and the consequent bad state of the roads it was deemed advisable not to move the Courthouse to Clam Lake this winter."

PART II:
THE COUNTY SEAT BATTLE

Chapter Eleven

PRELIMINARY SKIRMISHES: 1870-1873

The history of Wexford County from its organization in 1869 until 1882 is primarily the story of its county seat and the battle over whether it should remain at Sherman. The first page of that history, the legislative act incorporating the county, specified that the county seat was to be located "at or near Manistee Bridge." The next thirteen years caught up the county's most prominent citizens in the effort to change or affirm that designation. There was little that happened in county affairs, from the building of roads and bridges to the appointment of the superintendents of the poor, that was not colored by the regional controversy.

The influx of settlers and the organization of townships, villages, and cities to represent them, for instance, at once explain how the rivalry grew and illustrate the extremes to which partisans went in pursuing their goal. A treatise entitled "A Political History of Wexford County Townships," which suggests old election statistics and musty records, would probably attract few readers. On the other hand, a title such as "Your Sins Shall Find You Out"[1] hardly suggests a subject dealing with local government. It does more justice to our story, however, which is an account of deceit, election scandals, larceny, bribery and attempted bribery, rumors of blackmail, extortion, and larger crimes, and the final violence of 1882 that capped the political organization of the county.

The account includes names foreign to the present-day political map of the county. Even those most familiar with the county's township organization would be puzzled at references to the townships of Benton, Dover, Cleon, Concord, Sherman, Thorp, Summit, West Side, Wheatland, Nelson, Kysor, Linden, Garfield,

1. Closing words of Thomas Ferguson to the Clam Lake representatives, at the supervisors meeting Jan. 11, 1877.

Long Lake, and Copley, which appear in the old records, on some maps, and sometimes on the dockets of the Supreme Court.

Four things must be taken into account in considering our story: (1) The will and persistence of George A. Mitchell, (2) The growing population of the county, (3) The law governing a change in location of a county seat, and (4) The law dealing with township organization.

The first two we have already met. Mitchell's plans for his city on the Little Clam Lake assumed from the beginning that that city was to be the county seat. His plat set aside block F, Courthouse Hill, as the future site of the county's buildings. The determination and resourcefulness that marked his business planning was equally evident in his political planning.

We have also noted the population growth of the new county, from 650 people in 1870, to 3,011 in 1874 and 6,815 in 1880. The location of the new settlers along the east side of the county, and particularly in the village of Clam Lake, has also been noted, a fact of special importance, since the county seat could not be moved without a public referendum.

It would ordinarily be assumed that if the location of the county seat were to be determined by public referendum, it would inevitably go to the area where the majority of the people lived. The impediment to such logic lay in the fact that, while state law required an election to authorize a move, such an election could only be ordered by the vote of two-thirds of the members of the county board of supervisors. Had the "one man, one vote" constitutional principle been recognized then, there would have been no problem. Membership of the board of supervisors, however, had no relation to population. Which brings us to the fourth matter to remember in this story: where supervisors come from.

County government, until the "one man, one vote" changes of the past few years, was centered in the county board of supervisors. All of Michigan's constitutions have provided for local government within the counties in the form of townships, cities, and villages. The chief officer in each township is called the supervisor, and the county board of supervisors was made up of these officers.[2] If each township had one vote on the county board,

2. Villages had no representation on the county board, but each city was

through its supervisor, the next logical question is: where do townships come from?

Perhaps it would be well to begin by distinguishing between *survey* townships and *political* townships, before going into the legal basis for the organization of political townships. In Wexford County, as presently organized, each survey township is also a political township, but this is only a coincidence.

2.

Early in our history, when Congress passed the Northwest Territory Ordinance for administration of the Great Lakes area and its ultimate division into new states, it also provided for a systematic mapping and survey of the area. The system of the survey was simply to lay out a grid of squares, six miles square, called towns or townships, which were further divided into thirty-six sections of one square mile each numbered consecutively from 1 to 36.[3] An east-west line, called the "base line," was established, the eastern end of which is now eight-mile road in Detroit. Parallel lines six miles apart were then laid out and each strip was called a township and numbered. Thus, the first six-mile strip north of the baseline is called Township 1 North, the second, Township 2 North, etc. The southernmost row of townships in Wexford County are in Township 21 North.

A north-south line, called the Michigan Meridian, was established, and parallel lines were run six miles apart in each direction. The north-south strip of land was called a range and was similarly numbered east or west of the meridian. The easternmost row of townships in Wexford County are Range 9 West. The southeastern township in the county, then, is legally described by the two coordinates as Township 21 North, Range 9 West.[4]

entitled to as many representatives on the county board as might be authorized by the legislature.

3. We have already encountered this mapping system in our previous references to the railroad land grant setting aside the odd-numbered sections for the railroad subsidy.

4. The gross, or exterior, government survey was completed here in 1837, the year in which Michigan was admitted to the union. The area was completely wild,

A political township, as distinguished from the six-mile-square survey township, may be any area of land designated as such without regard to survey purposes. The county board of supervisors is given power to create, dissolve, and alter townships upon petition of resident landowners in the area affected. In addition to the desire of the petitioners for self-determination, there may be many other practical considerations involved in the creation of townships or the location of their boundaries. The only legal requirement, however, except for procedural technicalities, is that there must be at least five electors living in the area involved.

The pertinent fact for our purposes, however, is that the creation of a new township, which would thereby add a new member to the county board, was made *by the county board.* All suspicious readers will at once recognize the ability of a majority of an unrepresentative board to perpetuate their control over county government by refusing to organize any new townships, thereby preventing any increase in membership of the board.

One other body need be noticed: the state legislature. Cities could be created only by act of the legislature at this point in Michigan history, and they thus had only such representation on the county board of supervisors as the legislative act of incorporation specified. In addition, the legislature of the nineteenth century exercised a rather broad power of enactment of *local* legislation, which is a nice way of saying that it could stick its nose into whatever particular local problem it chose whenever it chose. One of the more common exercises of this power was the creation or dissolution of townships. Obviously, this power represented a safety valve against an existing county board arbitrarily refusing to create new townships. But it served to move local politics to the capitol at Lansing, usually under touchy circumstances.

Most local legislation of this kind presented the legislator with the most highly charged controversies of his district. His constituents were attempting to influence him instead of the local supervisors, removing the issue from hometown public debate. The legislator was particularly powerful in this respect, but he was also peculiarly on the spot. The lobbying for his support was usually

however, and the subdivision of the townships by establishment of the interior section lines was not finished until some fifteen years later.

private, or at least out of the public limelight, and therefore suspect. Woe to him if he misread the majority sentiment of his district.

3.

As presently organized, Wexford County is a neatly divided unit with sixteen political townships, whose boundaries coincide with the survey townships of the county, thus:

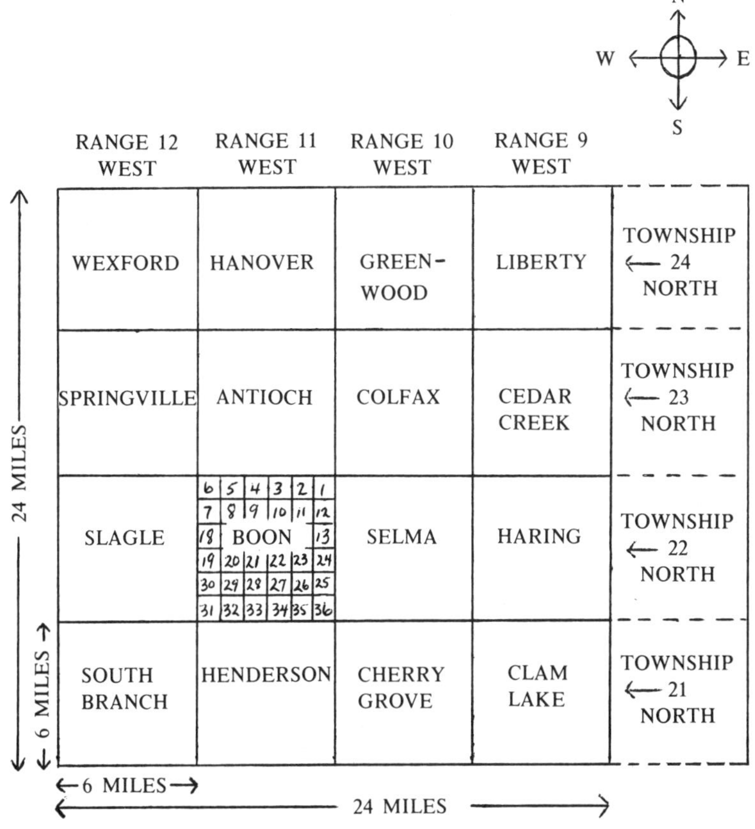

The original act incorporating Wexford County, divided it politically into four townships, in this fashion:

WEXFORD	HANOVER
SPRINGVILLE	COLFAX

In the northwest corner was Wexford Township, the smallest of the four, but containing the largest population in 1869. It consisted of Survey Township 24 North, Range 12 West, and has retained the same name and size thereafter, except for a brief period when section 36 was detached from the southeast corner to make up a township named Sherman.

The first caucus in Wexford Township was held under the direction of Isaac Davis, Isaac Cornell, and Lewis Carpenter and resulted in the election of Henry I. Devoe as supervisor. Over the next fifteen years, the office was filled by Judge Isaac Carpenter (who later moved to Antioch Township and held the same office there), Wilson Odell, J. W. Ransom (who was described by the *News* as incompetent while he was county treasurer, as corrupt when he fought Cadillac on the county seat issue, and, in between, as the most popular man in the county), J. Boylan, and Sylvanus Alexander (later a member of the legislature).

The three remaining townships in Town 24 North were organized as the township of Hanover. The first caucus was held under the direction of Lewis Dunham, Robert Henderson, and John Wheeler, and resulted in the selection of Clarence Northrup as supervisor, a position he continued to hold after Greenwood and Liberty townships had been organized and detached from Hanover. The next fifteen years saw the office filled by John Wheeler's brother Edgar (who was also to be a county treasurer), Solomon Worth, and Andrew Anderson.

The remaining twelve survey townships were divided in half. The six on the west went to make up Springville Township, and it remained the largest township in area for many years as its settlement lagged behind the rest of the county. A small settlement in the southern part of the county where the state road crossed the Pine River led to the detachment and organization of Henderson Township in 1871, but most of the population was in the northern part of Springville, where Antioch Township was detached and organized in 1872. The first Springville caucus was held under the direction of Aaron Baker, Daniel Jewett, and H. C. Duning, and resulted in the election of William Dean as supervisor, a position which he held for many years except for single terms by George Wheeler and George Hicks.[5]

East of Springville, the remainder of the county was set off as the Township of Colfax. Its only settlement of consequence was the cluster of Civil War veterans who settled in the northwest part of the township and called their area Unionville. In the same area, Survey Township 23 North, Range 11 West, which remains as

5. George Wheeler was a brother of John and Edgar, and later moved to Greenwood Township, where he was also elected supervisor. This gave all three brothers membership on the board at the same time. George was the black sheep of the family and found his way into the presence of the justice of the peace with dismaying regularity, an amiable disposition making it impossible to deny his friend John Barleycorn.

Colfax Township today, another settlement grew up near Lake Meauwataka. The most prominent of the group, Enos Dayhuff, gave his name to the settlement, and the lake became equally well known as Dayhuff Lake. The first caucus in Colfax was held at Unionville under the direction of Dayhuff, Lucas Gates, and William Goff, and resulted in the selection of Rascelas S. McClain as supervisor. The office was then held by George Manton, until Cedar Creek Township was detached and organized, and thereafter by Nathan Dayhuff, McClain again, John Goldsmith, J. W. Houghtalin, Ezra Harger (six times county treasurer), and Peter Will.

4.

As the county was settled, the board of supervisors began to receive petitions for the organization of more new townships. In 1870 a settlement grew up south of Dayhuff Lake in Colfax Township. The area, Survey Township 22 North, Range 10 West, was organized into the township of Thorp, named after its most prominent settler, Col. Thomas J. Thorp, who was to become county clerk and a powerful force in county politics during the years of the county seat struggle. The first caucus of the new township was held under the direction of Thorp, T. J. Thompson, Nathaniel W. Reed, and Eli Woodward (after whom Woodward Lake was named), and resulted in the election of Delmar Durphy as supervisor. In 1871, at Thorp's request, the name of the township was changed to Selma, and it has continued unchanged in name or size thereafter. Following Durphy as supervisor over the next fifteen years were C. J. Manktelow (later county clerk), George Otis, A. F. Tilyou, Peter Roberts, Charles Allaire, and Austin Collins.

In 1871 Henderson Township was organized in the southern part of the county, taking its name from its pioneer settler, Thomas Henderson, who became its first supervisor. His successors were Job Hoxie (who gave his name to Hoxeyville), Philip Frost, Elisha Caswell, and H. G. Owen.

Up to this point, the organization of the new townships had been scattered across the north, central, and southern portion of the county, without particular political significance. In the fall of 1871, however, another problem arose as the board was presented with a petition to organize Survey Township 21 North, Range 9 West, under the name of Clam Lake Township. The board rejected the petition because it wanted to do so, but assigned as its reason for doing so some apparent irregularities in the petition, suggesting that the circulator, George Mitchell, had been too diligent in obtaining signatures. Perhaps a few of the signers were migrant railroad workers or lumberjacks of doubtful residence or citizenship. The underlying cause was regional rivalry, which was beginning to become heated and to be expressed stridently at the board meetings.

There was no doubt, however, that the petition would be promptly renewed and that it would be hard to justify further denials. There were too many people settling in the southeast corner of the county to be ignored. Both the Hollister settlement and the new village of Clam Lake were already approaching the size of Sherman, and the new railroad would bring in more. Worse, the brash George Mitchell didn't disguise the fact that he intended to take the county seat from Sherman and move it to his village. His plat reserved a block for the courthouse.

To counter-balance the expected renewal of the petition, the people in the vicinity of Sherman planned the creation of another township to be taken out of the northeast corner of Springville and to consist of Survey Townships 22 and 23 North of Range 11 West. Among the petitioners for this new township named Antioch were Daniel Jewett, Dr. John Perry, Moses Cole, John Wheeler and his brothers George and Edgar, Harmony Carpenter, and J. S. Walling, who became the first supervisor of Antioch. He was followed in the next few years by Edward Austin, John Wheeler, Judge Isaac Carpenter, and Herman C. Meyer.

The Sherman group was surprised, however, when they presented their petition at the meeting of the board of supervisors on January 23, 1872, to find that there was not one but two petitions for the organization of new townships in the southern part of the county. To insure that their petitions had a fair hearing, George Mitchell had organized two delegations to attend the supervisors meeting at the Sherman House in Sherman. Supporting them was an escort of Mitchell's lumberjacks.

Representing one group was Mitchell (whose signature on the petition overlooked his continued legal residence in Indiana), Sylvester Stevens, Lester Sha, Thomas Whaley, C. W. Philips, and Chauncey Hollister. Their petition for the organization of the township of Clam Lake was granted, and Hollister was elected as the first supervisor in the caucus held at the Mason House. Following him in office during the next few years were William Kelley, Byron Ballou, S. S. Fallass, Judson H. Loomis, George Wade, A. T. Vance, James Whaley, and Fred Hector.

The other delegation consisted of Watson M. Smith, Charles Miller, Isaac Briscoe, and John Bonesteel, seeking the organization of Survey Township 21 North, Range 10 West under the name of Cherry Grove. The petition was in proper form. The board didn't dare deny it, and there were now nine townships where there had been six. Smith was elected as the first supervisor of Cherry Grove, and he was followed by Bonesteel and William East each of whom served several terms in office, off and on.

Six months later, the ambitions of another group were evident. At a special meeting of the board, a petition signed by George Manton, who was then supervisor of Colfax, John Carpenter, Damon Moore, James Hawthorne, Warren Seaman, and a number of residents of Manton Station, was granted, detaching Town 23 North, Range 9 West, from Colfax and organizing it as the township of Cedar Creek. The first caucus was not to be held until the next April (1873), and Seaman was elected supervisor on that occasion. His successors were Harry Brandenburg, H. C. McFarlan, Ward P. Smith, Ledra Hawkins, George S. Sloat, and newspaperman H. F. Campbell.

The regional fight blossomed at the annual meeting of the board in October of 1872, when Hollister of Clam Lake introduced a resolution calling for an election on the question of moving the county seat from Sherman to block F of the village of Clam Lake. Under the state law requirement of a two-thirds vote to carry such a resolution, the four supervisors from the northwest could block passage. They were joined by Henderson Township's Thomas Henderson, and the resolution was defeated, 5 to 4, Hollister being joined by Smith of Cherry Grove, Manketelow of Selma, and Manton of Colfax in support of the resolution. At the very next session in January of 1873, Hollister reintroduced the resolution. This time Henderson refused to vote, but George Manton abandoned the Clam Lake faction, because of his own regional ambitions, and the resolution lost, 5 to 3. No one was left with any doubt, however, that the question would be presented again.

5.

At the beginning of 1873, then, the county consisted of ten townships, four in the Sherman faction, four in the Clam Lake faction, with Cedar Creek entertaining its own ambitions, and Henderson waiting to be coaxed. The county map now looked like this:

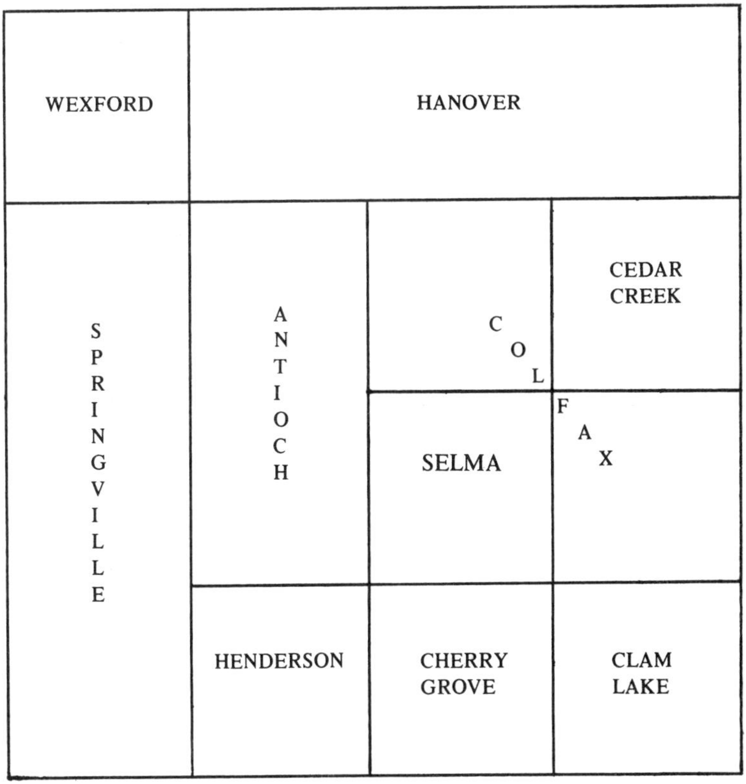

At the January, 1873, session of the supervisors, still another petition for the organization of a township was presented, this from R. D. Cuddeback, Ephraim Shay, Thomas McKinnon, Charles Ball, and others, asking for the organization of Town 22 North, Range 9 West as Haring Township. The supervisors rejected the petition on a regional split of votes, but it is likely that the objection that the petition failed to meet legal requirements was correct because of defective signatures. Except for a cluster of homes around the Shay and McKinnon mills at Haring Station and two farms being cleared on the road from Clam Lake, the area was largely unsettled.

There was another way, however, to skin the township cat and bypass the board of supervisors, and that was to go to Lansing for a local act of the legislature. The Mitchell faction at Clam Lake knew they could expect no help from the district's representative, for he was none other than Thomas Ferguson, just elected to the House after a term as prosecuting attorney. He was a resident of Sherman, the owner of business property there, and firmly dedicated to keeping the county seat where it was.

The area was represented in the Senate, however, by another Mitchell who had settled at Traverse City, and he was quite agreeable to introducing a bill to organize Haring Township. The bill passed the Senate easily, but its fate would depend upon the opposition of Representative Ferguson in the House. As a matter of privilege with his fellow representatives, since this involved his home county, he could have killed it. Instead he hit upon a scheme by which he could serve Sherman without actually voting against his Clam Lake constituents. He used his power to dictate the terms under which the bill might be considered. His condition was the matching of Haring by the creation of another new township, Greenwood, consisting of Town 24 North, Ranges 9 and 10 West.

Thus the legislative act brought two new faces to the board of supervisors. R. D. Cuddeback came from Haring but was matched by John Wheeler's brother George, who moved into the new township of Greenwood. Cuddeback held office in Haring until replaced by Charles Ford in 1880. Wheeler was followed as supervisor in Greenwood by William Briggs, Edward Cox, N. A. Reynolds, and William Rose.

Representative Ferguson was not content merely to match

Haring's admission, however, and he master-minded another slick bit of legislation that passed both houses of the legislature and was signed by the governor before the residents of Clam Lake woke up to what was happening.

At the time, Manistee and Wexford counties were in separate representative districts. Thomas Ramsdell, Manistee attorney and political leader, obtained the support of Ferguson on some bills favorable to Manistee, and, in return, Rep. Merrit Chafey of Manistee introduced a bill detaching Cleon Township from Manistee County and attaching it to Wexford County. The supervisor from Cleon who thus found himself evicted from Manistee County was Alonzo Chubb of Copemish and, as expected, he favored keeping the county seat at nearby Sherman. As a reward for his efforts and to tie Cleon's population more closely to Wexford County, he was nominated for probate judge in 1878, and was elected by a small majority. Unfortunately he was deprived of the office in 1881, when Cleon Township was finally returned to Manistee County to stay.

At the end of 1873, our map looked like this:

CLEON	WEXFORD	HANOVER	GREENWOOD	
	SPRINGVILLE	ANTIOCH	COLFAX	CEDAR CREEK
			SELMA	HARING
		HENDERSON	CHERRY GROVE	CLAM LAKE

Chapter Twelve

TACTICS, TREATIES AND BRIBES: 1874-1876

During 1874 and 1875, there were no formal matters before the board of supervisors pertaining to the county seat location. The question was never out of mind, however, and the regional rivalry between Sherman and Clam Lake was accentuated by the growing ambitions of Manton Station. Few issues were discussed before the board in which there was not an underlying web of regional political motives involved.

Clam Lake was pushing for dominance and made no bones about it. As a first step towards ultimate incorporation as a city and independent representation on the board of supervisors, the village was legally incorporated in 1874. Lumberman George Shackleton was elected village president at the first caucus held in George Mitchell's office in the Mitchell House under the direction of attorney Silas S. Fallas. Shackleton's partner, Holden Green, was elected justice. Another attorney, David A. Rice, was elected clerk, and the trustees were lumbermen Levi O. Harris, Daniel McCoy, and Jonathan Cobbs, blacksmith Fred Hector,[1] merchant George Holbrook, and saloonkeeper-harness-maker Alonzo McCardy. An interesting event of the caucus was the election for constable. Ninety ballots were counted for Eugene Saunders (the grocer who had dug the canal between the lakes) and fifty for contractor John G. Mosser. The total appeared suspiciously large to Chairman Fallass, so he ordered the caucus to stand and divide. The chair counted eighty-eight people present, forty-four on each side of the room.[2]

1. Hector later left the village, moving to a farm southwest of the village. He was almost continuously on the Clam Lake Township board and served several terms as its supervisor.

2. The tie was broken the following week when the candidates cast lots, Saunders winning.

The village trustees immediately demanded of the county that a full-time deputy sheriff be stationed in Clam Lake, and that the village have its own jail. After much bitter debate, the board of supervisors eventually approved a second jail at Clam Lake in 1875, but the only way the village could get county law enforcement was to elect a local man as sheriff. This it proceeded to do, successively electing Jeremiah Shackleton, William Kelley, and Charles C. Dunham to that office.

The discussion of the jail issue in the newspapers over a fifteen-month period in 1874 and 1875 sent the editors to their dictionaries in the quest for new and more calumnious adjectives with which to describe the opposition as they fanned the regional rivalry. Newspapers of the period were typically free-wheeling in style and language, usually politically allied, and often outright party organs. Both the Clam Lake *Weekly News* and the Wexford County *Pioneer* at Sherman were Republican. Democrats were never simply called such; an expressive supply of descriptive adjectives was necessary to properly identify them, "blackguard," "renegade," and "treasonous" being among the more polite.

The same vitriolic verbiage was equally useful in describing the opposite region of the county and its residents. To the Clam Lake *News*, the people at Sherman and those supporting Sherman's retention of the county seat were always the "Sherman ring" or worse. Editor Cooper at Sherman had made the *Pioneer* a temperance paper, so it was consistent—and at times perhaps accurate—to refer to Clam Lake as a "cesspool," "saloon city," "whiskey town," or to suggest that it ought to be "Clam Lake Vile-age and not Village."[3] Both papers were equally adept at labeling the opposing factions as grafters and "tax raiders," and individuals were described in terms so libelous that today's most aggressive editor would flinch.

3. Cooper started the newspaper war in 1872, following the first motion by Chauncey Hollister to move the county seat to Clam Lake, by calling Clam Lake a cesspool and its residents "cesspuddlians." Frazier's *News* got under Cooper's thin skin by replying: "Ill. We regret very much to learn that our friend Cooper of the Wexford County *Pioneer* is seriously indisposed. From what we can learn of the symptoms, we judge the disease is caused by too great a secretion of bile." From there on, Cooper pulled out all the stops.

On March 6, 1875, the Pioneer devoted a lengthy article to Clam Lake's demand for its own jail. Editor Cooper was generous to concede there was no doubt that Clam Lake had more people who needed to be jailed than all the rest of the county, but he viewed it as a wedge in the Clam Lake plot to bilk the treasury by moving the county seat from Sherman. The article concluded that:

> Everyone knows this to be a poacher's snare by a shyster counsellor in the hire of an Indiana money-grabber who will leech out the blood of our taxes to sell the land for a jail and the lumber to build it too. And won't he sell dear. And then he has his eye on the county treasury for the land for a court house in his sodden village where we will be expected to do our county business among the drunkards and bruisers who fill the place.

The Clam Lake *News* replied on March 20 in a relatively restrained tone:

> We have read three columns of filth in the Sherman Pioneer about the motives of the people in Clam Lake. Their motives in attaching Cleon Township by the most underhanded of political connivery doesn't leave them with very clean hands to talk about Clam Lake. Clam Lake has made an offer of free land for a county building and promises to build a better building free than there is at Sherman. The title to the county land at Sherman, we understand, is not even good and money has been squandered on buildings that have cost double what they are worth.

The cost of the county buildings at Sherman had been debated for some time. It was Thomas Ferguson of Sherman who as prosecuting attorney had first raised doubts about the payment to the builder and county treasurer, John Wheeler. The Clam Lake partisans, however, had been quick to pick up the charge and turn it into an accusation of negligence or worse on the part of the Sherman area leadership.

This article, however, was the first published charge that the title to the land on which the courthouse and jail were built was defective. When Henry Clark donated the courthouse site at Sherman, the deed contained language conveying the land to the county "so long as it shall be used for county purposes." In stating the charge, the *News* didn't bother to add that if there was any question about the title, it would be laid to rest by leaving the county seat where it was. Thereafter the statement would simply be made that the county had no title to its county seat.

2.

The part that really rankled the *News,* however, and against which it thundered issue after issue, was Cleon Township. When it was detached from Manistee County and tacked onto Wexford in 1873, adding another vote to the "Sherman ring" on the board of supervisors, Clam Lake had been completely taken by surprise. The author of the scheme, former prosecutor Thomas Ferguson of Sherman, had started his new career in the House of Representatives with an imaginative move. Nothing like it had ever been done by the legislature before, nor has it been done since. People in Lansing spoke of Ferguson as something of a political genius, and perhaps he was inclined to agree. Not the people of Clam Lake. To the southeastern part of the county, he was a traitor.

Notwithstanding that Ferguson was a Republican, or perhaps because of it, the *News* attacked him bitterly. Thereafter he was the "Sherman judas," "slick Tommy," "treacherous Thomas," or "shifty Tom." Any reference to Ferguson was designed to call his honesty or motives into doubt. Thus the usual *News* notice of notables passing through on the train would be expanded as to Ferguson by such comments as: "We are not so fortunate that the larcenous legislator is leaving us permanently," or, ". . . it is rumored that he and H. Brandenburg [his partner] contemplate making an exodus."[4] In its rage over the Cleon maneuver, the

4. In its attacks on Ferguson in his partnership in Brandenburg, Backus & Co., there is no doubt that the *News* was unfair and guilty of libel. It openly accused him of jumping timber claims, called him "pious, log-stealing Tommy," and implied that he was forging commercial paper. There is no evidence to support

Republican *News* even went so far as to support a Democrat, Clam Lake's George Holbrook, in an unsuccessful attempt to unseat Ferguson in 1874.

The Cleon issue was hot again in 1875. A legal opinion was jointly prepared by Clam Lake attorneys McIntyre and Rice with the cooperation of Silas Fallass, concluding that the 1873 act was invalid for technical reasons and recommending a suit to challenge it. It was hoped that this might aid the efforts to get the act repealed. Instead, Representative Ferguson introduced a bill to re-enact it, supported by dozens of petitions allegedly prepared by Manistee residents saying that they didn't want Cleon, and by Cleon residents asking to remain a part of Wexford County.

The *News* was supported by the Grand Traverse *Herald* in its charges that signatures to the petitions were obtained from Manistee saloons for the price of a drink of whiskey and that many of the names were fictitious. John Wheeler described the event this way:

> A messenger was sent to Manistee village with a properly drawn petition and a long list of names was secured. To show how easily one can get names signed to almost any kind of petition, this messenger reported that he would go into a saloon, call up all hands for a drink, pull out his petition and nine out of ten would sign it without reading it or hearing it read. To look at the petition when it came back, one would think that every last citizen of Manistee wanted Cleon to go, and would almost be willing to pay something if she would go.
>
> With petitions by the yard from Wexford County, the names upon which were too often fictitious, and such a formidable petition from Manistee county, it was not very hard to convince the legislature that Wexford county ought to have Cleon.

As one of the chief Sherman strategists, Wheeler undoubtedly understates facts of which he was surely intimately aware. At any rate, Representative Ferguson's colleagues in the legislature were

any of those accusations, and it appears that Ferguson was defrauded by Brandenburg, who really was "pious and log-stealing."

convinced, and Ferguson issued a tongue-in-cheek statement that the petitions persuaded him that the Cleon bill should pass for the benefit of both counties. And pass it did, leaving Cleon to rouse the editorial wrath of the *News* for another six years.

3.

The creation of new votes by organization of additional townships continued to engage the attention of the strategists. In the northeast corner of the county, Survey Township 24 North, Range 9 West, had enough people to justify its separation from Greenwood Township. A petition to do so and organize it as the township of Liberty was introduced in 1874. At the moment, Manton Station was nursing its own ambitions to become the county seat, and both the Sherman and Clam Lake factions viewed those aspirations as something that could be turned to their own advantage. In any case, each faction felt that it was not clearly within the territorial ambit of the other and saw little threat from its creation. The petition was granted without opposition.

Curiously, considering the lack of real controversy over the petition, the session was enlivened by the claim of Philip Frost of Henderson Township that he had been offered a ten-dollar bribe to vote against the petition and to support a move of the county seat to Clam Lake. The culprit, if there was one, was never identified, and no one was every prosecuted. Frost's claim may perhaps be considered suspect since he was the leader of a pro-Sherman faction in Henderson and known to be such.[5] An offer of a bribe to him would have seemed the height of foolishness. Ten dollars wasn't a very plausible sounding bribe, anyway, even with the dollar of 1874.

At any rate Liberty was organized. The first caucus was held under the direction of John Welton, Taylor Gray, and George Blue. Over the coming years, all three were to represent the township as supervisors, along with Rasmus P. Bredahl and M. C.

5. Frost himself was in trouble a few years later in an election fraud in Henderson in which it was charged that he was in the hire of the Sherman faction in a scheme to unseat a pro-Clam Lake supervisor and take office again himself.

Hoffman. As a member of the county board of supervisors, Blue was destined for an intriguing role, of which the inflation of Manton's ambitions was but a prelude.

In 1875 petitions were introduced to detach Survey Township 22 North, Range 11 West, from Antioch and organize it as the township of Summit.[6] The petition was first brought to a special meeting of the county board, called by the Sherman faction, an innovation opening a new period of parliamentary warfare. In this first step, Sherman was eventually successful, and the new township was organized under the name of Boon. The first caucus was held under the direction of William McNitt, John Perkins, and James and John Mansfield, with John Mansfield being elected supervisor. His immediate successors were McNitt and J. Daley.

Except for Cleon and Springville, which consisted of three survey townships, the township political map at the end of 1875 was the same as it is today.

CLEON	WEXFORD	HANOVER	GREEN-WOOD	LIBERTY
	SPRING-VILLE	ANTIOCH	COLFAX	CEDAR CREEK
		BOON	SELMA	HARING
		HENDERSON	CHERRY GROVE	CLAM LAKE

6. The name was derived from the first building erected in the township and called Summit Place. It was a log cabin built at the top of a steep hill on the state road and was intended as a way stop for the stage at which passengers could get shelter while the horses rested after climbing the hill.

4.

When the petition to organize the township of Summit (Boon) was made the subject of a special meeting of the supervisors during the summer of 1875, its sole purpose was to create another vote on the board for the Sherman group. It had no justification in population, for the area was a virtually uninhabited wilderness.[7] Many of the signatures on the petition, in fact, were of people who actually resided in what was to be left of Antioch Township.

The calling of the special meeting by the Sherman group to consider the petition also marked the opening of a new period of tactical parliamentary warfare which was to continue until the county seat battle reached its climax. The board of supervisors was frequently in an evenly divided condition over the next few years. In 1875 the Manton boosters, Warren Seaman and John Welton, from Cedar Creek and Liberty townships, were allied at least temporarily with the Clam Lake faction, and the board divided, 7 to 7, on most matters.

When a legislative body is rather evenly divided, the absence of a single member can be the key to passage of motions or resolutions which he has opposed. A special meeting provided a chance to exploit that possibility. One-third of the board's members could call a special meeting to convene at any place in the county at a stated time by giving written notice to the other members. The trick was to call the meeting on the shortest possible notice and at a place inconvenient for the opposing faction. If the scheme worked, one or more of the opposition might not get to the meeting on time, depriving his faction of a vote. And so a barrage of special meeting notices went out in the next few years.

As in chess or warfare, every offensive move tends to be balanced by a defensive counter-move, and one immediately appeared here. When the board was evenly divided, neither faction would enter the courthouse or any other place at which a special meeting had been called until all of its members were present. If one failed to appear, the rest would go home, leaving the

7. At the time, about the only bona fide residents of the area were the Mansfields, McNitt, Perkins, and Andrew and J. B. Denike. It was not until 1878 that there was any noticeable colonization in the township.

opposition unable to conduct any business for lack of a quorum of the membership.

The situation became so bitter that occasionally special meetings were called by each faction for the same time in different places, and each would demand that the other come to it, with some interesting legal maneuvers employed, as we shall see later.

At times meetings would degenerate into a complete stalemate when, with both factions at full strength, every motion would result in a tie vote. Even regular sessions of the board sometimes continued for days without the members being able to conduct any business, as the most inconsequential matters, and even motions to adjourn, were deadlocked by an evenly divided vote.

The sheer cussedness of most of these meetings is faithfully and wearily documented in the official minutes of the board. A few such meetings are not recorded, and we have only the written recollections of some participants and the newspaper accounts. Perhaps the county clerk grew tired of such fruitless notetaking, or, in the case of some special meetings, perhaps he knew in advance what was going to happen. It may be no accident that during the years when the county clerks were C. J. Manktelow and Thomas Thorp, both of whom were from Selma Township and Clam Lake partisans, there is no record of most of the special meetings called by the Sherman group. But during the term of Heman Sturtevant of Sherman, there is no record of two special meetings called to consider the petition to organize the township of Summit. Reports indicate that the first was a stalemate and that the second failed for lack of a quorum.

The same petition, amended to change the name from Summit to Boon, was resubmitted at the annual meeting of the board. On October 12 the stalemate was broken when the Manton area supervisors, Warren Seaman of Cedar Creek and John Welton of Libery, suddenly switched to vote with the Sherman faction, and the petition was approved by a 9-5 vote.

5.

Clam Lake had been frustrated again. With the growing population in its area, its supporters knew that a popular election to move the county seat to the village was bound to bring them the prize. The obstacle lay in getting the required two-thirds vote of the board of supervisors to call such an election. The addition of Boon Township brought the board membership to fifteen, of which Clam Lake had been left with only five after the defection of the Manton faction. And the presence of a pro-Sherman faction in Henderson Township meant that its vote couldn't be taken for granted.

The response of the Clam Lake strategists recalls the general who, on being told that he was outflanked, replied, "Excellent, I shall attack on all fronts at once." One weapon was the incorporation of the village of Clam Lake as a city. While villages had no representation on the county board of supervisors other than as part of the townships in which they were located, cities were distinct municipal corporations and given separate representation on the board. There was no municipal home rule in the nineteenth century, and cities were created by "local act" of the state legislature. The act of city incorporation would also prescribe the number of supervisors the city would have.

George Mitchell had planned the incorporation of Clam Lake for some time. The legal organization of the village in 1874 had been a step in that direction. In 1876 many of the Clam Lake citizens of consequence made quiet visits around the state calling on members of the legislature. By the end of the year, the groundwork was laid and Clam Lake was assured of the legislative votes to incorporate. The only question was whether it would be given the four supervisors its organizers were asking for.

It wouldn't be enough to merely add more votes to the Clam Lake strength, however. Somehow, if the two-thirds majority was to be acquired, votes had to be weaned away from the Sherman block. Alexander's strategy of "divide and conquer" could be as effective politically as it had been militarily. There were two places to look for weakness: the central and northeastern supervisors. The approach would be the same to each: an appeal to their own ambitions for the county seat.

George Manton, as supervisor of the larger township of Colfax before Cedar Creek had been organized, had voiced the first ambitions in that direction, and the rapid growth of the community bearing his name was matched by an equal growth of civic pride and optimism. The Clam Lake emissaries were quick to play on that pride and to assure Manton's businessmen that they sympathized with Manton's aims and thought Manton more deserving of the county seat than Sherman. It wasn't merely that Manton had several prosperous mills and a growing business district, nor that it had outgrown Sherman in population with every expectation of growing more rapidly in the future. The important thing, in Clam Lake's opinion, they said, was that Manton was accessible to everyone because of its good transportation, situated on the railroad, and with good state roads running east to Lake City and west to Sherman.

The Clam Lake sales pitch was a simple "soft sell." Tell Manton what it wanted to hear and human nature would do the rest: the county seat ought to be accessible by railroad; Manton was ideally located to have the county seat; the county seat would be better off located anywhere along the railroad, even at Hobart (and there was a committee at Hobart for that purpose), than at Sherman, where it was only accessible by stage; Clam Lake would be better off with the county seat at Manton, or Manton would be better off with the county seat at Clam Lake—or even Hobart; Sherman had nothing to offer Manton and had done nothing for Manton.

And so it went, repeated over and over in a dozen different ways. And Manton agreed with every word.

The merchandise sold, of course, was to be a secret treaty of sorts, an agreement by which Clam Lake would support Manton's aims. When a resolution was introduced before the board of supervisors to call an election for the purpose of moving the county seat to Manton, Clam Lake would support it. In return, if all efforts failed on behalf of Manton, Clam Lake asked only that Manton support a similar resolution on behalf of Clam Lake as second choice. The bargain ought to be kept secret, of course, and Clam Lake would continue to make public claim for the county seat. For one thing, it would lull Sherman into a sense of security and prevent it from taking counter-measures. For another, Manton could then be in the position of offering itself as an apparent compromise location which would be more convenient to the northern part of the county than Clam Lake.

The Manton area people were cultivated zealously by Clam

Lake, and they were receptive to the plan. Only one person of all those influential in the planning was really opposed to the idea, and that was Thomas Ferguson. The former prosecutor and legislator was beset by misfortune, and the continuous attacks on his integrity from the Clam Lake *News* had embittered him. He was in poor health, and his wife had died shortly after he was elected to his second term in the House of Representatives. She had taken the personal spite of the campaign badly; Ferguson said it had killed her. His law practice at Sherman had been neglected, and he had lost many friends there by his earlier attacks on John Wheeler. Now, having announced his intention not to run for re-election, he was dividing his time between Manton and Sherman and had opened a law office there. He was on the verge of entering the Brandenburg, Backus & Co. logging firm, and no doubt he had mixed emotions about seeing the county seat moved. After he had been taken into the confidence of the Manton planners, his position was complicated when John Wheeler sought him out as a friend, hired him as his attorney for several lawsuits, and made it clear that he had no hard feelings and respected his abilities. And, of course, his brother-in-law, Heman Sturtevant, was at Sherman and was a leader in his own right there. He was, in fact, presently the county clerk. Ferguson's loyalties were strained.

As events transpired, Ferguson made the move, sold his Sherman hotel, bought into Brandenburg, Backus & Co., and bought some Manton business properties for investment purposes. He worked hard on behalf of Manton's efforts for the county seat. He traveled the county, made trips to Lansing to lobby for incorporation of Manton as a village,[8] and spent his own money freely in the process. He couldn't bring himself to deceit or to make personal attacks on Sherman's leaders. And nothing could bring him to trust or like Clam Lake. He bitterly opposed the secret deal. He may have had a hand in sidetracking it temporarily.

Ferguson was the exception. The Manton leaders bit, hook, line, and sinker. Even George Wheeler of Greenwood Township

8. Noted by the *News* as follows: "Manton attorney T. A. Ferguson and Judge Mears were in town and later went south on the A. M. Train. What game of political jugglery is to be played now?"

joined the plan and kept it a secret from his brothers John and Edgar, who were also serving on the county board at the time. There was some wavering over the next few years, but Manton stuck loyally to its bargain. Had it known that Clam Lake was trying the same bargain with others, it might have suspected that the eventual success of the scheme would lead to betrayal.

6.

Unknown to Manton's leaders, who were committing themselves to the secret agreement with Clam Lake in the spring of 1876, spokesmen for Clam Lake were proposing the same secret bargain to the supervisor from Colfax Township, Nathan Dayhuff. It was the same sort of sales pitch: "Forget Manton and Sherman," it went; "they can't win in the long run. What the county needs is to have the county seat right in the center of the county, where it is equally accessible to everyone. When it finally comes down to a compromise, Clam Lake will support you and the rest of the county will have to go along. Clam Lake asks only one thing: If all our best efforts fail, you back us as second choice."

The Meauwataka settlement on the south side of Colfax Township was close to the geographic center of the county. Since the opening of the post office there in July of 1873, it had grown considerably. There were enough people living there that it wasn't unreasonable to stir up aspirations for a village charter and the county seat. Besides, there were always the economic factors to be considered. There was talk of a crosscounty railroad and it could very well go by way of Meauwataka. And, while the Dayhuffs were not the kind of people who could be approached crudely, it was true that the family's land holdings, including an ideal site for a courthouse, would increase in value if the county seat were moved.

If Clam Lake was zealous, it was also subtle. If Dayhuff bought the idea, he would undoubtedly seek support from Boon, an area where the Clam Lake supporters hesitated to tread because of the strong Sherman ties of the Mansfields. Dayhuff was non-committal, but they didn't press him. The seeds had been sown.

At the next session of the board of supervisors, on June 14, 1876, Warren Seaman of Cedar Creek introduced a resolution to call an election on the question of moving the county seat to

Manton Station. As promised, the Clam Lake faction supported the resolution, with the exception of Elisha Caswell of Henderson Township. George Wheeler of Greenwood abandoned Sherman to vote for the resolution, but it lost, 8 to 7.

William Kelley of Clam Lake then introduced a similar resolution for a move to Clam Lake. Manton supported it and Caswell returned to the fold. It carried by a simple majority, 8 to 7, but was short of the necessary two-thirds vote. Two more votes were needed.

During the remainder of 1876 efforts to get those votes were pursued feverishly. The lobbying in preparation for the incorporation of Clam Lake was completed, and perhaps as many as four votes for the new city seemed likely in 1877. The Manton deal was repledged, and Clam Lake supported Manton's legislative request for a village charter. More direct and personal efforts were also made, which were to have unfortunate repercussions.

7.

By township, the regional factions lined up like this in 1876:

Clam Lake — 5	*Sherman — 7*	*Manton — 3*
Clam Lake	Cleon	Greenwood
Cherry Grove	Wexford	Liberty
Henderson	Springville	Cedar Creek
Haring	Antioch	
Selma	Boon	
	Hanover	
	Colfax	

CLEON	WEXFORD	HANOVER	GREEN-WOOD	LIBERTY
	SPRING-VILLE	ANTIOCH	COLFAX	CEDAR CREEK
		BOON	SELMA	HARING
		HENDERSON	CHERRY GROVE	CLAM LAKE

Thus, even if Manton remained allied with Clam Lake, as it had been in the June meeting of the county board, Clam Lake still had only eight votes, two votes short of the necessary two-thirds. If Dayhuff of Colfax switched, there was still one more vote required. Looking ahead to the incorporation of the village, with three or four new representatives on the board, Clam Lake could get by with the Manton group and Colfax. But there was no assurance that Dayhuff would switch. Clam Lake set out to get itself another vote by direct means.

This was an era when politics was often a heavy-handed sort of proposition. Graft and corruption had been prevalent in the country and widely publicized. Politically allied newspapers were eager to publish evidence of the misdeeds of their opponents and just as quick to publish accusations without evidence. There was no reason to expect people to be any different locally, and accusations and rumors abounded to the effect that Clam Lake hadn't confined its county seat campaign to purely parliamentary efforts. Stories of threats, blackmail, and bribery were prevalent. Clam Lake had always claimed that money changed hands in Lansing when Cleon Township was attached to the county, and J. W. Ransom was to present evidence before the board of supervisors in 1879 that Clam Lake citizens had bought legislative support for an act dissolving the township of Sherman.

Some of the charges were undoubtedly true, some were merely gossip, and others were probably deliberate propaganda tactics. The first such claim of local corruption had been Philip Frost's 1874 allegation of a ten-dollar bribe offer. In the fall of 1876, however, there was a genuine and more lucrative bribe attempt made by one or more people in Clam Lake. The principals involved were never named in any public proceeding or newspaper account, but contemporary accounts indicate that the person offering the bribe, though unnamed, was well known. The finger of suspicion points rather strongly at George A. Mitchell himself.

Neither was the person identified to whom the bribe was offered. Accounts the following year, and by John Wheeler later, agree in describing him as living near Sherman, being a new member of the board, and having encountered financial misfortune. Wilson Odell, the new supervisor from Wexford Township, lived near

Sherman, and he was broke. In poor health,[9] which had prevented his farming effectively, he was in default in the payments on his farm and faced foreclosure. There isn't much doubt that he was the person involved.

Odell's financial problems became known in Clam Lake, and a friend was prevailed upon to sound him out with a job offer, an offer that would be alluring to a man in poor health. He was interested and the bait was enlarged. It was suggested that he might get some help in buying a house in Clam Lake, and perhaps a buyer could be found for his farm before the contract was foreclosed. Maybe he could use some cash right away to get on his feet financially. And maybe he could do a favor in return: if he were going to move to Clam Lake, he could just as well bring the county seat with him!

Odell couldn't refrain from telling a neighbor the good news that he was going to get $300, have his money out of the farm, and get a decent job and a free house and lot in Clam Lake, just for voting to move the county seat. The neighbor passed it on, and it soon reached the ears of county clerk H. B. Sturtevant. Sturtevant had just been defeated by C. J. Manktelow of Selma Township, an ardent Clam Lake supporter. While he would no longer be the clerk when the board of supervisors next met, Sturtevant proposed to see to it that there were some surprises for Clam Lake at that meeting.

Sturtevant contacted John Wheeler and attorney Charles Marr, and they called together the area supervisors and business leaders. Isaac and H. J. Carpenter, Alonzo Chubb, Sylvester Clark, Herman Meyer, William Dean, and Edgar Wheeler were among those at the meeting. The first thing that had to be done was to keep Odell in the fold. He was visited. No one minced any words. If Odell had troubles, he could expect the help of good neighbors. If he made trouble, Clam Lake wasn't far enough away to be safe. He was told to keep quiet and play along with the bribe offer—and to remember that there would be a lot of people at-

9. His health continued to deteriorate over the next few years, and he was bedridden and died in January of 1881.

tending the next supervisors meeting just to keep an eye on him. He was convinced.

Although the Sherman group was not aware of the secret deal between Clam Lake and Manton, the voting at the June session of the board of supervisors had made it clear that something was up and that the supervisors from the Manton area had to be spiked down. Of the three Wheeler brothers on the board, only George of Greenwood Township, who had voted with the Manton group, was not included in the Sherman strategy meetings. Shortly before the end of the year, his brothers called on him and warned him that there had been a bribery attempt made in the county seat matter. The supervisor who had been compromised, they told him, was Warren Seaman of Cedar Creek, and he should be careful not to appear to be allied with Seaman! The stage was set for one of the wildest sessions of the supervisors ever held—and for the incredible year of 1877.

Chapter Thirteen

A PLOT FOILED AND A CITY NAMED: 1877, Part I

With all the intrigue and conniving going on behind the scenes in 1876, as Clam Lake pursued its efforts to get the county seat, it is not surprising that rumors leaked out that something was afoot. In that respect, the unusual thing about the Clam Lake plan to buy Wilson Odell's vote is not that it was discovered by the Sherman group, but that their knowledge and counter-measures were such a well-kept secret.

It is impossible, of course, to pick and sort rumors. It seems to have been in the wind that Clam Lake was trying to buy *two* supervisors. Perhaps there was substance behind the rumor, for if Nathan Dayhuff wasn't buying the arrangement to give its second vote to Clam Lake, Odell's vote alone wouldn't be enough. There is no evidence that anyone else was contacted, and Wheeler refers to only the one case. But interestingly enough, Clam Lake did come up with another vote from an unexpected source.

Another interesting thing about the rumors is that, while there was never any mention of Odell, a story began to circulate late in December specifically naming Warren Seaman of Cedar Creek as the recipient of a large bribe from Clam Lake. There is nothing to indicate any truth to the accusation, and it seems quite inconsistent with the opinion his contemporaries held of his character.

Seaman was born in New York in 1834 and moved to southern Michigan while he was very young. He lived in Hillsdale, then Casnovia briefly, then homesteaded in Mecosta County in 1855. He sold his farm there at a profit and came farther north in 1869, having the first homestead in what was to become Cedar Creek Township. From the first log cabin, he moved to a frame home a few years later and added more acreage to his original eighty-acre farm, most of which he put into fruit orchards. He was one of the early members of the Methodist congregation at Manton, and he seems to have had an impeccable reputation for honesty and to have been known as a hard-working, generous, and kindly man. His neighbors gave him a variety of public offices, which included seven terms as township supervisor, those in later years being good indication that the bribe rumor was generally disbelieved.

If Seaman had no great loyalty to Sherman, there was no particular reason why he should have, or why he shouldn't feel a higher loyalty to Manton. He was one of the key men in the secret deal with Clam Lake which he thought would bring the county seat to Manton, and he had introduced the resolution for that purpose at the June session of the county board.

Because of the repercussions of the rumor, it is worth speculating about its source. If we begin with the assumption that Seaman was innocent and that the rumor was false, the course of events clearly warrants the further assumption that the story was deliberately and maliciously put into circulation to destroy Seaman's influence. From these assumptions, there seem to be three possible explanations.

The first possibility is that someone in the Manton area, seeing his vote on the second resolution at the June session, concluded that Seaman had betrayed Manton and started the rumor for vengeance or to destroy him politically.

A second possibility is that someone in the Manton area who had knowledge of the agreement with Clam Lake, and disapproved of Manton's commitment to support Clam Lake as a second choice, started the rumor as a means of getting rid of one of the leaders of the compact. Specifically, one of the members of the cast in our historic drama could fit the bill—Thomas A. Ferguson. He was willing, perhaps even eager now, to have the county seat in Manton, but he disapproved of the dealings with the Clam Lake leaders towards whom he was personally embittered, and he wisely felt they couldn't be trusted. The part that his partner, Harry Brandenburg, played in broadcasting the rumors about Seaman and stirring up local action against him might lend some support to the theory.

It is equally possible that the same explanation could place the blame on Brandenburg alone, either from his disapproval of the bargain with Clam Lake or to further his own personal ambitions. The handing out of liquor to a mob doesn't sound like Ferguson, a rigid prohibitionist and a devout Methodist. Of course, the

Reverend Mr. Brandenburg was a Methodist, too, and Seaman was a member of the same congregation, but there are some peculiar aspects to Brandenburg's character.

The third possibility is that the rumor was a plant by the Sherman faction, designed to put the heat of local public opinion on Seaman and the other Manton area supervisors. With reports circulating that Clam Lake had bought Seaman's vote, neither he nor Taylor Gray of Liberty Township would find it easy to abandon Manton and support Clam Lake. And if they merely held firm for Manton, the county seat was secure at Sherman. One of the circumstances supporting this theory is the call that John and Edgar Wheeler made on their brother George of Greenwood to warn him of bribery reports. George had voted in June for Manton on the first resolution and for Clam Lake on the second. Although his brothers had knowledge of the Odell bribe attempt, they did not disclose it to George. Instead, they told him that Seaman was involved. Whether they were starting the rumor, or had heard it and believed it, or were merely using it to try to separate George from Seaman, we can only speculate. The fact remains they did tell him, and they did conceal from him their knowledge of the real attempt.

At any rate, whatever the original source or reason, the story about Seaman spread in the Manton area. And whatever the motive, Ferguson opposed Seaman, and Brandenburg actively incited a rising tide of sentiment against him.

2.

At the other end of the county, things were getting a little thick in Henderson Township, where a special meeting of the township board was held to act on the resignation of supervisor Elisha B. Caswell. Caswell seemed to represent the majority sentiment of the township in supporting Clam Lake's ambitions for the county seat. The township, however, had a small but active pro-Sherman faction, led by township clerk George Johnson and former supervisor Philip Frost of the "ten-dollar bribe."

Among those present at the meeting were Harry Brandenburg from Manton and Charles S. Marr, an attorney who had settled at

Sherman in 1875. The presence of such distinguished outsiders at a town meeting in Henderson might be surprising. Even more surprising, the resigning supervisor, Caswell, was not present. In fact he claimed that not only had he known nothing of the meeting, he hadn't even known about his resignation! The board, however, accepted it and appointed Frost as supervisor to fill out the term until the election the following April.

3.

Special meetings of the county board had become customary in January, so there was nothing unusual about the notices which the Clam Lake area supervisors asked the new county clerk, C. J. Manktelow, to mail to the rest of the board. The meeting was called for January 9 at Sherman, and Clam Lake intended it to be the last such meeting there. In voting the previous June, Clam Lake's resolution had carried, 8 to 7, only two votes short of the necessary two-thirds. Clam Lake believed that it had one vote from Odell. It either believed that Nathan Dayhuff of Colfax had bought the same bargain as Manton and would go for Clam Lake as a second choice, or else there was truth to the rumor that there were *two* supervisors to be bribed. At any rate, Clam Lake was confident that after going through the motions of voting for Manton and Meauwataka, the Clam Lake resolution would pass, 10 to 5.

So confident were the Clam Lake partisans that a large delegation went to Sherman to watch the fun. The Clam Lake *News* reported that "a number of our citizens are spending this pleasant weather at Sherman, just twenty-eight miles from somewhere." Among those citizens were attorney S. S. Fallass, village clerk and attorney David Rice, and most of the village trustees. George Mitchell arrived on a handsome horse, accompanied by J. W. Cobbs and three wagon loads of mill hands, who, it was said, were prepared to load the county records into the wagons and return them to Clam Lake as soon as the board voted—and without awaiting the formality of the expected public referendum.

The Clam Lake faction began to suspect that everything wasn't going to be cut and dried when Wilson Odell, the man they thought they had bought, was accompanied into town by a sizable band of lumberjacks. The Sherman faction had an assist from lumberman William McClintock, who had a logging camp four miles upriver from Sherman. He had turned his men into town with pay to support the throng of residents of the Sherman area who were in town to see that things went the right way.

The possibilities of open warfare seemed increased by the arrival of the Manton delegation accompanied by an angry throng. Seaman was not among them.

4.

> MANTON-News that the Cedar Creek Twp. Supervisor would vote to move the county seat to Clam Lake brought out a large meeting at Town Hall and the supervisor resigned. Mr. Brandenburg replaced him. The whole delegation then went with him to Sherman. They have not returned so we don't know the outcome.
>
> (Dispatch from Manton, Jan. 9, 1877)

The weekend at Manton had been a nightmare for Seaman and his family. As Monday's special meeting had neared, the rumors against Seaman had reached fever pitch, fueled by an abundant supply of whiskey. The Manton saloons ignored the Sunday closing ordinance more openly than usual, and it was claimed that "the pious Tommy Ferguson and his Methodist angel, Rev. Harry Brandenburg," had something to do with it. By evening, a surly mob was an evident threat to Seaman's safety.

The events of the night and the parts played by Ferguson and Brandenburg are unclear, and the insinuation that they were the ringleaders comes from partisan Clam Lake sources. The climax came before dawn, when Seaman was forcibly taken from his home and escorted to the Cedar Creek Town Hall. There the mob called a caucus and presented Seaman with a choice of consequences. He chose the simplest and safest alternative by immediately resigning as township supervisor. The crowd then proceeded to elect Harry Brandenburg as the new supervisor and, whether to guarantee his safety, or to make certain he was seated as Cedar Creek's supervisor, or to be sure he voted right, set forth with him to the courthouse at Sherman. One can imagine the dismay of the Clam Lake faction when a new supervisor showed up from Cedar Creek, accompanied by Mr. Ferguson and a belligerent escort.

The meeting had been called for 10:00 that Monday morning. William East of Cherry Grove did not arrive and, after some delay, the Clam Lake faction decided to enter the courthouse without him. To their surprise, only Dayhuff, Odell, Brandenburg, and Gray were present. The Sherman faction was in town, but obviously playing some kind of game. There being no quorum, the meeting adjourned until after lunch.

When the meeting reconvened at 1:30, there was no question as to where the control of the meeting lay. Both Elisha Caswell and Philip Frost were present, each claiming to be the lawful supervisor from Henderson Township. What could have been the first battle of the regional war failed to materialize, as it was evident that the Sherman group had more than enough votes to seat Frost. John Wheeler's motion to the effect received only perfunctory objections. The seating of Brandenburg to replace Seaman was accomplished without objection.

The original Clam Lake strategy, which called for the introduction of successive resolutions on moving the county seat, was now impossible. The first resolution, to call an election on the question of a move to Manton, was to have been introduced by the deposed Seaman. His replacement, Brandenburg, was hostile.

The Clam Lake faction elected to play for time while it tried to work out a new plan. The afternoon was consumed by long debate on a few trivial matters, and the board finally adjourned until the next morning. Attempts that night to buttonhole individual supervisors, however, proved futile. Brandenburg attached himself to Taylor Gray of Liberty, and it proved impossible to talk to Gray alone. Wilson Odell spent the night with "friends." Nathan Dayhuff couldn't be found. George Wheeler couldn't refuse an invitation to spend the night at the home of his brother John.

Frustrated, the Clam Lake planners concluded that they would drag out the session as long as possible, try to rebuild their bridges, and hope that something would break eventually. They also decided that it wouldn't hurt to recruit additional delegations from other parts of the county to add persuasion and muscle to the parliamentary moves.

Tuesday was a boring, tedious, and frustrating day. Practically everything in the realm of county business except the location of the county seat was brought up and interminably discussed. In an attempt to conclude the session, the Sherman faction forced an evening meeting, but the Clam Lake group managed to put off consideration of several important matters, and the board finally adjourned until 8:00 the next morning. Off the floor, the Clam Lake strategists could accomplish little, but the crowded and already tense village saw an additional group of mill hands from Bond's Mill arrive, along with smaller groups from Selma and Colfax and a hastily organized rival group from Cedar Creek, to protest that Brandenburg was not their legal supervisor.

The town was jammed with "citizens" from around the county, many of whom were mill hands, jacks, and river drivers brought along by their bosses to lend strength to their regional claims. According to John Wheeler, the tension was heightened not only by whiskey, but by money as well, many of the Clam Lake group having wagered beyond their means at two-to-one odds that they would take the county records with them when they left. Now they could see their money taking wing. Tuesday night was a noisy one. The streets and the jail were full, and everyone knew things had to come to a head the next morning.

On Wednesday morning, the 11th, the courthouse was packed long before the supervisors' session opened at 8:00, and late-coming supervisors had difficulty getting through the crowd in the street. Several routine matters brought mutterings from the crowd. Then R. D. Cuddeback of Haring rose and offered a resolution calling for an election to move the county seat to the village of Clam Lake. There were to be no preliminary resolutions about moves to Manton or Meauwataka, just a desperation move: vote and get it over.

Cuddeback had not completed reading his resolution when the room exploded in sound and fury. Everyone who had crowded into the room wanted a chance to speak on the subject. The chairman, John Mansfield of Boon, finally brought the meeting to reasonable order by threatening to have everyone present arrested. An undisciplined argument among the board over who should be permitted to be heard was finally ended and chaos averted by the passage of a motion offered by Brandenburg.

The Brandenburg motion stunned the Clam Lake delegation. It had been obviously prepared in advance with the knowledge of the Sherman supervisors. Not only did the Sherman supervisors have things cut and dried, but they were using Brandenburg to rub salt in the wounds. The resolution provided reasonably that each faction present should have an opportunity to speak an hour on the subject; but only four delegations were recognized—Sherman, Manton, Clam Lake, and Bond's Mill. Either Colfax and Cherry Grove were being snubbed or their delegations hadn't been able to get inside the courthouse to be recognized.

A second motion by Brandenburg, again sweetly reasonable in the interests of order, specified that each delegation could have but one speaker for the hour. In order to insure that he spoke with authority, the delegation would have to caucus, elect a president and secretary, and pick its representative by ballot. The chosen speaker would then be admitted to the supervisor's meeting at 1:30 in the afternoon only upon presentation of written credentials signed by the caucus officers. The snickers from the Sherman supporters in the audience nearly drowned out the motion to adjourn for the morning.

When the board reconvened in the afternoon, it was apparent that the fun was over. The Clam Lake and Bond's Mill groups hadn't even bothered to caucus, and most of their leaders had pulled up stakes and headed home, taking their mill hands with them. Only a small, and brave, handful of loyal supporters remained with the supervisors of the Clam Lake group amid the jubilant Sherman backers. The only representatives to appear and present credentials to address the board were former clerk H. B. Sturtevant to speak for Sherman, and his brother-in-law Tom Ferguson, to speak for Manton.

And how they savored their victory! Both spoke well over the hour time limit, as they poured forth their best oratorical wrath on the supervisors from the southeast part of the county. Sturtevant dwelt at length on the attempt to bribe Odell and roused the bystanders to shouts of indignation and threats against the hapless Clam Lake supervisor, Byron Ballou. Ferguson started in where Sturtevant left off. And he, too, ultimately pilloried Ballou. This was the man, he said, who would speak for corruptors, who "would take our government into the halls of the bagnios and saloons." Clam Lake Village should be spelled VILE-AGE, he said, taking editor Cooper's line from the *Pioneer*. But the people of the county would never permit the seat of government to be corrupted by locating there. "It is written that 'your sin will find you out,' and it has," he said, pointing at Ballou. "The matter is forever done, for your sins have found you out and will never be forgotten."

When Ferguson finished on this note, supervisor William Dean of Springville, tongue-in-cheek, expressed amazement that there were no certified representatives from Clam Lake or Bond's Mill and offered a motion to permit anyone else interested in addressing the board to have fifteen minutes for that purpose. The motion carried and several other persons from Sherman spoke. The board then debated the question. The word "debate" is perhaps euphemistic, as is the clerk's minute that there was "an animated discussion." Ballou and Cuddeback attacked Ferguson and Brandenburg savagely in their remarks, and Frost and Cuddeback are reported to have come to blows.

When the roll was finally called, the resolution was defeated by a vote of 8 to 5. Brandenburg was excused from voting on the ground that there was a pending petition from Manton residents asking that the county seat be moved there. Clam Lake had not only failed to get close to the necessary two-thirds vote but had lost ground.

According to Wheeler's history, when the vote was announced to the crowd outside the courthouse, "a great shout went up from the people of Sherman over the defeat of their enemies. . . . The Sherman people were so sure that they would come out ahead that they had prepared to celebrate their victory by the firing of anvils, and had already commenced this work when Mr. George A. Mitchell came along on horseback, having started his return home, and begged the boys to desist until he could get by with his horse. This request was cheerfully complied with and after he had ridden past he was given a parting salute." Others remembered it differently or were not the beneficiaries of similar good cheer, as the crowd vented its wrath on the bribers and threatened a coat of tar and feathers.

But Ferguson was wrong. The matter was not forever done, notwithstanding the disclosure of Clam Lake's sin. The planning went on. From the wreckage of the special session, Clam Lake had picked up an ally. Board chairman John Mansfield had been an avowed Sherman supporter. For some reason, with the referendum resolution obviously doomed to defeat, he had switched to the losing side and had cast his vote with the Clam Lake faction. No one has ever explained his switch, and in the atmosphere of Sherman on January 11, it probably required considerable courage. Whatever the reason, he remained in the Clam Lake camp, as did Will McNitt, his successor as supervisor, after Mansfield was elected county treasurer.

5.

The efforts of Clam Lake to get a public referendum on moving the county seat seemed totally demolished after the debacle at Sherman. Far from obtaining the necessary two-thirds vote of the county supervisors at January's special session, the Clam Lake faction had lost strength, and the referendum resolution had been defeated by an 8-5 vote, with opponents Harry Brandenburg of Manton not voting and Chubb of Cleon absent. The disclosure of an attempt by unnamed Clam Lake supporters to bribe supervisor Wilson Odell would be presumed to cause a lasting public distrust of Clam Lake leadership, and, indeed, no one doubted the truth of the charge.

But Clam Lake was resilient. Right or wrong, more people lived in the southeast corner of the county than in the rest of the county combined, and they were as determined as their leaders to get the county seat by hook or crook. The attempted Odell bribery had been unsuccessful, but what about the Sherman scheming in Henderson Township and at Manton? With only a brief pause to assess the damage, Clam Lake returned to the attack, strengthened by the addition of John Mansfield of Boon, who somehow had been wooed away from the Sherman camp.

A look at Henderson Township indicated that its defection to Sherman was only temporary. The special board meeting at which Elisha Caswell's supposed resignation had been accepted and

Philip Frost named to succeed him as supervisor, had apparently been too crudely handled, and sentiment was considered to be running strongly against Frost and the township board. Job Hoxie was talking about running against Frost in the spring election, and it was believed that either he or Caswell could beat Frost easily, returning Henderson's vote to the Clam Lake side.

The "divide and conquer" strategy for splitting the northeast and central supervisors away from Sherman was not to be abandoned either. The secret agreement, by which Clam Lake had agreed to support the Manton area's aspirations for the county seat in return for the promise of the Manton area supervisors to vote for Clam Lake as a second choice, hadn't really failed. There simply had never been a chance to put the plan into operation after Cedar Creek supervisor Warren Seaman was literally run out of office by a mob. Clam Lake credited Thomas Ferguson with master-minding the event, since his logging partner, Harry Brandenburg, had been picked by the rump caucus to replace Seaman as supervisor. If Brandenburg could be beaten in the spring election, the strategy still might succeed.

The raw material was there. Seaman had many friends, and people were beginning to take a second look at the charges that had been circulated about him. And Ferguson and Brandenburg had their enemies. There were the rumors about the honesty of Brandenburg and the financial soundness of Brandenburg, Backus & Co. The Clam Lake *News* began to print such reports and on March 2, 1877, carried a story accusing Ferguson of claiming "phony tax titles" as a guise for cutting other people's timber. The story concluded: "This reminds us of the words used by Mr. Ferguson in his eloquent production before the Board of Supervisors at Sherman, 'Your Sin will find you out.' "

The *News* hammered at Ferguson and at the partnership. Brandenburg, Backus & Co. was on the verge of collapse, and Ferguson charged that its problems were the result of a political plot by his Clam Lake enemies. He claimed that Clam Lake merchants went so far as to file phony lawsuits against the partnership for the purpose of destroying it. Whatever their merit, the court files show that there was a flood of lawsuits commenced against the partnership. In a period when financial panics were easily caused, the publicity was undoubtedly harmful. The *News* comment that the partners of B., B. & Co. were preparing to skip for other parts may well have been the last straw, and the business closed its doors shortly after the April election. At the election, Harry Brandenburg was decisively defeated by a Seaman friend, Ward P. Smith. Brandenburg disappeared and the influence of Ferguson was ended.

In little over five years, Harry Brandenburg had made a big splash and had left bigger ripples in the Manton millpond. He came in 1872 as stationmaster for the G. R. & I., and was looking for ways to make a profit out of the new area from the beginning. He was also an organizer and a man with strong opinions, as Ezra Harger nicely put it. Others called him opinionated, overbearing, and bullheaded. He started the first Methodist church meetings, using the depot as the meeting place, and was licensed as a local minister by that church. Many of the early settlers were of that denomination, and he soon had a fair-sized congregation. He organized a union Sunday school for the village, but ultimately aggravated both his own congregation and the participants from the other churches so much that it was discontinued.

Brandenburg started the first sawmill in Manton, and the railroad was soon complaining that he was spending more time running the mill or hiking the countryside in search of pine land than he was in attending to railroad business. Most of their stationmasters did have other interests, so his neglect of duty must have been substantial to warrant complaint. Brandenburg chose to force the issue and found himself in the position of having resigned.

At almost the same time, however, he was appointed postmaster at Manton, and his lumber business seemed to be prospering. He soon linked up with Nathaniel Backus and James Glover in a partnership under the firm name of Brandenburg, Backus & Co.[1] When Thomas Ferguson came to Manton, he invested all the proceeds from the sale of his Sherman hotel, the Grant House,

1. Nathaniel Backus and his cousins Albert and Absolom did business as Backus Brothers. It was one of the leading lumber firms on the Lake Huron side of the state, and each of the members entered into a number of partnerships with operating loggers elsewhere as a means of reaping the extensive pine holdings they had scattered around the central part of the state. Brandenburg, Backus &

and more, for the purchase of an interest in the apparently profitable firm, not knowing that there were already rumors about fraud by Brandenburg in land dealings in Roscommon County. In retrospect, it appears that the firm was already insolvent when Ferguson bought in, and the substantial sum he paid for purchase of an interest was used by Brandenburg to cover his tracks and stave off the final reckoning. When Brandenburg left for Minnesota in the spring of 1877, never to return, it was found that he took the books of account with him, that there were many other unpaid creditors in addition to those who were suing, and that large sums of money had been diverted from the firm from the beginning.[2] Glover had nothing, so it was left to Ferguson and Backus to settle with the creditors as best they could. Ferguson's health took another bad turn, and he moved to Grand Rapids to practice law, returning to Manton shortly before his death in 1883.

If the Manton area did not rush at once to re-ally itself with Clam Lake, at least its ties with Sherman were weakened. The departure of Manton's two bitterest opponents of Clam Lake made it easier for Manton to allow itself to indulge its own ambitions without sufficient skepticism about the promises of Clam Lake.

6.

With the convening of a new session of the legislature in January of 1877, the immediate task at hand for Clam Lake was

Co. was one such venture in which Nathaniel Backus was basically an inactive partner, his contribution to the partnership being capital in the form of pine lands which he owned in Missaukee, Kalkaska, Roscommon, and Crawford counties. Brandenburg managed the business end of the operation and the sawmill, while Glover was a logger.

2. The shortage, which exceeded $25,000 over a period of twenty months, seems too large to have been caused by simple mismanagement. There is nothing to indicate that Brandenburg had secreted funds, nor is there anything to indicate where the money went, as by gambling, speculation, etc. In a book, *The Traverse Region*, published by H. R. Page in 1884, some unknown member of the Methodist congregation at Manton contributed this epitaph for the departed Brandenburg: "He seemed to gradually lose the place which he held in the hearts of the people and finally lost his power to accomplish good among this people."

the pursuit of its plan to create new votes for itself on the board of supervisors by incorporating as a city. The groundwork had been laid during the latter part of 1876, and the necessary votes for the incorporation act seemed assured in both houses. It was originally hoped that the act would divide the city into four wards, each with its own vote on the county board. This would have given the new city somewhat greater representation than other cities of comparable size. The bill was introduced by Sen. Marsden Burch of Hersey, a business associate of Delos Blodgett. Senator Burch felt that the bill would have a better chance of passing if it provided for only three supervisors, and it was introduced in that form.[3]

Clam Lake took great pains to conceal its plans to incorporate, hoping to avoid opposition from the remainder of the county. The bill was drawn by Silas S. Fallass and was prepared in its entirety with blanks where the name of the city and the area involved were to appear. Fallass, Mitchell, and Daniel McCoy spent the first part of February in Lansing following up the contacts of the previous year. Everything was in such good order, and Fallass and Senator Burch had things so well organized, that the bill was introduced and reported out of committee at the end of February with the name of the city still left blank.

In planning their legislative strategy, it had been agreed that, when the bill came to a vote and it was necessary to insert a name, some name other than Clam Lake would be used. Mitchell had been in favor of renaming the community for several years. With Big Clam Lake, Little Clam Lake, Clam Lake River, and the township of Clam Lake, he had grown heartily sick of the sound of Clam Lake Village. A new name would not only be more euphonious, but it might help the bill progress unrecognized by the opposition. The latter hope didn't materialize, the bill being promptly spotted and publicized for what it was, but it didn't matter.

On March 2, 1877, the *News* made its first reference to the bill although nothing in the carefully worded statement identified the place which was to be incorporated:

3. The three wards were laid out as follows: First Ward, west of Mitchell Street and north of West Mason Street; Second Ward, east of Mitchell Street and north of Cass Street; Third Ward, south of West Mason and Cass streets.

A bill has been introduced in the legislature to incorporate the City of Cadillac. The name is in honor of Antoine De La Mothe Cadillac who made the first permanent settlement at Detroit in 1701.

Several days later the Detroit *Post* carried a long story on the Burch bill to incorporate the city of Cadillac. The place was clearly identified. The actual population of the town, it said, was only about 800, but it was the "headquarters of a large floating population numbered by the thousands whose home is in the lumber camps or wherever they happen to be." The ordinary machinery of village government was inadequate to provide proper government in such circumstances, it said, since the town contained many saloons and houses of prostitution, and at any given time there might be as many as 500 "red sashed" woodsmen frequenting these disorderly places and behaving as disorderly persons.

With these problems, said the *Post*, and with its mills, lumber storage yards, factories, and wooden buildings, all peculiarly susceptible to destruction by fire, it was apparent that it required a regular city police force and fire department, available only under municipal machinery.[4]

The foregoing probably reflected an interview with Fallass, who was to stay in Lansing most of March keeping watch over the bill. The community's widespread reputation as a tough town would surely bring inquiry, and what better reason for the incorporation than an announced intention of cleaning up the vice? The *Post* article, however, went on to detail the real reasons for the bill. The settlement contained half the people of the county (untrue if its population was only 800), and paid half of the county taxes (also untrue), yet it shared with the rural township only one-fifteenth representation on the board of supervisors. If the bill became law, the city would have three wards, and it and the surrounding town-

4. This was the formal argument advanced in support of the bill, and it was repeated over the next few weeks by the *News*. A month after the city came into existence, however, the *News* referred to a petition for the hiring of a night watch as unnecessary, the sheriff being considered sufficient law enforcement for the city.

ship would thus have four supervisors on a board of eighteen instead of sharing one on a board of fifteen. Even then, said the story, the smallest ward of the new city would have a greater population than the largest township in the county.

The March 2 issue of the *News*, which first mentioned the Burch bill, carried another brief note: Former representative Thomas A. Ferguson had passed through town on the G. R. & I. en route to the state capital. On March 9, there being no further need to speak cautiously, the *News* was full of discussion about the pending legislation. Ferguson came in for his share of space:

> The Honorable T. A. Ferguson appears before the legislature in the light of a trifler. He is there opposing the incorporation of Clam Lake on the grounds of lack of population. All of his underhanded tricks for which his career as a legislator was solely notorious are being employed.

The article went on to predict that the lobbying efforts of "pious, log-stealing Tommy," would prove fruitless.

In this prediction, the *News* was correct. By the time the March 9 edition came off the press, the bill had already passed the Senate by a vote of 29 to 2. A few nuisance attempts were made to amend the bill in the House of Representatives by one of Ferguson's old associates, including an amendment to name the new city Clam Union, but they were defeated, and the bill was passed and sent to the governor in time to permit the first officers of the new city to be elected at the April election. The new city celebrated, and the former Clam Lake *News* proudly appeared on March 30 with a new banner, *The Cadillac Weekly News.*

Credit for the choice of the name Cadillac goes to lumberman Charles Ayers. In a conversation with Ayers and Henry May in which George Mitchell was telling them of the Lansing situation, Mitchell suggested that the two get together with Ayers' partner, Dan McCoy, and come up with a name for the city. May wanted a name with the word lake in it, but Ayers came up with Cadillac after the French governor.[5] McCoy was on the fence.[6] McCoy and

5. In later life, Ayers could not explain why the name occurred to him. He did have a vivid memory of the night the bill was passed by the House of Representa-

Ayers were not only partners but brothers-in-law. Mrs. McCoy made a deal with her brother. She was supposed to present a paper to a ladies' literary group. If Ayers would write the paper for her, she would persuade her husband to vote for the name Cadillac, which she liked anyway. He did, she did, and Dan did. Cadillac it was.

7.

Going back to the Clam Lake *News* of March 9, however, we find two other stories of interest. One sought to allay the fears of Manton over the addition of new supervisors should the Cadillac incorporation act pass. The story argued that it was only a question of fair representation, and the presence of 351 registered voters in Clam Lake was noted as compared to only 18 in Springville Township. But the real issue was what the public wanted, said the *News,* and Manton could trust Clam Lake to be fair. Referring

tives. At the time, the Ayers had just built a new house in "the wheatfield south of town." Its location was on the hill on the east side of Oak Street between Hersey and Evart Streets, although, of course, there were no streets and the wheat had been sown among the pine stumps in the area from the house to where St. Ann's Church now stands. McCoy had built a home on the northwest corner of Simons and East Mason Street, now occupied by Fred Roussin. On the southwest corner of that intersection was the home of A. K. Moyer, Mitchell's son-in-law, and George Holbrook's house was on the southeast corner. Ayers and his wife had driven

> into town to visit the McCoy's when a man came running over and said we were needed at Moyers. Thinking it was an emergency, we went hastily and found a party being organized by Moyer, Holbrook, Mitchell, May and the rest and which lasted all night. If you know how we celebrated here in those days, you'll know what I mean, for Cadillac was famous for its pure water and we had plenty, and also plenty of something to put in it, and I didn't get home that night.

6. McCoy was not always so indifferent to history. He acquired a keen interest in the history of Michigan's early days and was vice-president of the Michigan Pioneer & Historical Society at his death in 1908, before which group he delivered several well-done papers.

to Manton's own ambitions, the paper said: "If Clam Lake had a half dozen supervisors, when their vote would enable the question to be submitted to the people to remove the county seat to Manton, their vote would not be wanting. They would always be willing to let the people decide. If the majority of the people say Manton, we say Amen."

In fact, Clam Lake was going out of its way to make a showing of sincerity by giving support to a bill to give Manton legal village status, a possible first step to city incorporation, and the Manton Village Act was passed at the same time as the Cadillac incorporation.

The second story in the March 9 issue of the *News*, however, cried alarm over Sherman's counter-measures in response to the Clam Lake incorporation act. A special meeting of the board of supervisors had been called for March 30. Before changes and additions could be made in the board at the April election, the Sherman faction of the outgoing board intended to teach Clam Lake a lesson.

Chapter Fourteen

FALLASS FILIBUSTERS: 1877, Part II

As it became apparent that Clam Lake was not ready to play dead after its defeat at the special meeting of the board of supervisors in January of 1877, the Sherman faction took stock of its position. The position of the Manton area supervisors was subject to their own area ambitions, which made their continued support of Sherman uncertain. In several townships, divisions on county seat politics indicated that pro-Sherman supervisors faced strong opposition and that changes in the board's composition at the April election could reduce the Sherman majority. The bill introduced in the State Senate to incorporate the village of Clam Lake as a city with three votes on the county board, and another bill to organize Manton as a charter village, made it evident that time was working against Sherman.

A group of Sherman area supervisors and supporters met at the office of the Sherman *Pioneer* in mid-February. In addition to the editor of the *Pioneer*, Charles Cooper, there were three supervisors present, John and Edgar Wheeler and William Dean. Sherman attorney Charles Marr, who was negotiating to buy the *Pioneer*, was present, as were clerk H. B. Sturtevant and a half dozen Sherman businessmen. John Wheeler had heard from Thomas Ferguson that something was underway in Lansing to incorporate Clam Lake as a city. There wasn't anything definite, but something ought to be done and could be done to offset any gain in Clam Lake representation on the board of supervisors. After the April election, if Clam Lake became a city Sherman would probably still control the board, but a change of supervisor in one or two townships could make the margin very close. But until that actually happened, until the April election, the Sherman bloc had decisive control. While it enjoyed that superiority and the help of Manton, it could use its control to add to its own numerical advantage.

Under state law, the board of supervisors had authority to organize townships. Wheeler's proposal was simple: a special meeting of the board of supervisors could be called before the April election. At the meeting, the Sherman faction had the votes to pass resolutions dividing the existing townships in the northwestern part of the county so as to create two townships (and two votes on the board of supervisors) where there had been but one.

The idea sounded promising, and the group agreed to meet again on Saturday, the 25th, and to do some preliminary planning in the interim. It was also agreed that Thomas Ferguson and Harry Brandenburg could be counted on and should be invited to the meeting.

On the 25th, Marr presented an analysis of the law supporting Wheeler's ideas. It not only could be done, but a new township could be created by a simple majority of the board. Ferguson and Brandenburg agreed in principle. Cooper then told the group that he had surveyed the population centers of the area and had drawn up a proposed map showing the suggested lines of division. Two new townships were to be created in the Sherman area, and the northern part of Colfax Township was to be separately organized as well. The latter move was designed to counterbalance any renewal of proposals to move the county seat to Meauwataka in the Dayhuff settlement. Ferguson suggested that a division of Cedar Creek Township be added to the plan as a means of insuring support in that area and to boost Brandenburg's chances of re-election by putting Brandenburg and Warren Seaman in different townships. The proposal was accepted, a call was drafted for a special meeting of the board of supervisors to be held on March 30, and the planners dispersed to circulate petitions in the areas that were to be divided. Ferguson headed for Lansing to lobby against Clam Lake's city incorporation bill and to promote the bill creating an incorporated village of Manton.

Word of the scheme leaked out and the March 9 issue of the Clam Lake *News* devoted more space to the Wheeler plan than it did to the pending legislation to incorporate the village.[1] Even a

1. An interesting historical note, in terms of what was locally newsworthy, is found on the back page of that issue of the *News*. The presidential election of the previous November had been inconclusive because of fraudulent returns to the

copy of Cooper's map had found its way into Clam Lake hands and was printed in the *News.*

The Wheeler plan called for the creation of four new townships. A township of Sherman was to be organized consisting of four sections of the common corner of Wexford, Hanover, Antioch, and Springville townships around the village of Sherman. The north five miles of Springville, except for the section going into Sherman Township, would be separated and organized as the township of Dover. The north half of Colfax was to be independently organized as the township of Wheatland,[2] and all of Cedar Creek west of the G. R. & I. R. R. was to be organized as the township of West Side. As proposed, the county map would look like this:

CLEON	WEXFORD	HANOVER	GREEN- WOOD	LIBERTY
SHERMAN	DOVER	ANTIOCH	WHEAT- LAND COLFAX	WEST SIDE CEDAR CREEK
	SPRING- VILLE	BOON	SELMA	HARING
		HENDER- SON	CHERRY GROVE	CLAM LAKE

electoral college from four southern states. The nation had been unable to inaugurate a new president and had been on the brink of a new civil war. One line at the bottom of the last page of the *News* informed its readers that Hayes and not Tilden was to be the new president, a fact of only passing interest compared to the rape of the townships.

2. A small settlement in the northern part of Colfax township was known as Wheatland, and a post office had been established there in 1872 in the store of Jonathan Wheat.

As matters had ended at the January special session of the board, the Sherman faction had a clear 10-5 margin of control of the board. There seemed to be no way that its plan could be defeated. Clam Lake could do little but pursue its campaign to split off the Colfax and Manton area supervisors by encouraging their own ambitions to obtain the county seat. A lawsuit was prepared challenging the action of the Henderson Township board in replacing supervisor Caswell, and an attempt was made to obtain a temporary injunction barring his successor, Frost, from acting as supervisor until the case could be heard—which would have barred him from the March 30 meeting. Circuit Judge Harrison Wheeler of Ludington was serving as a visiting judge in Hillsdale, however, and when Clam Lake attorneys S. S. Fallass and David Rice sought the issuance of the injunction from neighboring Judge Henry Hart at Midland, they were refused on the ground that the matter would be moot before a trial could be held, since a new supervisor would be elected at the April election anyway.

2.

When the special session convened at Sherman on March 30, the hopes of Clam Lake rested squarely on the shoulders of Silas Fallass, who had barely had time to rest after returning from his long stay at the capital in Lansing. Byron Ballou was honest and forthright, but he knew his limitations as a debater and parliamentarian and agreed that attorney Fallass ought to speak for Clam Lake. He had resigned as supervisor and the township board had appointed Fallass to replace him. His parliamentary skill was known and respected and was perhaps the more feared because the chair was occupied by a Clam Lake ally, John Mansfield. When the first few matters before the board seemed to indicate that Fallass would assume command of the floor, John Wheeler attempted to put a spoke in his wheel by introducing a "gag rule" limiting each member of the board to only one comment on any item of business, with a ten-minute time limit. The rule was adopted.

Edgar Wheeler rose, but Chairman Mansfield recognized

Fallass, who moved to adjourn. The motion was defeated. Amid cries of outrage, Mansfield again recognized Fallass, ignoring many of the Sherman faction, and again an adjournment motion was made, argued, and defeated. Chairman Mansfield again ignored the Sherman faction, who were attempting to be recognized to introduce the new township resolutions. This time he recognized Nathan Dayhuff of Colfax.

Dayhuff had not been part of the Sherman planning meetings, but he had always voted with Sherman. John and Edgar Wheeler had called on him to explain the proposal to split his township and to explain that petitions were being circulated in the northern part of the township for that purpose. Unless he had some strong objection to the division, they honestly felt that since he was the Colfax supervisor he should be accorded the courtesy of introducing the petition. They came away from the meeting with the belief that he did not object to the division and that he would introduce the petition. When he was recognized by Mansfield, they expected to hear a resolution to organize the township of Wheatland. They were stunned as Dayhuff read a resolution proposing an election to move the county seat to lot 2, section 32, of Colfax Township on the shore of Dayhuff Lake!

Splitting the board on this issue before a vote could be reached on the new township petitions was the last thing the Sherman faction wanted. John Wheeler made the only possible move, a motion to take up the Dayhuff resolution as a special order of business at 7:30 that evening. The motion passed, leaving the Sherman faction the parliamentary means of taking up the new township petitions first, but leaving Clam Lake some time to bargain, and bringing into the open the conflicting regional ambitions with which Clam Lake could bargain. Another Fallass motion to adjourn until 1:30 met no opposition, and the factions fled the courthouse for private caucuses.

When the afternoon session began, Edgar Wheeler moved consideration of the new township petitions, and Fallass made only perfunctory objection. Brandenburg proposed adoption of the resolution to split Cedar Creek Township, creating the new township of West Side. There was a surprising silence, as no one offered to speak against it. When the roll was called, the resolution passed, 10 to 5, with everyone voting as expected. Chairman

Mansfield recognized Dayhuff. Another surprise: again he failed to move the resolution to organize Wheatland; instead, he moved to adjourn until 4:00. The adjournment was voted and the Sherman leadership tried to find out what was going on. They never had a chance to talk to Dayhuff; he was closeted with county clerk Manktelow, Fallass, and Cuddeback in Manktelow's office.

When the board reconvened at 4:00, John Wheeler proposed the resolution to create the township of Sherman. It carried, 9 to 6, with Dayhuff joining the Clam Lake faction to vote against it. Dean moved the resolution to organize Dover and Dayhuff re-joined the Sherman bloc as it passed, 10 to 5. That left only the petition to organize Wheatland. Dayhuff made no move. The chair recognized George Wheeler and the split between the Wheeler brothers reappeared. George moved to table the matter, and the other Manton area supervisors, Dayhuff, and the Clam Lake bloc joined in voting to do so. Nothing was making sense.

3.

Just before the board adjourned for the afternoon, John Wheeler was handed a note by his brother George. The Manton trio of George Wheeler, Taylor Gray, and Harry Brandenburg wanted an immediate meeting with the Sherman bloc. Former clerk H. B. Sturtevant offered his home for the purpose, and Brandenburg spoke for the Manton group. Friends of his predecessor, Warren Seaman, no doubt encouraged by Clam Lake supporters, were attacking Brandenburg's position. They were taking another look at Brandenburg's role in Seaman's forced resignation, and Brandenburg's chances of being re-elected were doubtful. A committee to seek the county seat for Manton had been organized, encouraged by promises of support in Clam Lake, and Brandenburg had no political choice but to speak for them.

The Manton trio had supported the Sherman plan for new townships, said Brandenburg, but the handwriting was on the wall for Sherman. The population was on the east side of the county and would continue to grow along the railroad. Sherman would be better off to have the county seat at Manton than at Clam Lake.

Without realizing it, Brandenburg was using the same arguments that Clam Lake supporters had advanced the previous year in making the secret agreement with Seaman.

Then Brandenburg overreached. It was perhaps typical of him that he could not make a point without making it an ultimatum. He told the Sherman supervisors that they had to support a resolution to move the county seat to Manton. If they didn't agree to do so, the Manton trio would not budge on the tabled Wheatland petition. Furthermore, they would move to reconsider the afternoon's resolutions creating the other new townships, and Sherman would never have their support again.

It was heavy-handed. It was also senseless. The three Manton votes were important, but he acted as if they were a majority. There is really no rational explanation for the move, and it was obviously not thought out in advance. There was no point in making Wheatland an issue; it was closer to Manton than to Sherman and could have fallen into Manton's block in the future. And why wait until now to make the point? The place to bargain would have been after the first township petition, the one organizing West Side, had passed, adding to Manton's strength, instead of waiting until after the next two in Sherman's corner of the county had been approved. At any rate, the threat didn't sit well, and the Sherman supervisors left the Sturtevant home in a group, leaving their host and friend Sturtevant alone with the Manton triumvirate and a full table of food.

When the board reconvened at 7:30, Dayhuff's resolution for an election to move the county seat to Dayhuff Lake received the Manton support. It carried by a vote of 8 to 7, but lacked the required two-thirds majority. True to his word, Brandenburg then moved to reconsider the resolution creating Dover Township. The three Manton and five Clam Lake votes carried the motion, and by the same vote Dover was then tabled.

Brandenburg was on his feet again with a motion to reconsider West Side, and when the motion carried, to table. It was tabled. There was still another, and he moved to reconsider the organization of Sherman Township. This time there was an interruption. John Wheeler moved to adjourn, and while the chair debated points of order with Edgar Wheeler and William Dean of Springville, and finally yielded to put the motion to a roll call, Wheeler penned a note to Brandenburg. As he recalled it in later years, it went something like this:

> This was your child you just recalled. You voted for it this afternoon. It would have voted for you Monday (i.e., at the election for supervisor). It would have given Manton another vote. How will you explain that? At least give us Sherman tonight and we will stay with you on West Side. The rest we can talk about later. Think!

The motion to adjourn failed. When the roll was called on the motion to reconsider Sherman Township, Brandenburg switched again, and the motion was defeated, 8 to 7.

At this point the meeting turned into chaos. William Dean moved to take up the tabled resolutions. Chairman Mansfield ruled him out of order. Dean demanded an appeal from the chair, and Clerk Manktelow finally called the roll on the appeal contrary to the chairman's orders, saying later that it would have been dangerous for him to have refused to do so. The vote was 9 to 6 to overrule the chair, but Mansfield announced that the motion required a two-thirds vote and was defeated.

One after another the members of the Clam Lake faction were recognized by Mansfield, who chose to ignore the furious Sherman supervisors who were trying to get the floor. William East of Cherry Grove moved to adjourn *sine die*. After long "debate," the motion lost. Cuddeback of Haring moved to adjourn until April 10. Again, after much wrangling, the motion was lost. Then, a motion to adjourn until April 9, and so it went.

Finally Fallass claimed the right to explain his vote on an adjournment motion and further claimed that this, as a matter of procedure, was not governed by the ten-minute limit on debate. Over strenuous objection he was sustained by chairman Mansfield and proceeded to launch the county's first filibuster. Frankly warning the board that he intended to talk until the April election, three days hence, he began reading the U. S. Constitution, followed by the Michigan Constitution and Volume I of Howell's *Revised Statutes of Michigan*. About ten o'clock, he paused between "Organization of the Legislature" and "Powers of Impeachment" to ask that a friend bring him some food. Somewhere

In the midst of "Claims Against the State," Sherman threw in the sponge. John Wheeler asked if Fallass would yield for the purpose of a motion to adjourn *sine die*. He did, the motion was made and carried, and everyone went home to await the April election.

From its position of strength, the Sherman faction had been able to bring about the creation of only one new township, Sherman. It was gained only at the expense of a deepened rift between Sherman and Manton which was ultimately to decide the county seat issue.

4.

The April 2 election did nothing to ease the peace of mind of the Sherman group. Considering that there was a wild snowstorm that morning, there was a heavy turnout of voters. The newly incorporated city of Cadillac elected three keen-minded men, S. S. Fallass, Holden Green, and William Kelley, as its supervisors. New faces included Judson Loomis from Clam Lake Township and A. E. Tilyou from Selma, both Cadillac supporters. William East of Cherry Grove, John Mansfield of Boon, and R. D. Cuddeback of Haring were back.

In the Manton group all three incumbents had been defeated. George Wheeler lost to William Briggs in Greenwood, George Blue defeated Taylor Gray in Liberty, and Ward Smith crushed Harry Brandenburg in Cedar Creek. All three of the new supervisors appeared to favor Sherman or at least were not favorable towards Clam Lake. In Colfax, Nathan Dayhuff did not run for re-election and was replaced by John Goldsmith, who was solidly in sympathy with Sherman.

In Henderson? Confusion. Supporters of Elisha Caswell had turned out in strength, but somehow they hadn't got to vote. The polls were closed, the ballot box had disappeared, and Philip Frost still claimed to be supervisor.

In the Sherman camp, the new township of Sherman elected John Wheeler as its supervisor, and his place in Antioch was filled by Judge Isaac Carpenter, who had formerly lived in and sat on the board from Wexford Township. Edgar Wheeler in Hanover did not seek re-election and was replaced by Solomon C. Worth.

William Dean of Springville and Wilson Odell of Wexford were unopposed, and Andrew Hannabal of Copemish was newly elected from Cleon Township. If the Manton group stayed with Sherman, as it appeared it would, the Sherman bloc still had apparent control of the board, 11 to 8 or 10 to 9, depending upon who was seated from Henderson Township.

5.

What did happen in Henderson Township on April 2? According to the *News*, most of the voters favored Caswell over Frost which was probably true. In order to defeat Caswell, the polls were closed early in the morning before most of the Caswell supporters could vote. The township records and the ballot box, said the *News*, were stolen by Frost and the township clerk George Johnson, and delivered to Howard Mesick and the devious Tommy Ferguson. Men and records were last seen heading north in Mesick's sleigh.

Prosecuting attorney David A. Rice of Cadillac issued warrants for Frost and Johnson, charging them with election fraud. In a rather unusual step, the warrants were placed in the hands of the city marshal rather than the sheriff, and the accused men were lodged in the city jail instead of being taken to the county jail at Sherman.

Cadillac supervisor Holden Green was also justice of the peace and presided at the preliminary examination. The evidence appeared rather damning. James Banker, Edwin Latimer, and John Denike all testified that they had gone to the polling place at the Van Antwerp or Banker school, arriving around 9:00 in the morning. A Harry Brandenburg and Howard Mesick were there, they said, along with clerk Johnson and Philip Frost, who were loading the township books and ballot box in Mesick's sleigh. Candidate Caswell testified that he arrived late because of the snowstorm and found the polls already closed.[3] Peter Sours testi-

3. It was brought out on cross-examination that he arrived in the company of Cadillac marshall Horton Crandell, and that Crandell disguised his identity, telling bystanders that he was circulating a petition for a change in the mail route. It suggests the possibility that news of the plot leaked out but the law arrived too late to catch the culprits redhanded.

fied that he came in the afternoon and was told by Frost and Johnson that the polls had been closed and that the ballots had been given to Mr. Brandenburg and Representative Ferguson to keep them from being stolen by the Clam Lake people.[4]

Even more damning, Johnson's brother-in-law John Henderson testified that he had been at the home of his father, Thomas Henderson, on the night before the election and that Johnson, Frost, Mesick, and Brandenburg had stayed the night there. They had said that they had Mr. Frost elected and that they had a box in Mesick's bag that was going to take care of the election. In the morning, Henderson testified, he had gone with the four men to the school, and they had never opened the polls. The defendants offered no testimony at the preliminary hearing, and Justice Green bound them over for trial in the circuit court.

A lawsuit was brought to compel the holding of a new election in Henderson Township, but neither it nor the criminal cases against Frost and Johnson were ever brought to trial. Frost's attorney issued a statement, gleefully reported by the *News*, in which Frost disavowed the office of supervisor. His defense to the election fraud prosecution would be that he could not be guilty of violating any election duties as supervisor since he had never legally held the office. To Cadillac's delight, Frost's attorney added that Frost had been unwittingly made a tool of the "Sherman ring." The *News* was willing to include its competitor at Sherman among the guilty, saying, "This will dispose of another of the innumerable falsehoods in the *Pioneer.*"

The Henderson town board quickly called a special election for May 4. Caswell was in poor health and decided not to seek election, but he was recognized as supervisor pending the election. Frost's name was filed as a candidate, but he was a beaten man and did not campaign against former supervisor Job Hoxie, who won by an overwhelming margin. The *News* reported that undersheriff Sanford Gasser and attorney Charles S. Marr of Sherman

4. This hearsay testimony was the only reference to Ferguson in the whole proceeding, and was inconsistent with the testimony of the other witnesses in that respect. It hardly warranted the *News* reporting that Ferguson was one of those driving off with the ballot box. The *News*, on the other hand, made no reference to the presence of Brandenburg.

were observers at the election, noting that they "did not offer to vote. Rather queer for those Sherman fellows." Things being well in hand for Cadillac, prosecutor Rice permitted both the civil and criminal prosecutions to languish, and they were ultimately dismissed.

Chapter Fifteen

ARRESTING A SUPERVISOR: 1877, Part III

Thanks to the prompt action of the prosecutor, the Henderson question was resolved and the pro-Cadillac Caswell was the acting supervisor. Thus it appeared that the Sherman majority on the board of supervisors was only 10 to 9 at best. Seeking an immediate advantage from their increased strength, the new Cadillac supervisors called a special meeting of the board of supervisors to be held in Cadillac on April 16 at eight o'clock in the morning. They were undoubtedly hopeful, in view of the short notice given, that some of the Sherman faction might not get to the meeting or would be late in arriving. In view of the nearly even division of the board, the absence of one or more members from the Sherman faction would give the Cadillac block an advantage which they might exploit. Cadillac had two things in mind.

One of the things the Cadillac faction planned, should it have a temporary advantage at the meeting, was to rush through resolutions dividing Haring and Cherry Grove townships in half, creating two new townships in the Cadillac bloc. The Sherman strategy of the March 30 meeting was a sword that could cut both ways. The other thing that Cadillac hoped to accomplish, if it could have a majority present at the special meeting, was to rescind the creation of Sherman Township and bar their nemesis, John Wheeler, from a seat on the board as the Sherman supervisor. At the same time, prosecutor Rice prepared a lawsuit against Wheeler, seeking to have the organization of Sherman Township declared illegal and Wheeler accordingly without office.

Promptly at eight o'clock on the morning of the 16th, the nine members of the Cadillac faction entered the city council room in Holbrook & May's Hall where the special meeting was to be held. Except for attorney E. F. Sawyer, specially deputized as a deputy county clerk, and prosecutor Rice, they were alone. They waited.

And they waited. After almost two hours, someone reported that some of the Sherman faction was at the American House. The report was false, but it was correctly surmised that the entire delegation had not yet arrived and that none of them were going to appear at the meeting until they were full strength. As long as they all stayed away, there would not be a quorum of the board and no business could be legally transacted. Chairman Mansfield quickly convened the session, the roll was called, and the presence of a nine-man Cadillac bloc was recorded. The clerk then noted the absence of *nine* members, naming them, and making no reference to John Wheeler. Sherman Township was to be ignored.

Cadillac's legal minds, Fallass, Rice, and deputy clerk Sawyer, had considered this possible Sherman counter-strategy. They had devised a counter-counter-maneuver in turn, and the board adjourned for half an hour to set the stage. There was sound legal precedent holding that it was malfeasance for legislative officers to fail to attend the meeting of the body of which they were members. Based on this, there was some precedent for the proposition that such bodies had power to compel the attendance of its members.

Prepared to act on this theory should circumstances require, the Cadillac faction had sheriff Frank Weaver on hand, ready to search out an absent supervisor and forcibly deliver him to the meeting room to make the quorum. The board adjourned until 10:30 while information was sought as to which of the absent supervisors were in town. That information indicated that there were two supervisors who hadn't arrived, Briggs of Greenwood and Dean of Springville. Not sure that Briggs and Dean wouldn't arrive momentarily, the Cadillac planners tried to be extra clever—they would adjourn until the following morning but would spread word that the meeting had adjourned without date. Then, after the Sherman faction had dispersed to their homes, the sheriff would take one of them into custody and deliver him the following morning. If it worked, they would not only have a quorum, but there would be little chance that any of the others in the Sherman bloc would be there, eliminating a full-strength deadlock.

At 10:30 the board was reconvened, the presence of the nine was recorded, and the nine absent names listed—Sherman Township and John Wheeler again omitted. A resolution was then passed directing the issuance of a warrant for the apprehension of John Goldsmith of Colfax, one of the absent supervisors, to be produced by the sheriff at the meeting room at eight o'clock the following morning. The board then adjourned until that hour. They dispersed, with the rural supervisors making a show of leaving the city and letting it be known on the street that they would try another meeting in May.

2.

The Cadillac supervisors had outsmarted themselves. Had they proceeded directly with their strategy and apprehended one of the absentees on Monday, they would have had a quorum and their majority, for Dean did not arrive in Cadillac until Monday evening and Briggs until the next morning. And as it developed, the attempt to decoy the Sherman faction into going home did not succeed. How they learned of the plot and what was going on that afternoon and evening we do not know. We know only that the following morning, when the board met at eight o'clock, only four Cadillac members answered the roll call, and they recessed till ten o'clock. We also know that the sheriff had been unable to find Goldsmith, who had learned of the existence of the warrant for his arrest. He had been kept under cover near Cadillac that night and remained out of sight until most of the other members of the Sherman faction had gathered at the American House Tuesday morning.[1]

1. He apparently had been kept north of town and had boarded the train at Haring or McCoy's Siding. The *News* of that week refers to the entire Sherman delegation arriving together on the train from Manton Tuesday morning. Two weeks later, however, the *News* said that: "The 'ladies' of the North Star have many stories about the doings of the 'Nine Muses' and their counsel, 'Liberty' Ferguson," during the April session, hinting that the Sherman faction stayed there and frolicked the entire week. It really must be doubted, in view of the long standing reputation of the North Star as a house of prostitution, that the Sherman faction would have stayed here. Ferguson and Wheeler always stayed at the American House, and Wheeler apparently did so during the April session.

Now both sides were worried. Neither knew what the other was up to. The Cadillac faction had no way of knowing where Goldsmith had gone or how many of the Sherman faction were in town. In the belated recognition that Goldsmith might not be easily found, warrants were drawn for each of the other absent supervisors to be issued when the board reconvened at ten o'clock so that the sheriff could apprehend whichever one he could find.

The Sherman bloc was nervous, too. They had ten voices if Wheeler could be seated. Otherwise the best that could be hoped for was a 9-9 deadlock. They weren't sure whether they could trust themselves; the Manton-Sherman fight at the March 30 meeting was fresh in their minds, and the new men from the Manton area were unknown quantities. For awhile Wheeler considered going to the meeting alone, thinking that perhaps the Cadillac faction would be so eager to get a quorum that it would recognize him as the supervisor from Sherman, and then he could stall things until the rest of his bloc got there.

On the other hand, there was a question whether he should let himself be seen at all. Rumors about some kind of action against him by the prosecuting attorney had reached his ears. Nothing had been filed at the courthouse in Sherman when he left there the previous morning, but perhaps it was part of the prosecutor's strategy to wait until he was in hostile Cadillac to start something. After all, Frost and Johnson had been thrown into Cadillac's jail. And if it was the intention of the Cadillac faction to have one or more of the Sherman faction criminally prosecuted for malfeasance in office, as was rumored, how could they prevent the board from meeting while they were in custody? Neither Thomas Ferguson of Manton nor Charles Marr of Sherman, the two attorneys allied with the Sherman cause, was in Cadillac. Wheeler sent telegrams to both, urging them to come to the American House at once. The sheriff got there first.

Whether the Cadillac leaders were tipped off to the contents of the telegram, thereby learning of the presence of the Sherman faction at the American House, as one version had it, or whether they were just conspicuous by their presence, is immaterial. Their presence did become known and Sheriff Weaver went after Goldsmith as the Cadillac delegation gathered at Holbrook & May's Hall.

Deputy clerk Sawyer called the roll and recorded nine present and nine absent, again without mention of John Wheeler. Within a few minutes, the sheriff, having accomplished the arrest of Goldsmith at the American House without opposition, delivered him "before the bar of the house" upon which Sawyer again called the roll. When Goldsmith refused to speak, Sawyer answered for him and declared a quorum present. He started to say something else but was interrupted by a booming voice from the doorway shouting, "STOP! STOP!" It was John Wheeler, demanding to know why his name had been omitted from the roll call.

The rumors of a lawsuit or prosecution of Wheeler and of the warrant for Goldsmith and perhaps for all of them, as well as the uncertainty about what was going on in Cadillac that morning, had left Wheeler and his colleagues undecided as to how they should proceed. For that reason, and out of fear of possible prosecution and arrest while in hostile territory, Wheeler had sent for Marr and Ferguson. On the arrest of Goldsmith, however, they were left with no choice. They couldn't wait until the attorneys arrived. And so, apprehensively, they followed to the Hall, and Wheeler entered to demand his seat.

The parliamentary niceties of procedure or what motion may have been made by whom isn't known. The brawl that erupted probably prevented the clerk from hearing or identifying any particular member, and he neatly disposed of the matter in the minutes by one sterile notation: "Mr. J. W. Wheeler asked for a seat on the board which was refused." Neither do we know what set off the melee, and only a few incidents are preserved from it. Gov. Fred Green once said that his father humorously ascribed the ill health of his late years to having been bitten by a rabid supervisor, apparently at this meeting. William Dean of Springville accused John Mansfield of Boon of having been bought by Mitchell money, and both men were severely bruised before order was restored. The Sherman *Pioneer* commented bitterly that the sheriff's authority, so bravely used on poor Goldsmith, remained unexercised while the Sherman delegation was set upon.[2]

2. Wheeler does not appear to have been harmed or involved in the outbreak, the extent of which may have been exaggerated by the *Pioneer*. Wheeler makes

Whatever the cause and duration of the fight, it eventually ended, and Wheeler left the room peacefully rather than cause further trouble. It nearly erupted again as Fallass moved that R. D. Cuddeback of Haring be elected temporary chairman and called for a voice vote. Deputy clerk Sawyer had no difficulty hearing a majority of ayes, and Cuddeback assumed the chair accompanied by shouts of protest. One of the Sherman group demanded a roll call, with the observation that he thought there was an equal division. He was ruled out of order. He then moved to appeal the ruling of the chair and proved his point, but lost the appeal when the roll call tally showed nine in favor and nine against the appeal. He then moved to adjourn to 1:30, and the vote was again tied, 9 to 9.

Dean moved to adjourn *sine die*. The vote was 9 to 9. Another motion to adjourn until 1:30 was tied, 9 to 9. Mansfield moved that nominations be made to elect a permanent chairman. Dean demanded a roll call on the motion and it was tied, 9 to 9. Fallass then introduced a resolution to call an election for the purpose of moving the county seat to Dayhuff Lake in Colfax Township. Goldsmith, the captive supervisor from Colfax, stuck with Sherman and voted no, and another 9 to 9 vote was tallied. Another effort to adjourn *sine die* was deadlocked, and they finally agreed to adjourn until 1:30.

Neither side could or would let go of the tiger's tail. Barring death, illness, or accident, the board was stalemated by an equal division of the factions. Both sides gave every indication that they were ready to stay there until one of those eventualities occurred. In the afternoon, all items of business, including motions to adjourn, were deadlocked, 9 to 9, and they finally agreed wearily to recess until the next morning.

They were no better off on the 18th and put in a long, irritating

no mention whatever of this session of the board in his *History of Wexford County*. In later correspondence with Perry Hannah of Traverse City, however, discussing various instances in the county seat struggle, he said that on two different occasions the Cadillac faction forcibly attempted to bar Sherman supervisors from meetings. This was very likely one of those occasions, with the Cadillac faction attempting to prevent the rest of the Sherman group from joining Goldsmith in the meeting room.

day of haranguing and balloting, motion after motion being deadlocked, 9 to 9.

On the 19th, it was the same dreary performance. Finally, Goldsmith was taken ill and asked for a brief recess to get some air, escorted by several of his friends. The chair granted the request, and the Cadillac faction huddled at one end of the hall. Suddenly, they realized that they were alone, and a hasty search failed to turn up any of the opposition. Without a quorum again, they adjourned until the next morning.

3.

Once again we are without evidence of what was going on in the secret councils of the two camps, and can only speculate about what they were attempting to do in the next ten days. Day after day, on the 20th, 21st, 23rd, 24th, 25th, 26th, and 27th, the Cadillac faction met at Holbrook & May's Hall, called the roll, found none of the Sherman bloc present, and adjourned until the following day.

Prosecutor Rice had filed his suit against John Wheeler on the 17th. It may very well be that the Sherman group was simply stalling to await the outcome of the matter, since it was hoped that it could be ruled on promptly. Wheeler's attorneys, Ramsdell and Gage of Manistee, had immediately filed a demurrer to the writ of *quo warranto*. It was, in effect, a motion to dismiss the writ as a matter of law and was designed to get a quick ruling on the legal questions involved. It had been scheduled for hearing before the circuit judge on April 27th. Ramsdell was confident that the judge would rule in Wheeler's favor, and, if that proved to be the case, the Sherman group could then re-enter the meeting as a majority.

On the other hand, perhaps Goldsmith really was ill. If so, the only way to prevent Cadillac from having a temporary majority was to deny Cadillac a quorum by all of the Sherman bloc boycotting the meetings.

It may well be that the Cadillac strategists were causing, or at least aggravating, Goldsmith's illness. There seems to be no doubt that they were busy in Colfax Township, again stirring up hopes there that the county seat might be moved to Dayhuff Lake.

Goldsmith's vote on the 17th against the resolution for such a move was being used against him, particularly in the southern part of the township.[3]

For some reason, Cadillac made no attempt to renew the arrest tactic to compel the attendance of any of the absent supervisors. Perhaps it thought it prudent to avoid further controversy pending a decision on the Wheeler case. Or perhaps it had something else in mind.

On the 27th, the courtroom at Sherman was crowded with spectators for the motion in the Wheeler case. They were disappointed. The attorneys agreed upon the facts in short statements. The judge declined to make an immediate ruling and asked the attorneys to prepare briefs. In twenty minutes it was all over, and the decision as to whether Wheeler was a supervisor or not was still unresolved.

But the composition of the board was determined on the 27th anyway. John Goldsmith resigned as supervisor of Colfax. If he assigned any reason for doing so, it was not noted in the *News*. After less than a month in office, perhaps he thought that if this was the way the board of supervisors did business, he could find a better way to spend his time and without the risk of being hunted by the sheriff. Maybe he really was sick and not just sick of the hassle.[4]

3. The Cadillac attempts to get Colfax support by this strategy were never taken seriously in Sherman. John Wheeler expressed the prevailing view there that "the insincerity of the talk . . . about moving the county seat to the center of the county . . . was so transparent that it deceived no one, although it may have had some little influence occasionally on the supervisor of the township." It was easier to believe that more malignant influences were at work when Colfax suddenly left the Sherman camp, as it did periodically.

4. If Goldsmith was ill, it wasn't particularly serious. He was still actively farming thirty years later at the age of seventy-one. He was a quiet, hard-working man of interesting background. He was born in Holstein, Germany, in 1836, to a mother of German-Danish extraction, and an Irish father who had been a revolutionary and had fled Ireland as a wanted man. The son took to the sea and had seen most of the world and had sailed twice around it before marrying in Germany at age twenty-five. He had, by then, seen the United States, and he returned to join the navy, fighting on the frigate Sabine in several naval battles of the Civil War. A friend knew Lucas Gates, who was "coming west to farm," and

The Colfax Township board immediately selected Rascelas S. McClain to replace Goldsmith. He had been on the first board and had argued against construction of the courthouse at Sherman in 1870. He had worked as surveyor and timber cruiser for George Mitchell, and the two men were friends. There was little doubt his vote would go to Cadillac.

The resignation of Goldsmith and the appointment of McClain to replace him were promptly attributed by the *Pioneer* to bribery, or worse. A merchant and postmaster of the Antioch Township settlement of Bandola, Herman Meyer, had a broadside printed over his name, claiming that both threats and money had been used to effect the change, and specifically charging county clerk C. J. Manktelow with having delivered the bribes by which "Cadillac bought the vote and soul of Colfax Township."[5]

Whether by circumstance, by bribery, or by more subtle politics, McClain became the new supervisor of Colfax on April 27 and presented himself at the adjourned meeting of the county board on the 28th. The meeting is another enigma in this strange episode. Again, none of the Sherman faction was there. McClain's addition to the nine members of the Cadillac faction not only gave Cadillac the quorum, but a 10-0 majority. Why Cadillac didn't go

Goldsmith decided to put as much distance between himself and the sea as possible. He had no means to go west except by sailing, and he worked up the St. Lawrence as a deckhand, then had a mate's berth on the Great Lakes for fifteen months to save the money to bring his wife from Germany. He ended up in the Unionville settlement in 1867, a few miles from the Gates homestead. He became a citizen and held office as justice of the peace, constable, township treasurer, and member of the township school board in the years after his short tenure as supervisor.

5. A bitter feud resulted between Manktelow and Meyer, largely maintained by the latter's hot temper, and highlighted by frequent offers to do violence. Meyer was elected supervisor of Antioch Township a few years later and proved to be the most volatile and aggressive member of the Sherman faction, both in word and conduct. His part in our history ends on a strange note: a brief story in the *News* rather casually reported that foul play was feared as Meyer had not been seen for several weeks after apparently leaving for Grand Rapids on a business trip. Not only was he never seen again, but he appears never to have been mentioned again in county newspapers or records except for notices of foreclosure on his mortgaged home and store.

on to exploit that advantage is a mystery. One of the purposes of the special meeting had been the division of Haring and Cherry Grove townships to create two more votes for the Cadillac area, and the petitions were ready to be acted upon.

Instead, the ten supervisors elected Cuddeback as permanent chairman, passed a resolution declaring Caswell the legal supervisor of Henderson Township pending the special election there, and passed another resolution declaring the organization of Sherman Township illegal and stating that neither John Wheeler nor anyone else claiming to represent it should ever be recognized as a lawful supervisor. They speedily disposed of some routine county business and then adjourned *sine die*, leaving the new township petitions unintroduced. Wexford County's version of the "Long Parliament" was finally over, and everyone was relieved.

4.

There was considerable public criticism of the expense of the marathon special session of the board of supervisors of April, 1877. The two county newspapers expressed their usual partisan, regional viewpoints, lodging their complaints against the opposing faction. *Pioneer* said the long session had no purpose except "to provide seed money for a few supervisors riding the coattails of Mitchell, Fallass, and Rice." It went on to charge that the Cadillac deputy clerk had been very carefree in recording attendance when only the Cadillac faction was appearing, and that some supervisors had collected per diem and mileage fees for days when they had been nowhere near the meeting hall. The *News* put the blame on the "Sherman-Manton clique which is determined to ruin if it can't rule," thereby introducing what was to be a badly overworked cliche in the next five years.

In the face of the criticism, the Cadillac faction called another special session of the board for May 29, again to be held at Cadillac. The stated purpose of the meeting was to dispose of many matters which had been undecided during the April stalemate, and it is true that by the time they adjourned on June 13, the supervisors had disposed of a great deal of routine county business. Even the most inconsequential matters, however, were marked by heated disputes, personal attacks, and petty parliamentary diversions. On most important matters, regional politics were bitter and often prevented fair consideration of local needs.

On June 2, for instance, arson destroyed the wooden bridges across the Manistee River in Liberty and Sherman townships. Petitions for county funds to rebuild the bridges were blocked by the Cadillac faction, and the allotment of money for the bridge construction and for road improvements during the next few years was handled according to position on the county seat issue, with the northwestern part of the county being treated rather shabbily. The only note of accord in the session was the prompt and unanimous acceptance by the board of an invitation to join Cadillac Mayor George Mitchell as his guests at a dinner at the McKinnon House. Editor J. A. Whitmore of the *News* said that none of the board was so rude as to decline the free banquet, and a few were sufficiently courteous to remain to listen to Mr. Mitchell's remarks about the future of the city.

The first skirmish of the session once again involved John Wheeler's right to a seat on the board as supervisor of the new township of Sherman. On April 28, with only the Cadillac bloc present, the board had declared that the organization of the township was unlawful and that Wheeler could not, therefore, represent a non-existent township. The circuit court suit against Wheeler to bar him from a seat on the board had not yet been decided.

Accordingly, when Wheeler appeared at the opening of the May 29 session, S. S. Fallass of Cadillac rose to protest his presence. Perhaps he had some doubts about the validity of the April 28 resolution, for he moved the re-adoption of that resolution barring Wheeler from sessions of the board. The motion passed, with the chairman graciously allowing the clerk to call Wheeler's name and record his "no" before ordering him ejected from the room. The astute Wheeler claimed a point of order based upon that recognition, but was forcefully expelled from the hall before he could complete his statement. An understanding was reached by which he was permitted to re-enter and to sit inside the door without participating in the proceedings. Thereafter, each session, morning and afternoon, opened with Wheeler's appearance and formal demand for admission, a refusal by the chairman, and

Wheeler's withdrawal to his seat by the door. It became a polite and formal ritual, apparently enjoyed by all and marked by the underlying respect of the two leaders, Fallass and Wheeler, for each other.

The real purpose of the May-June special meeting was evident as the Cadillac faction continued its strategy of winning support away from Sherman by encouraging the ambitions of other areas. Colfax was promised that Cadillac would support its claims to move the county seat to Meauwataka. Manton had the same promise. In each case, Cadillac "only" asked that the supervisors there support Cadillac in the event their own efforts failed. Thus, during the session, five different motions to call an election on moving the county seat were introduced—two for the move to Dayhuff Lake, one for a move to Manton, and two for a move to Cadillac. None received the necessary two-thirds vote of the board, but several produced a bare majority and indicated which way the wind was blowing.

The June 8 *Pioneer* carried a letter signed "Supervisor" which analyzed the Cadillac strategy well, described the promises Cadillac was secretly making to both the Manton and Meauwataka supporters and reasonably pointed out that since Cadillac couldn't be telling both camps the truth, it was possible that it was telling the truth to neither. The letter apparently stung, for the *News* reacted the next week, calling the letter . . . "completely untruthful. The author is generally supposed to be J. H. Wheeler. We have thought him to be a gentleman, but the article proves him a boor, untruthful and ungentlemanly."

The *Pioneer* in turn, replied on June 22 with another attack on Cadillac, and an equally scathing denunciation of the gullibility of the Manton area supervisors. The editorial unwittingly revealed, however, the extent to which Sherman was being worn down. Although Manton was accused of playing "dog in the manger," the *Pioneer* said that if the county seat had to leave Sherman, then let it go to Manton. Sherman would rather support Manton than "Cadillac treachery."

The session ended on June 13 with another breach of decorum growing out of Wheeler's daily presence at the meetings. At the end of the session, Wheeler's name was added by someone to the list of supervisors entitled to per diem and mileage. William

Kelley of Cadillac was the first to notice it and included in his remarks the comment that this was "just thievery." Andrew Hannabal of Cleon Township replied by reading the article from the Sherman *Pioneer* which had accused the Cadillac faction of chicanery in figuring per diem payments in April when none of the Sherman supervisors had been present. Kelley reacted violently to the inference that he was dishonest and the meeting was disrupted briefly. When order was restored, mutual apologies were made, but the Cadillac faction took revenge on the *Pioneer* by ordering the clerk henceforth to cease publication of official notices and minutes of the supervisors meetings in that paper and to publish them only in the Cadillac *News.*

Wheeler, of course, was above such petty motives. His daily presence in Cadillac was required by larger reasons of strategy. For one thing, he was now the unquestioned leader of the Sherman faction—they needed his presence. Additionally, the lawsuit against him involved some new questions and he did not want to do anything that might weaken his case or make it appear that he had abandoned his claim to be seated as a supervisor. Later that summer, the circuit judge sustained his demurrer and held that the *quo warranto* action could not be brought against Wheeler personally since it involved a township question.

Prosecutor Rice started a new case against the township in July, and in August this case also was dismissed by the court, the judge this time holding that a *quo warranto* writ could not be brought against a township. The Cadillac supervisors and the prosecutor couldn't understand why they shouldn't have been properly in court on one theory or the other, and special counsel from Detroit was hired to study the question.[6] He concluded that the judge was right in the second case but wrong on the first, and subsequent appellate court decisions bear out that conclusion. No appeal was taken, however, and after some minor opposition, Wheeler was finally seated during the October session of the board as the supervisor of Sherman Township. He was, incidentally, also awarded

6. The expense was later approved by the board on a regional 10-9 vote, another example, said the *Pioneer,* of Cadillac taxing the whole county to pay the cost of destroying it.

the per diem and mileage for all of the meetings from which he had been turned away!

5.

The *Pioneer* editorial of June 22 was the first open indication that there might be some grudging Manton support in the Sherman camp, if only as a matter of spite toward Cadillac in defeat. Over the next nine months, the position of the *Pioneer* fluctuated erratically, undoubtedly as a result of a change of ownership. In early June, owner and editor Charles Cooper sold the paper to Charles S. Marr. Marr was an attorney who had located in Sherman in 1875. He had immediately become involved in Republican politics and had been appointed acting postmaster at Sherman as soon as he bought the *Pioneer*. For some reason, he was not too warmly received by the Sherman leadership, and his closest ties were made in the Manton area, where he became very close to Harry Brandenburg and constantly sought the advice and approbation of Thomas Ferguson, with whom he tried to identify himself. There is more than a little evidence that the embarrassingly crude Henderson ballot box theft was his idea, engineered without the knowledge of John Wheeler and the older Sherman leaders.

After Marr's purchase of the *Pioneer*, there seems no doubt that its vacillating position reflected his personal ambitions and prejudices. The *Pioneer* did not so much support Sherman as attack Cadillac. In this, perhaps, Marr was a mirror of the old bitterness of Ferguson, whom he tried to emulate. Certainly the *Pioneer* was at its worst in the personal attacks it made against Ferguson's most personal enemies—S. S. Fallass, George Mitchell, John and Orrin Whitmore of the Cadillac *News*, and, occasionally even Sherman's own best leaders, John Wheeler and H. B. Sturtevant. On other occasions, Cadillac was sometimes described in such glowing terms that the *Pioneer* might well have been a carbon copy of the *News*. The *Pioneer* also devoted an inordinate amount of print to the talents and character of Sherman attorney C. S. Marr and to the likelihood that he would be the next circuit judge. This ambition of attorney Marr may well explain the inconsistency of editor Marr on the county seat issue.

The *News* indicated its understanding of his vacillation and his ambition in a biting comment on November 1, 1877. The *Pioneer* had carried two articles in October, one bitterly attacking the county's most prominent attorney, Cadillac supervisor S. S. Fallass, as personally dishonest and as the corrupt influence behind alleged attempts by bribery to buy votes on the county seat issue. The other article had been a fawning panegyric to Cadillac's leaders, Jonathan Cobbs, L. O. Harris, and others (ignoring George A. Mitchell). The *News* thought it no accident that the *Pioneer* had attacked the man best qualified in the county for judicial position and concluded:

> A new judicial circuit is being discussed and a certain Sherman lawyer whose name was mentioned had brains enough to know his location at Sherman was a drawback to his political aspirations. So he expressed a strong desire to move to the city which was alike to Sodom and Gomorrah . . . Fallass probably feels about the attack from the *Pioneer* like the boy kicked by the jackass who considers where it comes from.

During the latter part of 1877, things appeared calm on the surface while the two factions waited out the decision in the second Sherman-Wheeler suit and digested its meaning. The situation in Colfax seemed secure for Cadillac as the leaders in the southern part of the township agreed with the Cadillac promise supporting Colfax in its ambitions for the county seat. McClain resigned as supervisor in September to leave on a surveying trip, but Nathan Dayhuff came back on the board in his place and was sold on the bargain. Cadillac quietly kept up its pressures on the Manton area supervisors. The fall session of the county board, surprisingly, saw no resolutions about the county seat or petitions for new townships. This time there would be no action until everything was assured. In mid-December, notices went out calling a special meeting to be held at Cadillac in January.

Chapter Sixteen

1878: SHALL THE COUNTY SEAT BE REMOVED TO MANTON?

YES ☐
NO ☒

The New Year's edition of the *Pioneer* looked forward to 1878 with mixed emotions. The calling of the special session of the supervisors at Cadillac, it thought, probably meant more county seat election motions. How long, it wondered, before the supervisors would authorize an election to move the county seat? Without really saying anything bad about Cadillac, editor Marr acknowledged gloomily that perhaps Sherman ought to support a move of the county seat to Manton, if for no other reason than that otherwise it might wind up even farther away!

It was close to being an admission that Cadillac's "divide and conquer" strategy had succeeded. Sherman had only six solid votes on the board to nine for Cadillac. The four remaining votes, Colfax, Cedar Creek, Liberty, and Greenwood, were they to vote with Cadillac, would give Cadillac the two-thirds requirement of thirteen votes necessary to call an election on moving the county seat. The supervisors of those four townships gave every indication of having succumbed to Cadillac's blandishments. At the previous June's session of the county board, the five motions for elections to move the county seat to Manton, Meauwataka, or Cadillac seemingly demonstrated the truth of the warning contained in "Supervisor's" letter in the June 8 issue of the *Pioneer.*

The course of events and the analysis of "Supervisor" seemed to have no impact on those four supervisors, and attempts to reason with them over the following months had been met by polite yawns. They believed what they wanted to believe. At the end of the year, Wheeler and Sturtevant were convinced not only of the accuracy of their analysis of Cadillac strategy but that the strategy was working. They conferred with the other Sherman supervisors and made a desperation decision.

On the first day of the January, 1878, session of the board of supervisors, S. S. Fallass introduced a resolution for an election on the question of moving the county seat to Cadillac. Almost in the same breath, he moved that it be tabled and made a clever speech indicating that the citizens of Cadillac were interested only in moving the county seat nearer the center of the county's population. Should anyone else choose to introduce an election resolution for a move elsewhere, he said, he and Cadillac would willingly encourage a full debate and would gladly defer consideration of his resolution in favor of taking up any other resolutions first.

Fallass and the rest of the Cadillac bloc, of course, had prepared a script in which successive motions to move to Manton and Meauwataka would be voted upon. Cadillac would support them and they would probably have a majority of the votes, but each would lack the necessary two-thirds, as those areas voted against each other. Both being bound to vote for Cadillac as an alternate choice, the third resolution, for an election on a move to Cadillac, then would have just enough votes, thirteen, to meet the two-thirds requirement. The script, of course, assumed that the Sherman bloc would vote solidly against every resolution aimed at taking the county seat elsewhere.

The script seemed to be in order. Nathan Dayhuff introduced his resolution for an election to move the county seat to Meauwataka. The vote went as anticipated, and the resolution fell short of the necessary two-thirds vote. George Blue of Liberty then introduced the resolution for an election to move the county seat to Manton. The script went out the window. Fallass was stunned as the Sherman bloc, one and all, voted yes, and the resolution had passed with the necessary two-thirds vote.[1]

1. One can imagine the consternation of the Cadillac bloc and the dilemma in which it was placed when the roll call started by township and the first vote, that of Antioch's Carpenter, unexpectedly was "yes." Was this vote a single aberration from Sherman's solidarity, or was the whole Sherman bloc going to Manton? If the latter, only near unanimous opposition by the Cadillac bloc could stop it. And if Cadillac voted "no," its chances of ever again getting Manton

The Sherman switch was a desperate gamble, based on the assumption that sooner or later a resolution would get through the board of supervisors calling a public election on the question of moving the county seat *somewhere.* If the question was on a move to Cadillac, there was no doubt that the large population in the southeastern part of the county would pass it. On the other hand, whether the county would vote for a move elsewhere was far less certain. With the knowledge of Cadillac's strategy to get the votes of the northeastern and central supervisors, the Sherman leaders had decided that they could avoid the Cadillac resolution only by throwing their support to one of the other resolutions first.

It was a calculated risk, based on Cadillac's own "divide and conquer" strategy. If there was nothing that could be done to abate Manton's own ambition for the county seat which had split the Manton supervisors from the Sherman bloc, then something had to be done to keep Manton separated from Cadillac. Without Manton's three votes, nothing would get through the county board and things would stay as they were.

The heart of the strategy was the assumption that when things got down to brass tacks, Cadillac would never genuinely support Manton. If Cadillac's supervisors backed out on their promise when they saw the Sherman switch and voted against the election resolution, Manton could never trust them again. On the other hand, if they stuck by the promise and the election was held, a failure of Cadillac voters to support Manton would be equally damning. Of course, they might vote yes. If they did, Manton would have the county seat. Against that risk, Sherman was willing to gamble. If they were right, the county seat would still be in Sherman, and a permanent wedge would have been driven between Cadillac and Manton.

So there it was. The county seat question was finally out of the hands of the supervisors and in the hands of the voters. Sherman was honest with Manton about how it would vote at the election.

support were doomed. The second call, Mansfield, of Boon, responded "no." Cadillac's three supervisors all voted "yes." The township members of the Cadillac bloc then all voted "no," but it was not enough. Manton had the exact number of thirteen required. The city of Cadillac had kept its word to Manton, but the Cadillac bloc as a whole had not.

The vote of its supervisors, it said, had been intended only to give the people a chance to speak, but Manton shouldn't expect the people of its area to vote "yes." At Manton, the April election was approached jubilantly, with confidence that it would have the support of the the eastern half of the county. With that support, every last soul in the Sherman area could vote "no" and Manton would still win by a landslide. At Cadillac, the weeks before the election were strangely quiet. Cadillac had been out-foxed. It had never intended to go to the polls for any place except Cadillac. It didn't.

When the votes were counted, the Sherman area voted almost solidly "no," as expected. The Manton area voted almost solidly "yes," and the areas roughly balanced each other. Cadillac, Clam Lake, Cherry Grove, and Haring among them turned out 597 voters. Six voted "yes!" The question was defeated by almost that exact margin. Sherman had won its gamble. It was relieved. Manton was furious. Cadillac was embarrassed, but secretly pleased, and could reflect from the results that it had the votes for a move to Cadillac if it could but get the question on the ballot.

2.

During the summer of 1878, several events significant to the county seat issue seemed to strengthen Sherman's position. The first was the apparent return of Manton to the Sherman camp, or at least its estrangement from Cadillac, as a result of Cadillac's overwhelming vote against moving the county seat to Manton.

Then there were the apparently serious plans for the proposed Cadillac-Sherman Railroad. A route survey was completed during the summer which proved that construction of such a line was feasible, and incorporation of a railroad company was started. The construction of the railroad would mean increased population and economic growth for Sherman and would answer the arguments that Sherman was inaccessible to most of the county's people.

Another event of significance was the death of Cadillac's mayor, George Mitchell. If the *Pioneer* accurately reflected the views of its readers, Mitchell was generally supposed to be the malevolent force behind the Cadillac stratagems. Every hint of bribery or misdoing assumed Mitchell's wealth and power as the source. Every parliamentary trick was credited to some secret Mitchell plot. It was, perhaps, only a slight exaggeration. Now, on his death, the *Pioneer* paid a generous tribute to the departure of a great man, but a distinct note of relief can be sensed in its mention that he had been unsuccessful in only one of his ambitions, that of obtaining the county seat for his city.

Another series of events undoubtedly strengthened the Sherman leadership by removing a divisive influence. The arrival of attorney Charles Marr in Sherman in 1875 had led to the creation of an independent faction more disposed to further Marr's ambitions than to do anything else. Marr sought to dominate Sherman politics and considered as rivals and enemies those he could not dominate. He clashed with John Wheeler, thought him a rival, and considered Wheeler's friends his enemies. Marr's purchase of the newspaper at Sherman had resulted in a deterioration of the quality of the *Pioneer,* and a complete loss of editorial consistency. Personal animosities were impulsively and irrevocably preserved in cold print, along with the most fawning eulogies of those whose support Marr sought.

The announcement of the planned resignation of circuit judge Harrison Wheeler of Ludington in 1878 brought Marr's ambition for the judgeship into the open in the months just prior to the county seat election. It was unfortunate for Sherman and for Marr, for, both privately and through the pages of the *Pioneer,* Marr abandoned Sherman in an attempt to strengthen his position in Cadillac and Manton.

Marr also began an expensive round of campaigning which he could no more afford than the extravagant and inconsistent statements by which he revealed his character in the *Pioneer.* Setting out to woo the business and political leaders of the six-county circuit, Marr made himself a laughing stock. It was reported that a banquet given for the attorneys of Lake, Osceola, and Wexford counties at Reed City cost Marr over $1,500 for food, drink, gifts, and entertainment, a fantastic figure for the 1878 dollar, if true. The Osceola *Outline,* Hersey's newspaper, reported that Hersey's own J. B. Judkins "made a marked and sober contrast to the Wexford County host who is said to have never even been in a circuit court commissioner's trial."

In May, Judkins received the governor's appointment.[2] Two weeks later, Cooper repossessed the *Pioneer.* Marr had made no payments on the purchase price for seven months. Other creditors began to close in, and as the lawsuits mounted, Marr fled. In September, the *News* ran this account: "Where is Marr? Charles S. Marr has absconded. The recent editor of the *Pioneer* is accused of forgery, and there are also shortages reported in the postal funds."

The story went on to the details of an alleged forgery of a note and mortgage of Otis Morrell and a similar incident involving a Benzie County man. The following week, the *News* carried a classic of under-reporting: "C. S. Marr arrested. He is being taken to Calhoun County for trial."

Marr was born in New York in 1849 and had been raised in Battle Creek, where his father settled when he was a child. He had apprenticed to a tinsmith at twelve and learned the trade. Of more than usual intelligence and ambition, he had read law and been admitted to the bar there on his twenty-sixth birthday, moving to Sherman shortly thereafter. The *News* noted his presence in December, 1875, and said, "We welcome Mr. Marr and trust that nothing will mar his prospects." The newspapers treated him cordially for the next year and a half, referring to him as "promising," "gentlemanly," "dapper," "witty," and "adroit." Then he got into the county seat political battle and bought the *Pioneer.* The adjectives of the *News* became less complimentary, while those of the *Pioneer* became more so.

Now he was in trouble. Whatever his local sins, there is no record of any prosecution in Wexford or Benzie counties, nor is there any record left of the proceedings in Calhoun County. The records of the state prison at Jackson, however, show that he was received there on December 12, 1878, on a sentence from Calhoun

2. After thinking it over a few weeks, Judkins refused the appointment, the salary being something less than adequate, and the appointment then went to Samuel D. Haight. A few years later, the salary having been increased, Judkins accepted appointment to the bench on Haight's death. Judkins had practiced in Clam Lake in partnership with S. S. Fallass in 1874-75, and proved to be a competent and respected judge.

County. The sentence was commuted by the governor to permit his parole in 1880, and he was permitted to resume his trade as a tinsmith at Battle Creek. In 1883 he returned to Sherman and entered a real estate, loan, and insurance partnership with Sanford Gasser and soon resumed the practice of law. He apparently had won the respect of the community for his rehabilitation, had a good law practice, was elected Circuit Court Commissioner, and became much in demand as a public speaker. We meet him again after his election as supervisor of Concord Township. Late in 1889, he moved to Muskegon, where he held office as prosecuting attorney and developed into an effective and successful trial lawyer.

At any rate, when the *Pioneer* foreclosure sale was held in June, 1878, John Wheeler was the purchaser in partnership with H. F. Campbell, and the *Pioneer* became a better newspaper and a strong voice for Sherman. Marr's departure removed what had been a disruptive factor in Sherman's ranks. Wheeler and H. B. Sturtevant were able to repair the damage done by Marr's erratic behavior and end the disarray in Sherman leadership.

3.

An incident of the *Pioneer* foreclosure sale is also illustrative of how events of the national political scene began to assume more importance and to shape local issues to Sherman's advantage.

The panic of 1873 had had little effect on the struggling new settlements in Wexford County, and the Republican schism of the late years of President Grant's administration was largely unnoticed in northern Michigan. Even the Hayes-Tilden election of 1878 had been of less importance locally than the county seat issue. The county was staunchly Republican and satisfied to be so.

In Cadillac, George Mitchell was the dominant figure politically, as in everything else, and was a member of the state Republican committee. In the Sherman area, nominal partisan leadership had passed from Thomas Ferguson to Charles Cooper to Charles Marr, all of whom had acknowledged Mitchell's county leadership while chafing at the presence of party leadership outside the county seat.

By 1878, however, the local party was feeling the impact of

national affairs. The leaders of the so-called Republican reform group of the earlier seventies were now differing with the "regulars" over economic policy, and the growing strength of the "greenback" movement was stirring up controversy that carried across party lines and loyalties.

The lack of economic and monetary stability which yet plagues society produced particularly harsh consequences in the days before central banking and bank insurance had evolved. From the time of Andrew Jackson, banking and currency was a political issue of first order. Foreign money was accepted as legal exchange in the United States until after the Civil War, requiring Congress to pass an annual exchange act to establish the legal rate of exchange for the money of other nations. A shortage of money during the Civil War brought the issue of banknotes in small denominations of ten, twenty-five, and fifty cents called "shinplasters," and the issue of federal notes called "greenbacks" replaced silver and gold coins, or "hard money."

In 1873 the Republican administration proclaimed gold the sole basis of exchange, and silver coinage was halted. The recession of that year had a particularly severe impact on the farmers and settlers of the Middle West and Far West, who concluded that the government's gold policy was to blame. The issuance of paper money by private banks added to the monetary confusion, since such money was worthless if a bank failed from mismanagement, bad investments, or because of a general financial recession.

The "greenback" political movement resulted, advocating free silver coinage and an increase in circulating money by federal issuance of more paper money, or "greenbacks." A Greenback party was organized which elected several congressmen in 1878. In most areas, however, the issue only served to cause a realignment of the existing parties or the organization of rival Republican and Democratic slates. In Wexford County, the Greenback party was organized, but it failed to attract any substantial support.[3]

In Sherman, former *Pioneer* editor Charles Cooper advocated the alignment of county Republicans with a reform-greenback

3. H. B. Chapman of Hobart organized the first Greenback caucus in the county, one plank of the platform of which advocated that Hobart be made the county seat.

faction of the party but was outvoted. Cooper announced that he was bolting the party and organized a Greenback caucus in Antioch Township. When Charles Marr, to whom Cooper had sold the *Pioneer* in 1877, defaulted on his payments, Cooper started a foreclosure suit, and it was evident that he would convert the *Pioneer* into a Greenback organ if he reacquired it. Just prior to his sale to Marr, however, Cooper had given an option to purchase to his printer, H. F. Campbell, and the sale to Marr was made subject to Campbell's right to purchase. In order to prevent Cooper from reacquiring the paper, the Republican leadership urged Campbell to exercise his option. The only trouble was that Campbell didn't have the purchase price of $100. John Wheeler did have the money, but rather than make a loan to Campbell he advanced the money in return for a half interest in the *Pioneer,* thereby assuring himself of a voice in the editorial policy of the paper.

The closing of the transaction is unclear, since the record of the foreclosure sale simply indicates that Wheeler and Campbell were the purchasers. Wheeler says that he paid the option purchase price of $100 to Cooper only with great difficulty, since Cooper wanted the paper himself. When Wheeler tried to pay him with paper money, Cooper refused the tender, and it was necessary to obtain the money in gold coin and offer it in the presence of witnesses before Cooper reluctantly accepted it.[4]

4. It probably never occurred to Cooper that his demand for gold for personal purposes was inconsistent with his currency reform views. Cooper moved to Manton and bought the *Tribune* in 1880. He was soon broke again and sold it to Campbell, who had followed him there from Sherman. Within a few years, he had gained his first real financial strength by money lending, an activity which enabled him to repurchase the *Tribune* and resume his crusade against money lenders, Wall Street, and gold.

At Sherman, Campbell was named postmaster after Marr's disappearance, and the Wheeler-Campbell partnership continued successfully for two years. In 1880 Wheeler bought out Campbell, who moved to Manton, where he bought out Cooper, then resold and returned to Sherman, where he was elected to the state legislature.

Under Wheeler, the *Pioneer* proved a better business and a better newspaper than it had under either of the professional newspapermen, Cooper or Campbell. In 1891 Wheeler sold the *Pioneer* to Reuben Frederick, its best known editor.

The death of George A. Mitchell in the summer of 1878 undoubtedly slowed Cadillac's campaign to obtain the county seat. John Wheeler later expressed the opinion that it took at least two years to get over the loss of Mitchell's leadership and that Cadillac might well have acquired the county seat in 1879 had it not been for his death. Oddly enough, Wheeler thought this was largely because of the loss of Mitchell's leadership in the Republican party.

The man Mitchell had brought to his new villge to be his attorney, S. S. Fallass, was a Democrat. There were differing views as to whether Fallass was the brains behind the Cadillac county seat campaign or merely the agent to carry out the plans of Mitchell. In any event, there was no doubt that he had become the public spokesman for Cadillac, in and out of the board of supervisors, and that he was at once a scholarly man and a hard fighter.

Until the summer of 1878, Mitchell's control of the Republican party had been such that the presence of a Democrat at his side and as the city's spokesman had attracted no attention. The greenback issue had begun to cause some differences among the county Republicans, some of whom had threatened to form an independent Republican organization. Mitchell had kept unity with fair success. On his death, however, the party was fractionalized.

As matters developed, no independent Republican slate was organized that year and the Greenback party acquired no significant following. Instead, most of the Republican dissidents either switched to the Democratic party or announced their support of individual Democratic candidates. Ephraim Shay of Haring, later famous as the developer of the logging locomotive, was elected county treasurer. He was the only Democrat elected in November, but every contest was close.

Heresy in the Republican party was to continue for another eight years, but the "regulars" in the party never lost control.[5] In

5. The extent of dissatisfaction within the Republican party can be noted by the number of Independent candidates who ran in the next ten years and the appearance of unified "independent" slates in several elections, the individual candidates the meanwhile denying any intent to organize a new party or to leave the Republican fold. Several people ran for two or more offices, as Republicans

Cadillac, they were not disposed to place confidence in any Democrat, and Fallass and Sawyer, who had run for prosecuting attorney, found their county seat campaign handcuffed by personal animosity and party concern for returning greenbackers to the fold.

and Independents, and at least two had the dubious distinction of being twice defeated on two different tickets. David Rice went full circle. After three terms as a Republican prosecutor, he ran as an Independent in 1880 and was defeated. In 1884 he was elected as a Republican. In 1886 and 1888, he ran as a Democrat and was defeated. A Republican again, he was elected in 1892 and 1894.

Chapter Seventeen

COURTING: 1878-1879

COURT: noun, place of settling legal dispute; verb, to woo, solicit, persuade . . .

The fall election of 1878 gave Wexford County, and Cadillac, the district's representative in Lansing in Henry F. May, one of Cadillac's first settlers. His partner, George Holbrook, although a Democrat, had received considerable support in Clam Lake in 1874, when he ran for the House against Thomas Ferguson. Ferguson, then of Sherman, had negotiated the act by which Cleon Township had been taken from Manistee County and attached to Wexford County, thus creating another vote for the Sherman bloc on the county board of supervisors. Now, four years later, Holbrook's Republican partner was successful in getting the seat. He had two things in mind for Cadillac. One was to put Cleon Township back in Manistee County.

However, before tending to Cleon, May was determined to accomplish by legislation what Cadillac hadn't been able to do by litigation: Get John Wheeler off the board of supervisors, at least temporarily, and eliminate a vote of the Sherman bloc by eliminating Sherman Township.

As his first act when the legislature convened, May introduced a bill for a local act to dis-organize Sherman Township. The *Pioneer* editorialized vehemently against the bill. The county board, in the absence of some of the Cadillac area supervisors, slipped through a resolution to be sent to the legislature, calling the bill an unwarranted intrusion by the legislature into local affairs which should best be left to local self-determination. Nevertheless, the political weight of Wexford County now lay in Cadillac, and the legislature found convincing the argument of May and Cadillac that the tiny township of four square sections was a purely artificial creation designed to add an extra voice on the board of supervisors. The bill passed both houses without serious trouble and was signed by the governor on May 28, becoming Act 394 of the Local Acts of 1879.

Wheeler's answer was to try the same route again. If Sherman Township was to be dissolved by the legislature, the board of supervisors could create a different township to take its place. A simple majority vote of the board would be enough, and Sherman could probably manage that. The Manton area was still smarting at the way Cadillac had voted "no" on the public referendum for moving the county seat to Manton, and its supervisors would support Sherman. Colfax Township went back and forth like a pendulum, but in April it had elected a new supervisor, J. W. Houghtalin, who looked kindly on Sherman.

To add even more relish, a reading of Act 394 showed that Representative May had neglected or been unable to get an immediate effect clause. Had he done so, Sherman Township would have ceased to exist the moment the act was signed by Governor Croswell in May. Without such a clause, new acts become effective ninety days after adjournment of the legislature—and Sherman Township wouldn't expire until August 28. Until then, the vote of Sherman Township's supervisor would give the Sherman block a tenth vote and a majority. With its dying breath, Wheeler thought it only appropriate that Sherman Township could vote for its own successor.

A petition was immediately prepared calling for the organization of another new township, and a special meeting of the board of supervisors was called for August 21. The petition called for the first caucus of the new township to be held at Sherman post office on September 8, so that a new supervisor could be immediately selected and ready to attend the fall meeting of the board of supervisors. The new township, to be called Concord, was another dwarf of only four sections at the county seat, this time consisting of sections 31 and 32 of Hanover and 5 and 6 of Antioch.

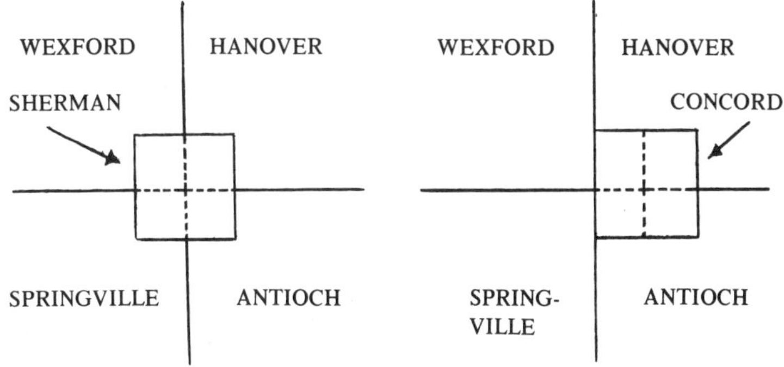

On August 21, John Wheeler, though no longer a supervisor, was on hand for the meeting of the board to guide the Sherman strategy, along with former clerk H. B. Sturtevant, his successor.[1] S. S. Fallass of Cadillac refused to answer roll call and then promptly moved to adjourn. He sufficiently disrupted the meeting so that before the Concord Township petition could be introduced, he had read and filed formal protests signed by Cadillac supervisor D. E. McIntyre and Boon's Will McNitt, asserting that they had not received legal notice of the meeting and that the meeting was unlawful. Fallass left the meeting and joined McNitt and McIntyre, who were waiting in the clerk's office.[2] In their absence, the Concord resolution was passed by a vote of 10 to 5.

The first caucus of the new township was held as scheduled, and Sturtevant was elected as Concord Township's first supervisor. On the following day, prosecuting attorney David Rice filed a suit against Sturtevant and Concord Township to enjoin Sturte-

1. After his acquisition of a half interest in the Sherman *Pioneer* in the fall of 1878, Wheeler had become the focus of increasingly personal attacks in the Cadillac *News*. He was disposed to think that his service to Sherman might be more effective if he had no apparent interest as a supervisor, and, accordingly, he did not seek re-election in the spring election of 1879. Perhaps he only wanted to avoid being voted out of a job by the legislature.

2. The cagey Wheeler sought to establish the presence of McNitt and McIntyre by having Sturtevant include them in the attendance list for per diem and mileage. Both returned the checks, and Wheeler found the checks still unclaimed in the treasurer's office when he became county treasurer nineteen years later.

vant from sitting as a supervisor and to declare the organization of the township illegal. A temporary injunction was issued by Judge Judkins. It was to be late in the following spring before a ruling would be made. In the meantime, Sturtevant was barred from sitting.[3]

2.

The fall session of the board of supervisors opened October 13 without Sturtevant. Without him, the board was reduced to eighteen members and was again evenly divided. Motion after motion brought a 9-9 vote. The stalemate had been restored.

In an effort to avoid a possible ruling that Concord Township was illegally organized, a petition was presented on the first day of the session calling for the organization of a new township of Sherman. The Cadillac bloc responded the next day with a petition to set aside the south third of Springville Township as a new township to be called South Branch. At the same time, Representative May filed a lawsuit to enjoin the county board of supervisors from organizing any new township containing any part of the former township of Sherman, and another temporary injunction against the board was issued by Judge Judkins.

The Sherman faction countered this move by still another township petition, this one to set aside the south half of Hanover Township, except for sections 31 and 32, as the township of Benton.

3. Rice started another lawsuit which had all the earmarks of a putup job. The newly elected county treasurer, Ephraim Shay, refused to keep his office at Sherman, alleging that it had never been legally designated as the county seat. Prosecuting attorney Rice then brought the suit against Shay to compel him to keep office at Sherman. In his private business, Rice was Shay's attorney. For this suit, he was represented by S. S. Fallass, and rumor had it that the suit was so cozy that Rice and Fallass, formerly law partners, worked together on the Fallass brief, demonstrating the technical deficiencies in the designation of Sherman as a county seat. In short, Rice was bringing the suit with the intention of losing it to his former partner. Judge J. B. Judkins, the third member of the old partnership of Fallass, Rice, and Judkins, granted Rice the relief he really didn't want and ordered Shay to Sherman.

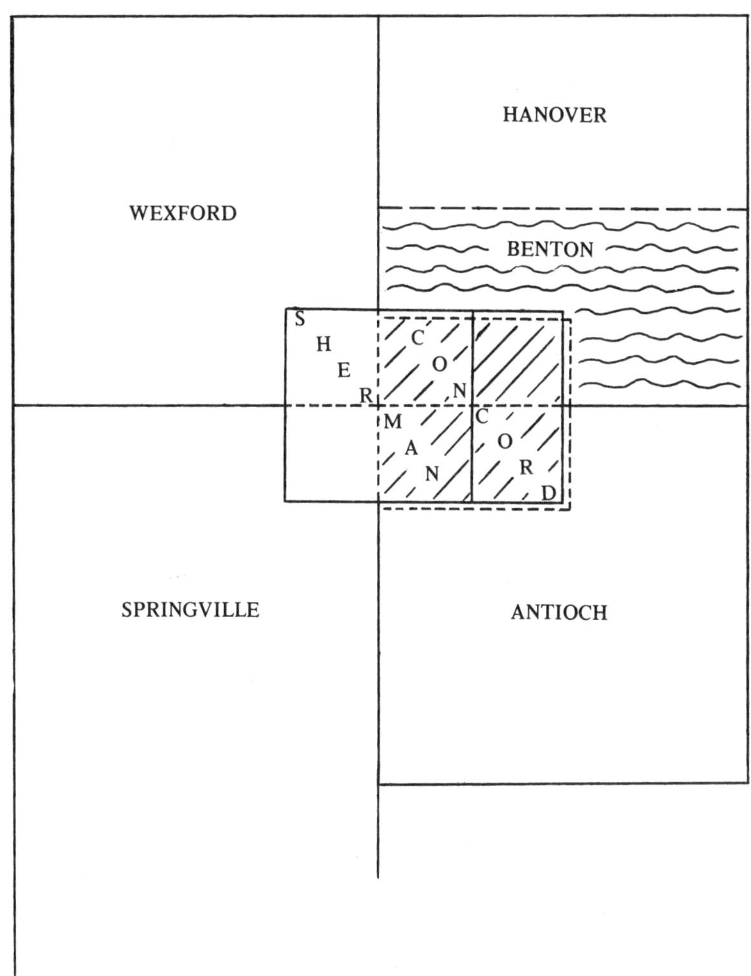

The fall session was lively and long. J. W. Ransom of Wexford Township declared war the first day. In supporting the petition for a new township of Sherman, he accused J. W. Cobbs and Holden Green of helping Representative May buy votes at Lansing for the bill to kill the old Sherman Township. S. S. Fallass of Cadillac requested a point of order but was overruled by Chairman H. C. McFarlan of Cedar Creek. Fallass demanded an appeal to the whole board unless Ransom withdrew the accusation. Rather than retract the statement, Ransom asserted that specific evidence of the bribery existed and would be placed in the hands of the governor.[4] The appeal to the board was then voted upon and Fallass was upheld on a 9-8 vote when Chairman McFarlan did not vote. Ransom declined to apologize, and the session turned sullen rather than violent. All serious business was brought to vote with a minimum of discussion—and deadlocked by a 9-9 vote. None of the new township petitions passed.

The board met again at a special session called at Cadillac on February 16, 1880. Nothing of consequence happened the first two days, but the Sherman faction came to the conclusion that Cadillac had a surprise of some kind in store. Whether it did or not, we do not know, but the suspicion that it did led Sherman to decide that something had to be done to disrupt the schedule. The strategem devised was desperate and exposed the entire Sherman bloc to punishment for contempt of court.

On the 18th, H. B. Sturtevant appeared at the Holbrook & May Hall with the Sherman delegation. He had the first word as the session opened, demanding amendment of the minutes of the previous day which showed a full board present. They were erroneous, he said, since he had not been present. County clerk Manketelow refused to call the roll because of the injunctions, so Chairman McFarlan called the roll and ordered the minutes corrected. Manktelow refused.

The meeting continued only briefly. McFarlan called the roll on every matter and permitted Sturtevant to vote. McFarlan announced every matter as carried by a 10-9 vote, while Manktelow stubbornly recorded a 9-9 tie in the minutes. The last such item was a motion to adjourn *sine die,* made by Sturtevant. The chairman called the roll, announced the meeting adjourned, and the Sherman faction left. Manktelow's minutes, on the other hand, record that, there no longer being a quorum present, the board adjourned on the motion of Mr. Green until the next day.

4. So far as we know, no such presentation was made to the governor.

3.

There was no meeting on the following day. When the meeting ended in turmoil on the 18th, the February session was over. Its disruption had been occasioned by the appearance of Sturtevant, claiming recognition as supervisor of Concord Township in violation of the temporary injunctions issued by Judge Judkins in the suits brought by prosecuting attorney David Rice and by Henry F. May.

The first suit was heard in April. Judge Judkins announced his decision from the bench, holding that Concord was illegally organized and that the injunction barring Sturtevant from a seat on the county board should be made permanent. For some reason, no written decree was ever filed. No attempt was made to bring contempt proceedings for Sturtevant's appearance at the February meeting in violation of the injunctions, nor was May's lawsuit ever brought on for hearing. Everyone was content to let matters rest, the ruling in the first case apparently having disposed of the question permanently.

An interesting legal footnote remained, however. In 1883 Charles S. Marr. after two years in prison and three years at his former trade as a tinner at Battle Creek, returned to Sherman. In some fashion, he became aware of the Concord story and examined the court files. May's case had never been heard. There was no decree filed in the suit by Rice. He promptly sought out the former officers of Concord, called a meeting, and induced them to appoint him supervisor. At the spring election of 1884, he put up a full slate of township officers, headed by himself, and undertook to operate the independent Township of Concord.

When Marr appeared at the county board of supervisors and demanded a seat as the representative of Concord Township, he was summarily turned away, and the newspapers laughed at his game. They were forced to take him seriously when he presented himself at the state treasurer's office in Lansing and demanded a share of the railroad tax for Concord Township. The treasurer's response was to delay all tax distribution to Wexford County and its townships. Finally, the attorney general commenced a *quo warranto* action against Marr in the Supreme Court, and Concord was decided at the highest level.

The Supreme Court ruled that Concord had never legally existed, and the Cadillac *News* crowed at the victory:

> The Supreme Court says Concord never was a town. That settles a long vexed question. Would-be supervisor Marr, who long has planned to represent an imaginary township of Concord in this county, will no longer appear at the regular meeting of the board and have his illustrious name presented only to be sat upon. That smiling face and petite figure, that eloquent tongue and proud step will no longer be witnessed in that great, impotent council of the county. Marr and Concord has sunk into oblivion. Their star is set. Peace be to their ashes.[5]

For all practical purposes, however, Concord was a dead issue after the circuit court decision in April, 1880. The Sherman bloc called a special meeting in May, hoping to force an appeal of the case at county expense, but only defendant Sturtevant and the five supervisors of the immediate Sherman area showed up at the courthouse. Thereafter, everyone accepted it as fact that the board had been reduced to eighteen members, and Sturtevant gave up the fight.

4.

After the walkout of, or adjournment by, the Sherman faction on February 18, 1880, the remaining nine supervisors had adjourned until the following morning. There was, of course, no meeting the following day, or the following month for that matter—or, if one were to judge by the clerk's minutes, for many months thereafter.

Actually, the Sherman faction made several attempts to call special meetings at Sherman in the next few months. Since Sturtevant was to be treated as the supervisor of Concord

5. The gloating in late October was correct but premature, based on erroneous reports that the Court had decided the case on the day it was argued, October 21, 1884. The Court's opinion was not handed down until January 4, 1885.

Township, clerk Manketelow refused to send out the notices or to attend the meetings, and no record was ever made of the meetings. No business was transacted, anyway, because there never was a quorum, even counting Sturtevant. The Cadillac faction was joined in boycotting the meeting by Houghtalin of Colfax! At some point between February 18 and the date of the first attempted meeting at Sherman, Houghtalin had deserted Sherman.

What changed Houghtalin is also a mystery. The southern half of Colfax had entertained its own ambitions, while the northern half had consistently favored Sherman. The Colfax vote had swung from one camp to another, depending on who was supervisor. Houghtalin, however, had always been firmly for Sherman; now he was with Cadillac.

At the next attempt for a special meeting in May, the only supervisors who appeared to join Sturtevant were Meyer of Antioch, Hannabal of Cleon, Worth of Hanover, Ransom of Wexford, and Dean of Springville. Manton's bloc had again moved away from Sherman. Cadillac was playing a variation of the game it had pursued from the beginning. Its plan to wean Manton away from Sherman by encouraging Manton's county seat ambitions had backfired in 1878, when Sherman had supported the calling of an election on moving the county seat to Manton, and the question had been badly beaten in the Cadillac area voting.

Now Cadillac was wooing again. It sounded sincere, humble, and persuasive. It disavowed any secret negotiations or underlying ambitions. It was resigned, said its spokesman, to the "true situation on the board of supervisors," which was that Cadillac could never get the necessary twelve votes to call an election to move the county seat to Cadillac. Cadillac would be content to have the county seat at Manton where it was accessible by railroad. No alternate or second ballot deals were sought. Just put up the one resolution and Cadillac would support it, and at the election, Cadillac's citizens would reverse their previous rejection of Manton.

Several things were working in Cadillac's favor. The anti-Cadillac sentiment of 1878 had dissipated quickly. Manton found no great comfort or community of interest with Sherman, whose residents had voted "no" almost as overwhelmingly as those of the Cadillac area. And Manton's ambition was still there, bruised, but needing only slight encouragement to blossom again.

Another voice had been joined to Cadillac's chorus of sirens in singing that encouragement, that of Col. Thomas J. Thorp. Thorp was born in New York to a distinguished father, who joined him soon after he homesteaded here after the Civil War. The township was named after him, but he modestly insisted on renaming it Selma. He had returned to his native New York, joining in the formation of one of the first great school book publishing firms, A. S. Barnes & Co., and traveling widely throughout the country in its behalf. He had also been superintendent of schools at Buffalo, New York. He returned to his Selma farm in 1879 and found that his eighty-four-year-old father had become one of the county's favorite personalities. With his father going everywhere with him, he plunged into Republican and county seat politics.

The father, Montgomery Thorp, was born in New York in 1795, named after Gen. Richard Montgomery, with whom his father had served in the French and Indian Wars. During the revolution, the family had been torn between allegiance to the crown and its sense of identity with its neighbors who sought independence. General Montgomery had resigned his commission with the British Army and had come to the colonies to take up arms for their independence. That swung the Thorps to the side of revolution, and they had served with distinction. Montgomery Thorp had fought the English himself as a boy in 1812, and the old gentleman, with his wit and exciting stories, was a favorite speaker at public gatherings around the county.[6]

Thomas Thorp was a graduate of Union College, where he had been a noted debater, his facility of speech giving him a rather considerable reputation throughout the Midwest in later years as

6. The stories apparently dwelt largely on his father's adventures, his own in the War of 1812 being a matter of chagrin to him. At seventeen he had enlisted in a unit of the New York militia which had disobeyed orders and refused to leave the American side of the Niagara River to go to the aid of the troops during the battle of Queenstown, Ontario. According to the story, Montgomery struck a cowardly officer who refused to give the order to embark, and he spent almost a month in the stockade before being vindicated. He advanced to captain by the end of the War but never saw combat.

he traveled around the country giving addresses on public occasions and ceremonies, large and small. He had enlisted during the Civil War and was commissioned as an officer, his lack of military experience notwithstanding. He found himself in action almost at once, and his bravery won him rapid promotions to the rank of full colonel. His bravery was better than his sense of tactics, however, and eventually led him into a position where his entire unit found itself comfortably bivouacked within the Confederate lines. He was awakened in the morning by an amused Virginia major, who broke the news to him that he was his captive.

In captivity, Thorp's bravery continued to exceed his good sense, and he distinguished himself by his intransigent refusal to co-operate in any way with his captors. His men loved him for it and perhaps were its beneficiaries, as a hapless prison camp commander attempted to placate his truculent captive. On a Fourth of July, however, he nearly overdid it. His men erected a platform a scant fifty feet from the wire which separated the prisoners from the Confederate commandant's quarters. The militant Thorp had planned an Independence Day ceremony for his fellow prisoners which he climaxed with an abrasive oration defending the Union and denouncing the rebels of the South. He never finished it, as the camp commandant finally lost his patience, sent his men to disperse the prisoners, and ordered Thorp hanged on his own platform the following morning. The camp erupted at the news, and the situation appeared so volatile that the execution order was finally countermanded at the last minute. Reports of the incident filtered back as prisoners were exchanged, and when Thorp was finally released he found that he had been promoted to brigadier general during his captivity. He refused the rank, saying it had not been meritoriously earned.[7]

Back in Wexford County in 1879, Thorp read law and was admitted to the bar, spoke widely at civic affairs and was soon in a position of leadership in his party. He was a doer, a thinker, and a remarkable speaker. His energy was devoted to the county seat campaign, and he was largely responsible for dissipating the dis-

7. As with many of the returned veterans, he did enjoy his military title, and signed his name Col. T. J. Thorp. The story of his renounced rank was well known, and the newspapers invariably referred to him as General Thorp.

trust of Cadillac. He was close to Houghtalin and may well have been responsible for winning him over to the Cadillac camp. In 1880 the divisions within the Republican party reached a peak, and it appeared that there would either be a complete Independent Republican slate of candidates or that the Greenback element in the party would capture the regular party convention. County clerk C. J. Manktelow, capable and popular, had joined the dissidents. Thorp announced his candidacy for county clerk and register of deeds, was nominated, and forced the dissidents into their own county slate.

In a remarkable series of letters for publication, Thorp discussed his candidacy, the issues of the parties, the role of the reform group within the Republican party, the silver-greenback issue, Michigan's future, the settlement of immigrants in the county, and, of course, the county seat. In a three-way race in which Manktelow ran as an independent and drew off some of the Republican vote, Thorp won a handsome victory.

The purpose of the Thorp letters, apart from advancing his own candidacy, was apparently two-fold. They were designed to heal the breach between the Republican "regulars" and the reform-Greenback group and to promote the marriage of Cadillac and Manton on the county seat issue.[8] On the latter, he came back time after time to one point: "If you don't believe us, try us. Manton has nothing to lose by an election on moving the county seat to Manton."

At Sherman, John Wheeler spoke to Manton in the *Pioneer.* "Beware—Cadillac has lied, connived, bribed and threatened to steal to get the county seat. Why should Manton buy from this same drummer [salesman] again." A few issues later, Wheeler returned to the attack but added too much. "Sherman," he said,

8. In the first aim, the success of the letters is open to question. The dissidents did bolt and put up a separate slate as Independents, headed by incumbent prosecutor David A. Rice and clerk Manktelow. The Republicans won everything, and John Mansfield of Boon beat the Democratic incumbent treasurer, Ephraim Shay, but the party was split. Two years hence, Donald E. McIntyre would be elected prosecutor as an Independent, and the Independents would make enough inroads into Republican votes to enable the election of a number of Democrats in the next few years.

"had never played the sharper to Manton but has always spoken honestly. Now, if it come to pass, Sherman would rather see the county seat go to Manton than to an undeserving Cadillac." Wheeler went on to express the hope that Manton would appreciate this honest co-operation and not let itself be demeaned by Cadillac. The damage was done. Thorp replied: "You [Manton] introduce another resolution to remove the county seat to Manton, and test the good faith of the Sherman people, and you will find that we will be as loyal to you as Sherman will. I speak for all the members of the Republican caucus in telling you we will be happy to make Manton our official home."

Manton wasn't sure Cadillac meant it, but Thorp was right; Manton had nothing to lose. Sherman was sure Cadillac didn't mean it, but it was now in the position where it couldn't afford to vote against Manton and probably couldn't stop Manton, anyway, if Cadillac kept its word. And, somewhat bitterly, Sherman did prefer Manton over Cadillac if it did have to lose the county seat. Besides Sherman could still hope that the election of '78 would repeat itself and that the Cadillac area would vote against Manton.

The fall meeting of the board of supervisors was subdued. It was as if the last session at Sherman was a requiem for the courthouse which had known so many brawls and arguments in its few years, as if everyone knew this was fated to be the last session there. The near riot of January, 1876, was not to be repeated. There were no crowds. The year's accumulation of business was dispatched quickly and quietly. A new township, South Branch, was organized in the southern half of the county, nearly completing the county governmental structure. The vote was unanimous, even though everyone knew that its principal citizens, James Banker, Neal Ford, E. P. Stocking, and Joseph Rossell, were Cadillac supporters.

On October 14, H. C. McFarlan, Manton merchant and supervisor from Cedar Creek, moved to call an election the following April on the question of moving the county seat to Manton. There were virtually no debate. The motion carried by a vote of 16 to 2. Once again the people would speak for or against a move from Sherman to Manton!

Chapter Eighteen

1881: SHALL THE COUNTY SEAT BE REMOVED TO MANTON?

YES ☒
NO ☐

As 1880 drew to a close, outward appearances seemed to indicate that the County Seat War was all but over. At the fall session of the board of supervisors, an overwhelming 16-2 vote had approved a county referendum on the question of moving the county seat from Sherman to Manton. Cadillac's leaders had supported the Manton bid and publicly renounced any claim to the county seat for Cadillac. The unanimous vote of the Cadillac area supervisors for the election resolution seemed convincing evidence of Cadillac's good faith. Except for some occasional rumblings from John Wheeler through the pages of the *Pioneer*, everything was peace and harmony.

That this should be so is nothing short of amazing in the light of Cadillac's past duplicity. In eight years, Cadillac had caused countless resolutions to be introduced before the board of supervisors, calling for removal of the county seat from Sherman—to Manton, to Meauwataka, to Cadillac—all but one failing for lack of the necessary two-thirds vote of the board. For control of the board, bribes had been offered and some allegedly paid; townships had been organized, some legally and some not; deals had been offered, threats made, and political rewards promised. A setback here could be converted to advantage elsewhere, as one faction and then another procured special legislation to create or dissolve townships, to incorporate the small village of Clam Lake as the city of Cadillac, and even to detach the township of Cleon from Manistee County and add it to Wexford. Supervisors had been arrested or threatened with arrest, and lawsuits had been frequent. Words and fists had inflicted a variety of bruises, some not easily forgotten by proud men. Township elections had been fixed, and one supervisor had been literally run out of office by a well-managed mob.

Manton had no reason from past experience to trust Cadillac's claims of support. The Cadillac leaders, beginning with George A. Mitchell and S. S. Fallass, had set about encouraging Manton's ambitions as early as 1874 as a means of isolating Sherman politically. At no time had Cadillac intended to deliver on its promises, and the duplicity of its dealings had been often enough revealed. The only previous election authorized by the board of supervisors had also been on moving the county seat to Manton in 1878, when Cadillac support had failed to materialize and the question was overwhelmingly defeated.

During the bitter fall session of the board in 1879, the Manton *Tribune* listed chapter and verse to enumerate these "Judas traits" of Cadillac's leaders. Referring to the 1878 election, it noted that the "whole half-hundred Cadillac merchants and townsmen who had pledged us their efforts must have been ill that election day for the "ayes" from Cadillac, Haring, Clam Lake and Cherry Grove were but an even half-dozen."

2.

But now all was forgotten. The *Tribune* had come into existence in 1879, in part to voice Manton's county seat ambitions. It was almost immediately bought by Charles E. Cooper, who had been the founder of the Wexford County *Pioneer* at Sherman in 1872. Cooper, the dissident Greenback-Republican, was a poor businessman, but he was aggressive and fluent. He made Manton into his image, creating a populist sentiment which endures there to this day. He was to hold almost every kind of public office in Manton and Cedar Creek Township over the next ten years. He was easily carried away with the picture he conceived of himself. In 1880 it was the picture of the great conciliator. Past wounds from Cadillac were forgiven. Now Manton was to be the place to which the whole county could repair for its government with mutual advantage; Charles E. Cooper was its leader and spokesman in bringing peace to the county and prosperity to Manton.

In Cadillac, another new paper had been founded by attorney

John B. Rosevelt, proclaiming itself the voice of an Independent Republican constituency, healing the scars of the Greenback rift in the party, and appearing to take an independent position on the county seat issue as well. The *Daily Enterprise* was slightly misnamed, appearing so irregularly that it might better have been called a monthly paper. It alternately railed against Sherman and editorialized on the need for peace in the county. It announced a "studied conclusion" that the prime concern for all was to have the county seat where there was rail service, and that it would be all the advantage that Cadillac could hope for to have the county seat at Manton. Soon the paper was transplanted and by the end of 1880 was being issued at the small logging settlement in Hanover Township which later became Buckley, challenging Sherman's political leadership in the heart of Sherman country and advocating removal of the county seat to Manton.

The Cadillac *News* "admitted" that events of the previous eight years were conclusive proof that Cadillac could never overcome the opposition of the rest of the county and that Cadillac merchants were acknowledging the validity of the out-county claim that Cadillac was too far removed from the rest of the county for convenience. But, said the *News,* it was equally true of Sherman, to which access by poor roads was a great handicap. It repeatedly spoke of a growing Manton support in Cadillac. On February 8, 1881, it put the issue squarely on Sherman's back, saying that Manton would get a strong vote in the Cadillac area and that whether there would be a removal to Manton for the interests of the whole county would depend in large measure on Sherman's willingness to join in co-operation with its fellow citizens of the county. What could Sherman say?

The *Pioneer* answered that the people of Sherman were well aware that, so long as Cadillac and Manton hung together, the county seat was going to leave Sherman. Said editor Wheeler:

> We are very pleased to note the spirit of conciliation and concession . . . that the *News,* together with the remarks heretofore dropped by prominent businessmen of Cadillac, evinces in furthering of so laudable an object as that of putting the county seat question beyond the power of further harm toward the development and prosperity of our county.

> There is another thing which we are glad to notice and that is the evident improvement in the feeling which is manifested by the members of the board towards those from other parts of the county. This has been particularly noticeable at recent sessions of the board and is undoubtedly the result of a desire to compromise on the one great question which has heretofore agitated the county... We can therefore as well afford to be generous on this occasion as can the people of Cadillac, for while we cannot possibly risk anything, should the vote carry we can have the proud satisfaction of making it as nearly unanimous as possible.

The personal salesmanship of Col. Thomas J. Thorp and his letters were undoubtedly influential in setting the stage for the smooth passage of the election resolution by the board of supervisors in October. The whole county was impressed when he pledged that if elected county clerk he would forthwith move to Manton in the assurance that it was to become the county seat. He was elected and he moved.

3.

In truth, Cooper and Wheeler had been taken in. The Cadillac game was the same. Colonel Thorp moved to Manton but as a renter and not a buyer. He intended only a temporary stay. Cadillac's *Daily Enterprise* had been deliberately created to further Cadillac's schemes to get the county seat. The apparent Republican owner, editor Rosevelt, had no money invested.[1] The real owners of the so-called Republican paper were among Cadillac's top strategists in the county seat war, attorney S. S. Fallass, and businessmen George Holbrook, John G. Mosser, and Daniel McCoy, all but McCoy being Democrats.

True, Cadillac was willing to move the county seat to Manton.

1. And anyway, he was a Democrat and had run for office as such. His move to "Republicanism" consisted of running for Circuit Court commissioner as an Independent at the same time that he again ran for prosecutor as a Democrat!

But that Wheeler could conclude that Cadillac would be content to leave it there was a great mistake, a mistake deliberately induced. Cadillac was looking beyond the Manton election to another referendum for removal of the county seat to Cadillac. And so, while the county discussed the probabilities of Manton's getting a majority vote in the 1881 spring election, Cadillac's plans were concerned with the means of getting the two-thirds control of the board of supervisors necessary to call another election the following year for moving the county capitol to Cadillac.

During the bitter sessions of 1879, the board had been stalemated, 9 to 9. The fight over Concord Township in the spring of 1880 had served to further separate Manton from Sherman but, more important, had brought supervisor J. W. Houghtalin of Colfax into the Cadillac camp. Cadillac now had a 10-8 majority but was still two short of the necessary two-thirds control.

In the harmony of the 1880 fall session, a new township, South Branch, was organized, sponsored by and giving its support to the southern supervisors. Plus one for Cadillac.

In the happy days prior to the 1881 election, it went almost unnoticed that Representative Henry May of Cadillac had introduced a bill in the legislature which was speedily enacted, returning Cleon Township to Manistee County, whence it had come.[2] Minus one for Sherman. Cadillac now had eleven votes on the eighteen-man board, just one short of the necessary two-thirds. By hook or by crook, it would get another.

4.

As winter turned to spring in 1881, the forthcoming April 4 election was the main topic of discussion in the northern part of the county. Manton's merchants happily played on the county seat theme in their advertising. One ad in January said; "County Seat fight may warm things up, but our stoves will do the job better . . . " Supervisor McFarlan had this ad for his department

2. The *Pioneer* briefly noted that of the thirty-eight registered voters in Cleon the names of thirty-six appeared on a petition to the Senate asking that Cleon remain a part of Wexford County. The petition was ignored.

store: "Some people make great fun about this "Concord" business, but there is one *accord* about our merchandise..." Lulled by the assurances of Cadillac, neither Manton nor Sherman had any thought but that this was the final determination of the county seat question. Sherman grudgingly admitted that it would likely be traveling to Manton for county business, and it resigned itself to its loss.

At Manton, the note was one of cheerful optimism as it devoted itself to efforts to get out a good vote in adjoining townships and to planning a bright future. There would be new business, so the merchants must expand. An influx of people would require new housing; streets would be improved. Manton had pledged to build a courthouse if the vote was favorable and, of course, there would have to be a jail as well. An advertisement of Fuller's Drug Store said: "In spring take Parmalee's great blood purifier. We want you around to vote for the county seat." It was an exciting time.

Election day found editor Cooper prepared, with his paper set in type except for two and a half columns on the front page reserved for the election story. That night, the township hall was surrounded by anxious watchers, Cooper included, as the ballots were counted, the special ballot first. The Cedar Creek vote was unanimous, all 188 ballots being "yes." With a cheer, the group headed for the G. R. & I. depot, where food and two kegs of beer were waiting. The refreshments were courtesy of the two candidates for supervisor, Ledra Hawkins and William Overhizer, neither of whom stayed at the town hall to await the outcome of the count in their race.[3] Instead, all awaited the telegram from Cadillac that would tell how the vote had gone there.

The vote from Cadillac's second ward came in first, almost unanimously "yes." The party was on and the bonfires lit. This wasn't going to be like '78; Cadillac was keeping its word. By 11:00 the total Cadillac vote was in, going "yes" by 436-17 margin. Shortly after midnight, it was "Haring gave you 177 votes." That clinched it even if every one else in the county voted "no." Hardly anyone noticed that the clerk from Liberty Township had arrived to report all twenty-seven votes there were "yes."

Cooper headed for the print shop to set his story. By daybreak

3. It was Overhizer's birthday, but he lost the race to Hawkins.

most of the results were in and the *Tribune* went to press, claiming a majority of 1,200, only slightly overstated from the final tally, which canvassed at 1,109 "yes" to 146 "no." Cooper devoted almost one full column to an editorial, recounting the history of the county seat war in a tactful way. Now, he said, the county could avoid the wasteful expense of special meetings, unite in peaceful accord, and prosper.

> Thus, it will be seen that though we have passed through trying times, the county seat war is at last settled, for from the verdict of Monday there is no appeal. Manton is the county seat!
>
> Now it is we look for better times as a county and more friendly feelings as individuals and citizens. No more "north" and "south" but a grand, united county, with peace, prosperity and happiness for its members . . . Let us shake hands over the memory of the past, and for the first time in the history of our county let us greet each other as friends.

5.

The next few days found Manton's residents sharing a sense of exhilaration, assuming as fact that it was to be the hub of county political power and bound to grow into a center of commerce. It was announced that H. B. Sturtevant, the former county clerk, Sherman merchant, and would-be supervisor from Concord, had bought the Woodward gristmill and was planning on living in Manton.[4] Former supervisor McFarlan broke ground on the day after the election for a new and bigger store building. Other merchants planned expansion, and a half dozen new houses were started within the week.

A first concern, of course, was a courthouse. Manton's merchants, speaking through McFarlan when he introduced the referendum resolution at the board of supervisors meeting the previous October, had pledged that a new courthouse would be

4. An erroneous report. Sturtevant bought the mill but stayed in Sherman.

provided for the county without public expense. McFarlan had men at work along the railroad park within days after the election, and within six weeks the building was up and enclosed. On May 17 the Tribune reported that it could be turned over to the county as soon as painting was completed, saying apologetically that it would have been done sooner had not the building boom in Manton made difficult to get lumber and labor. The next week the *Tribune* was full of business and personal briefs and casually noted: "Painting of the courthouse is being completed. There isn't a vacant house in town."

Actually, the "completed" new courthouse was barely a shell when the county officers moved in during the first week of June. It was a 22-by-40 building, located along the east side of the railroad, south of Closson and Gilbert's store.[5] It had been roughly partitioned to set off the county offices, but there was no room for a courtroom. Everyone assumed that plans for a more substantial building would have to be approved by the county board, and the Manton merchants undoubtedly were hopeful that tax money would be forthcoming at a later date for that purpose. In the meantime, the hall over F. A. Jenison's store would serve for court purposes and supervisor's meetings. Cadillac was later to claim that Manton had never really intended to provide adequate county facilities, and bills for use of Jenison's Hall for supervisor's meetings were rejected with that excuse by the Cadillac-dominated board of supervisors.

On April 26, a special session of the board met to canvass the vote. No one thought it peculiar that the board was called to meet at Cadillac rather than at Manton or Sherman. Declaring Manton the county seat, the clerk and sheriff were directed to move the records and county property from Sherman to Manton at once and to provide suitable accommodations for county purposes. On May 3 the *Tribune* rejoiced: "We are able to report the safe

5. The land was owned by Ward P. Smith, who took over the Closson and Gilbert store in 1883. The second floor of the store was leased to the Masonic order, and Smith leased the store on the first floor to L. Simon. Smith took over the courthouse as an office building about the same time. Both buildings were destroyed by fire in 1884. As nearly as can be determined, the courthouse apparently was located at about the site of the present Shamrock Tavern.

arrival of the county property to this place. We may now be recognized as the county seat of Wexford."

The new building, of course, was not completed when the move was accomplished. Colonel Thorp had rented a home in Manton and took the records for the clerk and register of deeds offices to the barn there, using a wagon for a desk until he tired of such sparse furnishings and moved the records into his home. The treasurer's records were taken to the home of former county treasurer Ezra Harger, who was named deputy treasurer under John Mansfield. The remaining county records and property were stored in Jenison's hall until they could be removed to the new building.

But by the time the new building was ready for occupancy in June, it was apparent that Cadillac was up to its old tricks, and nothing further was done toward building a jail or finishing or decorating the new courthouse. The Cadillac-controlled board of supervisors was not about to spend any tax money on a building in Manton, and the Manton merchants were not disposed to throw away their money until it became clear that the county seat was there to stay. Thorp later recalled a miserable winter for the county officers at Manton. One could see through the cracks in the walls in many places. The first order of business each morning was to remove the snow that had drifted in during the night through season cracks and a poor ceiling. The furniture, he said, had consisted of "a few more dry goods boxes."

6.

When editor Cooper announced the arrival of the county property in the May 3 issue of the *Tribune,* he also apologized for the tardiness of recent issues resulting from his illness. That illness may explain the lack of comment in the *Tribune* on some of the proceedings at the April 26 meeting of the county board. Had Cooper noted them, his elation would have been dampened. The board did direct the removal of county records and property from Sherman to Manton forthwith, but its proclamation closing the county jail at Sherman had specified Cadillac, not Manton, as the official site of the county jail. The thunderbolt, however, had come at the concluding moments of the session when Cadillac's Fallas rose to offer once again his familiar resolution, that an election be called on the question of removing the county seat to block F of the city of Cadillac. The board referred the matter to committee and adjourned, but the war was on again.

The Fallass resolution may have escaped the attention of an ailing Cooper, but it immediately became street knowledge, and rumor flourished. The following week, a legal notice was posted at every town hall and published in the Cadillac *News* over the signatures of Clerk Thorp and Sheriff Dunham. While Manton was driving nails in the new building, Thorp and Dunham proclaimed that there was no place provided for the holding of court by the village of Manton and that the "supervisors have failed to designate and provide at Manton any court house or other place of holding the circuit court," and that "accordingly until a court house or other place for holding said court shall be legally provided, the Council Room of the City of Cadillac in said County shall be and is designated as the place for holding the Circuit Court of said County."

Cooper, as with all Manton, was furious. The May 17, 1881, issue of the *Tribune* was headlined, "Rule or Ruin." Carefully wording his editorial so as not to alienate anyone unnecessarily, he aimed his attack at Thorp and Dunham personally. How was it, he asked, that these two men could assume the board of supervisors to be too ignorant to exercise its own powers? How could two alleged public servants defy the will of the people so overwhelmingly expressed but a few weeks before? They should be turned out of office at the end of their terms, and all right-thinking citizens of the county would "unite in opposing those who would rule or ruin."

In the *Pioneer*, John Wheeler ruefully allowed as how Cadillac was at it again. Sherman had lost the county seat but, he said, it could take some pride that it had never acted dishonorably, which was more than Manton could say. Now Manton was on the spit, and time would prove if it could stand the fire. In the past Manton, like Cadillac, had been willing to resort to chicanery, "willing to buy Greenwood for whiskey, and willing to call up a mob on an honest supervisor." Now Cadillac needed but a vote or two to call another county seat election, and Manton would know what Sherman had felt. The people of Manton could be assured that Sherman would not support Cadillac. Rather, "Manton had best watch its own." The same ambitions that led Manton to underhandedness to get the county seat in past years could be used by Cadillac to its advantage.

The *Pioneer* comment wasn't particularly bitter, except for Wheeler's reference to Manton having bought Greenwood Township for whiskey. His brother George, overly fond of strong drink, had been supervisor of Greenwood and had abandoned Sherman's faction to support Manton in 1876. There is apparently a story here, well known at the time, and referred to in Cooper's response, but which is lost to us now. At any rate, there seemed little in the comment to antagonize Cooper. But it did.

Cooper lashed back furiously. Referring to the Greenwood matter, whatever it may have been, he asked who "could trust this man who would drag up ancient history to the public and cover his own sins by accusing his own brother and his brother's partner of wrongdoing?" He called Wheeler a rogue who questioned the motives of others when caught in trouble himself. He accused Wheeler of being a party to a secret deal with Cadillac. He had sold out, said Cooper, for personal gain and was preparing to move to Cadillac to reap his reward.

From this point on, reason was lost to Cooper, and the *Tribune* attacked even those most needed for Manton's support. But Wheeler was honest. There was no deal with Cadillac. He was accurate in his analysis and showed considerable foresight in his prediction that Manton might find its downfall in its own ranks. Attention was again focused on the board of supervisors and on the fact that the Cadillac bloc needed but one more vote to have two-thirds control of the board.

Chapter Nineteen

LIBERTY? LIBERTY VOTES "YES!"

After the spring election of 1881, the board of supervisors was divided into three factions, Cadillac outnumbering the combined Manton-Sherman group, 11 to 7. The division was as follows:

Cadillac: C. R. Allaire, Selma; John Bonesteel, Cherry Grove: Robert Christensen, Cadillac, First Ward; Silas Fallass, Cadillac, Third Ward; James R. Bishop, Cadillac, Second Ward; James Daley, Boon; C. A. Ford, Haring; Neal D. Ford, South Branch; J. W. Houghtalin, Colfax; Judson Loomis, Clam Lake, and H. G. Owen, Henderson.

Sherman: John Boylan, Wexford; Andrew Anderson, Hanover; Isaac Carpenter, Springville, and Herman Meyer, Antioch.

Manton: George Blue, Liberty; Ledra Hawkins, Cedar Creek, and Norman Reynolds, Greenwood.

Cadillac did not yet know where or how it would get the twelfth vote necessary to pass a county seat referendum resolution, but it did not propose to give Manton time to plan or the county a chance to get used to having Manton as its county seat. It had made its intent clear at the April 26 meeting called to canvass the Manton election vote. It had done so by calling the meeting for Cadillac rather than for the new county seat, by designating Cadillac the official site of the county jail, and by the Fallass resolution for another county seat election. The following week Clerk Thorp and Sheriff Dunham had declared Cadillac the lawful place for holding circuit court.

The campaign was pressed. In mid-May, handbills turned up around the county stating that Manton had misled the county in its promises to build a courthouse superior to the courthouse at Sherman. Manton must have confused the courthouse with the adjoining horse shed, said the leaflet, for it was preparing to hand the county "a shack no larger than the horse shed and no better built." Cadillac's mill owners and merchants, sharing the county's sense of indignation, had met and were pledged to construct elite quarters for the county government if Cadillac should become the county seat, the handbill said.

On May 27 most of the Cadillac faction of the county board signed a call for a special meeting to be held at Cadillac on June 13. The *Pioneer* at Sherman acknowledged the notice with the brief observation that "its purpose we presume to be some move toward removing the county seat to that place since various callers from there have been in this part of the county that object to promote."

At Manton, the *Tribune* of May 31 appealed to the rest of the county without acknowledging the probable purpose of the meeting. Why was Cadillac attempting to hold all county functions there? There would have been a regular June meeting at Manton in any event, had not the special call been made for Cadillac. What end could Cadillac seek to achieve by avoiding a meeting at the proper place?

> What our Cadillac neighbors expect to gain by these acts so contrary to the expectations of the citizens of the county and at variance with the intent of the law is more than we can understand. It must be that the limit of hatred and patience will soon be reached. Are a few people huddled in one corner of the county to continue in their exhibitions of greed and lawlessness without interruption for all time? Will our people always exhibit the spirit of patience and forbearance that has thus far characterized their actions? Is there no limit in either case? We think there is and that it is within sight and that, like Satan, Cadillac has had its day, ruined by its determination to ruin.

The following week the *Tribune* exploded. Amid the rumors and wild stories, the mild response of the *Pioneer* the previous week was suspect. A letter from supervisor Hawkins attacked John Wheeler viciously, referred to the claims of Cadillac businessmen that they would spend $50,000 to $60,000 for a courthouse there, and charged that Wheeler and clerk Thorp had been influenced, hinting openly at bribery.

Editor Cooper commenced his editorial: "Cadillac is at the bottom of all the deviltry that ever was enacted in this county."

Cadillac, he said, had lied, bribed, corrupted, misrepresented, and cheated. Now he understood Cadillac supervisors were promising to give the old county building to Sherman for a school if Cadillac got to be county seat.[1] Once again he charged that Cadillac had made a corrupt deal to buy the support of John Wheeler in return for a political reward and that Wheeler was already making plans to move to Cadillac. Corruption, corruption, there was no end to Cadillac's corruption; and so, Cooper concluded: "Because Cadillac is that corrupt she may produce 9/10 of court business doesn't necessarily fit her for the location for the seat of justice."

Both Hawkins and Cooper were wrong about Wheeler. John, as was his brother Edgar, was to serve as county treasurer, to live in Cadillac at various times, and to invest in business ventures and land development there. But that was many years away. In 1881 he was not pro-Cadillac. But Sherman had lost the county seat. He had no reason to be particularly pro-Manton and he was undoubtedly worn out by his long efforts on behalf of Sherman.

2.

The leader of the Sherman faction now wasn't even a resident of the village. Herman Meyer of Bandola assumed the leadership of efforts to frustrate Cadillac, as a personal matter, for personal reasons. The only one of the Sherman area supervisors to accept editor Cooper's invitation to a strategy meeting at Manton, he informed those gathered there that he had already traveled to Traverse City at his own expense to consult with the law firm of Pratt & Davis. It was their opinion, he said, that the call for the special meeting was illegal. They should not ratify it by attending it. To do so would jeopardize their chances of attacking any action taken there. Instead, they should proceed with the regularly scheduled meeting at Manton, and he would guarantee the presence of the other Sherman supervisors.

And so, on June 14, there were two county board meetings. At

1. That was in fact what happened after the county seat was moved to Cadillac!

Manton, Meyer and the other six northern supervisors met, designated Meyer chairman and Hawkins clerk pro tem, sent a telegram, and waited. At the city council room in Cadillac, the eleven members of the Cadillac faction met, called roll, approved the expenses of Clerk Thorp and Sheriff Dunham in moving the county records from Sherman to Manton, and received a telegram. It said:

> Gentlemen: You are hereby notified that we, the undersigned supervisors, are at the county seat ready to do business. Your attendance is desired at such meeting.
>
> Signed, Herman C. Meyer,
> Ledra Hawkins, etc.

In response, from Cadillac to Manton, another telegram:

> Gentlemen: The lawful meeting of the Wexford County Board of Supervisors at Cadillac is compelled to adjourn by reason of your absence. It convenes tomorrow, June 14, at ten a.m. Members absent without cause are subject to penalty.
>
> Signed, T. J. Thorp, clerk.

On the morning of the 14th, the northern seven reconvened at Manton. Finding no quorum on the roll call, they recessed after sending another telegram, which was received at Cadillac by Thorp:

> Clerk Thorp and absent members: We recognize no meeting of board except at county seat.
>
> Signed, Meyer, etc.

The county had been through this before. In 1877 warrants had been issued for the arrest of supervisors to compel their attendance, and so it went again. The eleven-man session at Cadillac had the advantage of the prosecuting attorney and sheriff being with them. A resolution was passed directing the prosecutor to commence proceedings against those supervisors not in attendance at Cadillac and to enforce penalties against them for neglect of duty. The prosecutor issued subpoenas for the missing seven and Sheriff Dunham took the next train, a freight, to Manton where he found them at the county's new courthouse. All were served with their subpoenas except Hawkins, who left by the nearest window and fled, returning only after the sheriff had boarded the next southbound freight for Cadillac. They were quite aware that a refusal to appear at Cadillac the following morning would likely result in the issuance of warrants for their arrest. Carpenter and Blue had been through this before. It would be 1877 all over again. Agreeing on absence, they also agreed to drop out of sight for a few days. Editor Cooper of the *Tribune* would keep an eye on the Cadillac session and, in case of emergency, would telegraph attorney Edwin S. Pratt at Traverse City. And so the Manton meeting ended.

At Cadillac the following morning, Sheriff Dunham reported the subpoenas served and the clerk noted in the minutes that "Hawkins ran away."[2] After a recess, the board noted the continued failure of the seven to attend, found their absence a deliberate neglect of duty, and authorized the prosecutor and sheriff to cause the attachment of their bodies to be produced before the board at Cadillac. The warrants were already prepared, and Sheriff Dunham and his deputies headed north to seek out their quarry.

The next day, June 16, the Cadillac session reconvened. Only one of the fugitive supervisors had been apprehended, George Blue of Liberty. He did not answer the roll call but was presented to the board by the sheriff much as if he were being arraigned in court. Several routine matters were disposed of, and then, sur-

2. Hawkins had been a resident of Clam Lake for about five years then farmed downstate briefly before settling in Cedar Creek Township. He was close to many Cadillac residents and is reported to have approached the county seat maneuvering as a game, all the while realizing tht his Cadillac friendships would cause his Manton neighbors to watch everything he did with a suspicious eye. John Wheeler said he apologized for attacking him, saying that Manton still had "Brandenburg's old tar pot and feather tick ready for traitors, and we must all look ferocious."

prisingly, the board adjourned until August 15, again to meet at Cadillac.

No bombshell had been exploded, no tricky resolutions introduced. Even more interesting, no proceedings were to be commenced against Blue for disobedience of the call or the subsequent subpoena, although the possibility of such proceedings against the other northern supervisors remained open. Even more surprising, Blue's attachment was not extended to the adjourned date. Instead, the chair announced that the attachment was discharged. Something was afoot, but what?

3.

In the two months following the arrest of George Blue, and the adjournment of the Cadillac version of the county board session the Cadillac planners were busy. On the promotional level, the word was being spread that Manton was defaulting on its promise to provide adequate building for the county seat and that Cadillac was ready, willing, and able to erect "elite quarters" for the county government.

On the tactical level, equal effort was being made towards obtaining the one additional vote needed to give Cadillac the two-thirds majority needed to call a county seat election. There were hints dropped, invitations offered, and business opportunities suggested for the different members of the northern seven. Anderson of Hanover said he had turned down a sound position at Cadillac available "after the county seat election," and Reynolds claimed to have been offered an outright cash payment for his vote. Probably no effort was made to reach Carpenter or Meyer, their bitter opposition to Cadillac being of such long-standing duration and intensity that the effort would have been useless and would have resulted only in ammunition for them. But somewhere, Cadillac was going to get a vote. Would it be Boylan, Hawkins, Anderson, Reynolds, or Blue?

Recalling John Wheeler's warning about appeals to ambition, the Mantonites began to watch each other with suspicion. Specifically, what about Hawkins, who had lived in Cadillac and had so many friends there? And people began to ask how it was that Blue could have been found to be arrested when the seven northern supervisors had all agreed to go into hiding and the other six had in fact left the county? And how was it that Blue had been so promptly discharged and the Cadillac supervisors had adjourned until August without taking any significant action once they had Blue there?

4.

On a different tactical level, petitions were being circulated for the organization of new townships around Cadillac. Sherman had invented the game and had made history in the legislature and in the courts with Sherman and Concord townships. Both sides had played the same game with tentative organization of the townships of Dover, Wheatland, Westside, and Benton. Now it would be done again while the northern supervisors boycotted the Cadillac session. If there weren't enough votes from the existing townships to call the county seat election, more votes could be created by creating more townships—in the right places, of course.

On August 15 the adjourned Cadillac session of the county board gathered with all eleven members of the Cadillac faction present, plus George Blue. Blue's presence violated the agreement of the northern seven, but his vote seemed to be in Manton's interest. The first item of business was a petition for the organization of the township of Garfield from six sections in the southwest corner of Haring. Carried, Blue voting no.

Next, a petition to create the new township of Kysor in the six and a half sections of northwest Haring township where Frank and Dan Kysor were logging. Carried, Blue voting "no." Then a petition to separate the north half of Cherry Grove as a new township called Benson. Carried, Blue voting "no." Then back to Haring with three more petitions to organize the new townships of Copley (after lumberman E. J. Copley), Long Lake, and Linden. All carried, Blue voting "no." There would be six new supervisors in the Cadillac area. The meeting adjourned, leaving the former township of Haring looking like this:

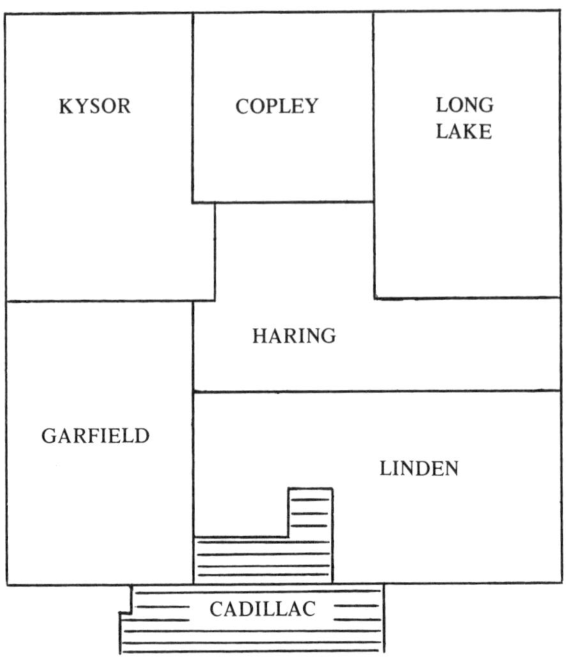

The election of the officers of the new townships was scheduled by the resolutions for the first Monday in February. Several considerations probably entered into the choice of date. State law required publication of notice over a period so extended that the election could not have been held prior to the fall meeting of the board of supervisors. In any event, with the volume of work facing the annual session of the board in October, county affairs would be brought to a standstill if the session were hung up on a fight over seating new supervisors.

The main consideration, however, lay in the timing of an election for removal of the county seat. It could not be held for at least a year after the last election on the question, which put the earliest possible election date at April 4, 1882. The meeting for calling the election would be scheduled at the latest possible date permitting election notices to be given, thereby reducing the possibility that a lawsuit could be brought halting the election. The supervisors in the new townships could be elected early in February, a meeting of the county board scheduled for mid-February, and, if all went well, a resolution passed for the county seat election.

As a result, a tranquil sort of mood set in that fall. The supervisors met at Manton in Jenison's Hall for the October session and disposed of business with a minimum of discussion and virtually no argument. The feeling of panic that had swept Manton in the first revelation of Cadillac's renewed campaign abated, as did the rumors that someone in the northern bloc had been reached by Cadillac's malignant influence. Blue's negative vote on each of the new township resolutions killed the speculation about his individual arrest.

Cadillac's strategy seemed clearly in the direction of padding the board to get extra votes, and Manton was confident it had a good legal answer to that. Pratt & Davis had briefed the question of the new township creation and had no doubt of the illegality of the proceedings. A long memorandum brief was prepared, and a form of complaint for an injunction type of lawsuit, called a writ of prohibition, had been drawn in co-operation with W. C. Haire, Manton's village attorney. The moment one of those new supervisors appeared at a meeting of the county board, the lawsuit would be filed and any matter voted upon by him would be blocked, specifically a resolution for a county seat election.[3]

In concluding the fall session, the board adjourned until February 14, 1882. In practice the board customarily adjourned its fall session without date, and thereafter a special meeting was traditionally called for mid-January. The adjournment to a specific date and the selection of a date in February were contrived by the Cadillac faction to coincide with the dates set for election of the supervisors in the newly created townships. It was expected by Manton, and no strenuous fight over the date was made. In the next few months the county waited. In early February the elections were held in the new townships, giving the

3. The only controversy of the fall session arose from Cadillac's anticipation of such a suit. By a vote following the regional division, the board passed a resolution authorizing the prosecuting attorney to obtain the assistance of outside counsel in the event of any lawsuit challenging the "right of any supervisor to a seat on the Wexford County Board of Supervisors," and appropriating $1,000 for that purpose.

title of supervisor to Watson Smith of Benson, A. E. Tilyou of Garfield, William H. Kellogg of Long Lake, John Downing of Linden, R. D. Cuddeback of Kysor, and Lester Macey of Copley. On February 14 they presented themselves at Manton for the county board's meeting.

5.

The course of the February 14 session was totally unexpected. No contemporary newspaper accounts for the month survive, and Wheeler offers no explanation of the direction that matters took. We know that Manton, in expectation of an attempt to pack the board with dummy supervisors, was ready to go to court immediately if the supervisors from the new townships were seated. When the session opened, a motion was made to refer to comittee the question of whether the six new supervisors should be seated. To the surprise of Manton, chairman Houghtalin referred it to committee without a vote. The first expected fight had not materialized, or had at least been delayed.

Then, surprisingly, without the new supervisors on the floor and without awaiting a ruling on their right to be seated, James Bishop of Cadillac offered a resolution to hold an election April 4, on the question of removing the county seat to the city of Cadillac. The next surprise: Chairman Houghtalin immediately ordered the clerk to call the roll on the question instead of referring it to committee. Down through the roll call, alphabetically by townships and city, the clerk went, every vote being as expected until he called Liberty. Blue replied, "Liberty votes 'yes!' "

Cadillac had its twelfth vote, the question was carried, and the supervisors from the new townships had not been needed. There would be an election at which the people of the county could finally vote on locating the county seat at Cadillac.

The rest of the session was anticlimax. The committee reported back that the Cadillac session at which the new townships had been organized was illegal and that the supervisors from those townships should not be seated. The board concurred. Cadillac had no further need of them, and Benson, Copley, Kysor, and the rest were never heard from again, except when claims were presented to the county board for their supervisors' expenses. The claims were tabled.[4]

As a legal footnote, Blue brought suit for false imprisonment against the deputy sheriff who had taken him into custody on the warrant issued by the rump session of the board at Cadillac the previous June. When the matter came to trial, the circuit had a new judge, none other than S. S. Fallass, who had sat on that board from Cadillac's Third Ward and who was undoubtedly the ringleader in the Cadillac planning. He was a model of judicial integrity. He instructed the jury that the meeting was in fact illegal and that Blue was entitled to recover damages as a matter of law, the only concern of the jury being to determine the amount of the damages. Blue was awarded $100.

But there remains an unanswered question: Why did Blue change his vote?

6.

It has been accepted since 1882 that the supervisor from Liberty Township was bribed to change his vote, the deciding vote, to support Cadillac on the county seat issue. There is no evidence available now. With control of the county government in Cadillac hands, there would be no official search for evidence then. All that remains is the view expressed by the *Tribune* and preserved over the generations that this was the way it had to be.

John Wheeler, who had fought Cadillac tooth and nail for a decade, who had bluntly described Cadillac's prior misdeeds and deceits, was tactful, saying: "What inducements were held out (by Cadillac) to gain this one vote from the enemy was not, and perhaps never will be known." The Manton *Tribune* bluntly said he had not only been bought but that it was the taxpayer's money that had paid for him.

With all the past chicanery, real and rumored, it would have

4. In mutual generosity, with public funds, the April 1882 session paid the six for their attendance and finally approved mileage and per diem payments for the Sherman and Manton seven who had held out at Manton the previous April while the Cadillac faction had been meeting in Cadillac.

been impossible for any of the Manton area supervisors to vot with Cadillac and against Manton without accusations of corrup tion following. Blue never offered any public justification for hi switch, but in the climate of the time he would have been wastin his breath to attempt to do so. And in that climate, it is only wonder that he escaped a tar and feather party at the hands o his neighbors.

Whatever the reason or price, the vote was cast, and the count board had set the county seat election for the regular sprin election date, April 4, only six weeks away. Manton had been con fident that it could block the election by legal action, but it planned lawsuit was based on the assumption that Cadillac coul only get the election resolution through the board of supervisor by the use of votes from the sham townships that had been create in August of 1881. Blue's vote gave Cadillac the necessar two-thirds majority without the presence of the contested super visors, and the proposed lawsuit was moot.

Chapter Twenty

THE BATTLE OF MANTON: 1882

We have no available copies of the contemporary newspapers for the early months of 1882, but it is not hard to imagine the nature of their comments on the forthcoming election. At Cadillac, the *News* would be confident and pointing out Cadillac's advantages and the promises made by its citizens for new county buildings. At Sherman, John Wheeler said later, his *Pioneer* took a philosophical attitude, the refuge of the defeated. Sherman had lost the county seat. There was no love lost for Cadillac, but it had the votes to take the county seat from Manton, and the fact had to be recognized. He added that Cooper's *Tribune* had seared him for that observation almost as badly as it had scorched Cadillac. We can only speculate on what Mr. Cooper said about Cadillac during those weeks.

On Monday, April 4, the ballots were cast. Responding to a later comment on how well Cadillac got out its vote, its largest up to that time, Cadillac's mayor, lumberman Dan McCoy, said that it hadn't been difficult. Cadillac's only voting problem, he said, had occurred the previous year in getting out a "yes" vote for moving the county seat to Manton.

How well did Cadillac get out the vote? On the first election to move the county seat to Manton, there had been only six "yes" votes in Cadillac and the surrounding townships. In 1881, with better coaching, Cadillac voted to take the county seat from Sherman to Manton by a 436-17 margin. Now voting for itself, it voted, 834 to 1. Somebody made a mistake in marking his ballot, the only mistake in Cadillac. The county canvass was never completed. Greenwood and Cedar Creek townships destroyed their ballots and refused to make a return. The other six northern townships all defeated the question by large margins, but the heavy population in and around Cadillac carried the day. The votes that were canvassed added up to 1,363 "yes" against only 309 "no."

Regional fights over county seat locations had not been uncommon in Michigan, but over the years the Wexford War had become famous. The efforts of the city, widely known as the wickedest place in the Midwest, had reached even into the legislature's proceedings, had involved names well known in state political and business circles. These efforts to get the county seat had become regular fare in the state's newspapers. There was one battle left in the war that would insure its lasting memory.

2.

As the election approached, Cadillac had only one other thing to worry about, and that was the possibility of legal action by Manton. It was assumed that Manton would seek an injunction or writ of prohibition before the votes were officially canvassed and before there could be a physical removal of the county records to Cadillac. Undoubtedly, consideration was being given to such a plan by Manton's leadership, and the destruction of the ballots of Cedar Creek and Greenwood townships may have been part of a plan preparatory to such a suit.

Cadillac's planning took the possibility of such a lawsuit into acount. It would move to canvass the votes at the earliest possible date and, accordingly, a special meeting of the supervisors was called to meet April 17—at Cadillac, naturally. Another plan was carefully thought out, based on one simple fact: An injunction or writ of prohibition could not be issued to stop the doing of something which had already been done.

The identity of the county officers made preparation easy. The Circuit Court Commissioner was James Riley Bishop. He also happened to be supervisor from Cadillac's Second Ward. The prosecuting attorney? Samuel J. Wall of Cadillac. The sheriff? C. C. Dunham of Cadillac. The clerk and register of deeds? One of the leading Cadillac strategists, T. J. Thorp. Treasurer? John Mansfield, a Cadillac backer. And the probate judge was Holden Green, formerly a Cadillac supervisor.

In the days before the election, the county officers quietly prepared their offices for a hasty evacuation. Personal belongings were removed and, on the Friday preceding the election, particular care was taken to get all records in order so as to permit their being packed and moved in the shortest possible time. And finally, in order to insure that there would be no convenient access to a resident circuit judge, Judge Rice would resign just prior to the election.

The 28th Judicial Circuit had only just been organized, and the unanimous choice in Cadillac for the judgeship had been Silas S. Fallass. His role in the county seat war had made him *persona non grata* to the northern part of the county, and his Democratic politics precluded majority support in the rest of the circuit. As a result, it had been agreed that Cadillac would push John Rice, who would then resign, and the governor would appoint Fallass. The program went as planned, and the plan was tailored neatly to the county seat election.

At Cadillac on election night, while the usual bonfires and celebration parties marked the returns, some people had turned in early, the better to get started the next morning. That next morning, before Manton was fairly awake, an unusual train made up of only the locomotive and tender, a caboose, boxcar, and a flat car, backed quietly into Manton and came to a halt in front of the courthouse, a scant 100 feet away. The train had been made ready by stationmaster E. L. Metheany at the G. R. & I. yards in north Cadillac before daybreak. With the dawn, it headed north carrying Sheriff Dunham and twenty men specially deputized for the occasion. As the sheriff's commandos disembarked, they were met by clerk Thorp, who opened the courthouse. Within a half hour, most of the county records and much of the furniture was aboard the train.

Although caught by surprise, Manton soon reacted, and a skirmish developed as the "deputies" were attempting to remove the safe from the county treasurer's office. In the Manton version, the city was virtually deserted, and only ten or twelve men were in town. They quickly gathered at the courthouse and confronted ten times that many heavily armed "Cadillackers." The sheriff was politely asked his authority, to which he rudely replied that he needed none. The safe was overturned, Cadillac produced firearms, and a drunken clerk Thorp urged the murder of the few brave Mantonites, who nevertheless managed to rout the attackers, who fled back to Cadillac in fear. The Cadillac version was that a mob of over 200 Manton men drove off the small band of deputies, which withdrew and returned to Cadillac solely to insure the safety of the county property already loaded on the train.

3.

If there was some discrepancy between the Cadillac and Manton versions of the first battle of Manton courthouse on the morning after the county seat election, there is no resemblance whatever between the versions of the second encounter of April 5. We are entitled to doubt Manton's claim that it had no cause to anticipate further violence and that the second invasion was totally unexpected, particularly since the Manton version also asserts that its inhabitants had agreed to make no forcible resistance to the removal of the three county safes remaining in the courthouse, an assertion which is doubtful in itself. In fact, when the sheriff and his deputies had returned to Cadillac on the "Dunham Express" earlier, the Mantonites had set to work to secure the courthouse, boarding over the windows and barricading the doors.

In Cadillac, a crowd was gathered at the depot awaiting the arrival of the county property on the special train. Newly elected mayor Byron Ballou, outgoing mayor Daniel McCoy, and most of the officers from Cadillac and surrounding townships were prepared to make speeches. Across the track, in the city park, a group of traveling entertainers known as the Marks Comedy Company appearing at the Forester's Opera House had situated its band and were providing entertainment in two hastily erected tents. By the time the "Dunham Express" arrived, the waiting crowd had spread along the track north of Pine Street, much liquor had been consumed, and a carnival spirit prevailed. It is perhaps fortunate that the mood of the crowd did not turn ugly when the people learned that the mission had not been a complete success.

Instead, most of the property was here, and it seems to have been in a good-natured mood that the second Manton expeditionary force got under way. A number of empty logging flatcars were attached to the train, and what Judge Holden Green called the First Volunteer Regiment, Cadillac Militia, was ready to invade Manton. It was a mixed crew consisting of the sheriff's deputies, most of the gathered officials, half of main street, and several hundred mill hands from the Cobbs and Mitchell, Cummer, and Haynes mills, accompanied by the Marks Comedy Company Band which provided music, coming and going. Provisions consisted of a barrel of whiskey donated by some volunteer quartermaster, more than enough privately owned bottles, and fifty repeating rifles commandeered from Sampson & Drury's hardware store and placed in the hands of the deputies and more sober citizens by Sheriff Dunham. Others brought their own armament in the form of clubs, poles and crowbars, and undertaker John Turner, feeling no pain, carried a broom.

According to the Cadillac version, the "Militia" numbered about 300 men, including train crew and Marks Company Band, who had been cautioned by the sheriff to avoid violence or damage to property. Arriving at Manton, they found a waiting mob made up of every able-bodied citizen of Manton, plus most of the farmers from miles around.

In the Manton version, it was an unopposed invasion by a drunken mob of 500 to 600 men, led by a drunken sheriff and clerk. Far from resisting, Manton said, a few brave citizens stood at the courthouse door to deliver a calm protest and to appeal to the sheriff to protect the village from the mob. His response was to order the courthouse demolished and to loose his men onto Manton's streets like a pack of crazed hounds. His fiendish deputies set out to find the handful of men who had repulsed them earlier and to take their vengeance upon them. Despite the great provocation, the only blows struck by Manton were those of the surrounded spokesmen at the courthouse endeavoring to fight their way out of the mob, and a few individual cases of self-defense against overwhelming odds.

To these versions, of course, is added a folklore of the Battle of Manton which grew through the years. Soon, everyone who had lived in the county in 1882, and hundreds of people who hadn't, were passing on their vivid remembrances of what they had done or seen in the climax of the great County Seat War. Even today, stories recur of the secret burial of a Manton casualty, axe still embedded in the corpse; of the attempt of the Mantonites to hang Thorp; of the rallying of the Manton women to spread lard and butter on the rails in an effort to halt the train, and of countless individual deeds of valor or violence.

There was violence. It was necessary to break into the courthouse with axes to remove the three safes, but the courthouse was not demolished—not quite. Clubs and knives were wielded; Dr. Martin and Washington Schyrer of Manton were seriously injured, with concussions and unspecified fractures. The repeating rifles probably accomplished their purpose simply by their obvious presence, but no shots were fired except in celebration on the ride home, and there were no corpses, with or without axe.

4.

The county election had been duly noted in the state press, but the Battle of Manton received nationwide attention. Cadillac was a young city, but it had already been well publicized. Its reputation as a corrupter of supervisors probably grew in part from the attention the city had previously received; it had been described by the Detroit *Post* as "the wickedest place in the Midwest," and by the Cleveland *News* as a "haven of harlots and saloonkeepers."

Then there had been the 1877 letter by Byron Ballou, published in the *News,* advocating legalized prostitution. The fact that the suggestion was made as an honest proposal to meet some of the problems of the community tells much about the rough quality of life in the early days of the city. But the fact that it had been proposed by an honest, sensible man was widely overlooked, as its author was labeled a Sybarite and his city a sink of iniquity.

To be honest, it must be added that Cadillac came by its reputation honestly and rather gloried in it. The local *News* reprinted without disclaimer the observation of the Detroit *News* that Cadillac was "the nearest thing to Sodom and Gomorrah since the original." It was not surprising, then, that editors, already familiar with Cadillac's name, should pick up the account of the county seat war and feature it.

There were two stories of note in the newspapers in early April. On the 5th, the state's papers reported briefly two events of the preceding day, the county seat election in. Wexford County and the shooting death of a man in St. Joseph, Missouri. On the 6th, the feature story in the Detroit *News* was headlined: "WEXFORD COUNTY SEAT REMOVED FROM MANTON IN SPITE OF ARMED OPPOSITION—A GREAT ARRAY OF FORCE ON EACH SIDE BUT LITTLE BLOOD SHED. The lesser story of the day was headlined: "THE MURDERED JESSE JAMES FULLY IDENTIFIED."

The story in the *News* concluded: "A large number on both sides received slight injuries from knives and clubs. This ends one of the worst local wars ever known in Michigan." It was not the end of the press coverage, however. Cadillac's mayor-elect, the nation learned, was the same Byron Ballou who had advocated the legalizing of prostitution. The story ballooned. Charles Cooper, editor of the Manton *Tribune,* furnished copy for a national news service, and so the continuing stories largely reflected Manton's viewpoint. The press had a recap of the past wrongs of the county seat war, of bribery, corruption, and intimidation, of drunken county officers and justice at the hands of a drunken sheriff, of a posse composed of the "offscourings of creation," including small children who had been led into a debauch of whiskey, armed with iron bars, and loosed on the streets of the peaceful village of Manton.

5.

It is the writer's greatest regret that there is no known available copy of the Cadillac *News* of that week or those immediately following. All we know of what it said is quoted in the *Tribune* of the following week:

> The county officers will be found for the present at Holbrook and May's Hall. They think the quarters preferable to those they occupied at the ex-county seat.

to which the Tribune replied:

> This condition is due to the fact that the devil and his imps are more at home in hell than Heaven.

We also know that the editor of the *News,* C. T. Chapin, chose to be humorous, the *Tribune* quoting the *News* as saying that:

> . . . probably one of the raciest events of the season was "dot leedle picnic" on Tuesday.

And apparently the *News* speculated also about the possibility of a lawsuit now that the transfer of the county seat had been physically accomplished, to which the *Tribune* replied:

> The *News* inquires after Supreme Court injunction papers? This is about as foolish as the *News* supporters. A supreme court injunction to quiet a mob! Soak your heads, you witless fools.

Virtually the entire front page of the *Tribune* of April 11 was given over to the editor's rage over the Battle of Manton. One article dealt with the plunder of the treasury to pay for bribing supervisor Blue (for which there is credible suspicion but no substantiation), to hire outside counsel at an expense of thousands of dollars (false, only an authorization was made which was never used), and to pay for the sheriff's posse (partly true, as the expense of the special trains and twenty special deputies was paid for by the county). The expense of special meetings, of the organization of illegal townships, all were recounted. In one last, hopeless appeal to his supporters, Cooper urged them to stand fast:

> Are we to lie down like a pack of cowering curs and be cuffed at the will of Cadillac's debauchery? . . . for the right there is no such thing as fail. Be firm, be united and victory will perch upon our banners and our county will be taken from the low pit of filth into which Cadillac has placed it, and lifted up to a higher level of honor and decency. Let every citizen do his duty.

Other columns of the *Tribune* recited Manton's version of the battle, assailed Cadillac's leaders, the treacherous county officers, and, of course, dredged up Mayor Ballou's former advocacy of licensed prostitution. Perhaps the most entertaining feature was a letter written by a Mantonite who claimed to have accompanied the "Dunham Express" on its return trip to Cadillac, and which described the leaders of the expedition. The letter is of interest in part because it tells us who some of the participants were without mentioning last names. There was former Mayor Danny, longing to be a congressman, and qualified because of his ability to hold more Washington or Philadelphia rot-gut than anyone in the district; the new mayor and vice-advocate, true B(al)lou; the clerk with the military title *too full* to speak, so he cried; a Napoleon Bonaparte and Daniel Webster boiled down into one drunken sheriff, and

> . . . one awfully tall fellow—they called him John—carried a broom, typical of the occupation for which he was best fitted, streetsweeper. He scared me terribly for in the highly fevered state of his brain, occasioned I suppose by too frequent draughts from the town pump, he flourished his weapon over my head and broke the handle . . . he was laid away for the night with prescriptions of strong coffee every five minutes until revived.
>
> Then there was another John who ran for justice on Monday, and ran some five hundred behind the other fellow. But he made a handsome record on Tuesday as he ran for Toad-Eater and was elected unanimously. I rejoiced at his success for he has heretofore been found running on the Democratic ticket for some office which he couldn't catch on to.
>
> Then there was another John who seemed nearly bursting with joy, either at the glorious victory achieved or at the numerous broken heads and consequent demand for "Tiger Oil." He danced around and turned summersaults equal to the learned bear. If you would like a little variety in the "cuts" you are receiving lately from the Cadillac *News,* please borrow the cut of this Dr. John's head; it appears weekly (weakly) over his advertisement, and your subscribers while cultivating their taste for the beautiful . . . could also see the Samson-like luxuriance of his flowing hair . . .
>
> Still another John was there who seemed so brave while piling throgh the window of the Court House with five or six hundred to back him. I admired his pluck to that extent that

I went straight to his "office" instead of going to the other nigger and asked for a clean shave . . . but found to my disappointment that he had been taken by friendly hands and laid in his bed. Oh there were big Johns and little Johns, but the captain who led the van was Demijohn. All his namesakes were blind drunk except Dr. John who don't have to get drunk to make an ass of himself . . . "

And so went the front page letter, under the headline, "AND THERE WAS ANOTHER JOHN." There were a number of these men who can be identified. The tall John was our undertaker, John Turner, who took his broom and broke it. Candidate for justice John, was none other than the supposedly Republican editor of the *Enterprise*, John Rosevelt, who ran for office then, and repeatedly thereafter, as a Democrat.

Dr. John Leeson, discoverer of the world's greatest medicine, Tiger Oil, is easily identified. Of him, suffice it to say for now that to this point in life he had been dignified by a head of glorious curls, extending below the shoulder; the engraving portraying him on his medicine labels and in his advertising would have done justice to the powdered wig of Louis XIV. A few days later, the good doctor had his hair cropped to ear level, below which point it never thereafter was allowed to grow.

Barber John was Johnny Sheridan, a Cadillac character from the days of the first settlement until well into the twentieth century, whom we noted earlier because of his renown for the whiskey he could drink, his pugilistic skills, and the all-time Cadillac record for misdemeanor arrests. He claimed to have been the tutor of Ad Wolgast, Cadillac's world lightweight champion. Other Johns present, contractor John G. Mosser and lumberman Jonathan Cobbs, we have also met.

6.

But it was accomplished. The county seat had been moved, and it had been in the best Cadillac tradition. It was an improvement over the 1877 precedent, when George A. Mitchell and Cobbs had gone to Sherman with three wagons and a backing of millhands, intending to remove the county records, only to be frustrated by a supervisors' session in which the Odell bribe attempt had been revealed.

For a few days the county business was conducted from a flatcar on the Mason Street siding and then from the second floor of Holbrook & May's building on the northwest corner of Mason and Mitchell streets. In 1884 the county made a five-year lease for occupancy of the second floor of the Cornwell & LaBar building at the southeast corner of Cass and Mitchell streets. This space continued to be used briefly for circuit court and for the supervisors' meetings after expiration of the lease, but the individual county offices moved into a brick building on Mason Street which had been built by the Cummer Lumber Company between the railroad track and the Holbrook & May store. Finally, in 1890, all county offices were moved into the second floor of the new Masonic building, where they remained until the construction of the present courthouse in 1911.

The county building issue continued to be a matter of agitation through those years. Block F, the Courthouse Hill on Mitchell Street, had been left vacant during George Mitchell's life, it having been his intention to donate it to the county for the site of a complex of county buildings. After his death in 1878, the involved process of settling his estate and the complicated secret partnership which lay behind his dealings ending any possibility of such a gift. The Mitchell heirs sold the property in 1883 to the Cummers, who were undecided for a time as to its development. Dr. John Leeson promptly offered to donate land for a jail and courthouse from his farm at the head of Harris Street, and the offer was accepted by the county, although prospects for building were remote. The original Courthouse Hill continued to be vacant, used as a commons on which farmers turned loose their horses while shopping or visiting in town.

Building a courthouse with county funds was out of the question. Cadillac had promised to build one free and had criticized Manton for the niggardly building it had put up in 1881. The truth was that no one was prepared to foot the bill. It was not until 1897 that anyone dared submit to election the possibility of building a courthouse with the taxpayers' dollars. Even Cadillac's voters turned it down solidly. From time to time political hay was made of the lack of a courthouse, of alleged excessive rents paid to Cadillac landlords, and the like. A jail was finally built in 1884 (and still stands on the northwest corner of Pine and Shelby streets) after much opposition from the northern part of the county, including a lawsuit. In 1897 there was a feeble effort made to promote the construction of a county center at Boon on the farm owned by attorney D. E. McIntyre, son-in-law of George Mitchell. It never was seriously supported. In this century, neither Boon nor Sherman, Manton nor Meauwataka, or even Hobart, has sought the county seat.

7.

And what of the principal characters? John Wheeler, the county's first treasurer, was defeated by Democrat James Haynes for that office in 1884, due in part to the antagonisms he had built up in the county seat wars. It was the mood of a moment on the part of the public, however, for he was an honest and capable man and later served two additional terms in that office, as did his brother Edgar. T. J. Thorp, the county clerk and register of deeds, was defeated by a Democrat, George Cummer, undoubtedly paying a price for his role in the battle. He moved on and prospered on the West Coast. Mansfield, the treasurer in 1882, went on to become probate judge, then moved away. Sheriff Dunham was to prove that the picture painted by the *Tribune* was not a reflection of the view taken of him by the electorate. He continued to grow in popularity throughout the entire county, served six terms in all as sheriff, and later became mayor of Cadillac and probate judge.

John Rosevelt had no more newspaper connections. His law practice was only average, and he suffered successive defeats in campaigning for a variety of offices as a Democrat, ultimately leaving the area and prospering elsewhere. Dan McCoy narrowly failed to get his nomination for Congress and shortly thereafter closed out his lumbering interests in Cadillac to move to Grand Rapids, where he prospered as a manufacturer and banker. He became a power in state politics and was elected treasurer of

Michigan in 1900 and again in 1902. Silas S. Fallass was appointed circuit judge by Governor Jerome a few days after the Battle of Manton, and became known as one of Michigan's finest jurists. He ran for Congress as a Democrat in 1884. The combined weight of the Republican and rural Wexford County vote, with long memories for the role he played in the county seat war, combined to defeat him by a narrow margin. Elsewhere we have noted his subsequent move to Chicago, where he headed one of that city's finest law firms, representing most of the major railroads, serving as an officer or director in many, and pioneering the construction of the first electric railroads in the nation.

Over the years Judge Green became known as one of Michigan's best horsemen, both as a rider and as a breeder and owner of racing stock. His stories of the great county war constituted a staple of the after-dinner speeches of his son Fred Green, Michigan's governor from 1927 to 1930.

Does anyone remember losers? At Manton, Henry McFarlan had wife trouble, then money trouble, and soon left the county. H. B. Sturtevant prospered both in Sherman and Manton, invested wisely and well in real estate throughout the state, and came to own a good portion of Owosso's business real estate. Warren Seaman was a pillar of the community, a prosperous farmer who held various public offices. The township was left with an abiding sense of shame at the way he had been run out of office in 1877. Charles Cooper sold the *Tribune*, rebought it, then sold it again and found himself in litigation with his buyer when he tried to start a competing paper. He held a number of township elective offices but twice lost county campaigns. He left the county to pursue his journalistic endeavors in several other communities.

George Blue? His career as supervisor ended a few days after the county board session of February, 1882, at which he cast his vote with Cadillac. He stuck it out and farmed in Liberty until his death, an outcast to a large part of Manton to the end.

And undertaker John Turner, who rode the "Dunham Express" with a broom and brought it back broken? He figures in several intriguing events in Cadillac in the next few years. His name graces the court docket with sufficient frequency that it is apparent his acquaintance with strong drink was not confined to

April 5, 1882. But on April 17, the supervisors closed their first meeting at the new county seat by perpetuating his name on the county records to prove that valor merits reward and that some of the supervisors, at least, had a sense of humor about the whole thing. The board appropriated thirty cents for a new broom for John Turner.

Cadillac Depot—The southbound passenger stands at the G.R. & I. depot in June of 1882, caught in a view across the city park taken from the observatory of the Foresters Opera House. The depot and park had been the scene of a wild celebration two months earlier when the "Dunham Express" brought back the spoils of the Battle of Manton. Central School is seen top-right. Near the depot may be seen the Scandinavian House and Saloon (above which can be seen the Sweed Lutheran Church in the distance), the Cadillac House and the McKinnon Hotel, from left to right on the north side of Harris Street. Behind the depot on the south side is the Balfour House.

William Slater collection.

View from the roof of the I.O.O.F. building overlooking the intersection of Cass and Mitchell streets. At the southwest corner is the Cobbs & Mitchell office. At the northwest corner is the George Mitchell, or bank, building and then the Mitchell Brothers office. At the left the Foresters Opera House stands on the lake shore. Across Little Clam Lake are the yards, stacks and sawdust burners of the Cummer, Haynes and Saunders mills.

The Michigan Historical Collections of the University of Michigan.

View northeasterly from the roof of the I.O.O.F. building. At left is the firehouse and hose tower. Beyond, on Harris Street, may be seen the Methodist and Presbyterian churches. On the hill between is the Wellington W. Cummer home, originally the home of George A. Mitchell. At top right is Central School. 1882.

The Michigan Historical Collections of the University of Michigan.

View from the hose tower easterly to the end of Cass (right) and Harris streets. Note the stumps. Central School is top center, the Presbyterian church top left. At lower right is the home of William W. Mitchell, behind it the home of Mrs. George A. Mitchell. The former was moved across Cass Street and demolished in 1971. The latter was moved to 219 Chapin Street, where it still stands. 1882.
The Michigan Historical Collections of the University of Michigan.

Looking easterly from the steeple of the Presbyterian Church. The first house east of Central School is the home of James Riley Bishop, attorney. 1882.

The Michigan Historical Collections of the University of Michigan.

Looking west from the belfry of Central School. The long building right is the Holbrook & May building at the corner of Mitchell and Mason streets. Beyond lies the north shore mill district. The large building to the left of the Methodist Church is the McKinnon House. At left, on the lake shore, is the Foresters Opera House. 1882.
The Michigan Historical Collections of the University of Michigan.

Looking northerly from Central School, Presbyterian Church at left. Beyond on the west side of the Simmons—E. Mason intersection (Piety Hill) are the homes of Andrew Keller Moyer (later acquired by Nathaniel Gerrish) and Mayor Daniel McCoy. At right front, an addition to the Levi Harris home is near completion. Beyond it may be seen the Swedish Mission Church. 1882.

The Michigan Historical Collections of the University of Michigan.

Looking southwest from Central School. At extreme left a trail is being cleared up Cemetery Hill. At left center, Cobbtown lies beyond the swamp. At center can be seen the new I.O.O.F. building. LaBar & Cornwell Roller Mills, the roof of James Haynes Planing Mill No. 2, and the stacks and cupola of Cobbs & Mitchell Mill No. 1. A raft of logs can be seen inside the Cobbs & Mitchell breakwater. 1882.
The Michigan Historical Collections of the University of Michigan.

Lawyer's Row—View from the roof of the Charles Ayers home on Oak Street, looking west down Hersey Street. The first three homes on the southside of Hersey belong, respectively to attorneys (and brothers-in-law) Eugene F. Sawyer, Samuel J. Wall, and Judge Silas S. Fallass. At left center a half-dozen pines mark the old cemetery. Beyond lies Cobbtown. On the far left lakeshore, smoke marks the mill of Milton J. Bond. Moving counterclockwise along the shore are the Cobbs & Mitchell yards and mill, James Haynes Planing Mill No. 2, the G.R.&I. icehouses (behind the Roller Mill), and the Foresters Opera House. 1882.

The Michigan Historical Collections of the University of Michigan.

Mitchell Street, looking north from Cass. At left, from the corner, the Bank Building, Mitchell Brothers, Hixson's Bank (and post office), LaBar, Cornwell & Company, grocers, Capt. Newson's saloon and Cloud & Morgan's Hardware. Note the wooden crosswalk through the sand. 1882.

The Michigan Historical Collections of the University of Michigan.

Mitchell Street, looking south from Holbrook & May's at the corner of E. Mason. At left, Dr. Leeson's drugstore. Note the suspended advertising signs at right, Olson's "Sign of the Big Boot" and Law's "Star Clothing." 1882.
William Slater collection.

Mitchell Street looking north in 1889 from a point opposite the I.O.O.F. building. At right, the new LaBar Cornwell building. Note the clay-improved street and the new electric light poles.

J.P. Craig, Cadillac Library.

PART III:
THE FINISHING YEARS:
1882-1900

Chapter Twenty-One

THE NEW COUNTY SEAT

The new county seat was really four different communities—Cadillac, Cobbtown, Harristown, and Frenchtown. The two "suburban" milltowns had grown up easily and naturally with a distinct atmosphere and more or less isolated from the main settlement. There could be no lakeshore avenue to unite them. The mills required large storage areas for the finished lumber. Each would need its surrounding yards with miles of track and tramways running through the stacks of lumber. Each mill with its surrounding yards was a buffer, through which there was no travel, and which divided the settlements one from the other. On the northeast shore, there were the Shackleton and Green, Haynes, and Harris mills. In the early years of the village, it was over three-quarters of a mile from the business district out to Haynes Road and around to the homes that were going up west of the Harris mill. A boardinghouse and bunkhouse for single employees was added to the cluster of homes, and in 1875 Harris started a general store for his employees about where Linden and Walnut streets intersect today. From 1872 to 1882, over thirty homes were built in the area, and as many as fifty men may have lived in the Harris bunkhouses. A hundred feet west of Harristown, or Harrisville, as it was sometimes called, there was still virgin forest in 1880.

On the south, the Cobbs mill and yards occupied the area between the railroad and the lake. The area across the track immediately to the east and northeast of the mill was a huge swamp. The area to the southeast was subdivided by the firm and lots sold to employees with the first homes built on high ground east of the railroad from South Street to Pollard. About twenty homes went up there by 1876 and another twenty in the next six years. This was the original Cobbtown.

When the county seat came to Cadillac, a trail led out to the southwestern part of the township following what is now Granite Street and Sunnyside Drive, but it went through solid forest. After ten years of steady logging, man had just scratched the surface and almost three-fourths of the area within the city limits was still covered by prime pine. There was no view of the hills on the horizon; it was obstructed by the solid wall of pine surrounding the settlement.

The central part of the city, Cadillac proper, had crept south of Howard Street. The new St. Ann's Church marked the southeast corner of the settlement. On the east, few homes had been built beyond Park Street, just ten or twelve on Cass Street and five or six on Harris. A clearing at the top of Cass Street Hill was called the circus grounds, or the ballgrounds, and was still the outer limit of homes on the east in 1891.

To the north, few people lived beyond Nelson Street except for a cluster of homes around Bremer and North streets between Mitchell and Simons, largely built by French settlers and forming the third suburb, Frenchtown, which gradually expanded to the north. Frenchtown and the Crippen foundry marked the north limits of settlement in the city.[1]

Early accounts of life in the settlement tend to be confusing unless the distinction among the four different communities is remembered. An account of an 1876 accident "a mile south of the village" happened during clearing at the cemetery. A logging camp "on the north shore of the little lake two miles west of here" was actually in the area now occupied by the Wesleyan Methodist camp grounds. A reference to Clam Lake or to the village meant only the central settlement. The communities were distinct from one another, and developed a considerable rivalry over the years, a rivalry acted out at the common meeting place of the baseball grounds or the saloons. The 1877 incorporation of the city did nothing to end the sense of separate identity or lessen that rivalry and it continued well into the twentieth century.

1. There was never any clearly developed "Sweedtown," although that name was briefly applied about 1880 to the area around the intersection of Simons and Nelson streets and, ten years later, around the north half of Lake Street and the intersection of Farrar and Wright streets.

2.

By 1882 the main business district was on Mitchell Street between West Mason and Chapin streets. The old business district along Lake Street and lower Mason Street had changed for the worse and consisted primarily of saloons and disreputable boardinghouses. At the northwest corner of Mitchell and Mason Streets, Kieldsen's store, the former Holbrook & May building, continued to dominate the street across from the open commons of Courthouse Hill. To the north of Kieldsen's was a saloon and boardinghouse, a private home, and Fred Hutchinson's meat market. Across the street, in the block between Spruce and Pine, there were only three homes, the largest being that of Jacob Cummer at the corner of Pine. It was a handsome but unpretentious home, in which the frugal millionaire was content to live during his stay in Cadillac.[2]

On the west side of the street, between Pine and the Crippen foundry at Bremer Street, there were only eight or nine residences, the George Hurst Shoe and Boot Shop, a blacksmith shop and livery stable, and one saloon.

On the east side of the street, Louis DeChamplain, son-in-law of James Haynes, had just bought the vacant lot on the northeast corner of Pine and Mitchell, on which he put up a grocery store late in the year, and that site was to remain a grocery store almost continuously for eighty years. Between DeChamplain's and Bremer Street were a saloon, the Central Hotel, and several residences.

South of Chapin Street, there were LaBar and Cornwell's flour mill and Osmund Reed's blacksmith and harness shop on the southwest corner of Chapin and Mitchell. On the east side of Mitchell, there was virtually nothing except residences south of Chapin Street.

The north end of the central district was dominated by Courthouse Hill on the east side of the street, which still remained

2. With the construction of the second Oddfellow Building in 1913, the house was moved to the southeast corner of Park and Bremer streets, where it still stands.

vacant. Beside it, looming over the city, was the George Mitchell home. South of Beech Street was Dr. Leeson's Central Drug Store, now being managed by O. L. Davis, with Leeson's office and drug manufactory behind. South of the drug store was Osgood's furniture store, A. M. Lamb's grocery store, John Turner's furniture and undertaking shop, and Sampson and Drury's hardware. Then, next to the McKinnon Hotel, the old Tobias Borne shoe shop, which was later occupied as a grocery store by J. N. McKinnon, had become the saloon of John Hassenfuss. Within a few years it was to be the site of Fred Reed's first jewelry store in the city. On Harris Street, behind the McKinnon House, was a small barn, then a Chinese laundry, and the Methodist Episcopal Church. Across the street was George Kirkbride's home and furniture manufacturing shop, and between that and the American House were Cutler's Livery Stable and a harness shop operated by city constable James English and T. W. Hawthorne. The two businesses were merged as Kelly and Mather's Livery Stable in 1887, after English left to manage the Blodgett farm in Missaukee County. On the corner, of course, was the American House, then John LaLone's barber shop, Abram Cohen's New York Store (later sold to M. J. Present), W. Boorem's grocery store, Dillenbeck's drug store, the O. H. Ellis Wholesale Liquor Store, John Sheridan's barber shop, Hunt's Jewelry, F. A. Koegel's harness shop, Kennedy's Bowling Alley and Saloon, and Morse's "Bankrupt Store" (cut-rate clothing). On the alley off Cass Street, Mosser & White had built a carpenter shop, and the first city jail had been built behind it.[3] In 1879 the city acquired the entire parcel and built a fire house, fronting on Cass, in which were kept the pumper, hose cart, and hook and ladder truck, with a fire bell on the roof. Behind the wagon house, sticking up like a miniature Washington Monument, was a fifty-six foot hose tower, in which

3. The village economized for several years by locking its prisoners in empty box cars on the G. R. & I. siding. Since they were usually only drunks, it presented no serious problem. Mike Corbitt, however, charged with breaking jail in 1874 was acquitted when he swore that he and two other "desperadoes" were wakened from a good night's sleep by a railroad detective in Grand Rapids, where the "jail" had been moved during the night. He had merely followed the detective's order "to leave the car and take foot."

the fire hose was hung to dry after use.

On the south side of Cass Street, the Ohio House had burned and the corner was vacant in 1882. Next door, Charles R. Smith had a grocery store, followed by E. Baruch's Great Western Clothing Store, Dunham's grocery, a meat market, the old Mosser & White building, in which was Crawford's grocery store, followed by Cheap John's Second-Hand Store (W.C. Davis proprietor), the meat market and bakery of Vosberg and Goff, and the new Oddfellow Building, occupied by grocers McAdam and Brown. On the corner was a vacant lot, where J.M. Ridlon's clothing store had burned down three years before.

Across the street was D.C. Kennedy's blacksmith and veterinarian shop. Moving northward, there was a residence, Mrs. Butler's laundry, Charles Dutton's furniture manufacturing and repair shop, a restaurant, Martin and Clary's grocery store, Fred Huntley's jewelry and sewing machine store, and the Cobbs & Mitchell office building.

On the north side of Cass Street was the large George Mitchell building, four stories in height, erected in 1874, and commonly called the bank building. On the ground floor was Rice and Messmore's bank. On the second floor, the city had rented space for a council room, and various attorneys and lumberman had their offices. The third floor was rented by the Masonic lodge. To the north was the office of Mitchell Bros., Jared Hixson's bank (formerly the Culver saloon building moved from Mason Street in 1875) in which was located the post office, LaBar & Cornwell's grocery store, the saloon of Capt. Lawrence Newson, Cloud and Morgan's hardware, Tress's grocery, Towle's photography, James Balfour's bakery (in the old Davis saloon building), a women's ready-to-wear and dry goods store, and Dr. R.J. Cummer's Drugstore.

At the rear of the block were the G. R. & I. depot, next to which were the Balfour House Hotel and Massey's Cigar and News Stand, fronting on Harris Street.

On the north side of Harris Street, the Cadillac House Hotel (formerly the Arnold House and about to be renamed the Jackson House) stood by the railroad track facing the street. From the corner of Harris to Mason, the block was known for many years as the "Star Block," and many of the businesses used the name. At the corner was J. W. Cummer's hardware, followed by L. J. Law's Star Clothing House, Phineas Medalie's ladies' ready-to-wear and dry goods store, the Chicago Store of W. R. Dennis and Company (men's clothing), the City Drug Store of Albert E. Smith, W. M. Gow's Fancy Goods, Rathmun's Star Bakery, S. W. Kramer's Men's Wear, John Plett's Star Market (meats), Pierce's clothing store (later Auer's) and John Olson's shoe store on the corner.

3.

The face of Main Street, of course, was changed repeatedly over the years by fire. Early construction was entirely of pine, and when a fire began, it was hard to control. The *News* was constantly lamenting the problems of fire insurance and fire protection and the need for brick construction. Even after George Mitchell's son-in-law Keller Moyer had opened the Clam Lake brickyard, brick construction was rare and the brickyard failed during the hard times of the seventies. It was only after it had been acquired by a better builder, John Mosser, in better times that the brickyard prospered and brick construction commenced.

Several major fires wrought havoc. On December 14, 1875, a good portion of the Star Block between Harris and Mason streets was destroyed on the west side of the street. On the north side of Mason Street, Holbrook & May's store was damaged. On the east side of the street, Dr. Leeson's drug store and the adjoining Osgood building were also badly damaged. On the west side of the street, the building owned by John Turner containing a grocery store, J. S. Duval's shoe store, two buildings owned by supervisor William Kelley, a clothing store of B. L. Meister, and O. F. Bloss's "Cheap Store" on the corner of Mitchell and Mason streets, were all destroyed.

In October, 1877, an even worse fire swept the Star Block. It started in the hardware store of J. W. Cummer at the corner. The Arnold House Hotel owned by Larson and Nelson behind it was totally destroyed, and the Balfour House Hotel across the street was badly damaged. The entire business block north to Mason was totally destroyed. Bloss had located next to Cummer after having burned out two years before, and he had recently become insolvent. The stock and merchandise being held by his assignee was still in the store and was destroyed. The next store north, owned by attorney John Rosevelt, housed his home and office on the second floor and the men's clothing and furniture store of Goodenough and Foster on the main floor. The fourth door north was Otto Lindahl's bakery. An attempt was made to pull it down to stop the blaze, but it was too solidly constructed and was soon blazing. Fire destroyed the next four buildings, owned by supervisor Kelley, and housing Ben Wolf's dry goods, the furniture store of alderman Daniel Peck, W. M. Gow's Fancy Goods Store (originally the Kelley home), and Kelley's new building replacing that burned down in 1875 and now occupied by Rock and Rathmun's bakery. Behind these buildings Kelley had a huge barn and livery stable which was also destroyed. In the remainder of the block, the shoe store of John Duval was again burned out, as was John Turner's new building, now occupied by Kramer and Medalie's Men's Wear, a vacant store building, and the clothing store of Samuel Wolf.

On the opposite side of the street, roof damage was done to the McKinnon Hotel, J. H. McKinnon's grocery store, the Lamb grocery and John Turner's casket and furniture store, but all were saved.

J. W. Cummer and Otto Lindahl promptly rebuilt with brick. Next to Lindahl, supervisor Kelley constructed a brick block seventy-five feet long and divided into three stores. Exceptionally well constructed, the building still stands with only minor alterations and renovations. The dry goods business of Ben Wolf and the men's wear store of Sam Wolf were joined in the south store of the building, which has remained in almost continuous occupancy as a men's wear store ever since, the Wolfs selling the business to W. R. Dennis, who operated it as the Chicago Store and sold in turn to James A. Smith in 1890. In 1901 Smith sold to Chris Jorgensen, who was the predecessor of the present owner and occupant, Ted J. Brown.[4] Jorgensen later bought the adjoining Lindahl building and moved the clothing store there, but soon brought it back to its original home.

4. Jorgensen's first residence on arriving from Denmark in 1874 was on the same spot as a roomer in the home of William Kelley.

Kelley's center store was re-occupied by Peck's furniture, and then leased to Albert Smith as the City Drug Store a few years later. After the death of the owner, William Kelley, his widow Nancy married George VanVranken, a pharmacist, and he bought out Smith, continuing the drug store operation there for many years. The third store continued to be occupied by W. M. Gow until he moved into the new Masonic Temple building in 1890. The store was then leased to Goodman's Shoe Store. Except from about 1928 or 1929 until 1931, it has been a shoe store ever since, being the site of Henne's Shoe Store for the past forty-one years.

In April, 1878, a disastrous fire started in the old part of town along Mason Street and destroyed the boardinghouse and shoe shop of alderman Lewis Lawson, Bergstrom's Sweed Saloon, the Mason House, Holbrook & May's old log building, the Gallinger building, and eight other buildings around the intersection of Lake and Mason streets, plus all of the boat houses. The fire took the life of Cadillac's outstanding surgeon, Dr. Nathaniel Blunt, and his wife.

In later years there were to be other spectacular fires. The rebuilt Jackson House, renamed the Burke, was destroyed in a spectacular fire in 1899, only the most heroic efforts preventing its spread and the loss of life.

Fires in 1896 and 1899 burned out all of the business block between Harris and Mitchell streets except the American House Hotel. The first fire started in Dr. Dillenbeck's drug store, which had been recently acquired by Louis Finn. It destroyed the neighboring Davis drugstore, Herrick buildings, Johnson and Ostenson's clothing store, Drebin's general store, and Olson's shoe store.[5] The only buildings saved were the American House at one corner and the store building at the south corner owned by Dr. Wardell. Most of the reconstruction was of masonry, which was fortunate in view of the fire of April, 1899, which started in the center of the block. The new masonry construction in the north prevented its spread, and only the southerly four buildings were destroyed: Sawyer and Hodges' news stand, Fred Reed's jewelry store, and the Wardell buildings occupied by Robert Wilson's

5. Olson had rented the building from Dr. Wardell after his old location at Mason and Mitchell was taken over by the Johnston and Kaiser grocery in 1894.

saloon and Rice and Casler's shoe store. Again, rebuilding was of brick construction, completing the renovation of the block which was to remain almost the same thereafter except for the fire which destroyed the American House in 1925 and the 1953 fire which destroyed the south central part of the block.

4.

Over the years certain sites have continued uninterruptedly in a particular commercial use. Besides those in the Kelley block just mentioned and the grocers at the northeast corner of Pine and Mitchell streets, we have noted the long succession of grocery stores in the Mosser & White building: LaBar, Cornwell & Company, Corneil and McDonall, Crawford Brothers, Wilcox Brothers, and others. The southwest corner of Harris and Cass streets is such a location. Several different business ventures were located on the corner in the early years of the village. About 1876 it became the site of the Walcott drugstore, which was the successor to Drs. Wilcox and Wardell, originally located in the Holbrook & May building. In 1877 it was bought by R. F. Lewis. The next year it was purchased by S. J. Case, and in 1879 Dr. R. J. Cummer acquired the building and operated a drugstore, maintaining his offices as a physician on the second story. In 1888 Cummer moved to Cleveland, selling his medical practice to Dr. Bartlett McMullen and the drugstore to Arthur H. Webber. The site continued as a drugstore until 1950, when the J. C. Penney Company acquired the lease and D. Bruce Wooley moved his drugstore to another location.

Another long-use location was that on the northwest corner of Harris and Mitchell streets. We have already noted that W. H. Hicks was the first hardware merchant in town, renting space in Larcom & Mott's building on the northeast corner of Mason and Lake streets. Hicks was in business before he had a site, selling directly from boxcars on the Mason Street siding until the Larcom & Mott building was ready for occupancy. In 1873 he put up a store building at the northwest corner of Mitchell and Harris. A siege of bad health required assistance, and he took in Daniel Peck as a partner in 1874. Peck's presence in the business was given time almost equal to his presence in the saloons, and neither Hicks' health nor the business was helped by Peck's addition to the firm. A buyer was found, J. Walter Cummer, brother of lumberman Jacob Cummer. He bought out Peck in 1876.[6] Hicks stayed about eight months to help Cummer in the transition, then left. The Cummer hardware store continued until almost the end of the century. Then it was occupied by M. J. Present, who had purchased Cohen's New York Store, until 1919, when it was sold to John Johnson for a clothing store. It has continued in that use until the present time. The building was destroyed by fire but rebuilt by J. Lawrence Johnson in 1965.

In 1879 Charles H. Drury came to Cadillac from Adrian. He worked briefly for Cloud and Mitchell's hardware store and in 1880 started a hardware store on Mitchell Street in partnership with Frank Sampson. Sampson retired after a few years, selling his interest to A. W. Newark, who later sold his interest to Frank B. Kelley. The original store was burned out in 1888 and a three-story brick building built to replace it, which presently is part of the Stephan drug building. The business was in operation in Cadillac for over fifty years, with Drury taking an active part in the affairs of the Methodist Church, the People's Savings Bank and various industrial enterprises of the twentieth century.

One of the American success stories was that of Solomon W. Kramer, born in 1850 in Courland on the Baltic, then part of Czarist Russia. Kramer came to the United States for a brief visit to relatives in 1872, returned in 1876, and located in Clam Lake in 1877, starting a clothing store with Phineas Medalie. At the end of the first year's operation, he bought out Medalie and continued

6. Peck worked at odd jobs for Osgood and Horton and John Turner, and when Fred Kieldsen had a heart attack in 1877 and temporarily retired, Peck leased his store from landlord William Kelley and tried his hand at a furniture business there. After burning out in the fire of 1877, he tried again, but failed after two years, going back to clerking for others. He was elected to several terms as alderman, but his drinking destroyed his effectiveness. The *Tribune* noted that a rider on Dunham's Express, by the name of Dan, "measured his happiness by the Peck," but not being sufficiently pugilistic at Manton tried his skills on his family when he got back to Cadillac and had to be cooled in the cooler. Shortly after, the family separated.

the business alone until his retirement in 1905. Kramer was a self-effacing, hard-working man with the mind of a builder. On several occasions he purchased rundown real estate and demolished it, putting up better buildings "to make the street look nicer." He sought no public office but was regularly sought out by city officials to serve in appointive positions and spent many years on the board of public works. In 1895 he was one of the organizers of the Cadillac State Bank and served as its vice president for years. In 1900 he acquired the store adjoining his property on North Mitchell Street and built a large brick building, which now houses Montgomery Ward and Company. He was organizer and president of the Cadillac Lumber Company, an officer of the St. John's Table Company, active in the Masonic organizations, and one of the community's builders for thirty years.

Levi J. Law came to Cadillac in 1881. He was born in Massachusetts and raised in Indiana, where, said the Republican *News*, he suffered from spring malaria and Indiana democracy. Law was one of the more successful merchants in Cadillac, largely because of his good humor and quick wit. He suffered the stigma of being a Democrat in a Republican community, was a frequent and generally unsuccessful candidate for public office on a city, county, and state level, although he did serve several terms as mayor, and was trusted with many appointive positions. He was four times chairman of the county Democratic committee, of which he was a perpetual member. On the state level, he was a member of the state Democratic committee for many years and attended five national political conventions as a delegate.

John Plett came to Cadillac in 1877 as a German immigrant. He became a member of the city countil in 1885 but professed not to care much for public life. He had a slaughterhouse on the west bank of the Clam River, near Thirteenth Street, and a residence on Pine Street. He operated a meat market on Mitchell Street for over twenty years. He was one of the organizers of the German Aid Society, but "in spite of that," said the *News*, "and his strong cigars, he votes the Republican ticket and is a mighty good citizen for Cadillac." His youngest son, Tom, was a familiar figure on Main Street for many years and still resides in the city.

5.

The professional life of Cadillac in 1882 consisted of two dentists, H. B. Ward and E. M. Hutchinson, eighteen lawyers, and thirteen physicians.

The legal profession had Judge Fallass, the Rice brothers, David, Rolin, and Judge John, William H. Cavanagh, who had moved back from Lake City, Eugene F. Sawyer, Probate Judge Holden Green, Donald E. McIntyre, James Riley Bishop, W. C. Haire, John B. Rosevelt, Samuel J. Wall, Eugene E. Haskins, William H. Parks, Robert Christensen, H. M. Dunham, M. L. Dunham, and J. Wight Giddings, who was in the process of buying the Cadillac *Weekly News.* Others had come and stayed but briefly, like James Byron Judkins, for a time partner of Judge Fallass and now serving as circuit judge in the Osceola, Mecosta, Lake, Ludington, and Manistee district, and George C. Worth. They were to be joined in 1883 by Fred Aldrich and Clyde C. Chittenden, both to be future circuit judges. Two other residents were soon to be admitted, Thomas J. Thorp in 1884 and Charles C. Dunham in 1885.

Drs. Leeson, Dillenbeck, and Wardell had had other compatriots come and go. Drs. Wilcox, McTaggart, Scott, and Morgan had left the area. Dr. Blunt burned to death in the fire of 1878, and Dr. R. Dundas, who arrived in 1875, had died of diphtheria in an epidemic in 1879. Newcomers were Drs. R. J. Cummer, Charles Keech. H. F. Askum, Edward C. Gray, Carroll E. Miller, R. W. Coleman, Joseph Raphael Brodeur, I. N. Coleman, Mott C. Heath, and C. Estelle Long. All except Dr. Long were prosperous and busy in 1882. Dr. Long had the fame and the misfortune of being the first university trained woman doctor in northern Michigan. It was, unfortunately, a time when women's rights were suspiciously viewed and people were not in a hurry to take their problems to a female doctor. She eventually became famous as a missionary in South America.

In the uncertain medical conditions of the times, several of the doctors themselves suffered from incurable maladies. Dr. Askum went to Arizona for his tuberculosis and died of it there. Dr. Gray and Dr. Heath remained, and died of it here. Some, like Dr.

Brodeur and Dr. Miller, were to join Drs. Wardell and Leeson as almost permanent fixtures in the medical community of the area.

6.

The town was well represented by newspapers. Besides the Cadillac *Weekly News,* there was the *Daily Enterprise,* a tool in the county seat battle, and ultimately to be removed to Buckley. In 1882 the Cadillac *Weekly Times,* a Democratic newspaper, was commenced. In 1885 the name was to be changed to the *State Democrat,* edited by M. T. Woodruf, followed by George Stanley, who continued its publication until 1911, the last few years under the name the *Weekly Citizen.* A competing Republican paper was commenced in 1886, the *Saturday Express.* In 1884 an independent reform Republican paper, the Wexford County *Citizen,* was founded by H. N. Enos.

The proliferation of newspapers seemed quite disorderly and self-destructive to the conservative Cummers. The Wexford County *Citizen* came to an end, simply shut down after it was purchased by the Cummers at a price far in excess of its value, with a covenant that Enos would not start another newspaper in the area. Nothing much could be done about the *Democrat,* but in 1887 the *Saturday Express* was acquired from its owners, C. T. Chapin and Henry Sill, by the Cummers, who also bought the Cadillac *Weekly News* from its publisher, J. Wight Giddings. The two papers were merged under the name of Cadillac *News & Express,* and Perry F. Powers was brought in to run it and given the opportunity to purchase it for less than the Cummer investment. The real purpose, said those who dared whisper about the Cummers, was to insure a single competent voice which would speak with the voice of Cummer.

Chapter Twenty-Two

GROWING PAINS

The new county seat bore little resemblance to the handful of buildings that had clustered around the end of Little Clam Lake ten years previous. The city claimed a population of "close to 5,000 stalwarts" at the end of 1882, bt it was an overly optimistic estimate, as was its estimate that it would reach 10,000 population by 1890. By 1884 it had 4,000 people. Despite its growth, it had only to look around it to see how short was the distance it had come. In any direction the forest was within a few minutes walk.

Some of the early millowners and merchants had come through the hard times of the seventies with a strong financial base, and the town was beginning to show a few evidences of luxury. For the most part, however, it was still a raw and poor frontier town. It was typical of the small rural towns of the period but molded by its one industry economy and colored by its newness. It had an unfinished air.

The streets were sand, "improved" with sawdust, largely ungraded, and with stumps still standing in most of the residential areas. Board sidewalks made foot traffic a little easier and cleaner in the business district and in some of the better residential areas. A few homes had neat lawns, landscaped terraces, and ornamental shrubs, but these were the exception and marked the homes of the more prosperous citizens. The first plantings of maple shade trees had begun in 1876, but the small trees were almost unnoticeable, and all of the original forest had been cut away. There was a naked look to the place.

Yards were fenced, for those who had no livestock had gardens to protect against the escaped beasts of those who had. Barns adjoined the homes or fronted to the alleys, adjoined by outhouses, woodsheds, chicken coops, and pens. There was a pound on Wood Street, usually having from ten to twenty-five stray cows as tenants, with an occasional horse or goat, and the dangers to gardens and shrubs from marauding stock was the subject of frequent editorial comment in the newspapers.[1]

Most homes were neither insulated nor centrally heated in 1882, and a cold snap in the winter froze the house plants and drove the occupants to bed-warmers under their quilts and comforters. As yet there were few pipes to freeze, since the impetus to a waterworks had been mainly for fire protection. The installation of running water in residences didn't become common for a few more years. Drinking water came from the lake by bucket, and those farther removed from the shore had open wells. Heating and cooking was done by wood stoves and furnaces, and the woodshed or woodpile was part of every home. Streets were unblemished by utility poles until 1878, when the first telephone line was strung between the homes of lumber partners Dan McCoy, at the corner of Mason and Simons streets, and Charles Ayers, at Oak and Hersey. It would be ten years before the practice spread and electric wire poles began to sprout.

All of this, of course, was to change rapidly in the next few years. Utilizing edgings and slabs for fuel, the Cummer Lumber Company built an electrical plant for its mills in the mid-eighties to more efficiently utilize plant and labor by enabling nighttime workruns. Around the clock shifts could now be scheduled when demand was at its peak. From this base, the Cummers formed a new company which was given a lighting franchise for the city. The contract first called for lighting from a half hour after sunset until ten o'clock in the evening except on moonlight nights. The contract was gradually amended until "all-night, every-night" lighting was provided "from dusk until dawn" in 1893, and the firm was beginning the promotion of household use of electricity.

Judge Green improved the waterworks, installing more powerful pumps at the pumphouse at the foot of Harris Street. In 1892 a new thirty-year franchise for the Cadillac Water Company brought extension of the system to the newly developed areas of the

1. With the adoption of the "loose cow" ordinance in 1887, the *Democrat* sniffed that the aldermen had "evinced similar concern for other strayed creatures in the past. It will be hoped that the ordinance is better enforced for our 'loose cows' than has that dealing with our 'loose women.' "

city, replacement of the old wooden mains,[2] and construction of a storage standpipe eighty feet high at the top of what was then called "Schoolhouse Hill" but which was thereafter known as "Standpipe Hill."[3] At the time of the transfer, the system had 430 subscribers and was pumping an average of a million gallons of water a day. The new system was operated from the Cummer Water Building and a new intake was constructed in 19 feet of water 475 feet offshore. It was soon running over 1.5 million gallons a day on the average, and ran as high as three million gallons during the dry summers of the mid-nineties, not counting water used in the Cummer industries.

2.

The household use of water, of course, not only provided drinking and cooking water, but revolutionized the bath and made possible the elimination of the outhouse. In 1886 the *News* began a campaign for a sewer system, and the first sanitary sewer construction began three years later. The system fed into a main trunk line running the length of Mitchell Street from Howard Street to the Clam River, where it emptied at the bridge.[4] The use of the Clam River as an outlet for the city's raw sewage and the weather extremes of the next few years led to more problems.

For one thing, the "crystal purity" of the lakes on which early observers remarked, had disappeared. Manmade changes around, and deposits in, the lakes had changed their character for the worse. The digging of the canal between the lakes in 1873 had

2. Broken mains and routine maintenance in recent years have disclosed that the contract was not completely met, since some of the old wooden mains were found still in use.

3. The standpipe was removed after twenty-five years, but the name stuck until recently, when the area came to be known as Diggins Hill after the park area donated by the Diggins family there. Neither a new standpipe put up in 1960 nor the construction of the new McKinley School there in 1957 caused a reversion to either of the old names.

4. The city was thus in violation of its own ordinance, adopted in 1887, prohibiting dumping any substance in Little Clam Lake or Clam Lake River.

scrved to move logs and facilitate boating between the lakes. But it had also served to speed the flow of water through the lake system and out the Clam Lake River outlet. The natural connection between the lakes, the Black River, had been shallow, winding and broken by numerous windfalls and other obstructions which tended to retard the flow of water from Big Clam Lake and keep the water table high in the areas to its west which constituted the great portion of the drainage basin. Now the spring runoff came with a rush and was gone, and man was further speeding the dispersion of surface water by filling the swamps around the lakes.

In consequence, a cycle of extreme high water in the spring and low water in the summer began, accentuated by repeated widening of the canal (in 1886, 1894, 1896, and 1900). During the spring, as the runoff of winter snow combined with spring rains, the swamps at the east end of Little Clam Lake were filled to overflowing. Mitchell Street from Chapin to its end at Howard, and Wood Street beyond, were often impassable for four to six weeks; Lake Street was often under water, and the mills had to be closed. Downstream, the farms and the slaughterhouses along the Clam Lake River were inundated. At the other extreme, during dry summers the bed of the river would be totally dry, and the lakes would be so low that tug operations had to cease, and, on a few occasions, the mills had to close down entirely.

Two attempts were made to control the flow of water through the lake system. The first was the unsuccessful series of locks in the canal, which were abandoned after washouts in three successive springs. At the river outlet, Levi Harris created a new channel and an island in an effort to use the flow of water for his mill. The new channel was opened at the mill to run north past it, then easterly parallel to the shore and into the natural channel. A dam was then built across the natural channel so that water escaped by that route only during periods of high water, and flow through the mill channel was controlled at the mill. In 1894 the dam washed out and it was never replaced.

In 1884 the Cadillac Veneer and Panel Company was organized and constructed a plant on the north side of the river. In order to have a floating pond, a dam was built across the river downstream from the plant, and large quantities of muck were dredged out of the swamp to make the millpond. Known as the Dutcher Dam, after Thomas Dutcher, president of the company, it stood until it was washed out in 1894, was rebuilt, and washed out again in 1897. It was relatively low, and did not afford an effective control of the lake level.

After the completion of the sewer to the river in 1889, it was not long until north city residents began to complain of the sewage odor, and the health board ordered that a wooden box sewer be placed in the bed of the stream to move the waste another 300 feet downstream. For reasons of health, an ordinance was enacted banning swimming in the river below the Haring (Mitchell) Street Bridge, but the *News* continued to note the presence of small boys swimming there, in several instances apprehended by chief of police Silas Huckleberry for their offense.

In 1893, as the new water system had filled its standpipe and was just beginning its operation, the water turned suddenly brackish. By June there was a large fish kill in the lake, and one account refers to the shores as being covered by dead lizards. It was a dry summer; the river bed was soon almost dry, and the lake water worsened. Samples were taken to the University Medical School at Ann Arbor. The water, said the report, "was quite pure, but boiling as a precaution against disease is highly recommended!" As matters got worse during the summer, the situation was the subject of debate before the city council. The aldermen concluded that stagnation, growth of weeds, and impurities "infusing the water" resulted from periodic low lake level. By the end of the summer, the stench of sewage in the dry bed of the river was intolerable.

For years it had been customary for the mayor-elect to give an inaugural address, invariably pledging to regulate the saloons and drive out the houses of ill fame. Commencing with the 1894 address of mayor-elect Samuel J. Wall, a new subject was introduced, which was to be a matter of concern for the next 65 years, long after inaugural addresses were passé. Although devoting about two-thirds of the address to saloons and prostitution, the mayor-elect spent most of the remainder of his time discussing the need for better sewage disposal, notwithstanding the city had just built its sewers; a better water system in the face of the new company's current improvements, and control of the lake level. The answer to all, he suggested, was the construction of a new dam, which would conserve the level of the lake, which in turn would keep the mills in operation and preserve the purity of the water. He continued:

> The experience of last summer warns us that we must protect the public against a recurrence of the condition when the bed of the Clam River was nearly dry. It may become necessary to extend the sewer even farther down the river and farther from the thickly built up portion of the city. In the meantime, the delivery of water from Clam Lake should be carefully attended to. The lake is the natural flushing tank of the river while the sewage is poured into it and the water should be held back by artificial means so as to insure sufficient volume for flushing during the dry season.

The new council promptly adopted an ordinance putting control of the river under the sewer commission. Nature vetoed it as a series of torrential rainstorms over the next ten days flooded the lakes, both the Harris and Dutcher dams being washed out on June 8. Capricious Mother Nature then turned it off. The lake level fell so low that no water was moving through the outlet at all by the end of July. The Veneer Pond was a dried-up mudhole, and the *News* exaggerated only slightly perhaps in saying that there was no water in the lake. The sewage problem was again atrocious, and the box sewer was extended down the riverbed another 300 feet. The Dutcher Dam was rebuilt, but the city failed to act. The year 1895 was a repeat of 1894, except that the Dutcher Dam didn't wash out, perhaps for lack of water. Jail prisoners were used to add another 200 feet to the riverbed sewer line, clean out debris, and straighten the course of the river downstream.

The following year was a relatively normal year and the matter was put aside, the city still being financially stricken from the continuing recession which started in 1893. In 1897, however, another particularly wet spring overflowed everything, closed the mills, and ultimately washed out the Dutcher Dam again. This time, the city forebade its reconstruction in private hands and directed the board of public works to build a controllable dam and to assure responsibility for maintaining the level of the lake and "flushing sewage down the Clam River." It was built by contractor M. L. Feury the following summer, and still stands, augmented by a modern lake level court order.[5]

In the meantime, the quality of the water pumped from the lake remained sufficiently bad that a number of wells were sunk around the city in 1897. These supplied the major portion of the drinking and cooking water for the community for the next sixty years.

3.

The Clam Lake River, by the time the new city dam was built, bore little resemblance to the stream Levi Harris saw when he came through the wilderness looking for pine and picked out government lot 2 through which the outlet flowed. For over two miles from its outlet across sections 33 and 27 of Haring Township, it meandered sluggishly through a swampland of cedar and marsh, overflowing even the higher pine land during the spring and retaining standing water most of the year. The cutting off of the trees, coupled with the heightened annual spring flow of water after the canal was opened, destroyed the natural capacity of the swamp to retain water and scoured off much of the surface growth. As a result, the area had the appearance of a vast lake or river for six to eight weeks every spring. For the remainder of the year, it was a desolate mudflat of stumps with a winding flow of water of varying size, depending on the annual rainfall. Perhaps the worst year was in 1877, when the water in the lakes was so low

5. The sewage problem was ultimately solved by a treatment plant, the capacity of which was always questionable. Modern health concerns brought state intervention and an order to terminate the use of the old plant, but the order was stayed from year to year on the basis of reports showing an operation of such efficiency that no raw sewage was escaping into the river. Plans for a lake level study in 1953 and 1954 led to rather strong suspicions that city reports showing incredible efficiency in operation of the antiquated plant were in the order of fiction. A quiet inquiry, without embarrassing publicity, and a hardened state stance, coupled with a more progressive city administration in a more prosperous time, resulted in the construction of a new sewage treatment plant.

that the mills closed and there was no water running through the outlet at all for over seven weeks, only small pools showing evidence of springs here and there.

At the time the Dutcher Dam was first built in 1884, the dredgings from digging the millpond were used to straighten the course of the river around Haynes Road and to build up the bank around the dam. The previous year, the work of beautifying and channeling the river below Haring Road was commenced by alderman Gilbert Anderson Bergland. Bergland was a Swedish immigrant of good education and immense energy. He logged, dealt in pinelands, and founded the logging towns of Sidnaw and Bergland in the Upper Peninsula. He owned the towns—stores, saloons, homes, mills, and churches—and prospered in everything. Among his early ventures, he did street contracting and, as the streets grades were cut into the hills of the town, the dirt removed was used for fill on his land through which the Clam flowed. Others, of course, stumped and channeled the river further downstream, farmed along and built on the banks of the river. But the Bergland improvement, running almost all the way to slaughterhouses of John Plett and Fred Hutchinson near Thirteenth Street, was a colossal undertaking before the days of modern earthmoving machinery. In 1886 the *News* noted the result:

> One of the greatest improvements to the City of Cadillac in the last few years is the work done by Alderman G. A. Bergland, known to his friends as Gilbert Anderson, on his property down by the river. Three years ago it was wilderness of stumps, marshes, with a muddy creek meandering through it. In fact, it looked like a wasteland. Mr. Bergland has gone to work and cleared, graded and planted the land until now it presents a beautiful, queenly, green slope which looks fairly like an oasis with a stumpland beyond. In addition to this, the course of the creek has been totally changed and from a dirty, winding stream, it is converted into a small river with a straight course, high banks with a wide hardwalk on each side and the channel made of such depth that three feet of water will go through it. The unsightly marsh has become dry, attractive land which will be made productive in time and

altogether the work done by Mr. Bergland, will be of great advantage to our city.

4.

There were other changes around the lakes. Around the east end of the lake, of course, were the mills, and they made their imprint. We have noted the Pioneer Mill of John Hale, built on pilings in the shallows of the lake the better to float logs, but eventually on solid ground, as the area around and beneath it was filled with sawdust, slabs and cinders and, eventually, sand. Under Cobbs' ownership, an earthfill, stone, and concrete dock was built into the lake.

The land between Lake Street and the water's edge was extended from fifteen to thirty feet outwards with pilings, stone, and fill dirt. From the foot of Pine Street to the Shackleton-Green mill, a marsh extended for a considerable distance north. In the first few years of the village, a sawdust road was built from the mill to Pine Street across the marsh.[6] Then it was gradually raised by more sawdust and fill dirt, as the marsh to the north was also filled and converted to building sites along Lake Street and to lumber yards from there to the mill. On the lake side of the road, fill was dumped several times after storm-driven waves had washed out part of the road.

The greatest incursion into the lake, however, resulted from the dumping docks at the mills. There was a great deal of fill around the Harris mill, but its dock was constructed on pilings, and Harris Point to the west served the same purpose, with tracks running to its end. When the Cummers bought the Bond & Green mill, they were prepared to enter into railroading as part of the enterprise. One landfill dock 250 feet long was built west of the mill in 1879, and in 1881 a second pier, almost 400 feet long, was

6. Known as Larcom's Marsh, it was really part of the lake and apparently was a spawning bed for grasspike. Water stood on the north side of the road until filling was completed during the dry summer of 1877. In 1876 the *News* reported grasspike over twenty-five pounds being taken in the marsh. In 1877 buildings were going up there.

built east of the mill. Railroad track ran its length, and an engine house and boathouse were built on the very end. The docks, of course, facilitated dumping of logs and booming of the floating logs. Three years later, the Cummers built a power plant on the lake to the east of the longer pier, and further filling of the lake front occurred at that time. With the end of the pine period, the portion of the piers above water was used to further fill the lakeshore, and the action of waves ultimately dissipated the subsurface portion of the piers.

Other docks served the heavy traffic on the lake. There was no road around Little Clam Lake for twenty years, and even travel around the east end of the lake was not convenient. A municipal dock near the foot of Harris Street was maintained after the early eighties, and several private docks between Harris and Pine streets were built by Gallinger and Blanchard, Andrew Larcom, Spencer Mason of the Mason House, and H. M. Wall.

Running west along the south shore, a small dock served the Sunnyside Bond mill. On the north shore, a landing dock was constructed at the end of Harris Point, and steamer service existed on a regular schedule between the city dock and Harris Point. Later, another dock was constructed farther west where Lake Drive meets the shore, and this was included in the service on an irregular basis. During certain seasons, it was a regular stop, as it was about due south of the fair grounds and race track located between Division & Chestnut streets.

In the area now known as Kenwood, but then called Taylor's Grove, a picnic area and park developed, and another dock was built there, as there was no means of getting there but by boat. The sole place of business was A. Poppino's Saloon and Dance Pavilion.

At the end of the lake, the area south of the canal and between the lakes came to be known as Idlewild, and excursions of picnickers were boating out there soon after the village was settled. A Sunday at Idlewild or a moonlight ride back on the steamer was an event to remember. In 1883 Gustav Helbing[7] started an enter-

7. In some of the warfare over the clearing of the Ann Arbor right-of-way, Helbing was shot and killed near Marion. Idlewild was continued by his father.

tainment resort called Twin Lake Park,[8] built a dance hall, and constructed a permanent dock there. The place was never referred to as a saloon, and it was the scene of Sunday school picnics and excursions. Nevertheless, it appears that liquor was sold there. A shooting and several drunken brawls are reported as having originated at Twin Lake Park, and on at least three different occasions nighttime drownings were blamed on whiskey when the deceased fell off the steamer en route home.

5.

The principal reason for the commercial steamer traffic, other than logging, was the lack of roads around the lake. The quickest way from downtown Cadillac to Harristown was by boat. The location of the mills along the shore effectively blocked off road construction. The sawdust road from the foot of Pine Street to the Shackleton-Green mill served only the mill and went no further. Lake Street, such as it was, ended a hundred feet north of Pine Street until late in 1875, when it was extended to meet the road leading to the Haynes mill from Mitchell Street, and it was not fully usable until two years later when the larger stumps were pulled. Beyond Harristown, there were no roads, nor was there any road around the south shore of the lake.

The town line road which is now M-55 East was cut in 1872 and 1873 but was just a sand trail until 1885, when it was made a plank road from the head of Cass Street to the city limit at Crosby Road, which took its name from the nearby farm of an early settler, T. W. Crosby. Beyond the city limit, the townships began improvements the following year by adding clay and gravel, and the city followed suit in 1892 when the plank road had deteriorated badly.

To the south, the only road was the Whaley trail, following the present course of Whaley Street to its present intersection with Lynn Street and then meandering along the east side of the old township cemetery to enter the village at the point where Shelby

8. The name so entranced editor Stanley of the Democrat on his arrival in Cadillac that he started a campaign to rename the community Twin Lake City. The name was commonly used for a decade as a by-name for Cadillac.

Street intersects with Howard, then the south limits of the settlement.[9] As the city spread outward, Lynn Street was graded and stumped and became the main traveled route until Cobbs Street was platted and cleared.

To the southwest, there was no established road until 1876. In 1875 Levi Harris, then township road commissioner, asked, and was granted, authority to lay out roads to the west on both sides of Little Clam Lake, recognizing the growing settlements in Cherry Grove and Selma Townships. Mitchell Street and the village ended at Howard Street, and Lake Street ended at Chapin. Outlot 7 was covered by a small lake extending from Chapin Street in an irregular hourglass shape all the way to the foot of Cemetery Hill. A sand and sawdust road had been built through it curving from the foot of Howard Street to the Cobbs mill, and a trail branched off southward along the railroad, part of which is now Hector Street, and ended at the foot of the hill. It was in this area along the railroad that the first cluster of homes for mill hands was built that came to be called Cobbtown.[10]

In deciding a route for the southwestern road, Harris elected to follow the section line to the foot of Cemetery Hill. State law required this where practical, but the choice wasn't made because of practicality but in anticipation of future extension of the road further south into the township. Another factor was the donation by George Mitchell of land on the hill for a cemetery which was named Prospect Park. Clearing work on the cemetery was beginning in 1875, and some grading on the hill was necessary to make the steep hill passable. The grading was utilized to fill the south portion of the swamp along the road right-of-way. A third factor was the existence of the Clam Lake brickyard, working on a clay hill which jutted into the swamp. There was already a trail of

9. The old cemetery was ill-defined, with graves scattered about in the area presently bounded by Hersey, Lynn, Hobart, and Cedar streets, with the greatest concentration lying in the west center of that area. An attempt was made to locate the graves and move the bodies to the new cemetery in 1889, but it was an impossible task. From time to time, old graves were turned up by the excavation of basements and in lowering the grade of Evart Street.

10. Isolated from the village of Clam Lake by the Cobbs mill and the swamp, Cobbtown gradually grew southward and onto the higher ground, and the trail turned south becoming modern Laurel Street.

sorts to the yard, and clay from the right-of-way could be used to build up the road.

Nevertheless, the first stretch of the road, to the foot of Cemetery Hill, was the most difficult construction and the most expensive. Cedar poles were laid in layers with sawdust, sand, and clay to build up the road most of the way, but two long bridges across the southern parts of the swamp were necessary. From the foot of the hill the road turned west, now Granite Street, then followed the railroad for a distance before turning straight south along the section line for about three-quarters of a mile and thence straight west. It came to be called the Hector Road after Fred Hector, an early settler and township supervisor, who had a farm there.

The northern route around the lake followed what is now Chestnut Street and continued on a straight line through the swamp around the Black River, then swung south to cross the canal at the Big Clam Lake end and meet a trail that followed the south shore of Big Clam Lake.

The road north commenced at the end of Mitchell Street, which extended beyond North Street on the map but in 1876 was only a trail through the pine trees beyond Bremer Street. Proceeding northerly, it followed the railroad across the river to the settlement of McCoy's Siding, then hit the section line at what is now Thirteenth Street and proceeded due north. This was the main route to Lake City, turning east beyond Haring to pass south of Long Lake and Crooked Lake, and then following the present Missaukee County Road around the south side of Sapphire and Muskrat lakes.

6.

Within the city, public works for the first decade were largely concerned with street improvements and filling the swamps. The beautification of the city park was entirely the private project of George Mitchell. In 1873 and again in 1874, his men were busy pulling stumps in the park "swamp" and hauling in fill sand. The work lay dormant for several years but was finally completed in 1877, when the remaining low spots were filled, walks were laid out, and a large number of small maple trees were planted. At what had originally been the highest spot in the park, one tree remained of those originally there when the first settlers came. The park was fenced and arched iron gates were installed at each corner. Within three months, the *News* was complaining that the beautiful park had become a rendezvous for the many gamblers infesting the city!

Mitchell's men were busy elsewhere. Whenever they were free from logging work, he had them busy improving the property which he had for sale around the town. They helped the Cobbs crew build up the road through outlot 7 to the Cobbs mill. Unwittingly, it aggravated the water problem there, preventing the usual drainage flow to the south. In 1875 all of South Mitchell Street from Chapin south was under water for most of the summer, and even the railroad right-of-way was submerged during the spring runoff. A sluice was put under the logging road to correct the problem, and Mitchell's men were busy building up Mitchell Street with sawdust, sand, and clay, and a start was made on filling the swamp south of LaBar & Cornwell's mill and along South Mitchell Street. The project was brought to an end after Mitchell's death in 1878.

The swamp was cut in two at its narrowest point by the construction of South Street, by another sawdust road, and by the Cobbs & Mitchell logging railroad which came from the mill part way down South Street, swinging south to cross Wood Street at what is now Cobbs Street, and swinging thence southeasterly past the "little lakes" behind Cemetery Hill. The north half of the swamp was really a lake, close to four feet deep in places during the high-water period in the spring. It provided excellent fishing until gradual filling and lack of flow caused stagnation. It was the site of an enclosed ice-skating rink in the winter time for almost a decade, and a toboggan was built there in the early eighties by Charles Dunham and Charles R. Smith, giving the riders a swift run across the ice after leaving the chute.

In 1883 the city's physicians began a campaign for the draining and filling of the swamp, citing it as the cause of malaria. The *News* was convinced and editorialized on the subject until the city fathers finally started work in 1885 and 1886. Only a small part of the work was done at city expense, however, as Cobbs and

Mitchell bought the site and donated most of the labor for the work. In 1886 the Ann Arbor railroad came through the northern portion, adding additional fill, and in the nineties Cobbs and Mitchell built their flooring mill on the south part.

The south half of the swamp was drained repeatedly, and Wood Street was built up gradually by repeated additions of sawdust, clay, and sand. The bridges were rebuilt in 1880 and more cedar poles laid in the roadbed. In 1882 the first gravel was added. But still it was periodically under water. From time to time the natural drain toward the southeast was cleaned, but with no lasting success. In the spring of 1893 the road was almost completely submerged and houses in the old Cobbtown were flooded. Tiles were installed that year, draining to the southeast, but they proved inadequate. Flooding again in 1894 led to an additional raising of the grade of Wood Street, by now already several feet above its original grade. The street up Cemetery Hill was cut down considerably that year, and large quantities of fill were graded down into the swamp. In the spring of 1895 the problem seemed even worse. William Mitchell asked the city for permission to do the work himself and permission was granted. New tiles were installed for drains, and the lower spots of the street were raised again. The high spot between Cobb and Mosser streets was cut down to establish a nearly uniform grade from the Ann Arbor crossing, and the clay was used to improve the surface of the refinished street. The old bridges were torn out and an earthfill was made over drainage tiles. Filling of the swamp has continued to this day, but the flooding has ceased, and Wood Street, now South Mitchell and U.S. Highway 131, sits high above its first cedar pole base.

Until the nineties, the area along Wood Street had remained unusable. Several houses had been built at the high ground where the Cobbs and Mitchell railroad crossed and along the high ground leading back to the brickyard east of the street. After John Mosser acquired the yard and subdivided the area, the road became Mosser Street. South of the brickyard, a reasonably high and level area was cleared in 1875 and became the baseball field. The only other structures were located on the west side of Wood street, between the two bridges. One was the city pound, the other the city pesthouse, to which those ill with contagious diseases were banished. It was convenient to the cemetery.

The streets were graded and regraded, dirt removed from the hills being used to even the low spots and fill the swamps. In 1881 the hill on Mitchell Street at the foot of Beech was cut down ten feet and Beech Street was graded down. In 1886 and 1887, in preparation for subdividing block F and the construction of the Cummer office building, immense quantities of dirt were taken from Beech and Spruce streets, block F, and Shelby Street at the top of the hill. G. A. Bergland, the contractor, was moving from 140 to 160 wagon loads of dirt a day, using it to channel the Clam River through his property. From 1883 to 1890, Harris, Cass, Chapin, and Stimson streets were regraded (leaving many homes high above the street level), and the newspapers noted approvingly that the dirt removed was going to fill gullies in South Mitchell Street, Lake Street, and the swamps. In short, much of Cadillac was relocated and rearranged over the years.

After five years of agitation, a program to build a boulevard following the shore around Little Clam Lake was approved. The chief impetus came from William Mitchell and Jonathan Cobbs, and the city would undoubtedly not have approved the project had it not been for their guarantee to underwrite a major part of the expense. The cost of construction was $10,000, of which the city paid $1,800. Cobbs and Mitchell were the principal donors of the remaining $8,200, but that tells only a small part of the story. The firm made the building of the road possible by laying out a railroad over which gravel was carried from the pit east of Cemetery Hill, furnishing the locomotive and cars and part of the labor. Cummer & Diggins finally agreed to do the same on part of the route along the north shore, but the greater portion of the work was done by Cobbs & Mitchell, who ran their road clear around the side of the lake, across a bridge at the west end and part way back on the north side. Starting from the old Graham dumping dock, the bridge was built by John Mosser in 1891. When the boulevard was completed, 1,700 Carolina poplars were planted along the route to replace the pines the early observer had urged preserving.

7.

The new county seat, of course, had grown in all forms of mercantile endeavor. Its saloons had multiplied, and such names as John Hassenfuss, William Kapnic, Frank LaRose, Alex Kennedy, Sailor McCauley, Joe Cicero, Sam Olander, Lavinus Lansing, Leon Robitaille, and Ole Borseth had become familiar. Over the next two decades, they would be joined by many others who came and went, the most prominent being Joe Journeau, Joe Cotey, Magnus Hansen, Adrian and Victor Erikson, Cornelius Burke, Robert Wilson, Tom O'Donall, and Frank Jacobson.

At the same time, religious, educational, and fraternal groups were thriving, and recreational and cultural activities were pursued with incredible vigor. The churches never came near to equalling the saloons in number, but their strength didn't lie in numbers. The new county seat had eight different congregations, five of which had their own church buildings, with a sixth almost completed. The Methodists and Presbyterians had put up their own buildings in 1873 after almost two years of meeting in saloons, the Empire Hall, and even on a barge in the lake (weather permitting). In 1875 the Free Methodists built on Pine Street, and the following year the "Sweed-Lutheran" Church was built.

A small Catholic congregation had been served irregularly by visiting priests, meeting in a private home in Frenchtown from 1875 on. In 1880 a building was put up and enclosed along the Whaley trail in the southeast corner of the village, and it was completed in 1882 except for the spire, which was added in 1889. The Swedish Mission fellowship had started in 1874, and it completed its building on Pine Street in 1882. A Baptist fellowship was meeting in various places and owned the land at the corner of Stimson and Shelby, while a Congregational group had just been organized and was holding services in the Forester's Opera House. They built their sanctuary the following year. The Baptists bought the Methodists' building in 1888 and moved it to their lot, the Methodists putting up a new brick church to replace it.

After getting a school district organized with its first sessions in the Empire Hall of Mosser and White, a slab building was constructed in 1872 on Schoolhouse Square, block 24 of Mitchell's plat, which he donated for that purpose. The block was another high prominence which has been cut down over the years until it bears little resemblance to its original condition. Children at the school in the seventies looked down on the roofs of the homes and stores between the school and Mitchell Street. Each successive construction resulted in a further lowering of the elevation, the process continuing with the construction of the Kirtland Terrace Apartments in 1966-67.

The first long school building was extended in 1873, then demolished and replaced by a pleasant two-story building which was added to in 1881 and again in 1883. With the commencement of a one-room grade school in Harristown in 1882, the main building came to be known as "Central School," by which name it was known until after the turn of the century, when its use was confined solely to the upper grades and it became the high school. On March 13, 1884, the Central School was destroyed by arson. It was rebuilt in similar style and again destroyed by fire in January of 1890. The new central school was of solid brick construction, to which north and south wing additions were added in 1911 to complete the school which served as a high school and junior high school until 1966, when it was razed after construction of a new junior high school.

In 1885 a Cobbtown, or Fourth Ward, school was built on Granite Street, followed by new Harristown (First Ward), Frenchtown (Second Ward), and Central (Third Ward) grade schools. All were built as two-room schools, and later increased to four. The Second and Third ward buildings were further enlarged in later years by the addition of new first floors. In each case, the existing building was jacked up and the new first floor built beneath!

8.

The hardships of life and man's natural instrincts for social life led to the formation of countless associations, mutual benefit groups, and fraternal orders. The Masonic and Oddfellow orders had been in existence in the community almost from its first days.

A Scandinavian Association, the German Workingman's Aid Society, the Knights of Labor. a cigar maker's union, a half dozen benefit groups, the Ancient Order of Hibernians, the Knights of Pythias, Royal Arcanum, the Redmen, Maccabees, Foresters, Woodsmen of the World, and others served to provide a means of group social life and collective security against the risk of early death. Most had some form of, or were organized primarily for, life insurance or burial benefits. Other groups, like the fire companies, blossomed into athletic and social organizations as well as meeting a civic need. The Cadillac Greys, composed entirely of cornet players (and one bass horn), provided volunteer fire protection, traveled throughout the state in hose-cart competitions, and claimed the north Michigan tug-of-war championship. As a cornet band, athletes, fire-fighters or lively dancers, the merchants, clerks, and bookkeepers who were the Greys were enjoying life with esprit de corps. They had their counterparts in the Wolverine Hose Company, the Vigilant Hose Company, and the Mechanics Hook and Ladder Team.

So it was with other diversions. There were debating societies, bands, choral groups, and theater clubs. While the town was competing in semi-professional and professional baseball by 1875, local competition on an amateur or semi-professional basis flourished, with Cobbtown, Harristown, Frenchtown, particular mills, and even occupations providing their own teams. Boating groups were organized periodically, and in the nineties a tennis club and several athletic and gymnastic clubs were formed.

The centers of social life, however, aside from the churches and saloons, were the lodges, of which the most important were the Oddfellows, Masons, Knights of Pythias, and Foresters. They carried on a constant program of education and fraternal teaching. All had benefit programs. They traveled extensively to found lodges in new communities and to share their fraternal and social activities with the lodges of other towns. They were a part of the member's life, the celebrant of his lifetime achievements, an escort to his burial, and a comfort to his survivors.

In 1881 the Oddfellows built their own building on South Mitchell Street, south of the Mosser and White building. In 1884 they put up a roller skating rink on Cass Street, capitalizing on the recreational and social rage of the moment,[11] but it did not prove a financial success in the long run. In 1881 the Foresters built an opera house on the lake shore just south of Harris Street. It was a large, frame, three-story building, topped by an observatory tower which gave a commanding view of the city. It served as the music hall, theater, public auditorium, political and town-meeting center, and social hall, as well as the meeting place for the Congregational and Baptist fellowships who then had no buildings. The opera house burned in 1885, and was never rebuilt. The Cummers would soon replace the loss. In the meantime, there were still the old Empire Hall, Kieldsen's Hall, the Oddfellow Hall, the third floor of the Bank Building, and the Masonic rooms on the third floor of the new LaBar-Cornwell Building for meeting places.

11. A similar venture at Manton by Dr. John Bostick and some friends also was instantly popular but eventually unprofitable.

Chapter Twenty-Three

CUMMER TOWN

On May 23, 1878, the *News* carried the account of a foot trip by its editor, J. A. Whitmore, and A. J. Teed, counting the ties along the G. R. & I. to the town of Haring.

> On the road we noticed that the clearing of Charles Ford and the Hortons show well from the track and give promise to refresh the weary eye of the traveler who has seen nothing but miles of pine, birch and maple forest with the sight of cultivated fields.
>
> After hoofing it for about an hour, we arrived at our destination. E. Shay is one of the most enterprising mill men in this section and his mill is in excellent shape and well equipped. It has a capacity of from 25,000 to 30,000 feet per day and is especially adapted to cutting bill stuff and is engaged a good part of the time in getting out special orders for heavy lumber dealers in this city. Among the many improvements we noted is a large elevated water tank from which water can be thrown on any part of the mill. This has the advantage of supplying water when the mill is not in operation.
>
> Mr. Shay was the first in this part of the state to employ a locomotive and cars for the purpose of lumbering. He has constructed many miles of road at a cost less than the cost of ordinary logging road. The gauge is two feet and the track is constructed with solid stringers on ties surmounted with a maple strip. On his road he runs a locomotive constructed by William Crippen & Son, machinist from this city. It works well and draws on two cars from 4,000 to 5,000 feet a load, making it much cheaper than team work. We enjoyed the trip over a mile or more of the road running north from the mill. The course was rough and winding, but grades and curves seemed no obstacles.

> Mssrs. Northan, Copley and Ruggles are now cutting timber on sec. 9 in Harring, which is being put in over this road and will be sawed at the mill.

The account of a rare cultivated field breaking miles of virgin forest was to remain typical of Wexford County for another decade, but Ephraim Shay of Haring was to do his share and more in turning that scene into one of endless stumps and burned-over slashings. Shay, Haring Township treasurer and supervisor, unsuccessful Democratic candidate for county clerk in 1874 and 1876, successful candidate for county treasurer in 1878, postmaster of Haring, made history by using a locomotive to move logs. The Whitmore account crediting him with operation of the first logging locomotive "in this part of the state," is correct locally but neglects the fact that he was very nearly the first man to use a logging locomotive anywhere. He was preceded only by Nathaniel Gerrish and his son Winfield Scott Gerrish in Clare and Osceola counties.

More important, however, Shay was to devise his own geared locomotive, patent its principle, and revolutionize logging. That is a story in itself. Suffice it to say that resourceful men were looking for ways to speed the cutting and transport of pine to the rivers or directly to the mills. When William Kelley built a pole railroad up Pine Street in 1873, he was simply utilizing the wheel and the railroad principle to help his teams move more logs more quickly.[1] And so loggers started building tram or pole roads, consisting of wood tracks on which horse drawn wagons carried the logs. Gradually they were improved and a better means of locomotion was sought.

Shay and D. C. McKinnon had located along the G. R. & I. tracks in 1872. The village that grew up around their mills, known briefly as Linden and then as Haring, became Shay's personal enclave when McKinnon failed. As logger, mill-owner, owner of the general store and postmaster, Shay was in little better condition than McKinnon. With much help from friends, parents and in-laws, he barely stayed ahead of his creditors. As he logged in an

1. Kelley's road was gradually extended until it reached a length of almost three miles in 1878, but it was discontinued after his death in January of 1879.

ever-widening circle, his costs for moving timber to the saw were increasing. Shay reflected on Kelley's pole road as a solution which would bring logs from many different locations to the mill inexpensively. He entered into a partnership with George Graham who owned an eighty acre tract of pine east of Haring, then hired Kelley on shares to supervise the logging. Included in the agreement was an undertaking by Kelley to put a wooden-rail tramroad into the tract.

The tramroad was so successful that Shay planned other roads. Without knowing of Gerrish's use of a locomotive, he came to his own conclusion that this was the next logical step and designed his own machine. It was built for him by machinist William Crippen and moved such loads in 1877 that Shay and Kelley spent most of the next summer building two miles of road northerly towards Long Lake which Shay called the Haring & Lake City Railroad.

Over the next two years. Shay built more track and more engines. He refined and patented his principle of a gear-driven locomotive. The design permitted manufacture of locomotives with sharp turning radius, capable of negotiating steep grades. It revolutionized the industry and logging railroads snaked out across northern Michigan.[2]

Others were building pole roads also. Shay's partner, George Graham, logged in Clam Lake and Cherry Grove townships with a pole road terminating at a dumping dock on the west end of Little Clam Lake. He abandoned horses for a shay-designed, Crippen-built locomotive on the wooden rails in 1878.[3]

In Missaukee County, several different small pole roads were

2. Shay assigned his patent to the Lima Locomotive Company of Lima, Ohio, in which firm he acquired an interest in return. Logging became a sideline for him and he left the area as he turned to the promotion of his invention. Refinements of design were added by James Henderson of the Michigan Iron Works, a Shay-licensee. Shay's machinist, William Crippen, also patented a design and manufactured locomotives. Between 1878 and 1882 the Michigan Iron Works, Crippen Machine and Shay works earned Cadillac and Haring worldwide attention and gave the area's loggers an advantage over their competitors.

3. Graham's dumping dock was eventually extended by John Mosser all the way across the west neck of the lake and became "long bridge" where M-115 causeway is now located.

eventually converted to locomotives. By 1878 Watson Brothers had a Crippen built machine operating on their wooden rails. But, the efficiency of the logging railroad having been demonstrated, it was the major mill owners who moved to utilize it on a large scale, enabling themselves to buy tracts of pine far removed from the mills, and justifying a greater investment in larger more modern mills, centrally located. Shay's locomotive guaranteed the continued prosperity of Cadillac's mills, which would continue to function long after the pine in the immediate vicinity was exhausted.

There were mills, of course, on all the lakes in the county, Meauwataka, Stone Ledge, Long Lake, Round Lake, at Bond's Mill, Woodward Lake, and on the artificial Billings Lake, created by damming the Cedar Creek at Manton. Other mills sprang up along the G. R. & I. at Haire and Putman's Siding, joining those at Hobart, McCoy's Siding, Haring, Hiatt's Siding, Bond's Mill, and Gilbert. Still more were to come into existence along the logging railroads laid out by Cobbs & Mitchell, Cummer Lumber Company, Mitchell Brothers, and others. Who remembers now where Six Corners was, or Simpsonville, or Bensher, or Collin's Siding? Man came in a flurry of sparks and sawdust and was soon gone, leaving old logging grades here, an overgrown concrete foundation there, and scatterings of charred wood everywhere as the memorials of his brief presence.

2.

Lumber and wood products were Cadillac's life, of course. A host of loggers and lumber dealers moved in and around the area. O. S. Whitmore & Co., Louis Sands, R. G. Peters, the McKinnon Brothers, A. F. Anderson, C. F. Ruggles, Tom Graham, Bill Kelley, Tom Kelly, Byron Ballou, E. J. Copley, the Bonds, Thayers, Kysors and Watsons, Chittenden & Herrick, and others. The logging railroad, however, enabled the mill owners to move out and operate their own logging camps, and the largest owners came to dominate all aspects of the industry. Cobbs & Mitchell, Mitchell Brothers, Mitchell Brothers-Murphy, and the Cummer family of enterprises: J. Cummer & Son, Cummer Lumber Company, Cummer & Cummer, Murphy & Diggins, Cummer, Diggins & Co., etc.

After the death of George Mitchell, Jacob Cummer became the dominant figure of the logging industry and of Cadillac. Canadian born, of Scottish ancestry, Jacob Cummer had been twice prosperous and twice insolvent following financial panics. In the late sixties he began speculating in pine lands. A profit of $100,000 in one transaction convinced him he was on the right track. In 1870 he moved to Cedar Springs, and in 1872 to Morley, operating a sawmill and logging business in partnership with his son Wellington. In 1873 he bought property in Clam Lake from George Mitchell and began to deal in pine lands and lumber in the area, finally moving to the village in 1876. In the period from 1868 to 1876, he had accumulated a fortune of half a million dollars. He doubled it by 1880.

Cummer's first operations were solely in land and timber, but as it appeared that the pine boom would continue, he moved into the mill operation. His frugal Scotish nature, the more sensitive from past losses, appreciated a dollar's profit as keenly as the $100,000 coup. In 1879 he bought Bond & Green's mill. In 1882 he bought out Levi Harris, giving him both of the mills on the northeast shore. His son Wellington, in partnership with his father-in-law, Nathaniel Gerrish, started a planing mill near sawmill No. 1. Two years later they bought out the nearby William Saunders & Son planing mill and then acquired Haynes planing mill No. 1 after the death of James Haynes in 1886. Almost everything west of Lake Street was now Cummer property.

Levi Harris had gradually retired from active operation of his mill, leaving management to a superintendent, and then leasing the whole mill outright for his last few years of ownership. He had commenced laying out a logging railroad north from Cadillac, and the Cummers had started one in a northeasterly direction as soon as they had acquired the Harris mill in 1882. Wellington Cummer, his brother Elmer, and their brother-in-law Wood Gerrish, had surveyed a route to Lake City in 1878. In 1883 the plan was renewed, and, as the logging road was gradually extended, more ambitious plans were entertained. In 1884 Cummer bought out O. S. Whitmore's mill and standing pine at Round Lake, and the railroad was extended there. In 1885 the Cadillac & Northeastern Railroad Company was organized with the Cummers and Gerrish as its owners and officers.

The C. & N. E. R. R. originated in Harristown, running on a straight line northeasterly across Haring Road south of the section line where the G. R. & I. roundhouse was built later,[4] angling across what is now the fairgrounds, and then following the north shore of the Clam River to the county line. They built a mill and settlement called Gerrish on Crooked Lake; from there the track ran to the northwest shore of Muskrat Lake, now Lake Missaukee. Jacob Cummer developed the area around the lakeshore terminus and called it Komoko Park, built a ball diamond, bath houses, a bandstand, and ran regular excursions there. Captain Towle of Cadillac put one of his steamers in service on the lake, and connections were made from the C. & N. E. dock to Lake City by boat. During the following winter, Gerrish ran a stage line to Lake City, but in the spring the C. & N. E. extended its track another twenty miles northeasterly, running a spur around the northeastern end of Muskrat Lake into Lake City. Plans were made to extend the road to Roscommon, but they never materialized.

The Harristown Depot in Cadillac proved unpopular, and a branch of the road which ran to the Cummer dock at the old Green mill was extended to Lake Street, ending at the northwest corner of Pine and Lake, where a depot was constructed in the fall of 1885. The business end of the road was largely the responsibility of Wood Gerrish, with the mechanical and logging part of its affairs handled by Elmer Cummer, who personally served as the locomotive engineer.[5] Although primarily designed to augment the Cummer logging interests, the C. & N. E. served as a profitable general carrier until 1892, when passenger service was discontinued in the face of competition from the G. R. & I. Missaukee branch. It remained in use as a Cummer industrial road until 1911, however.

4. And where the spur line now leads into Roundhouse Lumber Company. The original G. R. & I. roundhouse and turntable was south of River Street on the west side of North Mitchell Street.

5. He was killed in 1888 when he was caught in the gears of the Shay locomotive which bore his name, the E. C. Cummer.

The Cummers dominated the city government. In 1886 Judge Green made a proposal for a city lighting plant. The city turned it down, then, after the death of Mayor James Haynes, gave a franchise to Cummer Electric Lighting Company on terms less favorable to the city. When Judge Green's franchise for the water-works came up for renewal, the city decided to exercise its right to have the franchise transferred to another holder at a price to be fixed by arbitration. The new franchise was granted to the Cadillac Water Company, owned by the Cummers. Judge Green received $15,500 for the business which was giving him a profit of $6,000 on water rent receipts of $9,000 per year.

The Cummer influence came to dominate industrial Cadillac as well. Wages, hours, and conditions for the Cummer employees were the standard for other employers. Indeed, the Cummer image was cast over most community affairs. One paper was bought up and discontinued to end its irreverent chattering. Two others were bought and merged, and the selling editor of the *News,* Sen. J. Wight Giddings, found himself invited to devote his time and efforts to his speechmaking and legislative affairs. The combined *News & Express* was sold to Perry F. Powers, who was expected to sell not merely newspapers but Cadillac and Cummer as well. There were stories about how the Cummer employees had to vote, and that bad votes caused unemployment and black-listing. Employment became a strictly business matter, and the easy going days of the old mill operators was over. The company store, started by Levi Harris as a matter of convenience to his employees, became a dollar and cents Cummer enterprise which was expected to make the best profit possible. To the employees, living in the milltown west of the Cummer mills, there was resentment. They grudgingly joked that:

> Our fingers and hands can go through his saws,
> And our timechecks will go through his store;
> He'll take our last cent,
> For our daily rent,
> But someday we'll CUMM'ER no more!

They might grudgingly admit that Cummer owned them, but they'd be damned if they'd call their milltown Cummertown.

Harristown it remained, after their old beloved boss. It hardly mattered, however, since for all practical purposes the whole city was Cummer Town.

To a visiting editor in 1889, Cadillac

> . . . means CUMMER since they occupy the ground floor and all the other floors of Cadillac and the region about. It really consists of lumber yards, two sawmills, miles and miles of tramway, logging railroads, a railroad to Lake City, and 5,000 people devoted to serving the Cummer interest.

There were a variety of related firms: the Cadillac & N. E. Railroad; Cummer Lumber Company; Cummer & Cummer; J. Cummer & Sons; Cummer & Gerrish Planing Mills; the Cummer Ladder Company; Murphy & Diggins; Blodgett, Cummer & Diggins, and, finally, Cummer & Diggins. Other firms without the Cummer name had Cummer capital and Cummer directors. Cummer interests spread to Louisiana, Virginia, and Florida. Under Cummer initiative, every by-product was utilized in the lumber industry. Edgings and sawdust fired the boilers and the water and light plants; hardwood scraps were turned to charcoal and chemical by-products utilized. Later the charcoal would be moved a short way on the C. & N. E. to the furnaces of a pig-iron foundry. There was a ladder factory, a handle factory, potash works, and chemical works. As the century ended, the Cummer & Diggins Chemical Works being constructed in Harristown was the largest plant of its kind in the world. And, as if in imitation of Delos Blodgett, there was the 400-acre showpiece Cummer farm running from Holbrook Street on the west to Crosby Road on the east, with Thirteenth Street and Division Street as its north and south boundaries.

And there were Cummers. Besides Jacob and his sons, Wellington and Elmer, there was Dr. Robert J. Cummer, who practiced medicine and ran the drugstore. Franklin Cummer was an industrial and mechanical engineer, an inventor whose expertise was in demand around the world. J. Walter Cummer operated a wholesale and retail hardware business and for a time was the operator of the Michigan Iron Works. Herbert Cummer was the manager of the Cummer Ladder Works, and salesman of the specialty wood products manufactured in Cummer plants. William Cummer went where he was told. George Cummer, the political black sheep, was elected county clerk twice on the Democratic ticket. Through marriage, the Cummer interests were tied in with those of Nathaniel Gerrish and his sons, Winfield Scott Gerrish and Wood Gerrish. Wellington Cummer married a Gerrish daughter. There were ties to Delos Blodgett and his nephews and banking and business associates, Fred and Delos Diggins, both of whom became a part of the Cummer enterprises, Fred marrying Carrie Cummer and Delos marrying Esther Gerrish, another of Nathaniel's daughters. Family counted.

3.

There were others, of course, sharing the bounty of the forests. Just south of the Mitchell and G. R. & I. ice houses, Jared Hixson had a small sawmill on the lake front between the Haynes mill and Chapin Street. Along the southeast shore of the lake, in the area called Sunnyside, a number of sawmills and shingle mills operated over the years. Milton Bond had a mill there in the late seventies at about the point where George Street and Petrie Road now intersect. After Bond burned out, Byron Ballou had a shingle mill there. He too burned out in 1887, and being ready for retirement, didn't rebuild. The site was acquired by Fred Diggins, who built, burned out two years later, took in Joseph Murphy as a partner, and rebuilt as Murphy-Diggins Company. They burned out again in 1899, and again rebuilt, bigger and better. Just to the west, Peter Haifley had a shingle mill briefly in the early eighties until he too burned out.

Chittenden & Herrick operated a sawmill and had a crate factory a little closer to town. Westover & Company operated a shingle mill besides their brewery for at least three years, but the property was acquired by Cobbs & Mitchell when Westover went broke. Ultimately they built their No. 2 mill there. The G. R. & I. had a spur at Murphy-Diggins, and Cobbs and Mitchell ran a line of its logging railroad the length of Sunnyside so that the area from its No. 1 mill, beyond the No. 2 mill to Murphy-Diggins, was a solid length of track, tramways, and lumber storage yards.

Cobbs & Mitchell and Mitchell Brothers together were as impressive as the Cummer interests. With Mitchell Brothers centered in Jennings, however, they were less significant in nineteenth century Cadillac's industrial picture than the Cummer empire. Cobbs & Mitchell operated its two sawmills, had miles of logging railroad, and prospered in pine and later in hardwood. They eventually filled the swamp between Cobbtown and Cadillac and built one of the two largest hardwood flooring mills in the world on the site. The other was that of Mitchell Brothers at Jennings. William Mitchell, who was Jonathan Cobbs' partner and George Mitchell's nephew, had been joined by his brother Austin in several logging ventures. A venture in Missaukee County with Charles E. Haynes, one of James Haynes' sons, had become Mitchell Brothers after Haynes sold out. Jennings is a story in itself, as are the Mitchell brothers themselves. The Mitchell Brothers operations, however, are not part of the Cadillac story, being primarily at Jennings and elsewhere outside the county, and eventually outside Michigan.

Then there were the lumber-related industries. In many of them, the Cummer group or the Mitchells were interested. There was the Cadillac Veneer Box Company, organized by John McLaughlin but financed and controlled by a board headed by Wellington W. Cummer and Jacob Cummer. The Climax Blind Company manufactured a patented blind developed by Elliot Metcalf, but Metcalf was a minority stockholder. Control rested with the source of money and materials, as reflected in the list of its majority stockholders who were its officers and directors: Jacob Cummer, W. W. Cummer, R. J. Cummer, William Cummer, Herbert H. Cummer, George A. Cummer, and Delos F. Diggins.

Other Cadillac industries included the Cadillac Sash, Door & Blind Company, located on Cass Street west of the G. R. & I. tracks. In 1884 the Cadillac Veneer and Panel Company was organized with its plant on the north side of an artificial millpond created by damming the Clam River. There was the Cadillac Stave & Heading Company, the McRath Potash Company, and the Oviatt Basket Works. In the twentieth century, inter-company co-operation would result in the Mitchell and Cummer groups joining to create the Mitchell-Diggins Iron Company. And, of course, lumber-related in their own special way were the Crippen

Foundry & Machine Works on Bremer Street and the Michigan Iron Works on Harris Street, both building logging locomotives and serving as machinists and tool specialists for the lumber industry.

4.

At the northeast corner of Harris and Lake Streets, Levi Harris had started a small machine shop after the Davis saloon had been removed. In 1878 a disastrous fire had swept through the area at the foot of Mason Street and had taken the Mason House and the Harris building. James Henderson and Henry Wallin, Jr., acquired the land and built the Michigan Iron Works in 1880. Wallin had been assistant superintendent of the G. R. & I. and a frequent visitor to Clam Lake, staying at the Mason House in its early days. He started the Michigan Iron Works at Grand Rapids, and the Cadillac plant was originally intended as a branch of the business primarily to manufacture logging locomotives under Henderson's management. In 1882 J. Walter Cummer acquired Wallin's interest, continuing its operation for three years and turning its locomotive production primarily to the ends of the Cummer Lumber Co.

In 1880 a Canadian-born machinist named Robert Leslie came to Cadillac to manage the shop for its Grand Rapids owners, and he continued to do so under Cummer.[6] In 1885 a partnership comprised of William McAdie, John DeYoung, and Leslie bought the business, and for fourteen years it was the leading machine shop of northern Michigan, doing business under the firm name of McAdie & Co. and McAdie Iron Works. On Leslie's death from typhoid fever in 1899, the partners concluded that they would be unable to continue without him, and the business was eventually sold. The purchasers of the business, at the turn of the century,

6. Leslie's brother, John, also settled in Cadillac. For a time, he was the working partner with his brother in a dry goods and grocery store in the Turner building on Mitchell Street, but he ultimately returned to Canada when the business failed. Leslie's son, also Robert, was a well-known business figure in twentieth century Cadillac and held several public offices in the city.

were an interesting combination of nineteenth and twentieth century industry. The business was continued at first as D. S. Kysor Machine Company, after its principle partner, Daniel S. Kysor, who had first logged in the area and had been a partner in the Bond sawmill at Bond's Mill. When Col. Thomas Thorp left the area, Kysor had bought the Thorp farm in Selma Township, then logged in the south before returning to Cadillac. His partners were his nephew, Walter Kysor, and Frank Farrar, both to play an important role in twentieth century industrial Cadillac with the Cadillac Machine Company, Acme Truck Company, and Kysor Heater Company, predecessor of the present Kysor Industrial Corporation.

5.

In 1885 the Cummers bought Courthouse Hill, block F, from the Mitchell heirs. There was no intention of using it for a court-house site. Instead, the block was subdivided. After the Forester's Opera House burned in September of that year, the Cummers began to think about a building that would supplant the loss and meet their own needs as well. During the summer of 1886 Courthouse Hill was cut down immeasurably, the dirt being used to fill North Mitchell Street between Crippen Street and the river bridge and to improve the Clam River flats. That winter plans were prepared for a building which would replace the narrow two-story brick Mason Street office building from which the Cummers operated. More than that, it would have a separate wing to replace the burned out opera house and make Cummer Hall the community center.

The following spring, contractors from various parts of the state reviewed the plans. When all had examined them and been examined in turn, it was Cadillac's own John G. Mosser to whom the contract was awarded. Mosser, the G. R. & I. bridge builder who had been on the scene when the settlement was being cleared in 1871, had gradually been gaining in reputation as a builder in northern Michigan. A good share of Cadillac's industrial and commercial construction had been his work. The new three-story LaBar & Cornwell building had been built by him in 1884, and it was a handsome, sturdy structure, put up at less than the original estimates. The central school of 1876, its improvements of 1881 and 1883, and the new school of 1884 had been put up by him. When A. K. Moyer's Clam Lake brickyard had failed, it was Mosser who eventually bought it and made it a going proposition. Indeed, from 1883 until 1893, there was virtually no school, courthouse, or other public building of consequence in north central Michigan for which he was not the general contractor. Mosser's life, his faults, and his mysterious disappearance make a fascinating story, but equally fascinating is the evidence of his craftsmanship that surrounds us throughout the area to this day.

The new Cummer building was a two-story office building on the Mitchell Street wing, done in a blend of Queen Anne and British Gothic architecture, faced with cream colored brick manufactured in the Mosser brickyard. That wing, extended further along Mitchell Street in later years, is now the Cadillac *Evening News* building. The eastern wing, connected by a hall containing office space and a ladies parlor, was a 32-by-75-foot opera hall, which was the cultural center of the community for more than a dozen years.[7]

6.

The Cummer ambitions for the Cadillac & Northeastern Railroad in 1885 and 1886 represented only a part of the railroad planning that was going on in Cadillac. The Toledo & Ann Arbor Railroad of the Ashley family was looking northward and tacking together a system, piece by piece, that ultimately was to reach Lake Michigan. The days of the governmental land grant subsidies for railroads had ended, and various promotional schemes were devised to raise the capital necessary for right-of-way acquisition and construction. Guarantees from shippers were sought, at the same time that extravagant promises of rate concessions and rebates were secretly being made to secure

7. In later years, it became the Knights of Pythias Hall. Its ruins were torn down after the building was almost totally burned out in 1943 while being leased by the American Legion.

such commitments. Communities were set against each other in bidding for the railroad; their fears that they might be bypassed and a neighboring community favored were skillfully played upon by the promoters to obtain pledges of financial support. In some instances, construction was parceled out to local farmers, and sections of the track were built by small corporations which were merged into the parent company, leaving creditors and laborers unpaid.

The Ann Arbor thus came to northern Michigan, in an operation marked by warfare, unscrupulous financing, fraud, and a technical operation so inefficient and ramshackle that it would have been hilarious had it not been so tragic. But come it did, and the Cummers played a role in its coming.

In 1885 the Cummers were in contact with the Ashleys, and negotiations were pursued off and on for some time. In January of 1886 the Toledo & Cadillac Railroad Company was organized, one of several which would participate in the piecemeal construction of sections of the road and then go out of business. Its officers included not only the Ashleys but several Cadillac men, most notably Jacob Cummer and Fred Diggins. Cummer enterprises were major material suppliers, paid in cash while track contractors and laborers received credit chits redeemable when the city of Cadillac sold $35,000 in bonds which it had pledged to induce the railroad to come this route. The Cummer dredge and pile driver were "donated," said the *News,* to build up and extend the lakeshore from the foot of Harris Street around the corner of the lake where the track would be laid, but when other creditors of the T. & C. R. R. were crying for their money, the *Democrat* noted that Cummer Lumber Company had been well paid for its donation.

But whatever the inside story of its coming (and the *News* said no one would probably ever know the true story), the T. & A. A. did come. It suffered, it failed, and it was reorganized repeatedly, but it came. With it came some competition in the transportation industry, a new access to southeastern Michigan and Ohio, and the opening up and settling of more parts of northwestern Upper Michigan. The boom of the early eighties had boosted the county population from 6,815 to 10,518 from 1880 to 1884. There was little change over the next five years, but the commencement of regular railroad operations to the southeast made a difference, generating optimism about a further extension of the road from Cadillac to Frankfort. Work was begun almost immediately and from 1889 until 1894 almost 4,000 more people came into the county.

Chapter Twenty-Four

NEW RAILROADS, NEW TOWNS

As might well be expected, the coming of the Toledo & Ann Arbor Railroad not only brought additional growth to the existing cities and villages which it touched but contributed to the creation of new communities along its route. In Osceola County, the village of Marion already existed as a small settlement where two state roads and the middle branch of the Muskegon River intersected. The first settlement had begun in 1880, but aside from a sawmill, a general store in which the post office was located, and a blacksmith shop, it had little development until the coming of the railroad.

As soon as the railroad came, there was a Marion saloon. The *News* reported that there were opening night sales of almost $300, saying, "The next thing needed by the township will be a jail." Within a year there were three more saloons, a gristmill, a bank, several more general stores, a shoe store, a hotel, a union school, and Catholic and Methodist churches. Within the next two years, an electric light and power plant was constructed on the river, along with a small opera house. In 1889, Marion was formally incorporated as a village, the act of incorporation being necessary, said the sponsors, in order to permit adequate supervision of the thriving saloons.[1]

1. Marion's expectations of a promising future were further encouraged by the 1889 incorporation of the Manistee and Grand Rapids Railroad by Manistee investors. The ultimate destination of the railroad was intended to be Grand Rapids, but that destination was to be reached by a most circuitous route, doubtless in the expectation of capitalizing on contributions from the communities to be touched by the road. The railroad was completed between Manistee and Marion by 1893, with a branch line reaching Hartwick and Dighton. It was singularly unprofitable once the timber along the route had been logged, and it went out of business following World War I.

Four miles northwest of Marion, Park Lake Corner sprang up a mile south of the Missaukee County line, with several stores, a hotel, a blacksmith, and a saloon, but it had no further growth, except for the construction of charcoal kilns in 1889.

In Missaukee County, the T. & A. A. touched on the settlement of McBain, deriving its name from its early settlers, the McBains, who first subdivided it when the T. & A. A. came in 1887. Shortly after the arrival of the railroad, the federal government established a post office and touched off something of a furor by naming the place Owens on postal records. Local pride prevailed. A few years later the Cadillac *Democrat* noted the result of the village election and said that since John McBain was president, William McBain, clerk, and Gillis McBain, assessor, "it is little wonder that the name Owens didn't stick for the place."

The community had George Hughston's general store, Charles Sanford's sawmill and the McBains. Within a year it had two more sawmills (George Baker and Symes Brothers), a blacksmith, a dry goods and clothing store, and a hardware store. Over the next few years it attracted other industry—the Dewey Stave Company, Jessop's Clothes' Pin and Handle Factory, charcoal kilns, a shingle factory, and later the Cromwell Lumber Company, which manufactured wooden bicycle rims and chair frames. Around the end of the century it acquired a flour mill and a pickle factory.

The community was incorporated as a village in 1893. By the end of the century McBain had a population of over 500 people, with two dozen stores; a good hotel, the McKinnon House; a weekly newspaper, the *Chronicle,* and three churches. In 1907 it was incorporated as a city.

A few miles to the west, a settlement of Hollanders had grown up, taking its name from the first settler of the area, Harm Lucas. The cluster of homes and stores, plus two sawmills, was soon known as the village of Lucas and so known on railroad and post office records, although there never was any formal village incorporation.

In 1897 the Michigan *Tradesman* printed an article about the settlement, saying that there were between 150 and 250 Hollander families immediately around the settlement, mostly by the names of Lucas, Kole, Slaar, Pel, Eppink, Scholten, DeJongh, Hendricks, Elenbaas, VandenBosch, and Loeks. About the only non-Hollanders, said the account, were William Taylor and his sons and the Simmons family.

Lucas Station was to be the shipping point of some of the finest horses bred in Michigan. Lumberman Delos A. Blodgett, who owned showfarms in several parts of Michigan, had a 600-acre farm north of Lucas. It boasted a huge residence, several large barns, storage buildings, a blacksmith shop, a smokehouse, and stock pens. The farm was noted for its pure-bred work horses, particularly Clydesdales and Percherons. One Blodgett horse brought the unheard-of sum of $2,000 at the Chicago stock show in 1890. The Blodgett farm furnished employment for dozens of families and was a central part of the Lucas economy for over twenty-five years.

A short distance west of Lucas, Conklin's Siding existed mainly to serve charcoal kilns, and a store there soon went out of business.

Proceeding west from Cadillac on the Toledo, Ann Arbor & Lake Michigan branch of the railroad, there were many stops in Wexford County, at Selma, Bunyea, Millersville, Boon, Root's Mill, Harriette, Yuma, Mesick, and Bagnall. Most of these places were simply sidings put down to serve sawmills or logging camps. None of them had any existence before the coming of the railroad. Some survived and some did not, but settlers around each undoubtedly considered their own to be a prospective metropolis.

The village of Haskins, later renamed Boon, was platted in 1889. The location of two sawmills and two stores added impetus to the growth of the village. Bowen's mill and Haskins' mill were joined by a handle factory of Gardner & Haskins, and charcoal kilns were put up by Herkimer & Matevia Company. An additional subdivision was made in 1893. The village was not far from Deer Park, the showplace farm and game preserve of Cadillac attorney Donald E. McIntyre, and in the mid-nineties there was talk about moving the county seat there. Agriculture in the area seemed to thrive, and Boon became a buying and shipping center for farm produce, particularly potatoes. Another sawmill, a wooden bowl factory, two churches, and more stores were built. Supervisor Will McNitt made his residence there and headed a committee planning Boon's legal incorporation as a village.

The panic of 1893, however, put a virtual stop to the mill operations of Boon for almost four years and ended its ambitions. There was a lawyer in Boon for a few months in 1893 and also a Dr. Cardinal, who left the area in 1898, succeeded by Dr. Edward Brewster. At its peak, the Boon population probably never exceeded 150 to 175 people.

2.

The village of Harriette, now known as Harietta, had its start with the coming of the railroad in 1889. It was platted, and a major portion of the property in the area was owned, by the Ashley family, builders of the railroad. It took its name from Harry Ashley and his fiancée, Harriet Burt, and the streets bore the names of its founders and the railroad surveyors and engineers, Carland, Davis, Wells, Gasman, and Ashley. The Ashleys promoted the village heavily and succeeded in obtaining the F. D. Gaston Company Manufacturing Works, which had originally intended to locate in the city of Cadillac. Gaston, a Pennsylvania wood manufacturer, built a sawmill and large plant for the manufacture of hardwood furniture parts, bowls, and hardwood novelties. A partnership was formed for other enterprises with W. W. Campbell, and the partners built another sawmill and acquired additional land and subdivided it as an addition to the village in 1890.

In 1891 the Ogdens platted a further addition, and the city seemed to be growing by leaps and bounds. The Harriette Stove Company was founded by Ben Craig. Gaston and S. P. Millard commenced the Harriette Brick Company, which flourished for several years, shipping huge quantities of brick down the T. & A. A. to Owosso, Mt. Pleasant, Alma, Ann Arbor, and Toledo. One of the early industries was the Jenny charcoal kilns, which also built a small chemical plant for the production of wood alcohol. As it became apparent, however, that an expansion of the plant was necessary, the company made a decision to build closer to the center of the hardwood stand farther north, and moved to Yuma, an unexpected blow to the industrial hopes of the village.

Shortly after the original platting of the village, the post office at Springdale, a little over a mile north, was moved there, and for about a year, there was continual controversy between the Ashleys and the United States government as the postal department continued to refer to the place as Springdale. In 1891 a tentative understanding was reached for a name change, which further complicated things. By then the Ashleys had disposed of a large part of their holdings in Harriette, and manufacturer Gaston was the dominant figure in the village. With visions of further expansions of the community, it was incorporated as the village of Gaston in 1891. A three-way feud developed, as Gaston was adamant about his right to be commemorated on the map, the Ashleys refused to change the name on their railroad time tables, continuing to recognize it as Harriette, and the government persisted in calling the place Springdale. In 1892 Uncle Sam ignored Gaston and the Michigan legislature and sided with the Ashleys to rename the post office Harriette. In 1893 another act of the legislature amended the Village Incorporation Act to restore the name Harriette, but in the course of doing so, the final "e" was changed to "a," creating Harrietta, the name by which it remains known today.[2]

Hardwood logging was flourishing as Harrietta was born, and the area was a supply center for the logging camps. The site of the village was along the old state road. One of the earliest settlers of that area, Joseph Stanley, operated a flour, feed, and grocery store, and was the main supplier for all the independent loggers in the area except Cummer and Diggins, who supplied their own camps. Two blacksmith shops, the Hotel Forest, John Sage's hotel and livery stable, Rowe's restaurant and three general stores, the best known being that of Will & Larcom,[3] prospered in the village.

2. It took another thirty years before the government got around to changing the name of the post office accordingly.

3. Andrew "Jed" Larcom was one of the early settlers in Clam Lake, putting up some buildings on Lake Street, at the foot of Mason, and serving as justice of the peace in the township. In the mid seventies, he moved to Lake City, then came to Harrietta shortly after it was platted. He was the subject of considerable

In 1892 a bank was started. Counting the hotels and F. A. Rowe's restaurant, there were eleven saloons in the village. The panic of 1893, however, ruined Gaston, closed most of the lumber camps, or brought them down to half strength, and almost turned Harrietta into a ghost town. Tramps roaming the area did great damage in the lumber camps, and several bands of armed ruffians invaded the village.

That is not to say that the village couldn't take care of itself. Harrietta in the nineties was every bit as tough a town as Clam Lake had been in the early seventies. The courts were kept busy with the brawls and misfortunes of the community. Harrietta creditors were sometimes overly forceful in trying to collect their accounts, and more than one debtor profited enough from his creditor's assaults to offset the original debt, and more. Gaston was destitute and fled. The Ogdens were broke and stayed, resorting to an attempt to defraud the Maccabees Insurance Company. On two different occasions the village president was assaulted in the course of village meetings. John Garrett assaulted president John Sayes and did him serious damage with a piece of maple stove wood, and the following year, Dr. Hiram Chase, a somewhat eccentric physician, who was tried for perjury in the Ogden insurance fraud, was convicted of doing great bodily harm to president Razek during a session of the village council. Several years later Chase fought a duel to settle another "dispute of honor." The village constable, Phil Tobin, often took the law in his own hands, and on several occasions was convicted of offenses rather substantially outside the law. When federal marshals swooped into the village during the heights of the recession and arrested the town blacksmith, he was revealed as the leader of a ring of counterfeiters. The Harriette *News* lamented that things

interest in Lake City when he was implicated in the murder of a Mrs. Jagt at Vogel Center, but the real murderer later exonerated him. He served as president of the village and to him we owe the observation that election to the council of a village with eleven saloons was the next best thing to a gold mine financially, having all of the profit and none of the labor. Saloon licenses were issued by the village, renewable annually, and, said Larcom, "it made Christmas a joyous occasion. God and the council loved cheerful givers."

were so bad in town "that a craftsman cannot turn an honest dollar any more."

The recession ended and the village appeared to be on the way to recovery. By the end of the century the Feller brothers had a sawmill and stave mill in operation. The old Gaston works were again functioning with new occupants, along with the Simpson Lumber Mill and the Harrietta Brick Company, which had been taken over by a Cadillac saloon keeper, Robert Wilson, and William Heath. The state of Michigan was commencing construction of a fish hatchery on the Slagle Creek which is in operation to this day. At its peak. Harrietta had close to 400 residents, more than three times its present population.

So far as can be determined, the village never had a resident lawyer. There are references to a dentist having left in 1894, and at least three doctors cared for the citizens of the place in the nineties: a Dr. Hamilton, the volatile Dr. Chase, and Dr. John Barry, who proved to be the first citizen of the community. He was elected the first president of the village when it was incorporated in 1891, was postmaster from 1894 until 1897, served for many years on the county board of supervisors and was its chairman for ten, and was serving his second term in the state legislature when he died unexpectedly in 1913.

Harrietta had its misfortunes with newspapers, none seemingly being able to make a financial success. In December, 1890, William Eaton started the Gaston *Gazette* but was out of business by mid-February of 1892. Manufacturer Gaston tried to get it started again, but gave up. Later that year Thomas Jackson started a newspaper called, simply, *Harriette,* but he soon disappeared, and the Cadillac newspaper reported that when he left, the funds of the township and school district of which he was treasurer departed also. In 1894 Samuel Cooley started the Harrietta *News* but soon sold out to John Stone. His paper failed also, and Stone mysteriously disappeared in 1897 as did, once again, the township funds. In 1898 the Harrietta *Messenger* was commenced by W. N. Benedict. Benedict gave up and moved to Honor in 1900, but publication of the *Messenger* was resumed shortly thereafter by Thomas Campbell, who was able to survive for several years into the twentieth century.

3.

About half way between Mesick and Harrietta, the village of Yuma grew up around some logging camps and a sawmill located in the heart of a hardwood forest. In 1891 the Jenney Charcoal Kilns and Chemical Plant were moved from Harrietta to Yuma for convenience. Several blacksmith shops, saloons, general stores, and another sawmill went up around the camp. In 1892 the Union Iron Company built twenty-one charcoal kilns and a large chemical works for the production of wood alcohol at the site. A large school and a church were built, and for a time it appeared to people in the surrounding area that Yuma might well become an important industrial site. It was a one-industry town, however, devoted entirely to the charcoal and wood alcohol operation, and the equipment of the plants did not represent any substantial investment. When the hardwood in the immediate vicinity was gone, industrial Yuma was dead. Its population never exceeded 100 people.

In 1890 the village of Mesick was platted, taking its name from the Mesick brothers who came through the area working on the state road, remained as hunters and trappers, and ultimately were domesticated and became farmers. Having accepted construction money from the residents of Wexford Township to build a railroad to Sherman, the Toledo & Ann Arbor R. R. maintained a pretense of having done so by referring to Mesick for a numbei years as Sherman Station. That is undoubtedly the explanation for statements in several histories that Sherman was on the Ann Arbor line. It was not until 1896 that the railroad finally recognized the existence of Mesick on its timetables and advertising materials.

The village grew steadily. Almost immediately it had a sawmill and later a handle factory. In the mid-nineties, the Williams brothers operated a last block factory there. For many years Mesick was primarily known as a shipping point for lumber and wood products and was a typical logging town with a few general stores, a blacksmith, and a handful of saloons. By the end of the century, the Seventh Day Adventists had built a church, and the Methodists were holding regular meetings there. When Mesick was legally organized as a village in 1901, it boasted a large school; a doctor, J. M. Prentice; a weekly newspaper, the *Sun,* and over 150 residents.

4.

There were other railroads that came through the county. In 1886 the Manistee and Luther Railroad was organized. It was almost entirely devoted to servicing the logging camps in Manistee and Lake counties. For a time it was thought that it would pass through the settlement of Thorp in section 29 of South Branch Township, and plans were made to plat a village around the post office, which had been located there in 1883 and named after Col. Thomas J. Thorp, the Wexford County clerk. The M. & L. ended plans for the future development of Thorp by bypassing it a mile to the north. The road then swung south to the settlement of Eleanor in section 6 of South Branch Township, where it branched. One fork of the railroad swung south into Lake County; the other turned north and gradually circled back to the west in South Branch Township, following the areas that were being logged north of Peterson Creek. Eleanor, on Poplar Creek, was just a logging camp with a general store in which a post office was located. It never developed beyond the logging camp stage. Another general store was built and a railroad repair shop, but Eleanor was frequented almost entirely by railroad and logging men and had virtually no resident population. It did, of course, have a saloon.

In the northwestern part of the county, the hopes of Sherman to become a rail center were raised again when the Manistee and Northeastern Railroad made plans for an easterly expansion. There were a number of lines on the road, but one was designed to pass through Wexford County. It entered Springville Township, following the north bank of the Manistee River. One community, Miner's Rollway, consisted only of a saloon, blacksmith shop, store, and some bunkhouses for lumberjacks. For a time it was thought that the road might hit Mesick, but the decision to remain on the north bank of the river eliminated not only Mesick but also Sherman as a stop. There was a settlement at Glengary through which the railroad passed, and another at Walls, a half mile west of Manistee Bridge north of Sherman. Other stops along the railroad were Drake's Mill, Hopper's Switch, Buckley, and Baxter.

The so-called river branch of the Manistee and Northeastern swung north out of Greenwood Township through Walton Junction, then returned to Liberty Township and thence followed the Manistee River across country to its terminus at Grayling. Its deviation to Walton, where the G. R. & I. spur to Traverse City branched off from the main line, was an exercise in wishful thinking. There was no need to take that route in order to hit the G. R. & I. for an interchange, since it was crossed again in northern Liberty Township anyway. At the time, however, there were tentative plans for the Pere Marquette Railroad to run an east-west line into the central part of the state through Walton, and, at the same time, the Michigan Central was considering a line from Roscommon to Traverse City with a likely crossing at Walton.

Walton had once been wicked and prosperous but was now fallen on good days. The owners of the Manistee and Northeastern took an option on large tracts of land in the vicinity in the anticipation that the location of other railroads through Walton would turn it into a rail center of major importance, around which a large community was bound to grow. And they were hoping that the location of the Manistee and Northeastern through Walton might well stimulate the other railroads to proceed with their plans. As events transpired, neither of the major railroads made the decision, and Walton Junction, once the site of ten saloons, three hotels, five stores, a jail, at least four houses of prostitution, and a flourishing cultivated cranberry industry, rapidly sank into a one-hotel, one-store, and one-saloon town, mainly serving the G. R. & I. and M. & N. E. railroad crews. In 1895 it was described by the *News* as follows:

> Walton Junction was very properly called Hades when it flourished as an important place for distributing supplies for the lumber camps on the upper Manistee River. That was back in the seventies, when poor whiskey was dealt out on a

local option plan that every man was compelled to drink it or be whipped. It was the headquarters for every vice known to the lumber woodsmen, and in summer it was usually only the Indian braves who dared venture upon the prolific huckleberry plains that surround the place. A deserted looking locality it is today with its unpainted buildings going to decay and the grass and its trackless streets going to seed. Walton's redemption appears to be made possible only by way of a return to the conditions in which nature first adorned her.

5.

The rest of the settlements around Wexford County were nothing more than crossroad stores with a post office and perhaps a blacksmith shop located along the mail route. In South Branch Township there were Hoxeyville and Rodingen. In Henderson there were Angola and Stocking. In Cherry Grove Township there were Axin, Benson, Cherry Grove, and Six Corners. In Clam Lake there was Elton. In Haring Township the G. R. & I. ran a branch to serve Long Lake, Round Lake, Crooked Lake, and Missaukee County, and settlements at Missaukee Junction, Long Lake, and Round Lake grew up. In Selma Township there were Ballou and Thorp's Corners. In Boon there were Springdale and Summit. In Slagle there was West Summit. In Antioch there was Bandola. In Colfax, Meauwataka and Colfax. In Cedar Creek, Gilbert. In Liberty, there were Haire, Putman's Siding, and Mystic. In Greenwood Township there were Soper and Greenwood. Hanover had Wheatland, and in Wexford there were Cornell, Wexford, and Farnsworth. Somewhere else in the county, Viola had a brief existence, with its post office and identity discontinued after the town was destroyed by fire in 1881.

Sherman had reached its peak. The twentieth century did not deal kindly with it, and, after a disastrous fire razed the major part of its business district, it ceased to be a community of consequence.

In Manton, on the other hand, there was steady growth. The building boom of 1881, occasioned by the removal of the county seat from Sherman to Manton, abated somewhat as it became apparent that the county seat war was not over. The town, nevertheless, continued to grow even after the county seat was removed to Cadillac, although undoubtedly not as rapidly as if it had managed to retain the coveted political prize. Its woodworking industry continued to flourish, with new sawmills being built and with the location of the Williams brothers factory there in the nineties. The original Woodward flour mill, acquired by H. B. Sturtevant in 1881, was later acquired by Phelps and Baker and expanded. Frank Jennison had a large general store at the corner of Main and Seaman streets and a profitable branch at Jennings.

A Dr. Rhodes was the first physician known in Manton, and he was succeeded by Dr. D. S. Taplin, who started a drugstore in 1874. In 1880 Dr. Rinaldo Fuller bought the Taplin drugstore and remained until about 1892, although he practiced only briefly during the first years of this period. Dr. Hiram B. Wilcox, who practiced in Cadillac and Haring, came to Manton in 1876 and started his drugstore. He stayed only briefly and then sold to a Dr. Ketchum. In 1880 the store was purchased by H. Frank Campbell, the newspaperman from Sherman, and when he bought the Manton *Tribune,* he sold the store to Drs. John C. Bostick and Charles H. Bostick, father and son, who started a family business that continues today.

Other physicians who practiced in Manton were Amos Broughton; Thomas A. Corlett; J. L. Duston; Victor F. Huntley, who served as mayor and postmaster and was elected to the legislature; J. D. Martin; Edward Morgan, the early settler in Wexford Township, who had practiced briefly in Cadillac and then in Kalkaska; Nelson H. Parker, the herb doctor; Walter B. Wallace, and a Dr. Young. Of the sixteen, four are known to have acquired medical degrees and two others to have attended medical school.

Manton's first lawyer was Thomas A. Ferguson, who moved there from Sherman. In 1881 W. C. Haire and Henry Harpster commenced practice, with Haire following the county seat to Cadillac the following year. In 1883 Frank Waring opened an office but moved to Lake City before the year was over. The best established and most durable of the Manton attorneys was Isaac C. Wheeler, who arrived late in 1886 or early in 1887 and proved to be a successful and competent practioner for over thirty years. He was joined towards the end of the century by E. Perley Lott, and Arthur Bulkley, who commenced practice in 1897.

Repeated subdivisions added to the size of the city, as its population grew to about 1,300 people in 1900. Three hotels and a large business district served the community. A waterworks system was installed in 1895, and in 1900 work was commenced for the construction of an electric light plant which was continued as a municipally operated enterprise until recently.

6.

Typical of the hopes of the little settlements was this *News* note of 1892: "News from Bagnall Station indicates that the village is now being platted. Tell everyone you see there is an excellent chance for factories here."

Not counting name changes or a move of location, thirty-eight post offices had existed in the county in the nineteenth century, and Bagnall, Baxter, Buckley, Bunyea, and Coline were to be added to the list in the twentieth. Almost that many more settlements had been noted on a map or in the newspapers, and they were looking for factories, mills, and permanence. In truth, most of them had reached their peak by 1900. By 1919, the county's fiftieth year, the lumber was dwindling and the county's population was down by 10 percent from its peak of 20,769 only nine years earlier. Ten post offices remained. The crossroad and railroad siding settlements were withering away, if, indeed, not already lost into history.

Cadillac from Cemetery Hill in 1889, showing the ball grounds with Mosser's brickyard beyond (right center). The newly built Cadillac & Southeastern (Ann Arbor) railroad grade runs horizontally across the center of the picture. Beyond the pine at center can be seen the new Central School which burned in 1890, and to its right the Leeson and Austin Mitchell homes surmount "Observatory Hill." Arrows mark the Wood Street bridges over standing water in the south swamp. Midway between the arrows, a tree partially obscures the high ground on which the city pound and pest house were isolated.

Cadillac Evening News.

The Hotel McKinnon in 1890.

The American Hotel in 1890.

The old George A. Mitchell home after its new owner, Wellington W. Cummer, added an "Observatory Bay" on the southeast corner in 1889. Rear left, the Nathaniel Gerrish home; right rear, the Presbyterian Church.

J.P. Craig.

Into the Twentieth Century: The new Opera House at Shelby and Beech streets; The new city hall, corner of Mitchell and E. Mason streets. To the north, the old Holbrook & May building after being turned off its Mitchell Street axis.

Into the Twentieth Century. A view northwest from North Street hill, with the Clam River at flood. In the left foreground, the intersection of River and Wallace streets. Lying at the edge of the stumplands are the Williams Brothers mills, St. John's Table Company, and the Mitchell-Diggins Iron Company. Between St. John's and the river, the buildings around the intersection of Haring Road (North Mitchell Street) and Ayers Street date from the original settlement of McCoy's Siding.

Cadillac Evening News.

Chapter Twenty-Five

INTO THE TWENTIETH CENTURY

In Cadillac the coming of the Toledo & Ann Arbor Railroad seemed to presage a new era of prosperity, although not necessarily in the lumbering industry. For ten years the pessimists had been predicting that "the pine would be all gone in another year or two." So it was in the late eighties, and even the huge Cummer-Blodgett reserve of pine to the east of Cadillac didn't allay the feeling that it was all soon to end. The newspapers talked hopefully about the hardwood industry that might develop from the reserves in the county, but it wasn't a very confident prediction. No one as yet fully appreciated what had been happening in the past few years in the development of the logging railroads, and the enlargement of Cadillac's mills to handle logs shipped in from a hundred or more miles away simply wasn't anticipated except by a few leaders of the industry.

Rather than foreseeing an increasingly prosperous lumber industry, Cadillac's optimism steemed from the traditional agricultural nature of nineteenth century America. The greater part of central Wexford County remained unsettled, and the extension of the T. & A. A. to Lake Michigan would open this area up to settlement and farming. The science of soil testing was unheard of, and the sterile nature of the soil deposited by the glacial drift was yet unrevealed. It was assumed that the land which had produced such lush forests must be fertile beyond anything known in the central grasslands of the country. Real wealth in a stable society lay in a prosperous agricultural economy, and that seemed on the verge of becoming reality for Wexford County. Its county seat, crossroad of three railroads, would be the trading center for a fifty-mile radius.

The first few years following the coming of the T. & A. A. seemed to fulfill that expectation. Between 1880 and 1884 the county population had jumped by over 50 percent. Cadillac's population had doubled in that period, although predictions for an ever greater increase hadn't materialized. The 1890 census figures were discouraging, only a slight increase in county population being shown. With the extension of the T. & A. A., however, there was again a sharp jump shown in the 1894 census and an equal increase by 1900, amounting in all to another 50 percent increase in population between 1890 and 1900. The city of Cadillac had almost 6,000 people at the end of the century, while the county population had grown at an even greater rate during this period.

There were some who preferred the agricultural to the industrial climate. The churches, the temperence leaders, the genteel element of the community, all deplored the rough and tumble aspects of a milltown, periodically invaded by armies of woodsmen. Saloons and redlight houses might be profitable to some and tolerated by others, but it definitely didn't give the town class or serenity. Still others looked at the lumber-centered economy of the community as something less than an unmixed blessing, subject as it was to extreme fluctuations. The building boom of the late eighties was one of a number of periodic spurts in the local economy, and it shortly ran into the other side of the economic coin, the recurring recessions.

But at the moment, with two new railroads and the Cummer expansion underway, everyone was in an optimistic mood. There was more building going on than in any period since the building frenzy of 1873, when almost thirty-five commercial buildings and as many homes had been constructed. The Drury & Kelley hardware building burned and was replaced by a three-story brick building. John Turner put up a brick building next door to house his undertaking and furniture store and then replaced his frame store across the street with another brick building. The Methodists sold their frame church to the Baptists and contracted to build a new brick sanctuary. Additions were built on the Cummer No. 2 and the Cobbs & Mitchell No. 1 mills, and new homes were going up everywhere.

The town almost didn't notice the lumber recession of 1889. The mills were down for awhile, and commercial business was slow on main street, but no one was much concerned. Some of the lumber and furniture companies in the Middle West failed, but the Cadillac businessmen seemed sound. In contrast to the pessimism of previous years, the *News* looked realistically to another ten years of pine lumbering, urged planning to get hardwood industries to locate in Cadillac, and sparked the formation of an industrial committee, the predecessor to the modern chamber of commerce. The G. R. & I. was showing a handsome profit and Cadillac was its busiest station. Everyone thought the T. & A. A. was more prosperous than it really was; agricultural shipments were increasing on both railroads, and everyone took the hard times in a buoyant mood.

Aside from some dire predictions about where the Harrison administration's tariff and money policies were leading the country, even the *Democrat* was optimistic. It noted that more than twenty new homes were going up in Frenchtown in the summer of 1889, that Sweedtown west of Mitchell on both sides of Clam River was "building up mightily," and that more than a dozen new "luxury dwellings" had gone up in the past few years, reflecting the confidence in Cadillac held by such "swells" as E. C. Fosburgh and E. L. Metheany, who built on Prospect Street, A. L. Culliver on Stimson, Edward Lapham on Harris, E. E. Haskins on East Mason, and Austin W. Mitchell on Observatory Hill. In 1890 William W. Mitchell would dwarf them all with his huge home on the northeast corner of Cass and Shelby streets.

Another influential group spoke confidently for the city with the 1889 decision of the Masons to build their own building in Cadillac. Their first meeting had been held in the Holbrook & May Hall. Then the order had leased the third floor of George Mitchell's four-story office building at the northwest corner of Cass and Mitchell streets. In 1885 they had moved kitty-corner across the intersection to the third floor of the new LaBar-Cornwell building. Now they planned a three-story building of their own, to be financed by guaranteed leases and the sale of bonds in the amount of $20,000. Land was purchased from the Cummers in block F lying between the new Cummer building and Beech Street. The building would have three store sections on the Mitchell Street ground floor, and merchant W. M. Gow, one of the planners, led off by signing a ten-year lease for the corner store at $800 a year. The second floor would provide office space, and the Masons, in leaving its old landlords, LaBar & Cornwell, took their other tenant, Wexford County. The county agreed to a ten-year lease of the second floor at an annual rent of $1,000 for office space for the county clerk and register of deeds, county treasurer, sheriff, probate judge, and circuit court. The bonds were sold almost instantly.

The contractor for the building was John Mosser, who had just finished the Cummer building. The job was shared with Charles Dutton, who was beginning to prosper as a builder. John Born was prospering and had his share of the building work. The lion's share, however, went to John G. Mosser. He had acquired Moyer's old brickyard and made it prosperous. The former G. R. & I. bridge builder was still doing all the railroad bridge building, and its roundhouses and depots to boot. Everything on the G. R. & I. north of Grand Rapids was his work except the roadbed. Half of the town's new homes were his work. He had built the Congregational church, and was building the Methodist church. The Drury & Kelley and Turner buildings were his work, and, when the central school burned in 1890 and a three-story brick building replaced it, it was Mosser who built it. He owned a wholesale and retail building supply business and bought the old Ballou building on Mason Street for a warehouse. His new buildings used lumber from his own mill and brick from his yard. He was building all over northern Michigan. In the midst of prosperity, the Panic of 1893 struck the nation. Mosser was ruined and vanished.

2.

As a one-industry town, Cadillac had been particularly susceptible to the economic fluctuations of that industry, and doubly so to the panics and recessions that periodically shook the country. The mills and the banks particularly trace the effect of such cycles.

Cadillac's first building boom had come despite the panic of 1873, and the town had grumbled even as it bragged about its lusty growth. In 1874, with sales slow and the *News* reporting that some of the loggers were holding their crews out of the woods, the county's first bank started business. Daniel F. Comstock's Wexford County Bank started in one of Morris Bunyea's buildings next to the drugstore of Dr. Dillenbeck. Then, when George Mitchell was planning his office building at Cass and Mitchell streets, Comstock hastened to obtain the first-floor lease, and the building was commonly referred to as the "bank building" for the rest of the century. In 1878 another financial panic swept the country, and the Comstock bank was shaken by a heavy "run" against it. It survived only because George Mitchell intervened to shore it up. A few months later, after Mitchell's death, Comstock sold the bank to Frank H. Messmore of Pentwater and attorney John Rice of Cadillac.[1]

In 1883 another national panic swept the country. Banks closed, wholesale houses foundered, and credit was non-existent. In Cadillac the mills closed down for most of the summer, and commerce on main street was reduced to barter and hope. For the millhands, it was "fish, hunt, and tend your gardens, or starve." J. W. Cummer failed twice. He had taken in a partner the previous year to aid in the expansion of his wholesale and retail hardware business. Cummer and Rawles failed. A few days later Cummer and Henderson made an assignment for creditors as their Michigan Iron Works closed its doors. A dozen merchants locked up on main street. LaBar-Cornwell had planned to end their retail business and concentrate on the wholesale grocery and flour business. A sale of their retail business to Newark and Sorenson fell through when Sorenson's business went under. Six months later John Wilcox joined the firm of W. Boorem & Co. and they contracted to buy LaBar-Cornwell's retail store. Two days later Boorem & Co. failed. LaBar-Cornwell stayed in the retail grocery business. The Creitheon sawmill and several loggers went broke and, with them, their supplier, Crawford Brothers grocers and provisioners. There was a run on the bank, and Messmore & Rice couldn't meet the cash demands of their paper holders and depositors. The bank failed.

The panic passed. Some recovered; some didn't. The Cummer family remained sound, and Jacob financed his brother J. W. The hardware store resumed without partner Rawles. Within months Michigan Iron Works was open, producing logging locomotives

1. Comstock moved to Big Rapids and opened a bank there. He prospered until the panic of 1893, when he was wiped out.

and repairing lumbering equipment for the loggers and the mills, without partner Henderson who moved to Ohio to help build Shay locomotives at the Lima Locomotive Works.

In December of 1883 Delos A. Blodgett moved back into the Cadillac economy, buying the Creitheon mill, getting into the Westover partnership (brewery and sawmill), and setting up a bank, D. A. Blodgett & Co., in partnership with Delos F. Diggins, with whom he had been associated in various matters in Osceola County. The bank took over the assets and accounts of Rice & Messmore, assumed its lease in the Mitchell building, and prospered. Diggins moved to Cadillac to manage the bank and to look after his own lumber interests and those of Blodgett. In 1892 his own interests, in conjunction with the Cummer group, had become so extensive that he was instrumental in arranging the sale of the Blodgett pine reserve east of Cadillac to the Cummers. In 1895 he left Blodgett and became part of a new Cummer organization. Without his management, Blodgett closed the bank, and its assets were sold to a new corporation, the Cadillac State Bank.[2]

A second bank had been started in Cadillac in 1878 by Jared Hixson, who had first come to Cadillac as stationmaster for the G. R. & I. Hixson had a tobacco and stationery store[3] two doors north of the Mitchell building next door to Captain Newson's saloon. Politically active, he had been named postmaster of the new city of Cadillac in June of 1877, and the post office was located in his building until 1886. In those days, there was no mail delivery, patrons calling for their mail at the post office. As a result, his combined store, bank, and post office was the common meeting place of the community.

Hixson did well and weathered the panic of 1883 in good shape. In his prosperity he started a sawmill along the lake south of Chapin Street. From Prof. H. M. Enos he bought one of the nicest and newest homes in town at the end of Harris Street.[4] Then, in

2. Bank officers were F. J. Cobbs, son of Jonathan Cobbs, president; Solomon Kramer, vice president; Henry Knowlton, cashier, and Cobbs, Kramer, William W. Mitchell, Delos F. Diggins, W. W. Cummer, John Mansfield, and William McAdie, directors.

3. It was the former Culver saloon, moved from Mason Street in 1875.

4. Enos came to Cadillac as its superintendent of schools in 1879. In 1884, he started the *Wexford County Citizen* as an Independent Reform Republican

1886, the lumber markets went bad and the mills again were down. Hixson was in a double bind. The bank had extended credit to several loggers who failed. Worse, over a period of time commencing when he was city treasurer, Hixson had co-mingled city, postal and bank funds for personal log speculation. In this winter, he had contracted his largest timber purchases, giving notes payable at the end of the winter cutting season. Now, with the notes coming due and his logs unsaleable, his alternatives were few and miserable. The announcement by the new administration in Washington that James Croly would replace Hixson as postmaster brought the climax. Monday morning callers at the post office-bank found it closed. Hixson had departed on Saturday.[5] The largest loser was Jonathan Cobbs, who had been particularly fond of Hixson. Cobbs had been responsible for a measure of the Hixson success by giving his bank a large part of the Cobbs & Mitchell business, and by throwing some logging business his way. But Cobbs & Mitchell were too sound to fail with the bank, and the town breathed a sigh of relief.

The recessions of 1886 and 1889 had been relatively minor adjustments in the lumber industry. The town had tightened its belt but had not been severely damaged. No one quite anticipated the total collapse of the economy that came with the Panic of 1893. The country was sorely hurt. Cadillac was devasted. Two dozen merchants and small lumber dealers and loggers were ruined. The mills were totally silent. John Mosser disappeared. For almost four years the town was paralyzed. In 1894, at vastly reduced wages, some of the mills were in operation on a part-time

paper. He so antagonized the Cummers that they bought him out in 1885. This accomplished, the school board under President Jacob Cummer then fired Enos. He left Cadillac, selling his home to Hixson. After Hixson's disappearance, the house was sold at sheriff's sale to Jacob Cornwell's son, Monroe. For many years past, it has been the home of the T. Walter Kelley family.

5. Hixson returned two years later for the burial of his wife, Grace, daughter of Judge Holden Green, and to give testimony that shook the Cummer empire in a lawsuit growing out of the bank failure. Thirty-eight years later, when Fred Green was elected Governor of Michigan, he received a note of congratulations from California from "the postmaster who used you as a messenger boy." The Governor remembered his brother-in-law well and kept up a steady correspondence with the old man until his own death ten years later.

basis. At its very peak, mill employment for the year was down to 847 men, almost all of them working only part time. Two years before, almost 1,800 men were working twelve-hour shifts. It was not until 1897 that the mills got back to their 1892 strength.

3.

Main street had its new faces. In 1887 the McNitt brothers store was built at the corner of Mitchell and North streets.[6] Nephews of Boon supervisor Will McNitt, they had started a general store at Haring in 1879 then built a store at Round Lake in 1881 near the Haynes and Whitmore sawmills. The next year, with the beginning of a boom at Jennings, they started another branch store there. By the time they opened their Cadillac store, they already had thirty employees in their various branches. In 1892 the firm was dissolved when Henry McNitt sold out and turned to farming in Haring Township, but the McNitts continued to be active in local and state affairs. One of Henry's sons, Earl, served six terms in the Michigan House of Representatives in the first third of the twentieth century.

Cadillac's second directory,[7] published in 1894, listed twenty-three Smiths in the city. Some of them, descendants of Ansel Smith of Pennsylvania, by way of Ionia County, were a part of Cadillac life almost from its beginning. Of Ansel's thirteen children, several were prominent in Ionia. Vernor H. Smith became circuit judge, while Lewis was a prosperous merchant and postmaster there. Joel came to Cadillac shortly after its settlement as Clam Lake and married Hattie Caswell, the first teacher in the settle-

6. The McNitt building had a "hall" on the second floor which was a meeting place, and was in frequent use for dances, socials, and all kinds of gatherings. It was the site of most of the professional prize fights in Cadillac for almost two decades, until the fame of Cadillac's world champion, Ad Wolgast, produced such large crowds that outdoor fights became common.

7. The first directory was in 1883. The third, or Norton, directory of 1900 contained supplements on local history and extensive biographical material and immediately became a collector's item. An abridged reprint was issued in 1971 by the Cadillac Printing Company.

ment who had held classes in the winter of 1871-72 in the Empire Hall of the Mosser & White building. He was joined a few years later by a younger brother, James A. Smith.

After twenty years, Joel Smith moved to Lansing, where he and his second wife held positions with the boys training school. His two sons, Wallace Joel Smith and Charles R. Smith, were to be well-known figures in the community. The boys and their uncle James held a variety of public offices, Wallace and James between them holding the position of city clerk for fifteen years. Charles Smith operated a grocery store for a number of years and dabbled in a dozen or more entertainment or amusement projects, from roller skating, to a dance pavilion, to a toboggan slide. In 1887 he went to work at the McKinnon Hotel, finally buying it for $1,300 in 1891. In 1893, just before the panic, he sold it to Bert Spafford and C. E. Snow for $18,000. In order to get a healthy environment for his ailing son, Wallace Joel, he bought a 200-acre farm at Lima Center near Chelsea in Washtenaw County,[8] then left the family to run the farm while he worked as a salesman for various companies. He traveled through western Michigan, his jovial presence being noted in the Cadillac newspapers frequently. By 1896 the recession had nearly ruined Spafford & Snow, and the hotel was sold. Smith bought it back a few months later for a fraction of what he had sold it for three years earlier, sold his Lima Center farm for twice what he paid for it, and moved his family back to Cadillac. Wallace Joel became one of Cadillac's leading physicians, leading an active life, notwithstanding his childhood heart "weakness," until death took him in 1966 at age eighty-five. Dr. Joe's knack for judging real estate and poker hands was undoubtedly acquired from his father, who made the McKinnon House into the city's leading hotel for another twenty years but made his money and his fun in land and playing cards. The *Daily Citizen,* noting a party to celebrate his birthday in 1910, said: "If

8. The purchase was handled through attorney Eugene F. Sawyer, who learned of the availability of the farm. Sawyer and attorney Samuel J. Wall married two of the Sipley sisters of Ann Arbor, a third sister marrying E. D. Hepfer of Chelsea, and the farm had belonged to one of Hepfer's family. His daughter Emily moved to Cadillac in the nineties, working in the post office, and made Cadillac her lifelong home.

there ever was the likes of our dapper Charley R. elsewhere in the land, we should have heard it, but we hope he doesn't accept the invite to go to Washington to teach Taft how to bluff at poker."

Charley's uncle James was an equally gregarious and loved figure, but his knack with poker and money wasn't as keen. For six years he was in the shoe business. In 1890 he bought out the men's clothing business of W. R. Dennis & Co. in the Kelley block and stayed for eleven years. In all that time, he lamented, he never had an empty store but he seldom had a buyer. As alderman, as city clerk, and as a great conversationalist, he always had a store full of people. And he was always broke. He had some tough competitors in Levi Law, S. W. Kramer, Drebin's Boston Store, Auer's Clothing, Aldrich & Kubeck, Johnson & Ostensen, and a half dozen tailors who sold men's custom made suits as cheaply as the ready-mades from his racks. In 1897 he gave up, advertised his remaining stock, lease, and home for sale—and couldn't find any buyers. In desperation he hung on another four years, finally going under and making an assignment for his creditors in 1901. The new buyer, Chris Jorgensen, proved just as popular, but knew his merchandise and a dollar, and he prospered.

There were new faces. John and William Wilcox prospered in the grocery business, then bought out the old Mosser brickyard and were equally successful there. Fred Lentz bought out Rathman's grocery store. He failed to survive the Panic, but the Lentz family became fixtures in Cadillac's affairs. Fred Reed had been in and around Cadillac for over ten years before finally starting a jewelry store in the old Borne building next to the McKinnon Hotel,[9] starting a business which continues as Reed & Wheaton to this day. There were Johnston & Kaiser in the grocery business, M. J. Present in fancy goods and dry goods (succeeding Cohen's New York Store), Gustafson & Johnson's hardware, Ostensen & Johnson's clothiers, Nilsen & Stone grocers, Snider &

9. The preceding tenant had been saloon-keeper John Hassenfuss, who left town after a scandal involving his relationship with undertaker John Turner. Hassenfuss died suddenly in Grand Rapids, and Mrs. Hassenfuss moved to Indiana, where she was tried for murder a few years later. During the trial, it was suggested that her late husband was but one of several of her male acquaintances to meet a sudden end.

Hoag's grocery, Aaron F. Anderson (later merged with John Olson and John Coffey) in the shoe business, Aldrich & Kubeck's clothing, the Torrey family's Cadillac Granite Monument Company, Mather & Kelley's livery stable, William Cassler in fuel, shoes, and undertaking, and George Giuffra's fruit market.[10] There were new trades: Robert Thayer, John Dersch, John Wolgast, and Rybold and Clausen were cigarmakers.

The professions added new faces, men and women who were generally better trained than their predecessors. In 1888 Drs. David Ralston and Bartlett H. McMullen came to Cadillac to serve three decades and more as outstanding members of their profession. In the nineties there were others: Drs. Henri Berghall, William Dwyer, Mary Seehouse, A. B. Watson, Archibald Thompson, and Philip A. Wolfe. The field of dentistry found newcomers Edward Sangster, Gaylor Brown, Frank Fletcher, Charles Edwards, and Howard Kneeland. Two veterinary surgeons, D. W. Curtis and J. R. Knauf, located in Cadillac.

At the bar, F. C. Moriarity, Fred S. Lamb, Russell Tinkham, Elwood Peck, Fred Wetmore, Ulysses S. Albertson, and John Mansfield (the former Boon supervisor, county treasurer, and probate judge) were admitted to practice. Lamb and Wetmore in particular had most distinguished careers, both in private practice and in public life. Judge Lamb became known as one of the state's most distinguished jurists in a thirty-nine-year career as judge of the twenty-eighth judicial circuit from 1909 until 1948. Wetmore served in the Michigan Senate, then became United States attorney for the western district of Michigan and moved to Grand Rapids.

4.

Cadillac in the nineties was growing up. There were new church congregations: the German Lutherans, Seventh Day Adventists,

10. Giuffra moved to Albion and became a part of the college experience of three generations of Albion College students who made his Campus Eat Shop their hangout until after World War II.

and Christian Scientists. An off-again, on-again Salvation Army effort finally took firm root. The Presbyterians built a new church. There were more hotels: the Co-Operative Hotel and the Montreal House, and the Central was rebuilt after being destroyed by fire. The town had two telephone exchanges; the Cadillac exchange operated by former printer, Henry W. Sill, and the Michigan exchange operated by attorney Eugene E. Haskins.

There were more newspapers. In 1890 Karl (later anglicized to Charles) Thornmark, started the *Arbitaren,* a Swedish language paper which flourished for many years. Thornmark was admitted to the bar then moved to Chicago, and the paper was taken over by Axel Burman, who came to Cadillac in 1893. In 1894 George S. Stanley, owner and editor of the *State Democrat,* a weekly, started a daily Democratic paper, the *Daily Citizen.* If we recognize that the *Daily Enterprise* had never really been a daily, the *Citizen* was the first daily paper in the city, continuing until 1911, when Stanley sold both his daily and weekly papers to Perry F. Powers of the *News.* In 1898 John Terwilliger started an Independent paper, the *Globe.* This, too, was eventually acquired by Powers.

The town had a fairgrounds bounded by West Division and Chestnut streets on the north and south, Colfax Street on the east, and Dr. Leeson's farm road on the west. The grounds, Cadillac boasted, had the best race track in the state. The streets were being improved with clay and gravel, and cement sidewalks were going in everywhere in 1894 at twelve cents a square foot. There was the new boulevard around the little lake, the new central schoolhouse and another dozen large homes, of which the F. J. Cobbs home on the northeast corner of Chapin and Park streets, the Fred Diggins home at the head of Harris Street, and the Joseph Murphy house on the northeast corner of Park and Cass streets, were the most elaborate.

On Mitchell Street, Arthur Webber replaced his frame drugstore with a new brick building, now occupied by the J. C. Penney Company. And after the fires of 1896 and 1899, all of the block on the east side between Harris and Cass streets was rebuilt. The largest and most ambitious building was the Granite Block built for Dr. J. M. Wardell. It was constructed entirely of masonry and faced with granite, with pillars from the Torrey works to frame the entrance and ends of the building. Less grandiose but equally modern were the brick buildings put up by Dr. Wardell, George Herrick, and Fred Reed farther down the block.

Industrially, the mills were expanding. Two mills were torn down and replaced by bigger and more intricate works. The flooring mills were built and then enlarged as the hardwood age arrived. The chemical plants, a veneer plant, the hardwood specialty manufacturing plants—all these came with the nineties. More important, the industry reached out, as the giants expanded to dominate the field, and the best stands of timber in northern Michigan were being purchased for shipment to Cadillac to be processed. Cadillac's lumbering manufacturers were now the acknowledged leaders of the industry. Cadillac became its trade center, the location of the hardwood manufacturers' association. and publisher of half the trade journals for the industry. It was also the pricing point for hardwood flooring and lumber for the entire nation, a practice that was eventually to lead to federal anti-trust prosecution.

5.

While Cadillac's industrial leaders were dominating their business nationally, Cadillac's leadership was extending throughout the state politically as well. The area's legislators, Tom Ferguson and Henry May, had begun a long succession of local representation from among names already familiar herein. Judge Mears, Nathaniel Gerrish, William H. Mitchell, Fred Wetmore, Dr. John Barry, Dr. Victor Huntley, Ben Bonnell of Pioneer, John Caldwell, publishers Orville Dennis and H. Frank Campbell, and Sylvanus Alexander.

But Cadillac, in particular, was to have its period of dominance. Editor and publisher J. Wight Giddings of the *News* was elected to the Senate in 1886. From then until the end of the century, he and attorney Clyde Chittenden would control the Senate seat except for the terms of Judge Mears and J. W. Milliken of Traverse City. Former mayor Daniel McCoy, at Grand Rapids, had become a power in the Republican party, and he, with Gidding's successor at the *News,* Perry F. Powers, were to figure prominently in the state organization for twenty years. McCoy was twice elected state treasurer. Powers was elected to the state board of education in 1888, starting a twelve-year stay, for a good part of which he was president of the board. He went on in the twentieth century to two terms as auditor general and the chairmanship of the state labor commission. Senator Giddings became lieutenant governor. And behind the scenes, quietly directing the traffic, was Wellington W. Cummer. A term as mayor of Cadillac had shown him the risks of exposure to the criticisms and barbs of public life. Except to serve on the state Republican committee and to cast his vote as a presidential elector for Harrison, he never sought the limelight of public office. There were few who doubted the role he played in state affairs, however. When other men spoke, it was the voice of Cummer that was heard.

6.

Cadillac ended the nineteenth century in a cloud of optimism and a frenzy of building. It shared the uncertainty of much of the country as to whether the twentieth century started in 1900 or 1901, and so it set out to make both years monumental in achievement. Its board of trade had a sizable bank account again, to be used in subsidizing incoming industries. Cobbs & Mitchell doubled the size of its flooring plant. Cummer & Diggins incorporated, as William Saunders, its local superintendent, became a part owner, and started the construction of its chemical plant, the largest of its kind in the world.

Commercial building flourished. After the Hotel Burke burned, the Anheuser-Busch Company bought the Harris Street property and put up its three-story building to serve as a combination beer-storage building, saloon (with billiard parlor), and office building. Across the street the G. R. & I. built a new luxury depot at the foot of Cass Street. Charley Smith built an additon on the McKinnon House and veneered it with Ionia sandstone. Solomon Kramer built a two-story brick building in the star block, occupied today by Montgomery Ward & Co. The business district was extending northward along Mitchell, and a half dozen smaller brick store buildings enhanced its appearance.

Another floor had just been added to the Third Ward school

(soon to be renamed the Emerson), and the burned out Second Ward school was rebuilt bigger and better (and would shortly be named the McKinley after our assassinated president). Several churches were making plans to build and St. Ann's did so, replacing the old frame building started in 1880. Funds were raised and the land acquired for a huge new opera house which would face the Wellington Cummer home across Shelby Street at the top of Beech Street. By June 30, 1900, the *News* reported that over fifty new homes were under construction in town and another fifteen to twenty remodeling and improvement projects were underway.

The public's mood of optimism was revealed when a vote at the spring election to bond the city for $10,000 for a city hall carried by a margin of 723 to 124. The village and the city had never had a building of its own except for the fire house on Cass Street. Early council meetings had been held in Holbrook & May's Hall and then in the Mitchell building above the bank. In recent years, some offices had been scattered around in the Kelley block, the Herrick block and elsewhere, changing from year to year. Now the city wanted one building in which all of its offices and the council room could be under one roof.

Three aldermen, logger John Reiser, Charley Smith, and butcher Cornelius Wager were in favor of a relatively modest building on the city's Cass Street lot. The majority of the council, however, led by William Saunders and Warner Peterson, had more grandiose ideas. Mayor Henry Knowlton appointed Saunders to head a site committee, the report of which was promptly assailed by the *Citizen,* the *Democrat,* and the *Globe.* Like Saunders, Peterson was a Cummer executive. Their site, said the opposition papers, had been personally selected by Wellington W. (W. W.) Cummer.[11] They had recommended lot 1 of block D, directly across the street from the Cummer Building. The reasons given by the committee were central location and "the historic significance of the site going back to the early village and county

11. This was not Saunders' first exposure to public attack for being a Cummer spokesman. When an issue of Cummer performance of its water contract was being raised, his appointment to the board of public works by Mayor Diggins was rejected by the city council three times.

supervisor's meetings in the Holbrook & May Hall prior to its having been moved onto lot 2." The opposition papers said it was chosen to permit Cummer to keep his hand on city government from the comfort of his office and to allow him to make a profit on the transaction.

The significance of the latter accusation isn't clear. The lot had just been acquired by Delos A. Blodgett in several separate purchases. The east end of the lot had been vacant since the old Holbrook & May building had been turned lengthwise on lot 2, but the west end of the lot had a two-story brick office building on it, the former Cummer office building.

By a 6-2 vote, Reiser and Smith voting "no," the council voted to offer Blodgett $2,000 for the lot. Ten days later Blodgett replied that his price was $2,250 plus the city's Cass Street property. A counter offer was made and rejected, and Blodgett's terms were accepted.

Six weeks later the *News* printed the architect's plans for the new city hall. It was considerably larger than Smith or Reiser would approve and on a grander scale than the public had anticipated. The *News* called it a fitting home for the business of a city as important as Cadillac. The *Globe* doubted that there would be enough left of the bond money, after paying Blodgett for the lot, to do much more than get the walls up. The *Citizen* charged the plans had been known from the beginning, that there had never been any intention of going anywhere except "within W. W.'s call," it being quite apparent that the planned hall could never have been built on the Cass Street location. When the bids were opened, the low bid was that of a Grand Rapids contractor at $18,492. The opposition papers wondered how it could be built at that figure and wondered even more sarcastically how the council could accept the bid when it would have less than half the necessary money. The *Citizen* noted sarcastically that no one had yet heard of any Cummer donations to make up the difference. No one ever did. Nevertheless, the contract was let and the work begun.

The twentieth century year, 1901, saw a continuation of the building boom. The opera house was looming over the city, a truly impressive structure. On Mitchell Street, the Cadillac State Bank had acquired the Mitchell building and had decided to replace it with a smaller, two-story brick building. The four-story frame bank building was moved onto "Cass Street lawn" and kept open for business during the summer while the new building was constructed on the old site. In excavating the footings, workmen found two huge pine stumps that had been buried beneath almost four feet of fill dirt, attesting to the once wild state of the city site as pine forest, and showing the extent of filling to level the grade of Mitchell Street. When the stumps were pulled, the adjoining Mitchell Brothers building on the north collapsed into the excavation!

While the city council was holding its meetings in the relocated Mitchell building that spring, things were going badly with the new city hall. It couldn't be built for the contract price. The $18,492 figure had been a desperation bid by a contractor who was in financial trouble. He failed, and it appeared that there was not an adequate performance bond. The city had been short of funds to begin with. Now it would have to dip into funds appropriated for other purposes and borrow additional money to complete the job. In retrospect, the city hall does not look overly elaborate for a city the size of Cadillac. At the moment, however, the only heroes to the people were those who could say, "I told you so," John Reiser and Charley Smith. Mayor Knowlton and most of the pro-city hall aldermen were defeated, and the city elected as its mayor its oft-unsuccessful Democratic candidate, editor George S. Stanley.

By the end of the summer, Mayor Stanley had scrounged the money to finish the building, and it was completed that fall. The new bank building was ready for occupancy. On November 11, the last city council meeting was held in the old bank building, and the work of demolishing it was commenced on the thirteenth. George Mitchell's Main Street landmark had no place in the twentieth century. On the eighteenth, the first council meeting was held in the new council chambers on the second floor of the new city hall, across the street from Courthouse Hill.

The county still didn't have a courthouse, and the name, "Courthouse Hill" had almost disappeared from use, superseded by a new name, Cummer Hill. The town didn't have time to notice the difference. Blodgett's view from Courthouse Hill had been of things past, and of an uncertain and unfinished town groping towards the future. Now, the view was of expanding mills and growing wealth, a view of a maturing city whose raw energy had been veneered by the patina of success and the assurance of knowing that it shared the seats of power.

APPENDICES

APPENDIX A

WEXFORD COUNTY POSTMASTERS
1865 — 1900

ANGOLA	Cappitolia M. Wait	—	Dec. 20, 1899
	Francis O. Wait	—	Sept. 14, 1900
AXIN	J. Axin Morgan	—	Aug. 1, 1899
BALLOU	Elmer C. Lewis	—	May 16, 1892
	Discontinued	—	Sept. 6, 1893
BANDOLA	Herman C. Meyer	—	Jan. 20, 1879
	Martin B. Mix	—	Feb. 16, 1887
	Discontinued	—	Oct. 2, 1890
BENSON	Swan Benson	—	Nov. 17, 1884
	Axon Morken	—	Feb. 17, 1899
	Swan Benson	—	Aug. 1, 1899
BOND'S MILL	Myron H. Bond	—	Oct. 30, 1872
	Frank Kysor	—	Sept. 2, 1873
	Daniel S. Kysor	—	Jan. 23, 1882
	Charles Mastin	—	Nov. 1, 1883
	Discontinued	—	Nov. 30, 1883
BOON	Joseph Matevia	—	Dec. 19, 1889
	Elwood Griffen	—	July 3, 1893
	William Haskin	—	April 21, 1897
	Albert C. Fessenden	—	May 31, 1899
CHERRY GROVE	Sven A. Benson	—	Feb. 7, 1879
	Discontinued	—	March 3, 1879
CLAM LAKE	John S. McClain	—	Jan. 3, 1872
	Henry F. May	—	April 18, 1872
	Byron Ballou	—	Feb. 24, 1874
	J. A. Whitmore	—	April 12, 1875

(Cadillac)	Jared Hixson	—	June 15, 1877
	James Croly	—	Feb. 19, 1886
	Byron Ballou	—	Feb. 6, 1890
	Levi J. Law	—	March 1, 1894
	Samuel J. Wall	—	March 9, 1898
CLAY HILL	Elizabeth Van Antwerp	—	Nov. 21, 1878
	Antoinette C. Banker	—	June 23, 1882
(Hoxeyville)	Charles Bigelow	—	April 25, 1891
	Charles E. Hawley	—	April 1, 1892
	W. F. Chittenden	—	June 4, 1892
	Edwin B. Brooks	—	July 3, 1895
COLFAX	Joseph Richardson	—	Oct. 20, 1877
	John Carvin	—	June 17, 1880
	H. C. Foxworthy	—	Nov. 14, 1883
	John J. Stackus	—	Nov. 19, 1885
	Laura Wait	—	April 27, 1889
	Discontinued	—	Oct. 12, 1889
ELTON	James L. Felton	—	July 6, 1897
ELEANOR	W. F. Chittenden	—	Nov. 14, 1891
	Discontinued	—	June 4, 1892
FARNSWORTH	Stephen Farnsworth	—	June 20, 1889
	Oliver J. LaBatt	—	June 18, 1898
GILBERT	Andrew Carlson	—	Nov. 1, 1883
	John Carlson	—	Jan. 29, 1889
	Jacob Larson	—	Feb. 27, 1896
HAIRE	Samuel R. Hepburn	—	Aug. 21, 1883
	Rasmus P. Bredahl	—	June 23, 1884
	Fred Moore	—	July 3, 1884
HARING	Dr. Hiram B. Wilcox	—	Dec. 18, 1872
	S. R. Stewart	—	May 2, 1873
	Samuel J. Wall	—	June 11, 1873
	Ephraim Shay	—	Dec. 7, 1875
	Lucius L. Fuller	—	Oct. 17, 1881
	Horace McNitt	—	Dec. 6, 1881
	Discontinued	—	Nov. 14, 1891

HOBART	John Copper	—	July 7, 1876
	Simon L. Rouse	—	Aug. 23, 1880
	Richard F. Corwin	—	May 13, 1887
	Simon L. Rouse	—	June 18, 1889
	John H. S. Copper	—	June 24, 1898
MANTON	George Manton	—	Jan. 3, 1873
	Oscar P. Carver	—	April 7, 1873
	Henry M. Billings	—	Oct. 28, 1874
	Harry Brandenburg	—	Sept. 28, 1875
	Mathew P. Gilbert	—	Oct. 1, 1877
	H. Frank Campbell	—	Jan. 19, 1883
	Charles E. Cooper	—	Jan. 6, 1885
	Frank Weaver	—	April 24, 1889
	Charles E. Cooper	—	Aug. 5, 1893
	Dr. Victor F. Huntley	—	Sept. 13, 1897
MEAUWATAKA	Enos C. Dayhuff	—	May 2, 1872
	Elijah Smith	—	Sept. 7, 1886
MESICK	Henry N. Brooks	—	Jan. 9, 1891
	Willis W. Galloway	—	Aug. 31, 1893
	Eli L. Gates	—	Oct. 13, 1897
MILLERSVILLE	Humphrey Miller	—	March 8, 1890
	Discontinued	—	March 30, 1895
MYSTIC	David B. Cox	—	March 3, 1900
RODINGEN	Fred Rodingen	—	Aug. 13, 1884
	Discontinued	—	Feb. 1, 1887
ROUND LAKE	W. H. Stewart	—	May 26, 1882
	William H. Gordon	—	April 5, 1884
	Discontinued	—	Dec. 28, 1887
SHERMAN	Dr. John Perry	—	Feb. 3, 1868
	Lewis J. Clark	—	Aug. 10, 1869
	Edward W. Stewart	—	Sept. 6, 1871
	Joseph S. Walling	—	Jan. 3, 1872
	Charles E. Cooper	—	Nov. 25, 1874
	Heman B. Sturtevant	—	Oct. 17, 1877
	Charles S. Marr	—	Dec. 21, 1877

	H. Frank Campbell	— Oct. 5, 1878
	John H. Wheeler	— Jan. 3, 1881
	Isaac N. Carpenter	— Aug. 27, 1886
	Edgar W. Wheeler	— March 27, 1889
	Mrs. Mabel Ramsey	— June 8, 1893
	Mrs. Mabel Rose	— Jan. 13, 1896
	Leroy P. Champenois	— Oct. 6, 1897
SOPER	William Grandholm	— March 23, 1900
SPRINGDALE	Andrew J. Green	— July 17, 1874
	James Daley	— June 17, 1880
	James Z. Stanley	— Sept. 16, 1885
	John R. Begle	— May 24, 1890
	James Daley	— Sept. 10, 1891
(Harriette)	Mrs. Letitia Daley	— Sept. 27, 1892
	Dr. John Barry	— March 6, 1894
	Samuel J. Doty	— Sept. 18, 1897
STOCKING	Erastus P. Stocking	— Aug. 21, 1883
	Discontinued	— Feb. 2, 1885
THORP	Neal D. Ford	— Aug. 21, 1883
	Olive B. Lewis	— Jan. 14, 1887
UMATILLA	Marilla B. Johnson	— July 3, 1876
	Discontinued	— July 20, 1877
VIOLA	Thomas C. Thornton	— Feb. 12, 1879
	Abner D. Kinney	— Aug. 19, 1880
	Discontinued	— Jan. 27, 1881
WEST SUMMIT	Hanson S. Carrier	— April 10, 1872
	Discontinued	— Feb. 6, 1874
WEXFORD	William Masters	— Feb. 17, 1865
	Israel Foust	— Jan. 8, 1872
	John Lennington	— Aug. 10, 1887
	George Cook	— April 3, 1889
	George M. D. Clement	— Aug. 24, 1893
	John Lennington	— Dec. 14, 1896
	Miss Belle Carl	— Sept. 27, 1897

WHEATLAND	Jonathan Wheat	—	March 4, 1872
	George Bolster	—	Nov. 14, 1876
	Jonathan Wheat	—	Jan. 3, 1877
	Discontinued	—	Jan. 24, 1878
YUMA	Rollin H. Jenney	—	Jan. 3, 1893

APPENDIX B

VILLAGE PRESIDENTS OF CLAM LAKE, AND MAYORS OF CADILLAC

Clam Lake: George Shackleton President 1874-77

Cadillac: 1877 George A. Mitchell
1878 Jacob Cummer
1879 Daniel McCoy
1880 Daniel McCoy
1881 Daniel McCoy
1882 Byron Ballou
1883 Eldon L. Metheany
1884 Fred Huntley
1885 James Haynes
1886 Jared Hixson
1887 James McAdam
1888 Wellington W. Cummer
1889 Levi J. Law
1890 Eldon L. Metheany
1891 Eldon L. Metheany
1892 Fred Diggins
1893 Fred Diggins
1894 Samuel J. Wall
1895 Samuel J. Wall
1896 Fred Diggins
1897 Fred Diggins
1898 Fred Diggins
1899 Fred Diggins
1900 Henry Knowlton
1901 George S. Stanley

APPENDIX C

WEXFORD COUNTY CIRCUIT JUDGES

As part of the 13th Judicial Circuit:

Jonathan G. Ramsdell	(Rep.)	1866-1873	Traverse
Shubael F. White	(Rep.)	1873-1874	Traverse

As part of the 19th Judicial Circuit:

Harrison H. Wheeler	(Dem.)	1874-1878	Ludington
Aaron V. McAlvay	(Rep.)	1878	Manistee
Samuel D. Haight	(Rep.)	1879-1880	Ludington
James Byron Judkins	(Rep.)	1880-1881	Hersey

As part of the 28th Judicial Circuit:

John M. Rice	(Rep.)	Jan. 1, 1882-April 1, 1882
Silas S. Fallass	(Dem.)	April 5, 1882-Dec. 31, 1887
Fred H. Aldrich	(Rep.)	1888-1899
Clyde C. Chittenden	(Rep.)	1900-1909

APPENDIX D

WEXFORD COUNTY PROBATE JUDGES

Isaac N. Carpenter	(Dem.)	1869-1872
William Mears	(Rep.)	1873-1876
Alonzo Chubb	(Ind.)	1877-1880
Holden N. Green	(Rep.)	1881-1884
H. M. Dunham	(Rep.)	1885-1892
John Mansfield	(Rep.)	1893-1900
Fred S. Lamb	(Rep.)	1901-1909

APPENDIX E

WEXFORD COUNTY OFFICERS
1869-1900

Year of Election	Prosecuting Attorney	County Clerk and Register of Deeds	County Treasurer	Sheriff	Circuit Court Commissioner
1869	O. H. Mills	Leroy P. Champenois (R)	John H. Wheeler (R)	Harrison H. Skinner (R)	T. A. Ferguson (R)
	Thomas A. Ferguson (R)				
1870	Thomas A. Ferguson (R)	Heman B. Sturtevant (R)	William Masters (R)	Joseph Sturr (R)	T. A. Ferguson (R)
1872	Silas S. Fallass (D)	Heman B. Sturtevant (R)	Ezra Harger (R)	E. D. Abbott (R)	S. S. Fallass (D)
1874	David A. Rice (R)	Heman B. Sturtevant (R)	Ezra Harger (R)	Jeremiah Shackleton (R)	David A. Rice (R)
1876	David A. Rice (R)	C. J. Manktelow (R)	Ezra Harger (R)	Frank Weaver (R)	John Rosevelt (D)
1878	David A. Rice (R)	C. J. Manktelow (R)	Ephraim Shay (D)	Wm. Kelley (R)	D. E. McIntyre (I)
				Charles C. Dunham (R)	
1880	Samuel J. Wall (R)	Thomas J. Thorp (R)	John Mansfield (R)	Charles C. Dunham (R)	D. E. McIntyre (I)
1882	Donald E. McIntyre (I)	Thomas J. Thorp (R)	John Mansfield (R)	David Cook (R)	William Park (I)
1884	David A. Rice (R)	George Cummer (D)	James Haynes (D)	Charles C. Dunham (R)	C. C. Chittenden (R)
1886	Clyde C. Chittenden (R)	George Cummer (D)	Ezra Harger (R)	Charles C. Dunham (R)	Chas. S. Marr (R)
1888	Clyde C. Chittenden (R)	Samuel J. Wall (R)	Ezra Harger (R)	W. L. Sturtevant (R)	E. E. Haskins (R)
1890	Clyde C. Chittenden (R)	Samuel J. Wall (R)	J. W. Ransom (D)	W. L. Sturtevant (R)	R. F. Tinkham (R)
1892	David A. Rice (R)	Samuel J. Wall (R)	Ezra Harger (R)	Charles C. Dunham (R)	Fred S. Lamb (R)
1894	David A. Rice (R)	Samuel J. Wall (R)	Edgar Wheeler (R)	Charles C. Dunham (R)	Fred S. Lamb (R)
1896	Fred S. Lamb (R)	Henry Hansen (R)	Edgar Wheeler (R)	George Troy (R)	Elwood Peck (R)
1898	Fred S. Lamb (R)	Henry Hansen (R)	John H. Wheeler (R)	George Troy (R)	Elwood Peck (R)
1900	Fred Wetmore (R)	David Garver (R)	John H. Wheeler (R)	Silas Huckleberry (R)	David A. Rice (R)

R = Republican
D = Democrat
I = Independent